THE GOOD,
THE BAD,
AND
THE GODAWFUL

Also by Kurt Loder

I, Tina

Bat Chain Puller

THE GOOD,
THE BAD
AND
THE GODAWFUL

21st-Century Movie Reviews

Kurt Loder

Thomas Dunne Books
St. Martin's Griffin ≈ New York

THOMAS DUNNE BOOKS.
An imprint of St. Martin's Press.

www.thomasdunnebooks.com
www.stmartins.com

Book design by Meryl Sussman Levavi

Library of Congress Cataloging-in-Publication Data

Loder, Kurt.
    The good, the bad and the Godawful : 21st-century movie reviews / Kurt Loder.—1st ed.
        p. cm.
    ISBN 978-0-312-64163-4
    1. Motion pictures—Reviews.   I. Title.
    PN1995.I57 2011
    791.43'75—dc23

2011032782

First Edition: November 2011

10   9   8   7   6   5   4   3   2   1

For Jennifer

Contents

CREEPERS   43

A collection of horror films, some actually scary, some scary-stupid.

THE TORTURE NEVER STOPS   75

Into the dark land of cinematic excruciation.

FUNTIME

Some comedies worthy of the name.

THE LAND THAT LAUGHS FORGOT

Some comedies best avoided, or possibly fled.

OTHER WORLDS

Sci-fi flicks, some great, some entirely otherwise.

THE HIT FACTORY   155

Big movies impressive for more than the size of their budgets or the salaries of their stars. Well, mostly.

NEVER-ENDING STORIES   177

Franchise players—movies that keep on giving, like it or not.

THE HOLLYWOOD VERSION 197

Moral instruction from movieland millionaires.

REAL DEALS 217

Documentaries: wild tales brought back alive.

AUTEURS 259

The director as movie star.

BIG BANG BOOM   295

Action movies with and without redeeming features.

ONE MORE TIME   307

The dwindling rewards of endless remakes.

WILD THINGS   325

Movies that defy classification. In a good way.

STRANGE CARGO   341

Wild, weird, and (mostly) worth seeking out.

CRITICAL LIST   363

Movies that reviewers just loved, and we're still wondering why.

DECLARATIONS OF INDEPENDENCE
                                                                    375

Big stars, vast budgets—who needs 'em?

FOREIGN PARTS
                                                                    401

Some worthy imports that didn't get lost in translation.

THE COMIC-BOOK CONQUEST 429

An avalanche that never ends: graphic-novel escapees and blue-chip superheroes (some not so super).

LOOKING FOR LOVE 469

Movies that deserved a lot more attention, and still do.

PLEASE SHOOT ME   487

Some movies that no one should ever have to sit through.

NICOLAS CAGE   523

The man, the mystery.

Acknowledgments

A ll of the reviews in this book originally appeared at MTV.com, with the exception of *The Rite, Rubber, Atlas Shrugged, The Adjustment Bureau, Unknown, Cool It, Client 9: The Rise and Fall of Eliot Spitzer, The Way Back, Wall Street: Money Never Sleeps, The Mechanic, Jackass 3D, The Girl Who Kicked the Hornet's Nest, Burlesque, The Tourist,* and *The Green Hornet,* all of which were first posted at Reason Online.

Introduction

I wish I could say I'm a "film critic," but I'm not, really. I'm a *movie reviewer*. A real film critic—the late Pauline Kael springs immediately to mind—is a scholar of the art, tirelessly sorting through the Hollywood offerings that course through screening rooms and theaters, but also patrolling the cinematic fringes and uplands. The formidable erudition of such people is always instructive. Real critics are immersed in the history of the movies; they have an organized interest in their subject, and they've devoted a vast tranche of their lives to studying it. Reading their work can be part of an ongoing education. Having devoted my own vast tranche mainly to music—listening to it, writing about it—my knowledge of film has been acquired more haphazardly. Anyone who has been watching movies for decades, and who still sees three or four pictures a week, as I have and do, is bound to acquire some degree of knowledge in certain areas. But I suspect I won't be catching up with the true critics—the monklike devotees of world filmmaking—any time soon. It's a sad fact that I probably know more about lesbian vampire movies than I do about, say, Iranian cinema or the lesser works of Harold Lloyd. One plugs away, but time is finite.

On the other hand, over the course of many years I've also written quite a bit about movies and the people who make them. I've sweltered with George Miller in the Australian outback and interacted with the Davids Fincher, Lynch, and Cronenberg. I once did a phoner with the great John Huston. And I once found myself, astonishingly, in the presence of Alfred Hitchcock. I remain amazed that one can make a living meeting such people.

Even more amazingly, over the course of many years as a semi-familiar face on television, I have sometimes been approached to actually appear in movies, almost always as "myself"—which is to say, as a semi-familiar face on television. This is the most inconsequential of accomplishments. One is essentially being used like a flake of confetti sprinkled on a parade—or, more often, a sequin pasted on a pig. I've passed fleetingly through a couple of pretty good Hollywood films, like Ron Howard's *The Paper* (that's me in a two-second shot of a pair of eyeballs peeping over the top of a restroom stall) and some low-budget gems, like Rusty Cundieff's underseen hip-hop takedown, *Fear of a Black Hat*. Most of my dubious movie credits, however, have been accumulated in pictures so dreadful that I've never had the heart to watch some of them all the way through. (Let us not speak of *The Adventures of Ford Fairlane*.)

Among the things I've learned from these experiences is one key thing: making a movie is hard work. I mean maddeningly, exhaustingly hard. The first movie in which I took part was the 1993 *Who's the Man?* This was an "urban comedy," as they say (code for pictures aimed at a black audience), directed by the late Ted Demme, a onetime MTV colleague who broke into the film business with this movie. Ted rashly offered me a nonspeaking part in the film as a mob hitman. The shot in which I figured required about thirty seconds of on-camera exertion, and yet the scene of which it was a component took the better part of an afternoon to shoot. This is not unusual. Moviemaking hours are invariably long, and many of them are spent waiting—waiting for new camera setups, for lighting tweaks, for the rain to stop, or the damn sun to come out, or the twilight "golden hour" to begin. The endless inactivity is draining. As a crew member once explained to me, "This is factory work."

I try to keep the heavy labor of filmmaking in mind when reviewing a movie. Even the most mediocre film represents very hard work on the part of many people, none of whom set out to make a lousy picture. In assessing a movie that's not very good, it doesn't seem right simply to sneer at it. On the other hand, some movies are so flagrantly bad—the worst work of talented people who should know better or the flailings of untalented and sometimes pretentious people who one feels should be discouraged from making even one more film—that a certain cruel candor must creep into any critical assessment. As you might suspect, this sort of review is the most fun to write.

What follows is largely a winnowing of the hundreds of weekly movie reviews I wrote for MTV.com over the course of six years, beginning in 2004. The MTV site not being a natural home for critical discourse, I must thank its overseer, my longtime friend Dave Sirulnick, for his encouragement and his forbearance in the face of occasional advertiser displeasure. Also included here are a number of reviews I've since written for Reason Online, the Internet outpost of *Reason* magazine. This libertarian political site would not seem a natural home for movie writing either, and yet managing editor Nick Gillespie has made room for it. I suspect Nick's experience in another life as a music and movie journalist himself, and his association with the late, lamented Suck.com, may explain this. Gratitude is also due to my Reason editors, Damon Root and Michael Moynihan, and to my invaluable agent, Sarah Lazin. Above all, I must thank my colleague and co-vivant, Jennifer Vineyard, whose idea this book was, and whose own vast movie knowledge was invaluable in assembling it.

In going back over these reviews, I've tried to trim away the dead words, bloodless phrases, and infestations of linguistic overkill that are so often a byproduct of deadline writing. I have not, however, adjusted any of the original opinions in these pieces. What you have here are immediate responses to a disparate array of movies, tapped out by a simple movie enthusiast. Like yourself, perhaps.

—K. L.
New York City
March 2011

SCHLOCKBUSTERS

There's something especially dispiriting about a big movie that fails. We may stumble out of a small, brain-dead comedy like The Dukes of Hazzard figuring the $50 million it cost to make must have been spent mostly on cash-kindled after-work barbecues for the cast and crew; but we know that making movies is an expensive gamble, and we accept that this was simply a dumb one that didn't pay off. However, when a picture's budget swells beyond the $100 million mark, the huge outlay can stir larger thoughts, usually involving starving third-world children. Some of these big gambles do pay off. James Cameron spent a reported $200 million to make the 1997 Titanic, but the movie had a cast of nearly 140 performers and a behind-the-scenes crew—from editors, designers, and effects technicians to drivers, accountants, and animal trainers—that numbered more than 1,500 people, none of whom was working for free. No one now begrudges that expenditure, least of all the movie's producers: Titanic was a well-made film that went on to gross more than $1.8 billion worldwide.

On the other hand, twelve years later it was decided that a good use for $200 million would be to hand it over to the director of the Charlie's Angels movies in an attempt to revive the moribund Terminator franchise. The result, Terminator Salvation, was a botch of such sobering proportions that even the producers' thoughts may have turned to starving third-world children. Bad *big movies like this are often connected to franchises—either in the hope of sustaining one, as with* Terminator Salvation, *or of launching one, as was the purpose of* The Golden Compass *(a movie that cost $180 million to make and was stillborn at the American multiplex). Other big-budget bombs are uninspired exploitations of evergreen genres, often involving swords, sandals, or sorcery; popular novels, cartoons, or video games; endlessly time-tested stories, like Ridley Scott's* Robin Hood *(another $200 million down the drain); or of the movie-epic form itself—a determined attempt to paint a huge, sprawling picture that no one wants to see (*Australia, *coming up).*

"Bad" is a subjective term, of course, and many movies that a rational person—that would be you and me—might dismiss as dreck actually make money. This is annoying. Despite my conclusion in the review that follows, The Mummy: Tomb of the Dragon Emperor *sucked in sizable grosses worldwide, such that yet another installment of the franchise is apparently in the works.* Tomb *is still a silly movie, in an uninteresting way, but there's clearly a large audience—presumably with a lot of spare time on its hands—that doesn't care. I envy them their spacious capacity for cinematic pleasure.*

What all bad big-budget movies have in common is the central question they raise: not why they were made—like other movies, they too were gambles—but how. *Did no one notice how rickety the script was, how lifeless the performances, how dismal the cinematography? These are questions that have no answers—none that anyone involved will volunteer, anyway—but let us nevertheless contemplate them once again.*

Australia

There's a truly heartbreaking moment about two-thirds of the way through *Australia,* director Baz Luhrmann's cinematic tribute to his Antipodean homeland. Although the story is set Down Under, the picture is essentially—in fact proudly—an old-fashioned western, complete with plucky widow trying to save her ranch from an evil cattle baron and handsome cowboy helping her do it. After sitting through about two hours of campfires, cattle drives, and mad stampedes, we feel that the movie must soon come to an end. But then—this is the heartbreaking part—it suddenly turns into a World War II battle film and it *just keeps going.* For almost another hour. I nearly cried.

It's hard to imagine what Luhrmann thought he was doing with this picture. Clearly he intended to make an epic; and if we were to judge only by the film's interminable running time and its blockbusting budget (reported to be north of $120 million, although eased by Australian tax breaks), he might be said to have succeeded. But while the movie is packed with ravishing sights—palm tree'd billabongs, baking outback vistas—its story is such a fusty mélange of western-movie clichés that we might as well be camped out in the old cowpoke canyons of Utah, listening to the ghost of John Ford wondering who forgot to shoot the writers.

Briefly—to employ a word that's clearly not a part of Luhrmann's professional lexicon—it's September of 1939, the year Australia joined the U.K. in declaring war on Germany. Oblivious to this development, the posh Lady Sarah Ashley (Nicole Kidman) has pursued her wandering husband from England to the Australian cattle ranch he owns in the parched outback. Upon arrival, she discovers he's been murdered, allegedly by an Aboriginal shaman called King George (David Gulpilil). The cattle baron, Carney (Bryan Brown), makes an oily offer of assistance: he'll take the ranch off the widow's hands for a price, and in the process complete his monopoly of the country's beef supply. Sarah decides instead to make a go of the place herself; but the only way to raise enough money to do so is to herd the fifteen hundred resident livestock off to Darwin, hundreds of miles away, to be sold. This seems an unlikely possibility—until a master cattle drover named, well, Drover (Hugh Jackman) turns up.

Naturally, these two are an ill-matched pair. Sarah is a prissy tenderfoot (Kidman might be auditioning for the Katharine Hepburn role in a remake of *The African Queen*), while Drover is a rough-hewn natural man, most at home under the sun and the stars, venturing into town only for an occasional round of hearty barroom fistfights. (Jackman's matey charisma is at full voltage here, but it's no match for the picture's energy-draining sprawl.) After Sarah fires her late husband's devious ranch foreman, Fletcher (David Wenham), who takes the spread's best men along with him on his way out the gate, Drover is forced to assemble a new crew of cowpunchers from a slim list of candidates. He winds up with an alcoholic accountant (Jack Thompson), a pair of Aboriginal ranch hands, a mixed-race boy named Nullah (thirteen-year-old first-time actor Brandon Walters, who narrates the picture and is a real find), and, of course, Sarah herself. ("I will have you know, I'm as capable as any man!") So off they ride, into the flatlands of cowboy banality.

Fletcher and his nasty-looking henchman are of course secretly in league with Carney—thus the stampedes and water-hole poisonings as they harass Sarah's party from every perimeter in an effort to prevent her from reaching Darwin. At this point, it's heavily inevitable that Sarah and Drover should come together in the desert wastes for a silly silent waltz and a chaste kiss—although the very Spielbergian starry sky under which they do so is a little unexpected. What I couldn't figure out was how the skeletal King George—Nullah's grandfather, we learn—kept turning up at various far-removed locations saying things like, "I will sing you to the place where the rivers meet," when Drover and company were all on horseback and he was on foot. (This is perhaps unremarkable in the Aboriginal worldview.) As for the strange, continual references to *The Wizard of Oz,* I'm sure they're a salute to the transcendent magic of movies and not to the director himself.

In any event, Drover gets the cattle to Darwin, scotching Carney's nefarious scheme and saving Sarah's ranch. In any sane picture, credits would now roll. But no. Having secured the money to keep her ranch, Sarah suddenly decides to sell it. Then she decides not to. Then she invites Drover to accompany her to a fancy-dress ball. He refuses to go; then he changes his mind, and eventually makes an entrance amid the party lights in a blindingly elegant white dinner jacket. Then Nullah is snatched by missionaries and taken to a nearby island reserved for the forced housing of mixed-race children (an Australian historical issue that may not resonate here). Then the Japanese navy, fresh from its assault on Pearl Harbor, unleashes a fleet of bombers on Darwin, engulfing the city in a transparently digital conflagration. Then Drover disappears. Sarah thinks he's been killed. Then he returns, and he thinks Sarah's been killed. Then they realize they both were wrong. Then it looks like they may finally come together for good, with Nullah—who's not dead either—as their honorary offspring. But no. And still no credits are rolling.

Luhrmann's highly operatic sensibility (he directed his own production of *La Bohème* on Broadway a few years back) seems best suited to over-the-top pop material like *Moulin Rouge.* Here, his attempted blendering of some of the hoariest elements of old cowboy and war movies with squirts of historical instruction and sloshes of social consciousness lacks the wild style of that earlier film; it's just ungainly. Did he really think there'd be an audience thirsting for nearly three hours of this? Or was he simply too long out in the brain-roasting Aussie sun? (November 2008)

The Golden Compass

Dusted

Here's a magical-mystery movie with everything money can buy: big-name stars, boffo effects, a story presold (somewhat) in a British cult fantasy novel. The only thing *The Golden Compass* lacks, alas, is magic. And its mystery is a little too mysterious.

The picture looks great—director Chris Weitz and his town-size team of digital technicians have created a dazzling fantasy world of misty cities, gleaming dirigibles, and intricate steampunk gadgetry. But in attempting to cram as much as possible of Philip Pullman's four-hundred-page novel into a two-hour movie, Weitz—who wrote the script after nixing Tom Stoppard's pass at one—gives us both way too much and much too little. We're so pounded down by all the exposition in the beginning, and then by the stampede of daemons and bears and mechanical insects arriving in its wake, that fans of the book may slump in despair, and nonfans in simple indifference.

The story is set in a parallel world that resembles Victorian England. There's even a parallel Oxford University, where spunky little Lyra Belacqua (Dakota Blue Richards) is happily installed as the ward of the scientist-explorer Lord Asriel (Daniel Craig, who's in the movie for about as long as it might take you or me to hail a cab). The freethinking Asriel is a heretical figure to the sinister Magisterium (think the Catholic Church—Pullman did, although New Line Cinema really hopes you won't). Both Asriel and the Magisterium are obsessed with something called Dust, a shimmery substance that no one entirely understands, least of all us. About the time Asriel decides to take off for the northern polar regions in search of the source of this stuff, the glamorous Mrs. Coulter (blazingly blond Nicole Kidman) arrives on the scene, making a runway entrance into a vast university dining hall that's so blatantly Hogwartsian, you half expect to see Albus Dumbledore go tottering by.

By this point, you'll have noticed that all the characters in the movie are walking around with little animals perched on their shoulders or yipping around their feet. These are the above-noted daemons—advisers, protectors, stand-ins for the soul, you might say. Little kids have cute daemons: butterflies, birds, fuzzy quadrupeds of various endearing sorts. The evil operatives of the Magisterium lean more toward serpents. Mrs. Coulter's daemon is a monkey, which I found to be a stumper.

Anyway, Mrs. Coulter offers to take Lyra to "the North," as it's called (think Norway), unaware that Lyra had already been hoping to follow in Asriel's footsteps and maybe get to the bottom of this Dust thing. By now we've also learned that a group called the Gobblers—nefarious minions of the Magisterium—have been kidnapping children, and before long we're further informed that they've been spiriting the kids off to a snowbound laboratory to perform alarming experiments on them. Lyra is enraged, but Mrs. Coulter takes a suspiciously sympathetic view of the Magisterians: "They keep things working by telling people what to do."

I haven't mentioned the alethiometer—the titular Golden Compass. This is a nifty device that can tell all truths and reveal all that others wish to hide (if I may slip into the fancy-speak of the story for a moment). Nor have I touched upon the armored Ice Bears—and there's a whole kingdom full of them. Lyra recruits one of these lumbering creatures, named Iorek, to accompany her on her polar quest. She also gets backup from another outfit called the Gyptians, who sail about in a piratey schooner. Then there's a drawling cowboy "aeronaut" named Scoresby (Sam Elliott—even his rabbit daemon has a cracker accent) and a sky full of fierce witches armed with bows and arrows. I'm leaving stuff out, believe me.

Admirers of Pullman's book, who've invariably followed this tale through to its third-volume conclusion, marvel at the story's scope and purpose. The movie strives mightily to cram in hints of those things, but the result is mostly clutter and confusion. (In this regard, lopping off the first book's ending, which had actually been shot, is something of a puzzlement.)

I'm guessing part of the fault for the picture's shortcomings must lie with New Line micromanagement. Having grossed billions with its *Lord of the Rings* trilogy, the company surely latched on to the similarly tripartite *His Dark Materials* with visions of another corporate cash-wallow. But this one ain't that one. The first *Rings* movie set up its story with ravishing clarity: good Hobbits, bad wizards, evil ring. *The Golden Compass* (which reportedly cost $180 million to make, approximately two-thirds of the budget for the entire *Rings* trilogy) buries us in so much desperate explication that the shape of the story never emerges. The picture ends with the promise—or the threat—of a sequel. Given the numbers, and this movie's probable reception, I'm betting it never gets made. (December 2007)

Angels & Demons

Talk Show

The hardest thing about wrestling a Dan Brown novel into submission for movie purposes would have to be the wads of undigested explication that clog the author's narratives. Brown and his reclusive wife-cum-research assistant, Blythe, appear never to have encountered an arcane factoid they could resist cramming into one of his tales. It needn't even be factual. (Their inaccuracies have been widely derided.) The result of this book-crafting technique has been to give Brown's wooden characters far too many things to explain and instruct us in. This was already a problem for director Ron Howard in his film version of *The Da Vinci Code* three years ago. Now, taking a whack at *Angels & Demons*—the opus that preceded *Da Vinci* but has been extensively re-wrought into a sequel here—Howard has thrown up his hands and gone native.

Tom Hanks is back, minus the mullet under which he wandered through *Da Vinci*, as Harvard symbologist Robert Langdon. And once again he's teamed with a female sidekick—this time a "bio-entanglement physicist" (an actual career path, wonderfully enough) named Vittoria Vetra (Ayelet Zurer). Like Langdon, Vittoria is a stick figure whose sole purpose (*no chemistry, please!*) is to stir the vats of esoteric Brownian blather. She spends most of her time listening to Langdon say things like, "It's the ancient Illuminati threat!" Occasionally, though, she gets to inject some big science into the proceedings, causing Langdon to make superfluous comments like, "You're talking about the moment of creation!" There's more to the movie, it must be said; but mainly it's more of that.

Langdon has been summoned to Rome by the Vatican, which is having a terribly bad day. The pope has just died and the church has gathered its cardinals from around the world to elect from among themselves a successor. But the four frontrunners—the *preferiti*—have been kidnapped, and word has been received that one of these hostages will be killed at the top of each hour in a countdown to midnight, at which time the entire Vatican will be blown up by a single drop of antimatter stolen from CERN, the big physics research center near Geneva. (In his book, Brown offers an earnest explanation of antimatter which, unfortunately, has been dismissed as fantasy by CERN itself. So the antimatter we're dealing with in the movie is essentially just some pretty nasty stuff, and let's move on.)

The outlandish conspiracy has pronounced Bondian overtones—you half expect a cutaway of Auric Goldfinger cruising down the Via Veneto in his gold-plated Rolls, checking his watch and chuckling in homicidal anticipation. But alas no. Langdon knows what's going on here—it's the return of the science-loving Illuminati, sworn enemies of religious superstition for centuries, now making their most hostile move. The only way to stop them is to uncover the Path of Illumination, a sort of obstacle course that wends its way through four Roman landmarks, at each of which a cardinal has been scheduled to be sacrificed in some colorful way related to the elements of earth, air, fire, and water. As the hours tick down in on-screen updates, Langdon and

Vittoria scurry from one of these sites to the next, littering the streets with clots of scholarly discourse about art and architecture and such-like, some of it accurate. Meanwhile, even more stuff is being explained back at the Vatican, where the late pope's chamberlain (Ewan McGregor) is trying to hold down the fort until a new pontiff can be elected, and a harried head cardinal (Armin Mueller-Stahl) is having the devil's own time getting that done, and the chief of Vatican security (Stellan Skars-gärd) is proving mysteriously uninclined to evacuate the place.

Brown's familiar hostility to the Roman Catholic Church is too reflexive to be of much concern to believers, I'd think. However, it's interesting to note that the filmmakers have been careful to change the ethnicity of the killer. In the book, he's an Arab; here he's a garden-variety European. This suggests an unspoken awareness that while there are some faiths you can push around with impunity, there are others you'd be wise not to annoy. Hollywood's celebrated political boldness is clearly not unbounded.

The whole story is hokum, of course (especially the elaborate non-sense about the Illuminati). But then so are the plots of the Indiana Jones movies. Those pictures, though, have an exuberant pulp spirit— they're fun. *Angels & Demons* is humorless and way too talky. And it leaves Hanks, one of the most likable of actors, stranded, unable to use his skill and his warmth to turn the one-dimensional Langdon into an actual character. He's too busy trying to keep us clued in to what's go-ing on to do much more than breathlessly hoof it from one picturesque tourist site to the next.

Some of the cardinals are dispatched in arresting ways (human bar-becue is something we don't get nearly enough of anymore); a lethal confrontation between Langdon and the shadowy killer at a Bernini fountain is rousingly (if implausibly) depicted; and the shot in which we see rats chewing off somebody's face is pretty memorable, too. If only there were room for more such cinematic inventions—for more real action, more high spirits. If only, in short, the movie would shut up. (May 2009)

Robin Hood

Ye Olde Bait-and-Switch

Ridley Scott's *Robin Hood* is brilliant, in a way. Faced with the fact that filmmakers have been cranking out pictures about the scalawag of Sherwood Forest for more than a hundred years now, the director and his writers must have pondered at length how to put a unique spin on the oft-told tale. Their brainstorm: don't tell it. Scott's movie, very oddly, is a *prequel*—a sort of origin story prefiguring a better Robin Hood movie that doesn't yet exist. And on the evidence of this one, probably never will.

So Robin Hood fans hoping for some of the dash and wit of the classic films that starred Douglas Fairbanks and Errol Flynn should set their expectation meters to OFF. The simple pleasure of a few acrobatic hours with Robin and his Merry Men—and the blundering Sheriff of Nottingham, the chubby Friar Tuck, the evil Prince John, and the lovely Maid Marion—is not forthcoming. True, there is a Sheriff of Nottingham loitering around the new film's perimeter; also some men called Little John, Will Scarlet, and Allan A'Dayle, although they're not very merry. Mark Addy's mead-sipping Friar Tuck is a robust character; but Prince John, played here by Oscar Isaac, is a witless buffoon, and Marion, played by Cate Blanchett, is hardly the elegant beauty of lore—at one point we're given a closeup of her washing clots of mud off her bare feet.

Russell Crowe, in his fifth collaboration with Scott, dispenses with Robin's traditional tights and feathered cap, which is not a great loss; but he also dispenses with the character's traditional high spirits, which is. The Robin cobbled together by writers Brian Helgeland, Ethan Reiff, and Cyrus Voris isn't the jaunty rogue nobleman of earlier versions of the story; here, he's just a glum yeoman called Robin Longstride, a loyal archer in the service of the good King Richard the Lionheart (Danny Huston). As the movie opens, in 1199, Richard and his weary men are returning from the latest crusade in the Holy Lands. They're plundering their way through France en route to England, where Richard's conniving brother, Prince John, is coveting the royal crown. John is planning to dump his current princess and marry sultry young Isabella of Angoulême (Léa Seydoux), niece of King Philip of France (Jonathan Zaccai). Then, with the help of his henchman, the devious Godfrey (Mark Strong in a villainous black cloak), John will terminate his hated sibling, creating an agreeable vacancy on the English throne for him to fill. Across the Channel, King Philip is salivating over this scenario, too—with the weakling John in charge, the French monarch feels he will have no trouble invading England and bending it to his imperial will.

Much research has gone into getting all this medieval backstory right (or somewhat right). But the heavy scholarship turns the movie into what seems like a very long history lesson delivered in a loud, dark, and unusually muddy lecture hall. The endless battles, skirmishes, and castle-stormings, accompanied by the usual arrow swarms, head axings, and boiling-oil downpours, are nothing we haven't seen before. (Although in one seaside battle, with enemy ships crashing up onto the beach and much slaughter in the water, we half expect Tom Hanks to come wandering through in search of Private Spielberg.) Even more familiar are the roistering peasants, with their campfire rabbit roasts and sloshy revels. ("More wine!") And while some of the dialogue is newly minted, that's not always a good thing. ("An English princess shut out of her husband's bedroom by a piece of French pastry?")

In the midst of one bloody fray, Robin is beseeched by a dying knight to take his sword and return it to the knight's father in faraway Nottingham. ("I've heard of Nottingham," says Crowe, as if dimly recalling a more enjoyable movie.) The father is the ancient Sir Walter Loxley (Max von Sydow), and he implores Robin, upon his arrival, to remain at the family castle and impersonate his dead son (surely the servants won't notice). This also entails moving Robin into the bedchamber of the son's now-widowed wife, Marion. At this juncture we get the priceless scene in which Robin, preparing to turn in on their first night together, but still encased in battle gear, says to Marion, "I'll need some help with the chain mail."

Crowe and Blanchett are too good for these roles. Crowe is heavily morose throughout the film, and Blanchett is photographed in unflattering ways that subvert her angular beauty. And the emotionally anemic script doesn't allow them to work up a romantic glow—a serious shortcoming in a story set in the age of chivalry.

After two hours and twenty minutes of watching charmless characters slogging about in grim, mucky conflict, we're more than ready to celebrate the rolling of the end credits. But then we get a final scene in which the Sheriff of Nottingham asks for a nail to hang a wanted poster on a tree—and an arrow comes flying in to do the job for him. This, of course, is where the traditional Robin Hood story begins. As Scott's misbegotten prologue demonstrates, there's a good reason for that. (May 2010)

Speed Racer

Massive Attack

On one level, the Wachowski Brothers' *Speed Racer*, with its frantic action and ultrascrumptious Jolly Rancher color design, is a kid flick unlike any other. Viewers of more advanced years, however—say, twelve—may feel like they're being beaten to death with lollipops. The picture is also kind of long (two hours and change). Will the tykes sit still for it? Will anybody?

It is said (although not by them personally, since they no longer do press) that Andy and Larry Wachowski were childhood fans of the *Speed Racer* TV series, a Japanese anime import of the 1960s that was dubbed into English for U.S. syndication. In choosing to turn this property into a feature (it's their first directorial foray since the *Matrix* trilogy collapsed in exhaustion five years ago), the Wachowskis opted for an almost totally computer-generated comic-book look. Actual actors are involved in the film (and some pretty snazzy actual cars, too), but the world in which they operate clearly orbits Planet Manga: jewel-like cities shimmer in the night, pools like puddles of Jell-O beckon wetly, and fat white marshmallow clouds drift across impossibly perfect cerulean skies. If the colors in this movie were any more saturated, they'd be dribbling off the screen.

The story is pure milk-and-cookies. The Racer family—Pops (John Goodman), Mom (Susan Sarandon), teenage Speed (Emile Hirsch), and preteen Spritle (Paulie Litt)—are all car nuts. Pops builds them, the kids race them, and Mom cheers the gang on. An older son, Rex (Scott Porter), has already bought the farm in pursuit of the world racing championship (we see him in flashbacks). Now his brother Speed—installed in one of Pops's most awesome creations, a screaming white Mach 5—is preparing to follow in the family tradition, with the chaste support of his girlfriend Trixie (Christina Ricci—with her pert bangs and big liquid eyes, she looks like an anime character herself).

Speed is obviously a Grand Prix ace in the making and has thus drawn the attention of a sinister industrialist named Royalton (sneermaster Roger Allam, of *V for Vendetta*). When the idealistic young hotshot turns down a big-bucks sponsorship deal Royalton has offered him, the malevolent mogul taunts him with an ugly secret: the top car races are fixed and always have been—nice guys *do* finish last. Then he dispatches a gang of thugs to take the potentially troublesome kid out of the running, permanently. Also endangered, for more obscure reasons, is another young driver named Taejo (South Korean pop star Rain). These two outnumbered wheelmen aren't on their own, though. Weighing in on their side are a tenacious sleuth, Inspector Detector (Benno Fürmann), and a mysterious masked outrider called Racer X (Matthew Fox).

It's a simple story, but the Wachowskis don't play it for camp; they appear to be genuinely engaged with its themes of faith and family. Not that anyone's likely to care. The picture is a monument to kinetic excess. The overpowered race cars on display crash, careen, and sometimes fly along endless looping tracks that wind through tropical islands, desert wastes, and ice-glazed mountain tunnels. There are a few amusing James Bond touches (built-in automotive weaponry, and a poison-dripping scene straight out of *You Only Live Twice*) and some passing enchantments (a shot of Trixie piloting a pink helicopter over snow-capped Alpine peaks). The picture looks great. In fact, it looks astonishing. But nonstop astonishment is exhausting—sometimes you *want* it to stop. *Speed Racer* kicks off in overdrive, but quickly runs out of places to go. (May 2008)

The Mummy: Tomb of the Dragon Emperor

Undead Again

*T*omb of the Dragon Emperor, the third installment of the sub-Indy *Mummy* series, achieves a new level of subness. Along with the usual lifts from the Jonesian canon—this time, an Ark-like sarcophagus, an arrow barrage blasting out of booby-trapped walls, a rickety rope bridge swaying over a mountain chasm, even a stage full of dancing girls in a Shanghai nightclub—we have an ill-omened romance between a mere man and his immortal sweetie (in the manner of *The Lord of the Rings*) and a leaping trio of big, hairy Himalayan yetis who look as if they're very late for a *Golden Compass* audition.

With Rob Cohen (*The Fast and the Furious*) taking over from Stephen Sommers, who directed the first two films, *Mummy 3* is an assembly-line action movie clogged with special effects of a sort that will seem special only to those who've been bricked up in an ancient tomb for the last twenty years. It helps that the likable Brendan Fraser is back as stalwart explorer Rick O'Connell, and that Maria Bello has been recruited to play his equally intrepid wife, Evie, a role previously occupied by Rachel Weisz. (Weisz presumably had better things to do; in a better world, Bello would have, too.)

In the customary prologue, set in China "long ago," the fanatical King Han (Jet Li) is wiping out a succession of provincial warlords to become emperor of all the land. Han also has an interest in immortality ("I have too much to do in one lifetime"), so after attaining royal supremacy, he dispatches a beautiful sorceress named Zi Juan (Michelle Yeoh) to find the secret of eternal life. Unwisely, when she returns with a Sanskrit spell suited to that purpose, Han double-crosses her, and she pronounces a curse that turns the emperor and his legion of soldiers into life-size pottery statues. (The story is based, rather closely as these things go, on the tale of the historical Emperor Qin Shi Huang, whose own long-buried terra-cotta army was one of the more striking archeological finds of the last century.)

Flash forward to England in 1946. Mummy hunters Rick and Evie are now retired in their mansion in the Oxford countryside and bored stiff. When His Majesty's government offers a new assignment—transporting an item called the Eye of Shangri-La (it looks like a Fabergé Easter egg) back to its native China—they quickly dig out their old adventuring gear and hop on a plane. Meanwhile, their son, the now-grown Alex (Luke Ford), is already in China on an adventure of his own—and he's dug up the crockery-encased Emperor Han. All of this draws the attention of the sinister General Yang (Anthony Wong Chau-Sang), who wants to seize the immobilized emperor, use the Eye of Shangri-La to lift the ancient curse off him, and employ the revivified monarch as a terrifying weapon in the raging Chinese civil war.

An awful lot of stuff transpires. There's a kick-ass ninja girl, a rather perfunctory betrayal, a mad horse-and-emperor chase through the teeming streets of Shanghai (where the movie was partly shot), a vast cavern full of those terra-cotta warriors (pretty impressive, actually), and reams of dialogue both archly anachronistic ("You don't really believe in the concept of personal space, do you?") and simply limp ("I hate mummies—they never play fair!"). Toss in a magical dagger, a three-headed dragon, and an Elixir of the Pool of Eternal Life and you have a movie that should be more fun than it is. There's abundant action—all the usual shoot-outs, punch-ups, and acres of exploding real estate—but by the second half of the film, it has all blurred into rote frenzy; and it's so choppily edited (and pumped up with blaring horns and overbearing choirs) that our attention drifts away toward niggling details. How likely is it, for example, that a character of Brendan Fraser's age (thirty-nine) would have a son the age of Luke Ford (who's twenty-six)? And how odd is it that a movie called *The Mummy* should have no actual mummy in it? And why is the picture's most intriguing character—the clairvoyant Colonel Choi (Jessey Meng), a young woman with an exotic scar running the length of her face—left to languish on the sidelines of the plot?

The two previous *Mummy* movies cleaned up worldwide, but the many fans of those films may be disappointed by this one. *Dragon Emperor* cost twice as much as the first two pictures combined, partly because of its extensive Chinese location work (note the attempted synergy with the upcoming Beijing Olympics, to be televised by Universal's broadcast arm, NBC). But the result is a flairless clutter of digital tumult. The *Mummy* producers might profitably take a tip from the old Indiana Jones movies they so often mine. The original Indy series came to a graceful conclusion with its third installment. This franchise is already living on borrowed time. (August 2008)

10,000 B.C.

Time Bomb

The new Roland Emmerich movie *10,000 B.C.* can be recommended to those who have (1) never seen Mel Gibson's vastly superior *Apocalypto*, (2) never seen the *Lord of the Rings* pictures, or (3) never seen a movie before in their lives. To call the film derivative would be to overpraise it. Much of the story and several key sequences—especially one set in a vast pyramid city swarming with slaves—are ripped straight out of the Gibson movie, while the stampeding mastodons and snowy New Zealand mountaintop panoramas (along with some sub–Howard

Shore soundtrack symphonizing) will surely stir feelings of familiarity among Frodophiles.

More than anything else, though, the movie recalls the overblown Hollywood biblical epics of the 1950s, with all their attendant anachronisms and free-floating cheese. The story, which is blandly generic, is set in the late Stone Age, a period in which the filmmakers appear to have had no particular interest—they've blithely readjusted the inceptions of navigation, textile manufacture, and fortress cities by thousands of years. The tale concerns a mountain tribe called the Yagahl and centers on three of its members: the handsome young hunter, D'Leh (Steven Strait); his beautiful childhood sweetheart, Evolet (Camilla Belle); and his wise mentor, Tic'Tic (Cliff Curtis). The question of whether people might really have had apostrophes in their names back in Paleolithic times is quickly subsumed by the larger question of why the Yagahl speak English while everyone else they encounter in the film rattles on in the colorful gibberish ("Naht'm gahtzi!") traditionally reserved for movieland primitives. Other puzzlements include the fashion-forward dreadlocks on the men and Evolet's plucked-and-penciled eyebrows, not to mention the mascara-tinged tears she sometimes sheds.

In any case, one day the Yagahl are attacked in their peaceful village by a gang of marauding horsemen, who carry off several Yagahlis as slaves—among them, of course, the lovely Evolet. D'Leh, Tic'Tic, and the other male survivors of this onslaught give chase through mountains, jungles, and deserts and along the way have hair-raising encounters with saber-toothed tigers, giant woolly mammoths, and ferocious, proto-ostrich "terror birds." (The birds actually are scary; if only anything else in the movie measured up to them.) Finally, D'Leh and company, together with some other tribal guys they've recruited along the way, arrive at the evil pyramid city, which is ruled by a towering, heavily veiled god-king called the Almighty (an initially intriguing figure who turns out to be just some old coot, and so what?).

Throughout all of this, a fruity voice-over (by Paleolithic Egyptian star Omar Sharif) has been droning on about "ze Legend of ze Child with Blue Eyes," a reference to Evolet's contact lenses. This limp myth-mongering is only a mild annoyance until we realize that its sole purpose has been to facilitate what must be the most preposterous ending of any movie of the century to date. (At the screening I attended, even small children groaned.) Advice for anyone who actually *has* never seen a movie before: don't start with this one. (March 2008)

2012

The End Again

Even if most of Earth were to be destroyed by a natural cataclysm predicted long ago by the ancient Mayans, director Roland Emmerich would surely survive, if only to crawl back and polish off what little was left.

Going in to Emmerich's *2012,* I was prepared to set my brain on spin cycle and just roll with it—who doesn't enjoy a good CGI soak now and then? And there is in fact some snazzy digitalia on display here: a monster tsunami crashing over the Himalayas; a spectacular White House takedown (yet another); and some monster-wave ship-twirling that's truly, uh, titanic. An L.A. freeway buckles and falls, Las Vegas craps out, and the coast of California rears up and slides right into the ocean. All that, plus lots of fireball storms, collapsing high-rise real estate, and geysers of boiling black magma.

But there's an awful lot of this stuff; and since the movie is more than two and a half hours long—and since we are a nation of very jaded FX gluttons by now—surely there are some who'll find much of it grindingly monotonous. We should probably be grateful to Emmerich for not larding the picture with the endless eco-blather that burdened his last disaster special, *The Day After Tomorrow;* but this one is sprinkled with little We Are All One sermonettes that are almost as irritating.

Disaster movies always have a high baloney count, so there's no point in nit-picking the premise that launches *2012.* As a scientific possibility, the Ancient Mayan Prophecy presented here ranks one notch above Y2K. So let's just accept what's happening, which is . . . what? Something about planetary alignments, raging "sun eruptions," things like that. As one agitated science guy says: "For the first time ever, the neutrinos are causing a physical reaction!" (To which another script victim later replies: *"We're all gonna die!"*)

But let's meet the characters, and pretend we actually care about them.

Jackson Curtis (John Cusack) is a small-time sci-fi writer in exile from his wife Kate (Amanda Peet) and their winsome kids. Kate is now cohabiting with a nice-guy plastic surgeon named Gordon (Tom Mc-Carthy), who knows how to fly a plane—well, a little bit—which will soon come in handy. Adrian Helmsley (Chiwetel Ejiofor) is a top government geologist and number one (perhaps only) fan of Jackson's obscure book, *Farewell, Atlantis*. Adrian also has eyes for Laura Wilson (Thandie Newton), who's some sort of art expert and also the daughter of the president of the United States (Danny Glover). Yuri Karpov (Zlatco Buric) is a rich Russian thug whose mistress, Tamara (Beatrice Rosen), is the proud owner of a pair of fine new breasts that were installed, as it happens, by nice-guy Gordon.

Then, off in the woods on his own, there's Charlie Frost (Woody Harrelson), a doomsday loon who broadcasts his ravings from a little radio setup in his battered trailer. (Charlie's on hand to fill us in on that Ancient Mayan Prophecy.) There are also a number of excitable scientists in places like India and Canada and a wizened old lady in subtitle land who says things like, "We are all children of the Earth." (Great, just when Mom's pitching a fit.)

Oh, and Carl Anheuser (Oliver Platt). He's a White House weasel who, as Zero Hour approaches, is overseeing a secret escape plan for the world's top politicians and their billionaire friends. (We hope they've all booked lodgings in Hell.) And who was it that came up with the cutting-edge technology to effect this big getaway? You'll never guess. In any case, the gargantuan conveyances that have been devised, when we finally see them, look as if they drifted in out of a Carnival Cruise Lines commercial.

While the snickering fat cats prepare to sail away, the unticketed masses are deep in prayer. The director's heart is probably not with them, though—not after he's blown away a Buddhist monastery, the Sistine Chapel, and the giant Jesus statue overlooking Rio de Janeiro. (Not that Emmerich holds *nothing* sacred. In an online interview, he's quoted as saying that he had wanted to wipe out a sacred Islamic shrine, too, but then thought . . . maybe not: "You can [let] Christian symbols fall apart, but if you would do this with an Arab symbol, you would have . . . a fatwa. So I kind of left it out.")

Emmerich's best movie to date was 1996's *Independence Day.* The reasons for this are instructive. *ID4,* as you may recall it being called, had a highly personable top-rank star, Will Smith. The *2012* actors are all fine, but they lack A-list presence. *ID4* was witty (this one's mirthless) and its effects were stylishly deployed (this one just piles them on). *2012* may be a must-see movie this weekend, but you might not feel that way after the dust clears. (November 2009)

Prince of Persia: The Sands of Time

Boys Town

It's true that Jake Gyllenhaal's sudden, suntanned muscularity suggests Malibu Beach more than it does ancient Persia; and one wonders if the ancient Persians said things like "Watch your back" and "I need a drink." Still, *Prince of Persia: The Sands of Time* seems like a pretty good Arabian-adventure movie for kids. It's made in the classic Disney style: no sex, no swearing, and lots of action with very little blood. So if you know a kid—of the male persuasion, ideally—you might want to take him to see it. You might also want to wait at a bar somewhere while he does so.

The movie is based on a long-evolving video game created by Jordan Mechner, who came up with the story for the film, too. It's the sort of story whose hazy details could only be ignored by a kid waiting impatiently for the next eruption of swordplay, rope-dangling, and bad-guy head-bashing. Gyllenhaal plays Dastan, a commoner who was adopted as an urchin, for reasons we can hurry right past here, by the good King Sharaman (Ronald Pickup), who raised the boy along with his two sons, Garsiv (Toby Kebbell) and Tus (Richard Coyle). Also lurking about is the lads' uncle, Nizam (Ben Kingsley, wearing enough eye shadow to put him in line for harem duty).

As the tale gets under way, Nizam brings news that the holy city of Alamut is supplying weapons to Persia's enemies. The now-grown Dastan is heroically helpful in storming Alamut's battlements and, once inside, draws the attention of the resident Princess Tamina (Gemma Arterton). After some preliminary squabbling (the traditional prelude to a chaste Disney kiss), she informs him that Alamut is the repository of "the beating heart of all life—the sandglass of the gods." This turns out to be located in the handle of a golden dagger, of which Dastan, for some hazy reason, is in possession. Pressing a button on the magical artifact summons a fiery wind that allows the dagger's wielder to go back one minute in time and undo whatever terrible things may need undoing. Just such a situation soon arises: King Sharaman dons a robe that someone has given him as a gift and . . . it kills him. (The haze thickens.) Dastan is quickly fingered as the malefactor and must flee into the desert with Tamina.

Out among the dunes they encounter a character named Sheik Amar (Alfred Molina), who presides over a desert settlement where he stages ostrich races "every Tuesday and Thursday." (As you always suspected of ostrich races, they're fixed.) When the duplicitous Amar learns that there's a reward out for Dastan's capture, the prince and his princess are forced to flee again, this time under cover of an ostrich *stampede,* which I must say is something to see.

Dastan unwisely decides that the time is now right to return home to attend the funeral of his father and to determine who was responsible for his death. (Men with an overabundance of eye shadow should be prime suspects.) Various trials must be endured along the way. There's a trudge through the Valley of the Slaves and an onslaught of black-clad, whip-flicking Hassassins (the hashish-stoked killers of legend, but here—this being a Disney film—apparently drug-free). In the end, Dastan and Tamina make it back to his native castle and . . . so forth and so on.

Producer Jerry Bruckheimer knows his way around this sort of great big money-stuffed movie, and here he delivers everything you might expect. The action is excitingly staged (some of the wild roof-leaping suggests that the urban acrobatics of parkour were devised far earlier than we'd thought), although the CGI varies from beautiful (the hilltop city of Alamut) to whatever (that fiery wind). There are some funny touches, too—Molina in particular seems to be having a ball. And of course in the grand tradition of Hollywood movies about long-ago foreigners, all the main parts are played by Brits—except for that of Gyllenhaal, who nevertheless affects a British accent in solidarity with his fellow Persians.

Despite his bronzed buffness, however, Gyllenhaal is too laid-back for serious swashbuckling; and Arterton, a better actress in other pictures, here falls back on her basic gorgeousness, occasionally inflected with a curious lip twitch that she really ought to have looked at. But then if you feel that acting quality is a serious concern, you're not the target audience for this hard-charging fantasy epic. Hope that there's a bar right down the street. (May 2010)

Clash of the Titans

Myth Mash

C *lash of the Titans* probably wasn't intended to be a lotta laughs, but Lord knows it is. Unfortunately, that's not the same thing as being a lot of fun.

The picture is a 3-D remake of the 1981 film of the same name, which was itself a throwback to the muscle-bound sword-and-sandal epics cranked out in Italy in the 1950s and early 1960s. Once again we are in a world of haughty gods and fearsome monsters drawn rather loosely from Greek mythology. Our hero, Perseus (Sam Worthington, of *Avatar*), is the half-human son of the mighty Zeus (Liam Neeson), who has a longstanding affection for humans (and an eye for their ladies—thus Perseus). Gazing down from the cloud-bound realm of Olympus, Zeus and his fellow gods—who with their strange silvery glow bear an amusing resemblance to an ABBA cover band—have become worried by signs of unrest in the coastal city of Argos, whose residents are fed up with the gods' capricious reign and the disasters and tragedies they regularly inflict. The angry Argosians have ceased offering up prayers to their heavenly rulers, and revolution is in the air. As one upstart citizen cries: "Should we be trembling and soiling ourselves in fear?"

Zeus is hesitant to clamp down on these ingrates; but his brother, Hades (Ralph Fiennes), is made of sterner stuff. Hades drew the short straw when godly dominions were handed out and has been consigned to rule the dismal Underworld. He is thus in a perpetual bad mood and turns up on Olympus offering the services of a fearsome pet monster in subduing the whiny humans. "In ten days," he announces, "I will unleash the Kraken!"

Meanwhile, down below, Perseus, who was raised among mortals, has now fallen in with the Argos rebels. Tipped to his demigod heritage by a mysterious beauty named Io (Gemma Arterton), he sets off with a detachment of soldiers on a quest, the object of which is to rescue an endangered princess, Andromeda (Alexa Davalos), and, while he's at it, to smite all manner of loathsome magical creatures. First there's an attack of giant scorpions, then an encounter with a trio of crones, the Stygian witches, who offer little in the way of encouragement. ("You will die.") Next stop is a confrontation with the ghastly Medusa (Natalia Vodianova), whose snake-wreathed face can turn those who gaze upon it to stone. Luckily, before Perseus sets off for this deadly challenge, Zeus appears and bequeaths him a special sword ("a very rare and high-quality item"), which of course soon comes in handy.

The Medusa confrontation is the movie's most imaginative sequence. (Well, it was imaginative when we first saw it, back in 1981.) The frightful demon's body is a lashing reptilian horror; and the battle that ensues when Perseus calls her out is, relative to the rest of the movie, fairly thrilling. (Even more so than the concluding fray with the Kraken, a CGI confection that manages to resemble both the goofy mountain troll in the first *Harry Potter* film and the huge squidlike guardian of the door to Moria in the first *Lord of the Rings* movie.)

But apart from the recycled feeling of some of the creatures (one character with an eye in the palm of its hand recalls the Pale Man in *Pan's Labyrinth,* and some extra-tall desert nomads exude a vague Chewbacca vibe), the movie has other problems. In unflattering contrast with Neeson and Fiennes (both slumming, as Laurence Olivier was in the original *Titans*), Worthington is a colorless hero—he lacks the outsize personality that might have made his character a commanding presence. And the film is a visual jumble: it wasn't conceived or photographed in 3-D, but instead hastily converted in the wake of *Avatar,* and the effect is flat and pointless. Combined with the chaotic camera work (the whole picture looks as if it were shot from the back of a moving truck), it makes the movie an eye-wearying chore to take in. Despite the picture's many laughable moments, the box-office gods may not be amused. (April 2010)

Alexander

Ancient Evenings

There are many worthwhile things that might be done with $150 million; a movie like this isn't among them. Back in the fourth century B.C. Alexander the Great took eight years to conquer the known world of his time. The best that can be said about *Alexander,* the movie, is that it isn't quite that long (although it does run nearly three hours). The picture is so thoroughly silly, it's hard to know where to begin in listing its infelicities. But let's try.

First of all, Colin Farrell, who plays Alexander (with a blond dye job), is twenty-eight years old; Angelina Jolie, who plays his mother, Olympias, is twenty-nine. Olympias has a thing for snakes—she purrs through the film with vipers thrown over her shoulder or wrapped around her leg or just left lying all a-squirm on the floor of her palace boudoir. Why? Dunno. She also speaks in some sort of indeterminate Carpathian accent, for reasons that eluded me, if they even exist.

The movie is narrated—and narrated and narrated—by Alexander's boyhood friend, Ptolemy (Anthony Hopkins). At a point many years after Alexander's death, we see Ptolemy, now old and tiresome, doddering about his palace recounting the Great's many exploits and trying to shovel in as much ancient historical context as possible, in vain hope of giving the audience some idea of what's going on. His incessant drone, clotted with phrases like "the loins of war," is the picture's overriding annoyance. Although you do kind of chuckle when he lets rip with "It is said that Alexander was never defeated, except by Hephaistion's thighs." Hephaistion (Jared Leto) is another of Alexander's childhood chums, although in this case, one with whom he has a sexual relationship. We're not about to actually see these two men in carnal entanglement, of course—not in a big Hollywood movie—so we're treated instead to many sultry looks and steamy sighs, all of them risible. ("You have eyes like no other," Hephaistion murmurs at one point.) The director appears to be aiming for a tone of bold homo-eroticism. (Who knew that ancient armies traveled with contingents of simpering young sex slaves?) But since Stone has no knack for the erotic, the result is just silly. For example, after Alexander marries a woman named Roxane (played by Rosario Dawson, lumbered with another indeterminately foreign accent), she catches him in their bedroom trading smoldery confidences with Hephaistion. "You luff heem?" she asks, with understandable pique. "There are many different ways to love," Alexander replies, as Roxane backs away, possibly not wanting to see any of them demonstrated. (Dawson later features nakedly in the movie's only heterosexual interlude.)

There are two big, expensively staged battles in *Alexander,* but their tumult is largely a matter of blurry camera work and whip-bang editing. Somebody shouts, "Prepare to repel chariots!" Then there's a lot of leaping and grunting and clanging. Then Alexander, riding ahead of his men into battle, yells over his shoulder, "Left turn!" And then . . . no, I can't go on. Or wait, yes I can: the soundtrack score of this movie, by the Greek synthesizer eminence Vangelis, is a trial in itself, an ugly mush of oozing string washes, pounding tympanis, swooning chorales, and wee tinkling chimes. There's no one up on the screen at any point suffering as much abuse as the audience enduring this aural assault.

Colin Farrell's career will survive this movie. So will Angelina Jolie's. And of course Anthony Hopkins, having previously lent his presence to the execrable *Hannibal*, obviously feels secure about his own professional future. But Oliver Stone hasn't directed a movie that anyone took seriously since the 1994 *Natural Born Killers*. His career disarray continues. (November 2004)

YOU GIVE LOVE
A BAD NAME

Romance being an eternal human concern, romantic comedies will surely always be with us. The screwball (and nonscrewball) classics of the 1930s and 1940s set a high bar for the form, which had slumped by the dawn of the 1960s into the sort of cuddly fluff most profitably exemplified by the Rock Hudson–Doris Day pictures. Stylish rom-coms have continued to be made—Moonstruck, Groundhog Day, The Princess Bride. But fluff, like love itself, and its attendant overpriced chocolates and Valentine's Day doggerel, is a hardy cinematic species. As we see here.

Bride Wars

What a Girl Wants

Girls are so dumb. They say they want to grow up and become, you know, lawyers and stuff; but all they *really* want to do is grow up and lasso some poor guy and make him buy them a cauliflower-size diamond ring and then throw themselves a monstro wedding and invite all four hundred of their pathetically unmarried girlfriends to duke it out over the bridal bouquet. You know it's true.

Or you do now that *Bride Wars* is here to break the news. "It all began at the Plaza Hotel twenty years ago," says an opening voice-over—although it's soon clear that the movie's view of women and their wants dates back much further, possibly to the Late Pleistocene. The script may have started out as an attempted satire of the American wedding industry (two of its three writers are female), but the picture in which it has resulted is a prolonged honk of derision aimed at the women who get caught up in our national matrimonial mania. Granted, anyone who longs to drop $10,000 on a simple Vera Wang wedding gown needs a good talking-to. But this movie has a curdled nastiness (especially in its depiction of secondary characters) that's unlikely to play well even on the chick-flick circuit.

Kate Hudson is Liv, a hard-charging New York lawyer. Anne Hathaway is her lifelong best friend, Emma, a doe-eyed schoolteacher. Ever since they were kids, both of them have dreamed of one day getting married at the Plaza—which, if I may explain for out-of-towners, is a place where room rates start in the spine-tingling vicinity of a thousand dollars a night and the eggs Benedict in a Palm Court breakfast will set you back thirty bucks (or would have, if the hotel hadn't been forced to close the Palm Court last week, presumably for lack of enough out-of-towners willing to pay thirty bucks for eggs Benedict).

For different reasons, both girls have to finance their weddings pretty much themselves, once they become engaged (to male characters whose roles in the proceedings are entirely vestigial). This might not be a problem for lawyer Liv, maybe, but Emma? A schoolteacher? Oh, wait: "I've been saving up for this since I was sixteen." Ah.

Since it's an article of faith in wedding world that no mere civilian can organize one of these extravaganzas, Liv and Emma consult a high-end wedding planner (Candice Bergen), who's happy to confirm their belief that the big-ticket nuptial blowout is a peak life experience. ("You have been dead until now," she tells them. "You are dead *right* now.") The planner screws up, though, and books both girls' Plaza weddings on the same day. Since there are apparently no other venues in Manhattan suitable for marrying—no others quite so pitifully ostentatious, anyway—this means war. Soon, in a sly effort to fatten Liv up beyond the confines of her Vera Wang frock, Emma is anonymously sending her boxes of chocolates, baskets of snacks, and a membership in the International Butter Club. (After a dismal beginning, the movie does strike some funny notes.) Liv retaliates by sabotaging a tanning session that ends up turning Emma's skin orange. Emma strikes back by infiltrating a beauty salon and arranging to alter Liv's dye job to an electric shade of blue.

Some of this might have passed for funny in a TV sitcom, although probably in an earlier decade than the one in which we're dozing through this movie. The plot has the rigid predictability of a wedding march; and while it's sort of amusing to hear one of the girls' bachelorette guests desperately yelping, "I'm gonna do a quick head count of the hot drunk single guys," there's also something predatory and off-putting about it. The director, Gary Winick, may have been hoping to give the picture some of the urban gloss of a movie like *The Devil Wears Prada,* but even with the esteemed Frederick Elmes behind the camera, *Bride Wars* isn't much to look at. More remarkably, neither are its two stars, both well-known beauties. Someone has contrived to keep Hathaway's lustrous hair yanked back from her face for much of the film, putting an unflattering emphasis on her outsized features; and a shocking makeup miscalculation has Hudson looking like a gingerbread cookie that's been left in the oven too long. The upbeat outcome of the movie's titular bridal battle is never in doubt, but the two stars suffer unexpected collateral damage. (January 2009)

All About Steve

Clueless

All About Steve is a plateful of stale crumbs swept up off the floor of the Hollywood rom-com factory. It's one of the worst movies on which Sandra Bullock has ever wasted her talent or our time. The picture was written by Kim Barker, whom one might have thought still to be under house arrest for penning the wretched Robin Williams anti-comedy *License to Wed*. Barker's script has been given the direction it deserves by Phil Traill, who came to the task from TV and shorts. Bullock is one of the producers, which brings the fiasco full-circle.

The story is a laborious trifle. Bullock plays a cruciverbalist—a professional maker of crossword puzzles—named Mary Magdalene Horowitz (half Catholic, half Jewish, no payoff). Mary somehow makes a living creating one crossword puzzle per week for a small Sacramento newspaper (a publication that appears to be stuck in an age other than our own—its editor pastes up pages by hand, rather than composing them on a computer). Laboring in her chosen field, she has accumulated a vast store of arcane knowledge—obscure geographical factoids, stray phrases from foreign languages—and it comes spilling out of her in an unstoppable flow, short-circuiting all attempts at social interaction. She's also strangely partial to cheesy miniskirts and knee-high boots of a screaming red hue, which she wears at all times. The movie wants us to see Mary as a good-hearted eccentric, undervalued by the world. But her overbearing oddity is indistinguishable from mental defect.

This is another of those pictures in which a character who looks like Sandra Bullock can't get a man. Thus, Mary's mom and dad conspire to set her up on a blind date with another couple's son, Steve (Bradley Cooper—yes, it's also the sort of picture in which a guy who looks like Bradley Cooper can't get a gal). Steve is a cameraman for a CNN-like news channel, and he's such a godsend that the love-starved Mary jumps him the minute she gets into his van on their first date. Steve is terrified by this eruption of psycho-neediness, and greatly relieved when a call comes in at that very moment dragging him away to cover a breaking news story with his producer Angus (Ken Jeong, wasted) and their pompous on-air reporter Hartman (Thomas Haden Church, way overqualified for this picture). Left hyperventilating in Steve's dust, Mary decides to make it her life's work to follow him hither and yon from that point on.

When she learns that Steve and his crew are covering a hostage situation in Tucson, Arizona, Mary hops on a bus to make the trip—which would take more than thirteen hours from Sacramento—and is puzzled to find the story long over and Steve and company long gone when she finally arrives. She catches up with them in Oklahoma, covering the birth of a three-legged baby, and then doggedly pursues them down to the Gulf Coast of Texas, where there's a big hurricane blowing in. At this point we might note that keeping a production crew racing around the country in an expensive satellite van to cover things like hurricanes is not the way TV news operations operate.

But then the movie itself is a demonstration of the ways in which comedy doesn't operate. It collapses in its long concluding section, which involves a group of deaf children who've been swallowed up in a Colorado mine-shaft collapse. This is where we're supposed to see a realization of Mary's many admirable qualities—her hyperintelligence, her good heart—dawning on the main characters. But Mary hasn't evolved—she's not a good soul out of step with everyone else; she's an idiot. (Bullock's familiar appeal as an actress is straitjacketed throughout the picture by her character's glued-on, moronic smirk.) And so there's no preparation for the moment when Steve suddenly has a complete change of heart about Mary, because there's no plausible reason why he should have one.

The level of dialogue doesn't evolve either. Early on, when Church's character learns that Steve is being followed around by a woman in red boots, he says, "You bangin' a fireman?" This might have been amusing if firemen in fact wore red boots; but they don't. And when we finally do learn why Mary has been wearing those damn boots all through the picture, the answer turns out to be, "Because they make my toes feel like ten friends on a camping trip." This, alas, is the movie's most memorable line. Now that you've read it, there's no need, believe me, to see it spoken. (September 2009)

The Back-up Plan

Ladies Only

I saw *The Back-up Plan* at a very special screening. On Venus, I believe. The audience was larded with contest winners, brought in to catch a sneak peek and to fill the air with free-admission laughter. And yet there's no denying that the women of all ages sitting around me appeared to really like this movie. They laughed all the way through it—laughed at the vintage corn (when was the last time a movie dredged up the old boy-girl meet-cute in a taxi they both think they've hailed?), laughed at the adorable little handicapped dog (a gag-on-wheels that was more diverting in *Babe: Pig in the City*), and laughed long and hard at the shocks and wonders of pregnancy and childbirth with which the picture is centrally concerned. At the risk of sexist condescension, I'd say that being a woman—or a woman of a certain kind, anyway—is a prerequisite for enjoying this film.

Jennifer Lopez plays Zoe, the owner of a Greenwich Village pet shop—not a "puppy mill," as she disdainfully puts it, but a store that offers up proudly un-bred mutts for adoption. Despite her strong resemblance to Jennifer Lopez, Zoe has had no luck finding a good guy. Now, facing forty and longing for a family, she's decided to have herself artificially inseminated. But then, mere moments after undergoing the procedure, she has the fortuitous taxicab encounter with a guy named Stan, who's played by Alex O'Loughlin, an Australian actor so appealing in his own right that he might as well have a "good guy" tag affixed to his wrist (or perhaps stapled to his frequently shirtless chest). Stan is instantly smitten. He follows Zoe down the street and then down into the subway, where any New Yorker will be surprised to note that she doesn't seek out a transit cop.

Zoe and Stan—whose crunchy vocation is creating artisanal cheeses at an upstate farm—are of course made for each other. They share their dreams. His is to open "a sustainable gourmet shop," although he's also studying economics on the side (a pointless plot splinter). After some preliminary nuzzling, Zoe tells Stan she's pregnant by someone she knows only as a number on a sperm-bank shelf. Stan is taken aback, but not for long, and soon he's dealing with the complications of having (PG-13) sex with a pregnant woman, and with her impromptu vomiting and her hilarious inability to fit into her favorite clothes and her sudden lust for lapping up ice cream in bed. (There's also a bit in which the ever-famished Zoe, overcome by the aroma of a pot of tomatoey goop bubbling on a stove, submits to temptation and begins shoveling the stuff into her mouth with her bare hands—a scene that might best have been left in its entirety for the blooper reel at the end of the film.)

In addition, there are infusions of predictable wisdom from Zoe's garrulous grandmother (Linda Lavin) and a father of three (Anthony Anderson) whom Stan meets in a park. There's also one funny line—when the slowly swelling Zoe tells Stan, "I miss my hot ass"—that will strike a chord with longtime Lopez watchers. Then there's a fateful penny that keeps turning up in an entirely rom-com manner, a drum-thumping single-mothers group ("We do what we have to do when we don't have a penis partner"), and a birthing scene in a wading pool that struck me as grotesque, but which had the laughing women at the screening I attended laughing even harder.

The Back-up Plan was scripted by TV sitcom veteran Kate Angelo, and despite its obstetrical candor, it has a flat sitcom blandness. It seeks to take us to the heart of female functions, and it leaves the men in the picture with little to do but stand around looking love-struck, heartsick, or, for the most part, clueless. It's not a date movie. If anything, it's a girls' night out. Depending, as I say, on the girls. (April 2010)

The Switch

Fluid Situation

The Switch is set in that fantasy Manhattan, familiar from Woody Allen movies, in which everyone seems to be a highly compensated white professional and all ethnic coloration has been drained away. The movie wants us to care about such people's problems—which include things like imaginary medical maladies—but many viewers may wish that such trifling complaints were the only ones *they* had.

Jennifer Aniston plays Kassie Larson, a top TV producer who's nearing forty and desperate to have a child. Jason Bateman is Wally Mars, a stock trader who was once Kassie's boyfriend but is now simply her best pal—although of course he still secretly pines for her love. Kassie has never found the right guy to have a family with, so she's decided to go the artificial-insemination route. She's found the ideal donor in a guy named Roland (Patrick Wilson), who's both a hearty jock *and* an assistant professor of feminist theory at Columbia University. Obviously Mr. Right, at least for purposes of impregnation.

Do women desirous of offspring actually throw I'm Getting Pregnant parties at which their chosen sperm donor arrives bearing baby juice in a plastic cup? Kassie does. Unfortunately, Wally is among the many friends in attendance, and he gets drunk, stumbles into the bathroom, finds Roland's cup, accidentally spills its contents, and then—using a magazine photo of *Diane Sawyer* for stimulation!—brings forth his own seminal contribution, which he leaves to be passed off as

Roland's. Wally is so drunk that the next day he doesn't remember doing this. Two weeks later, Kassie announces she's pregnant. She relocates to Minnesota in order to raise the child she'll soon be having.
Seven years later she returns to New York with her little boy, Sebastian
(Thomas Robinson). She reconnects with Wally—who's still in the dark
about what he did at the party that night and doesn't realize Sebastian is
his son—but also with Roland, who now develops an amorous interest.
Et cetera.

Romantic comedy isn't often an arena for violence, but this film's
different: the movie's script continually manhandles its characters into
situations of brazen implausibility. The picture does have some funny
moments, mostly provided by Jeff Goldblum as Wally's distracted boss
(Goldblum always seems to have another, more interesting conversation going on in his head while he's delivering his lines); and by Juliette
Lewis, who sparks a few scenes with her blowsy, wisecracking energy.
("I've had orgasms that last longer than his relationships.")

It's too bad that Bateman, so expert at underplaying comic characters, has a character here that's so thinly conceived it can't bear much
underplaying. Wally—who exhibits none of the sharkish traits we might
expect of someone in his line of work—is a downbeat lump, and after a
while, as he fails over and over again (and ever more unconvincingly) to
break the news that he's the father of Kassie's son, we understand why he
might seem a poor romantic choice for any woman. This leaves a charisma deficit that would have to be filled by Aniston. She's an appealing
comic actress, but after seventeen years of making feature films, she's
still handicapped by the mild effect of the TV star she once was. Will she
ever really turn us on? Or will we always just be friends? (August 2010)

Valentine's Day

Heart-Shaped Schlock

Looking for a rom-com fix this Valentine's weekend? Rather than fall for the calculated come-on of *Valentine's Day*, you might want to revisit some much better films instead. *Jerry Maguire*, perhaps. Or *Moonstruck*. Or *House of 1000 Corpses*.

Okay, I exaggerate. *Valentine's Day* does have a few good lines, and a couple of lively performances. But the movie is overstuffed with plot and characters; they're confusing to keep up with, and uninteresting even when you're able to figure them out.

The story takes place on . . . well, you know what day it takes place on. Ashton Kutcher is a love-struck Los Angeles florist who has just proposed to his sleepover girlfriend, Jessica Alba. "I can be a sappy moron all day," he crows, with unwarranted presumption, "because it's Valentine's Day." His best friend, Jennifer Garner, is happy for him, in part because she's finally found Mr. Right—a doctor, played by Patrick Dempsey, whose many endearing qualities include a talent for juggling fruit. (Really.)

Meanwhile, Anne Hathaway is a lowly temp secretary (sure) who moonlights as a phone-sex dominatrix in order to pay off her college loan—a sideline that weirds out her boyfriend, Topher Grace. Bradley Cooper finds himself seated on a plane next to Julia Roberts, an army captain (uh-huh) en route all the way from the Middle East to spend one day with someone special in L.A. At a local high school, Emma Roberts is planning to have first-time sex with her boyfriend, Carter Jenkins, while another student couple, Taylor Swift and Taylor Lautner, is heading in that same direction. Football star Eric Dane is contemplating quitting the game because he has no sweetie; his cynical publicist, Jessica Biel, is preparing to throw her annual I Hate Valentine's

Day party; TV sports reporter and commitment-phobe Jamie Foxx is fuming over being forced to shoot a man-on-the-street Valentine's Day piece; little Bryce Robinson is struggling with the pangs of first love (he's nine years old); and Shirley MacLaine and Hector Elizondo are celebrating fifty-one years of happy marriage when she suddenly confesses a long-buried secret (which drives him off to a screening of . . . an old Shirley MacLaine movie).

Is Kutcher in for a surprise with his new fiancée? Has Garner possibly found Mr. Wrong? Can Grace learn to accept Hathaway for the lovable kook she is? Will Foxx and Biel see the Valentine light? Surely these are questions no one need ask. And the picture is so crowded (George Lopez, Kathy Bates, and Queen Latifah also wander through) that there's little room to develop most of the characters beyond simple personality doodles, and thus make us care about them.

In any case, it's hard to relate to people who are so maniacally excited about Valentine's Day. Fortunately, Foxx's outsize presence juices each scene he's in, Swift makes a winsome ditz, and Lautner gets off one of the movie's few wry lines. ("I'm a little uncomfortable taking my shirt off in public.") But the rest of this trite confection is a flavorless goop of exhausted clichés about the varieties of romantic love. The movie is designed to exploit the date-night ferment of its opening weekend and nothing more. It has the radiant glow of a Hollywood pitch meeting. (February 2010)

Ghosts of Girlfriends Past

Payback

In a time of tight money and ridiculous ticket prices, *Ghosts of Girlfriends Past* offers an excellent opportunity to save yourself ten bucks. The movie aspires to nothing beyond its flat premise—it's *A Christmas Carol* with Scrooge replaced by a clueless womanizer in need of comeuppance. But the picture has some laughs, and a couple of punchy comic performances, and rom-com fans, so often underserved, could do worse.

Matthew McConaughey plays Connor Mead, a New York fashion photographer of such genius that he only needs to saunter into a shoot after everything's been set up (lights, camera, bosomy models), press the shutter release, and—*click*—his job is done. Connor is so awash in adoring girlfriends that he has to break up with them in groups, via laptop video conference. He agrees to drive up to Connecticut to attend the wedding of his younger brother Paul (Breckin Meyer) mainly so he can service whatever bridesmaids are on hand whom he hasn't already nailed.

Also present at this affair are Jenny Perotti (Jennifer Garner), the childhood sweetheart Connor never had the good sense to stick with, and the ghost of his late Uncle Wayne (Michael Douglas)—the man who set him on the path to horndog-hood with advice like, "The power in any relationship lies with whoever cares less." ("He invented the word 'milf,'" Connor says admiringly.) Wayne has belatedly seen the error of his earthly ways, though, and now, back from the beyond, he's arranged to have three ghosts visit Connor over the course of one night and try to wise him up, too.

The movie takes off with the arrival of the first ghost, Allison, a teen throwback in ratty red hair, scrunchies, and braces, who's played with gleeful abandon by Emma Stone (*The House Bunny*). Allison was Connor's first hookup, at a high school party ("We dated for the next thirty-nine minutes!"), and Stone has such exuberant comic energy that we kind of wish the movie would just follow her and forget about the self-infatuated Connor (a character McConaughey inhabits with unsurprising expertise).

Another lively presence in the film is Noureen DeWulf, who injects the role of ghost girl number two, Melanie, with bracing sarcasm. (Mel is actually Connor's worked-to-death assistant, and she's about had it: not only does she slave for this guy all week; now she has to spend her weekend acting as one of his spirit guides. It's best not to think too hard about this.) Lacey Chabert brings a surge of ditzy fizz to a few scenes as Sandra, the bride-to-be; and of course Michael Douglas carries off the

Scotch-sipping libertine Wayne with an old pro's expansive ease. (He also anchors the movie's best scene, when Wayne, standing outdoors with Connor, triggers a downpour of rain, and explains that it represents all the "lady tears" that have been shed over his narcissistic nephew. Then he brings a bunch of *other* representative things pouring down, which is pretty hilarious.)

Despite the best efforts of all these people, though, Matthew McConaughey is still the star, and the better he is at playing Connor as a self-infatuated sexual predator, the more off-putting the character becomes. (Garner's Jenny, meanwhile, has little to do but wait around for him to come to his senses, allowing the actress to demonstrate her appealing sweetness, and to get off some tart lines, but not much else.) The picture is boxed in by its concept. The one-joke setup is cute, but the plot mechanics are familiar and we know the punch line in our bones. When Connor says, toward the end, "I'm an empty ghost of a man," he speaks for the movie itself. (May 2009)

CREEPERS

A good horror movie has to be imaginative, of course, and stylish. But how many really are? How many rely instead on rote shivers and shocks to achieve their predictable effects? The industrial nature of movie production—the need to keep the pipeline filled with product—ensures that most horror films will be of this uninspired variety. Although there are always bracing exceptions worth seeing.

The Midnight Meat Train

Blood on the Tracks

Well, here it is, the little movie that Lionsgate dumped unheralded into about a hundred second-run theaters last month, consigning it to the trash heap of horror history—or so a legion of ticked-off Clive Barker fans feared. *The Midnight Meat Train,* based on one of Barker's 1984 *Books of Blood* stories, is now scheduled to make a proper debut on the FearNet channel on October 1, and on the channel's website on October 30. The picture deserved better treatment.

Unexpectedly, this is not completely a gore movie. Not in the way that most brain-dead blood feasts are, at least. True, there are some savage attacks, some queasy dismemberments, and a meat-mallet head-bash that knocks a victim's eyeball straight out at the camera. But these are fleeting, for the most part. Japanese cult director Ryuhei Kitamura maintains cool control of the narrative, ratcheting up tension along the way toward startling bursts of terror.

The story seems simple, at first. Struggling photographer Leon Kauffman (Bradley Cooper) is determined to capture with his camera the nighttime heart of his big city (unspecified, but actually Los Angeles). One night, down in a subway station, he sees a young Asian woman being harassed by thugs. He drives them away, and she gratefully boards her train—never to be seen again. (Although *we* see what happens to her—not pretty, of course.) Before long, Leon is on the trail of a strange, unspeaking figure in a too-tight suit and a tie, carrying a large satchel. This, we eventually learn, is a character called Mahogany (Vinnie Jones), and the train he rides on a regular basis is a very special one—not just because of the glistening blood lakes that slick its floors, but because of a special stop it makes. As Leon draws closer to penetrating this mystery—and seriously alarming his girlfriend, Maya (Leslie Bibb) in the process—the story opens up into something I wasn't anticipating and won't hint at here.

Kitamura bathes the proceedings in rich washes of light—not just the septic blues and greens of so many contemporary horror flicks, but dustier illuminations that enhance the film's feeling of enclosure and entrapment. The cast, which also includes Roger Bart (*Hostel: Part II*) and Peter Jacobson (*House*), is stronger than most movies of this sort ever deserve; and Vinnie Jones, with his big bullet head, grim visage, and case full of fearsome implements, is a very scary monster. Spotting him onboard this infernal train, you might rather walk. (September 2008)

The Haunting in Connecticut

Housing Crisis

Just because the "true story" on which a horror film is based doesn't pass the hogwash test is no reason, in itself, to dismiss the movie. (Consider *The Exorcist*.) *The Haunting in Connecticut*, however, offers additional reasons. What we have here is a simple haunted-house flick, pure and silly. Demons lurk and loom, characters make straight for the cellar stairs leading down into darkness, and every time a reflective surface comes into view, you know with a sigh of certainty that some spectral presence will soon be glimpsed in it: *boo!*

What the picture does have going for it is a more skilful cast than you'd expect, and some effective shocks and scenes of shivery dread. The story has been trimmed of the more asinine elements of the "real" haunting, which took place, if that can actually be said, in a Hartford suburb in the mid-1980s. Now we have out-of-towners Pete and Sara Campbell (horror vets Martin Donovan and Virginia Madsen) moving into a spooky old house in order to be close to the hospital where their son Matt (Kyle Gallner) is undergoing cancer therapy. Also on hand, for reasons clear only to the writers, are Sara's niece, Wendy (Amanda Crew), and Wendy's two cute little kids (Sophi Knight and Ty Wood).

Upon arriving at the house, Matt immediately calls dibs on the dismal basement for his bedroom. We know this to be a knuckleheaded decision even before it's revealed that the house was once a funeral home (thus the embalming slabs and corpse cutlery still cluttering the basement); and if that weren't unsettling enough, we learn that the former owner also conducted séances down there, with his son acting as a spirit medium and channeling thick gouts of otherworldly ectoplasm out of his mouth (an activity seen in creepy flashbacks—it looks like slo-mo barfing). There are also a lot of vintage dead-people photographs lying around (very *Wisconsin Death Trip*), a nice grisly interlude of eyelid-severing (very Buñuel), and some blather about a nearby cemetery that's missing a lot of cadavers (very whatever). Also wheeled in, inevitably, is a priest (Elias Koteas, Madsen's costar in *The Prophecy*, a much niftier horror film) to explain all this stuff for us.

Any movie set largely in gloomy rooms and corridors is going to be low on illumination, but the murk here is oppressive. The lights do go up for some scenes in the cancer hospital, but this plot strand is talky and it slows the story down; we want to get back to the maggots, the worms, and the charbroiled room wraiths. First-time feature director Peter Cornwell has a flair for claustrophobic horror (the séance scenes have a smothering chill); but he also has an unfortunate affection for that weariest of cheats, the hair-raising jolt that turns out to be "just a dream." Wake us when it's over. (March 2009)

Orphan

Our Little Monster

Little Esther has been a bad girl. A *very* bad girl. For most of her nine years, in fact—although as the new horror movie *Orphan* opens, all we know of her earlier life is that she was left homeless when her adoptive family died in a fire. How fortunate that she managed to escape. Now she's available to be re-adopted by another family, and here come the well-to-do Colemans to scoop her up. Naturally they haven't thought to hide the matches or anything, but they'll learn soon enough.

Orphan is an evil-child movie with an interesting twist at the end. It's a twist that doesn't stand up under retrospective contemplation, but how many do? And the picture is so strongly cast and sleekly filmed that when the crafty ending arrives, we accept it out of simple consumer gratitude.

We join the Colemans—architect John (Peter Sarsgaard) and his pregnant wife Kate (Vera Farmiga)—as they arrive at a hospital, where Kate is ready to give birth. Then, in a bloody half-dream sequence, we see that her baby is born dead. The couple is bereft. They already have two children, but now decide to adopt a third to join their six-year-old deaf-mute daughter Max (Aryana Engineer, who actually is hearing impaired) and her twelve-year-old brother Daniel (Jimmy Bennett). At a Catholic orphanage they meet little Esther (Isabelle Fuhrman), a raven-haired, dark-eyed Russian girl. Esther loves to paint and sing and dress in old-fashioned frocks and even wear ribbons in her hair—a perfect little angel. With the blessing of Sister Abigail (CCH Pounder), the head nun at the orphanage, the Colemans decide to adopt Esther, which makes her oh so happy. "Nobody's ever talked to me before," she says sweetly. "I guess I'm different."

Director Jaume Collet-Serra (the 2005 *House of Wax*) is intent on not rushing the horrors to come. The first thing we learn after the Colemans bring Esther home is how shaky their marriage is. John had an affair some years back, which may have been what drove Kate to drink—she's an alcoholic, now on the wagon, who almost caused little Max's death when she passed out while the girl was playing by a pond. Esther, who's eerily devious, quickly perceives John's ambivalence about his wife and determines to exploit it. She begins by appearing in the couple's bedroom one night and announcing, "I want to sleep next to Daddy."

Esther's strangeness comes into focus slowly—a crushed bird here, a crippled schoolmate there. When she breaks into the safe where John keeps a pistol, we also learn she has a very unchildlike expertise with firearms. She neutralizes her new siblings through cold-blooded intimidation (a threat of castration gets Daniel's attention); then she sets her sight on Kate, intent on driving her crazy. (Farmiga has been through this before, in the 2007 demon-kid dud *Joshua*.) The only ray of hope in this march toward disaster comes from Sister Abigail, who sounds an alarm—she's discovered that Esther may not be the little princess everyone thought. But Esther is eavesdropping when this information is conveyed, and by the time the nun's car comes speeding onto the Colemans' extensive acreage, she's waiting by the side of the road, with a hammer.

The picture was shot in Canada, which afforded an appropriate wintry chill. Snow blows and drifts outside the Colemans' home, whose austere interiors—slate grays and dark wood, with brushed-metal lamps providing puddles of light—are elegantly captured by cinematographer Jeff Cutter. Sarsgaard and Farmiga give a full account of the Colemans' troubled union—which in a lesser fright flick might have been only a plot twitch—and Fuhrman proves to be a remarkable young actress. Her pale, freckled face can shift from winsome innocence to malignant hostility as if a switch had been thrown in her character's soul. (She also has a scene with Sarsgaard that's spectacularly creepy—it couldn't have been easy to do, for either of them.) Unusually for a child performer, this unsettling moppet holds our attention for two full hours. We're happy she's not holding anything else. (July 2009)

The Unborn

Waiting for Jumby

Even really bad horror movies can be watchable. I don't know how many times I've returned to Roman Polanski's *The Ninth Gate* in an effort to penetrate the mystery of how someone can turn a terrific book into a truly terrible film. I still haven't figured it out, but I'll probably keep trying.

That won't be the case with *The Unborn,* all reasons for the wretchedness of which are immediately clear. Director David Goyer's new picture isn't precisely unwatchable—it's so flagrantly derivative, so oppressively idiotic, that it drains you of the energy necessary to get up and walk out. You just wish it would stop. But it won't. You give it every opportunity, but it continues not to. It may be the longest eighty-seven-minute movie ever made.

This is an exorcism flick that rips off *The Exorcist* right down to the head spin and the spider walk. The "twist," if one can be bothered to call it that, is that it's a *Jewish* exorcism flick. Well, sort of. Instead of a Catholic priest battling the dark forces of whatever, we now have a rabbi—but a rabbi played by *Gary Oldman.* (Since Oldman also appeared in *The Dark Knight,* which Goyer scripted, there's the feeling here of a major favor being done—one that Goyer may never be able to repay.) Oldman's Rabbi Sendak is the last resort of a tormented college student named Casey Beldon (Odette Yustman, of *Cloverfield*), who lends the movie its only really gripping moments when she walks around in her underwear. Casey has been seeing some way-strange things lately: a weird neighbor kid, an even weirder dead kid, a dog in a mask. One night, puking her guts up in a nightclub toilet stall, she notices an oddly ornate, well, glory hole in the wall—and all of a sudden a legion of slimy beetles comes pouring through it. (Porn adepts will know it could've been worse.) And the weird neighbor kid keeps telling her that "Jumby wants to be born." She doesn't know what the kid's problem is, but she fears it'll soon be her problem, too. *We* know this with a weary certainty.

For reasons too convoluted to concisely relate, Casey hooks up with an old woman, a Holocaust survivor named Sofi (Jane Alexander), who's also a psychic. Sofi informs Casey that she is a twin and that she should beware of mirrors, "because what is a twin but another kind of mirror?" Okay. Now the plot takes a squealing left turn into Auschwitz, where, according to Sofi, Nazi doctors were "obsessed with twins" and conducted "horrible experiments that blurred the lines between science and the occult." Sofi then fills Casey in on the evil spirits called dybbuks and recommends to her a Hebrew exorcism manual called the *Book of Mirrors*. Conveniently, Casey is able to locate one of these ancient books in her college library. She casually stuffs the priceless tome into her backpack, lugs it over to Rabbi Sendak, and tells him, "I need an exorcism." "I'll make some calls," he says.

I'd ask you to bear with me, but I don't think I can bear with me myself. There are all manner of cheap jolts, of the sort that require people to go poking about in dark basements; and there's a basketball coach who's actually a priest (well, an Episcopal priest), and a couple of pals on hand for hideous deaths. And of course Jumby. There's also a generous supply of lines that snap your head back with the force of their inanity. Trying to describe the hellspawn dybbuk that's turning her life into a blood feast, Casey says, "It's not like us. I don't think it even comes from the same universe." Something similar might be said of this movie. The picture is such an embarrassment, Goyer must now be hoping that very few people will see it. He may get lucky. (January 2009)

The Uninvited

I'm Not There

Anna has been having a terrible year, even by teen standards. It started, as so many of these things do, with her mother. Mom was bedridden for the longest time with some awful disease, and she'd exiled herself to the boathouse down the hill from the family's island mansion—possibly to escape the sounds of her husband having it off with Mom's live-in nurse, a frosty blonde named Rachael. Then the boathouse burned down, and Mom along with it. Anna, in a fit of acting out, slit her wrists and woke up in a mainland bughouse. Now the shrinks have turned her loose and sent her back home to her father and her sister Alex and . . . Rachael, who's *still* living in. Can things get any worse?

Need you inquire? *The Uninvited* is that too-seldom-seen thing: a traditional psycho-horror movie made with smarts and style, which arrives at a creepy conclusion with its honor intact. Looking back on its artful feints and misdirections, you realize that the key to its knotty puzzle is as plain as the knife in your neck, if you'd only been paying attention.

The movie is a faithful remake of South Korean director Kim Jee-Woon's 2003 shocker, *A Tale of Two Sisters*. This English-language version approximates the gorgeous visual design of that film—a considerable achievement in itself—while at the same time paring away or tightening up some of its more ambiguous elements. The Guard Brothers (Charlie and Tom to their agents) are the latest English directors to make the ever-shorter trip from TV commercials to feature films, and with this picture they've delivered a solid debut. Both brothers also write and shoot (although not here, apparently), and they're keenly attuned to story-shaping and gradations of color and mood. They've also been especially sharp in casting the picture. Australian actress Emily Browning (last seen here in the underacclaimed *Lemony Snicket's A Series of Unfortunate Events*) brings a persuasive sense of beleaguered resilience (along with pillowy lips and gull-wing cheekbones) to the role of Anna; and Arielle Kebbel (*The Grudge 2*) is a convincing visual match as her older sister, Alex. David Strathairn does everything that can be done with the role of their dad, which isn't a lot (it was a stick-figure part in the original film, too); but Elizabeth Banks (of *Role Models* and *Zack and Miri Make a Porno*) is a real surprise as the malevolent Rachael. Who knew you could look cute brandishing a carving fork?

And what are all these characters up to? Oh, the usual: Something's Not Right. If Mom's so dead, what's that thing oozing around in the corner? And those three corpse kids in the cemetery—why're they still traipsing about? And that nice delivery boy with the urgent news to impart—what ever happened to him? Did he stumble over one of the bulging bloody trash bags? As for Rachael, she may come on all step-maternal now that she's lassoed Dad, but she whips out a snarl—and a syringe!—whenever he leaves the room. "She's like a crack whore without the dignity," Alex says.

The Uninvited shares its dark, sneaky secret with . . . oh, let's say a number of other crafty psych-out movies starring people like Brad Pitt, Johnny Depp, and Robert De Niro (not to mention Cécile De France). It's not a picture likely to set off any cultural tremors, but its modest scale is part of what makes it so enjoyable. Uninviting it's not. (January 2009)

The Wolfman

Furball

The new *Wolfman* lacks snarl. There are plenty of bared fangs and flesh-rending claws, and of course much howling at the moon, too. But the movie is mainly an exercise in gothic atmosphere. It's lavishly produced, sumptuously scored (by Danny Elfman), and beautiful to look at. It's just not very scary.

But how could it be? Is there anyone who doesn't know the familiar story? Or who needs to have it told yet again? Given the film's troubled production—the last-minute director switch, the reshoots and reediting, the year's worth of release-date delays—it has probably turned out better than anyone involved might have hoped. But it still feels redundant.

The movie is a remake of, and inevitably a tribute to, *The Wolf Man*, the 1941 Universal horror classic that introduced silver bullets to the werewolf genre, as well as the snatch of spooky doggerel that begins, "Even a man who is pure in heart, and says his prayers by night . . ." In this new version, director Joe Johnston (who replaced Mark Romanek) has pushed the story back from the 1940s to 1891. He retains the misty moors and twisted trees of the original film, as well as the big wolf-rousing moon that seems to be stuck on full every night of the year. But he and the writers, Andrew Kevin Walker and David Self, have enlarged the tale in enterprising ways. Now, Larry Talbot (Benicio Del Toro), the doomed hero, has been called back to England from America—where he was sent as a child following the bloody and still-mysterious death of his mother—by Gwen Conliffe (Emily Blunt), the fiancée of Larry's brother, Ben, who has suddenly gone missing. At Talbot Hall, the decrepit family manse, Larry reconnects uneasily with his frosty dad, Sir John (Anthony Hopkins), who in this version of the story is a, shall we say, more complex character than in the original film.

Brother Ben soon turns up, unfortunately dead, and the story gathers shape. We already know that Larry will be bitten by a werewolf, that he'll seek enlightenment about his alarming new condition from the Gypsy crone Maleva (Geraldine Chaplin, stepping in for the incomparably shriveled Maria Ouspenskaya in the 1941 movie), and that he shouldn't bother making any long-term plans for his future. Newly added, though, is a sequence in a London insane asylum (a place so hellacious that when Hopkins's Sir John pays a visit, we half expect a sly smirk of acknowledgment at its resemblance to the Baltimore bin in which Hannibal Lecter was incarcerated in *The Silence of the Lambs*).

There's also an early form of waterboarding; a ferocious escape; and a chase across the rooftops of London, with the transformed Larry being pursued by a new character, Scotland Yard's Inspector Frederick Abberline (Hugo Weaving). Abberline is a real historical personage—the lead investigator in the Jack the Ripper case of 1888. Presumably, he's been brought in to help out with the wolf hunt because of the expertise he displayed in failing to catch Saucy Jack. Let us only say that he's more successful here.

As Larry, on the run, attempts to get to the root of what now appears to be the Talbot family curse, there are a lot of expensive gore effects—gut ripping, entrail flinging, arm yanks, and head severings. And the seamless, digitally assisted wolf transformations are of course a far cry from the stage-by-stage lap dissolves of yore. And whenever these effects abate for a bit, we can savor Talbot Hall's lush decay—the candles and cobwebs, the dead leaves drifting across the marble floors, the fireplace big enough to roast a Jeep in.

But the movie never catches fire, and the only thrills in it are cheap fake-outs—a sudden eruption of birds, a hideous creature crawling up on the foot of a bed (only a dream!). Del Toro is a master of hulky brooding (and of course a better actor than Lon Chaney Jr., the original Larry Talbot), but hulking and brooding are pretty much all he's given to do here. Hopkins brings his usual razory gleam to the part of Sir John, but the character's expansion for this film, although inventive, has left it awfully thin. And while Weaving, with his familiar clenched glare, contributes a bracing sourness to the proceedings, his Abberline seems to be on hand mainly to set up a sequel—a more moonstruck notion than anything else in the picture. (February 2010)

Thirst

Drinking Problem

A movie about a priest who's transformed into a vampire would seem designed to prompt deep thought about Roman Catholic ritual. And that could be what Park Chan-wook, the waywardly brilliant South Korean director (and onetime philosophy student), had in mind in making his latest film, *Thirst*. But just when we've set our minds on ponder, the picture sidetracks contemplation with flashes of the fearlessly eccentric imagery for which Park has become famous, and some of the slurpiest sex scenes to be found in any recent R-rated movie.

Park's narratives are . . . challenging, you might say. Here, the virtuous priest, Sang-hyun (played by frequent Park associate Song Kang-ho), after volunteering to be a test subject in the search for a cure for a mysterious disease, finds himself developing a taste for blood. At first, being a gentle soul, or possibly just lazy, he simply siphons the juice out of comatose patients at the hospital where he ministers. Then he becomes involved with Tae-ju (peppery Kim Ok-bin), the unhappy wife of his childhood friend Kang-woo (Shin Ha-kyun, another Park vet). Tae-ju soon learns the priest's secret and is intrigued. ("Vampires are cuter than I thought.") Before long, he puts the bite on her—but quickly regrets it. Tae-ju has none of Sang-hyun's spiritual conflicts (she's not Catholic!), and soon she's mocking his timid approach to slaking the ancient thirst. ("You easy-blood-drinking coward!") She embarks on a lusty solo round of throat-ripping depredations among the local populace, resulting in the sort of problems that a hundred years of vampire movies would lead you to expect.

The picture is deliberately paced and rather long (it meanders for well over two hours), and there are the director's usual confusions. Tae-ju's tiresome husband keeps dying and then reappearing. (I quickly gave up trying to figure out what his deal was.) The point of the priest giving the girl his battered shoes to wear at one point is likewise puzzling. And there are more mah-jongg games going on in the picture than a clueless Westerner might prefer.

But working once again with cinematographer Chung Chung-hoon and lighting director Park Hyun-won, the director has created another series of swooningly strange scenes and images. The lubricious sex interludes, slathered in blood and heightened with overamped heavy breathing, are certainly audacious. And while the picture may not be as spellbindingly gorgeous as some of Park's previous films—*Sympathy for Lady Vengeance,* say—the long concluding shot of the star-crossed couple on a cliff high above the sea is a stunner. All of this, plus lines like "We can put the blood in Tupperware and keep it in the fridge"—who can resist? (July 2009)

The Fourth Kind

Impossible Dreams

With the fumbled release of *The Fourth Kind*, sneaky-hip viral movie marketing shoots itself in the foot. It's been ten years since the makers of *The Blair Witch Project* used the Internet to plant suggestions that the eerie events in their film were real. Today the Web is patrolled by a legion of bull-sniffing bloggers, so any attempt to do the same thing again is doomed to fail. And this picture expends so much energy trying to sell its preposterous assertions as fact that there's very little left over to animate the story, which is in any case a hopeless jumble.

The movie is an attempted alien-abduction thriller. It begins with what is probably the most laughable opening scene of the year. Walking through some misty woods and straight up to the camera, the film's star,

Milla Jovovich, informs us that everything we're about to see is true—that it's "supported by archived footage" and is "extremely disturbing." But then we're also told that the names and professions of the characters have been changed. Why would that be? The silly premise instantly begins to crumble.

In fact, nothing in this movie is real, starting with the aerial shots of Nome, Alaska, where the story is set. What we see is a city surrounded by mountains and forests (the picture was mostly shot in Bulgaria). But the real Nome, as actual residents have noted online, is situated in a vast, strap-flat snowy landscape. From this point, the film's bogosity only builds.

The picture has an awkward duplex narrative. In one part of it, Jovovich plays a "real" Nome psychologist named Dr. Abigail Tyler, whose husband was recently murdered (an unwise red herring that eventually sandbags the whole story), leaving her to tend to their young son and daughter. Back in 2000, Tyler's patients, under hypnotic regression, all began telling her the same strange tale—that they were being awakened in the middle of the night by a weird dream. Something was lurking outside their bedroom window. Something was opening their bedroom door. Something (insert shrieks of horror). Tyler videotapes these sessions with the help of a fellow psychologist (Elias Koteas), and we're shown the tapes at wearying length. They're certainly intense—much shouting and crying, even a brief bit of irrelevant levitation. This long section of the movie is maddeningly repetitive, with most of the tension conjured up on the soundtrack—an onslaught of nerve-pinch strings, doomsday percussion, and stray tiny tinklings. The movie itself seems more terrified than any viewer is likely to be.

Mixed into all of this are scenes of the director, Olatunde Osunsanmi, conducting a solemn interview with the "actual" Dr. Abigail Tyler—a mercifully uncredited actress in puzzling land-of-the-dead makeup. We also see *her* "real" tapes. Then there's a visit by a professor (Hakeem Kae-Kazim) who's conversant with the language of ancient Sumer. He's called in by Jovovich's Tyler after she hears a strange tongue being spoken through the static on one of her tapes. The professor arrives, listens to the tape, and unsurprisingly confirms that this is, indeed, the language of ancient Sumer. Why this should matter is left to our incomprehension.

There's little more to be said. The patients have all become nightly rentals for alien abductors (the Fourth Kind being the category of extra-terrestrial encounter that follows the slightly less alarming Third Kind). We never see these creatures, although at one point we do briefly glimpse some big blurry figures. These aren't especially scary, either.

At the end of the film we're informed that the "real" Abigail Tyler now lives somewhere "on the East Coast," under medical supervision. The implication here may be that some sort of government conspiracy has contrived to silence her. But since both incarnations of the good doctor have seemed so demented throughout, we can more readily con-clude that she's just nuts. Good thing she's only "real." (November 2009)

Blood and Chocolate

Wolf Bane

Along with being a bargain for low-budget filmmakers, the Roma-nian capital of Bucharest also turns out to be the only city on Earth run by werewolves. It's an unusual setting for *Blood and Chocolate,* author Annette Curtis Klause's 1997 teen-wolf romance novel, which takes place in a suburban Maryland high school. But the German di-rector Katja von Garnier makes a stylish go of it, feasting on the city's cobbly streets, moody churches, and vintage Wallachian charm. True, the interiors mostly look like bombed-out tailpipe factories, but that's probably the low-budget thing kicking in.

The story revolves around Vivian (Agnes Bruckner), a pretty young werewolf from Colorado who's not happy about it—the werewolf part, that is. Following the murder of her parents by anti-werewolf activists, she has relocated to her family's ancestral home and now works in a Bucharest chocolate shop. (The chocolate theme suggested by the film's title begins and ends right there.) Vivian spends her nights reluctantly hanging out with the local lycanthropes, whose leader, a brooding, leather-clad character named Gabriel (Olivier Martinez), thinks Vivian is the long-promised embodiment of some ancient wolfish prophecy and aims to make her his mate. ("Bride" seems too gentle a word for what he has in mind.)

Then Vivian meets a young Englishman named Aidan (Hugh Dancy), an artist who's in town working on a graphic novel—about werewolves. Why? Well, he tells Vivian, when he was seventeen, he punched out his abusive father; now, "there's an assault warrant out for me," and he's been on the lam internationally ever since. Vivian buys this story, and we worry for her.

You can see where this tale is going, and it goes there, as I say, rather stylishly. The movie has considerable problems, though. It's not just the impoverished visual effects (the werewolf transformations are effected in an odd flare of light, and the snarling wolves themselves might as well have "Cheap CGI" engraved on their fangs). There's also the wobbly tone: Wolfie doings in the moonlit woods outside of town are lumpily interspersed with frolicsome young-love montages and a few over-burnished images that would seem more appropriate to a fashion shoot than a feral passion. And since this is a pan-European production, cast with Americans, Brits, Germans, Hungarians, Frenchmen, and Romanians, some giggle-triggering line readings were probably inevitable. ("You know our *tradeeshun*," says Gabriel, who also says, "No one *effer* reaches the *reever*.") The writers, however, have to take full credit for muddled guff like, "If you cared about me, you would've left me before we ever met."

The movie's heaviest burden, unfortunately, is its star. The undeniably lovely Agnes Bruckner's acting skills—as directed here, at least—range from a sullen stare to a slightly less-sullen stare with a mild smile going on down below. She may one day become an expressive actress, but that day does not seem close at hand.

All of these defects, which aren't unusual in pictures of modest budget, could be overlooked if *Blood and Chocolate* were actually scary.

But it isn't; not even a little bit. Werewolf devotees may feel that it bites. (January 2007)

Predators

Buffet Dining

The strapping beastie of the *Predator* franchise remains pretty much the same after twenty-three years—dread of lock, moist of mandible. It's the humans in his life who seem to have devolved. In the first film, his chief antagonist was played by that pregubernatorial muscle mountain, Arnold Schwarzenegger. Now, in *Predators,* the crafty alien faces off against willowy Adrien Brody—not an opponent to strike fear in the heart (or whatever) of any self-respecting behemoth, you'd think.

Predators is a B movie that knows its job, and does it. Which means, among other things, that making sense is not on its to-do list. The picture opens with a group of people falling from the sky into a jungle. What are they doing here? None of them knows. One minute each of them was sleeping, the next they were plummeting through the clouds. That's that. Where are they? The group's lone woman, Isabelle (Alice Braga), looks around suspiciously. "I've never seen this jungle," she says. "And I've seen most." Isabelle hails from Guatemala, where she no doubt saw quite a bit of jungle, but has lately been employed as a sniper by the Israeli Defense Force, whose missions are not often thought to be jungle-related. But whatever.

The movie germinated from an unproduced 1994 script by pulp fan Robert Rodriguez (one of the producers here), which was more recently refined by Alex Litvak and Michael Finch. Faced with the challenge of revitalizing a creature that has already been the subject of four previous films (if you count two transfranchise dalliances with the slobbery Alien), they and director Nimród Antal have come up with a new plot wrinkle. The humans—who include among them a black-ops mercenary, a drug-gang enforcer, an African warlord, a Russian soldier, a mass murderer, and a Yakuza killer—are all predators themselves back on Earth. Well, except for one, who's a doctor. (A clever plot twist, it turns out.)

Now they're all prey on this strange planet, which turns out to be an off-world hunting ground for Predators, whose day-trip spacecraft is parked invisibly nearby. As you'd expect, the picture consists—with the exception of a visit to a batty survivor played by Laurence Fishburne—of each of the human interlopers being put away like finger food by the wily monsters. Fortunately, the cast, which is better than you'd expect, makes this an enjoyable exercise. Topher Grace, as the doctor, is a fine sufferer, and Walton Goggins, as the mass murderer (fresh from death row), brings the same redneck flair to his role that he does to the hillbilly schemer he plays on *Justified*. The effects are also first-rate. We've seen the nasty-looking Predators before, of course, but there's a new creature on the scene—a tusky attack beast (it's like a cross between a wild boar and a Doberman)—that enlivens the action memorably.

The movie remains boldly nonsensical throughout—would we have it any other way? How likely is it, for example, that the Japanese Yakuza guy (Louis Ozawa Changchien) would just happen to find a samurai sword lying around on the alien planet? (What next? we don't wonder.) And there's a priceless moment when the exasperated Brody walks right up to one of the Predators and says, "I want off this planet!" Then, as an afterthought: "You understand me, don't you?" As if it mattered. (July 2010)

High Tension

Low Blood Pressure

You'd figure that any slasher movie that got under way with a guy having sex with a severed head might be a slasher movie with something new on its mind. But no. *High Tension* isn't just a slasher movie; it's a "tribute" to old slasher movies of the 1970s and 1980s. And like tribute bands and tribute albums, this low-budget French quickie, directed by Alexandre Aja, is essentially a footnote to the originals. Miss it and you miss nothing.

The most memorable slasher flicks have some sort of backstory. In *Halloween*, Michael Myers is an escaped psycho returning to his unfondly remembered hometown. In the *Friday the 13th* films, the hulking Jason Voorhees is driven to murder by serious mother issues (or something). And in *A Nightmare on Elm Street*, the razor-fingered child-killer Freddy Krueger haunts the dreams of the kids whose parents once burned him alive. We understand why these guys are pissed.

High Tension, on the other hand, is simply a checklist of familiar gore effects pasted onto an unusually uninvolving story. Two young college friends, Marie (Cécile de France) and Alexia (the monomial Maïwenn) are driving through the South of France as the movie opens, on their way to the remote farmhouse of Alexia's parents, where they intend to study for their finals. Almost immediately, they start doing classically dumb things, like pulling off the road at night and running out into a dark spooky cornfield for no reason (and then traipsing back to their car again after nothing happens). There's also the traditional ration of skin. Alexia takes a shower and we get to watch. Marie has been watching, too, and is moved to return to her room for a bit of self-fondling. We're still watching.

Then a big guy in a greasy jumpsuit walks into the house and starts killing people: hack, slash, rip—just like that. He overlooks Marie, who has hidden under a bed, but he catches Alexia and drags her outside to his battered old panel truck and locks her in the back. Then he drives off—unaware that Marie has managed to slip into the back of the truck, too . . . somehow. There follows an axe murder at a roadside gas station and an episode in a greenhouse way out in a forest (what?), where someone is bloodily beaten and wrapped in barbed wire. Inevitably, a chain saw is loudly cranked up.

There's a trick ending that *is* kind of clever, I suppose, especially if you didn't see the Robert De Niro quasi-slasher movie *Hide and Seek* earlier this year. And especially if you don't mind a plot hole big enough to drive whoever's truck that *really* is right through it. The movie's only eighty-five minutes long, but that's eighty-five minutes you might need some day for something more engrossing than this. Sorting socks, maybe. (June 2005)

Piranha 3D

Don't Go in the Water

Piranha 3D is a genre horror film that delivers exactly what you'd expect: gushers of blood, ripped flesh by the kilo, and acres of bare booty and boobs (some of them real). But the movie has been fashioned with considerable skill: the effects are top notch, the camera work is fluid, and the 3-D is genuine (none of that postproduction add-on stuff). The thrills here may be traditional, but they're still kind of thrilling.

The picture rips off *Jaws* with tremendous enthusiasm. Taking the part of the local lawman played by Roy Scheider in the 1975 classic, we now have Elizabeth Shue, with Adam Scott signing aboard as the science guy played back in the day by Richard Dreyfuss. (Dreyfuss himself actually pops up here, in a very small part that requires him to be rendered into even smaller parts.)

The setting is Lake Havisu, Arizona (here called Lake Victoria), where a seismic event of some sort has opened a subaqueous crack, up through which pour a legion of primordial piranhas ("more than two million years old!" one knowledgeable character gasps). And wouldn't you know, this ominous event has occurred right in the middle of the annual spring-break invasion of drunken college boys and knockout bikini women. (There are lingering shots of the inevitable wet T-shirt contest.)

The story is unabashedly by the numbers. While the college kids frolic on the lakeshore, a creep named Derrick (Jerry O'Connell) is out on the water in his cabin cruiser with local boy Jake Forester (Steven R. McQueen), son of the sheriff (Shue); nice-girl Kelly (Jessica Szohr), on whom Jake has his eye; and two bisexual babes (Kelly Brook and Riley Steele) who swim around naked beneath the glass-bottom boat so that Derek can film them for a skin flick he's making. There are also two little kids stranded on an island and wading out knee-deep to shout for help. All of this solicits the traditional audience response: "Don't go in the water!" But does anyone listen? Need you ask?

Director Alexandre Aja (*High Tension*) knows there's no point in using 3-D for subtle depth effects—what we really want is vicious multi-fanged piranhas shooting right off the screen and into our face. And working with cinematographer John R. Leonetti, Aja has also concocted some ripping subsurface scenes (beyond the pull-'em-under shots familiar from *Jaws*) and some lively stunts. We expect Sheriff Forester to start running around on the beach in a panic pleading with the college kids to get out of the lake (to no avail until the water is running red with blood), and so she does. And when Derek's boat founders on some rocks with one of the girls trapped below deck, we know that somebody has to jump in the water and dive down to rescue her. We know, we know. But we still want to see it all again, one more time. (August 2010)

The Rite

Magic Man

Anthony Hopkins has made many fine films over the last forty years; but unavoidably for an actor who works so much, he's also figured in some unfortunate paycheck junk, movies like *Freejack* and *Beowulf* (in which he unwisely bared his loins) and the horrid *Hannibal,* which turned his great Dr. Lecter into a depraved cartoon. What's interesting about even these misfires, however, is the actor's unflagging commitment: no matter how impoverished the script, or how clamorous the inanities unfolding all around him, Hopkins always gives a complete performance—he just can't stop being a terrific actor.

Such is the case with his latest, a minor exorcism venture called *The Rite.* The movie is not entirely without interest. Unusually, it makes an earnest case for religious faith over rote atheism; and it has a rich dark look. (The picture was shot in both Italy and Hungary, but a Magyar gloom prevails.) Hopkins plays Father Lucas Trevant, a Catholic exorcist based in Rome, who takes under his wing an American seminarian named Michael Kovak (the bland Colin O'Donoghue), who's having a crisis of faith and second thoughts about entering the priesthood. Lucas sets out to demonstrate to Michael that the Devil—and therefore God—does exist. The key exhibit is a pregnant girl who's been possessed by a demon, which is turning her into Linda Blair, complete with roll-up eyes and crackling neck twists (although she vomits nails, too, which is something new). Also on hand are a red-eyed donkey demon, a devilish frog, and a herd of cockroaches that are clearly up to no good. You get the picture.

None of this nonsense has the pulp charge that would make it fun. But Hopkins is once again unstoppable, enlivening the slumpiest scenes with his fleeting tics and twitches, and that oddly unsavory smile. Only he could have brought off one scene, in which Lucas is interrupted, while dealing with a flailing demon child, by the ring of his cell phone. "I can't talk now," he whispers into it. "I'm in the middle of something."

Hopkins transcends all of this, but he still leaves us wondering: how does such a superb performer become involved in a project so unworthy of his talent? Maybe it's just the eternal actor's plight. As Lucas says at one point, "It's very difficult to predict how any of this stuff is going to work out." (January 2011)

Let Me In

Vampire Chronicle

Fans of the revered 2008 Swedish vampire film *Let the Right One In* were not universally enthused to learn that an American remake was in the works. Nor were they reassured to learn that Matt Reeves—the *Cloverfield* guy!—had been chosen to direct it. So it's a relief to find that Reeves has done a smart and respectful adaptation of the earlier movie, carefully replicating its formal restraint and its chilly tone. There's a new character or two, and some unobjectionable new narrative touches; and there's also a bit more blood and quite a bit more action—which, as it turns out, is entirely fine.

So here we are once again—not in the snowy suburbs of Stockholm this time, but in a snowy suburb of Los Alamos, New Mexico. And once again we find a lonely twelve-year-old boy, here called Owen (Kodi Smit-McPhee, of *The Road*), peering out the window of his mother's apartment one chilly night when a barefoot girl arrives outside, accompanied by much baggage and a bedraggled man, presumably her father. These are Owen's new next-door neighbors. Maybe he and the girl can be friends (she turns out to be twelve, too). Owen could use a friend. His parents are divorcing, his mom's a drinker, and at school a hulking bully named Kenny (Dylan Minnette) makes his life an every-damn-day living hell.

Of course the girl, Abby (Chloë Grace Moretz), isn't at all what Owen imagines. As we see, in a succession of scenes taken directly from the original movie, she's just as lonely as Owen but a lot stranger. "Just so you know," she says, when they first meet in a snowy courtyard, "I can't be your friend. That's just the way it is." And soon we understand why.

Abby is an ancient vampire, condemned to be twelve years old and friendless herself forever. The unnamed man with whom she lives (played by the invaluable Richard Jenkins) isn't her father, he's her slave, dispatched on nightly rounds to create fresh corpses and return home with their blood in a jug for Abby to drink. When he fails in one of these missions, Abby is forced to leave their apartment, with its blocked-out windows, and forage for herself. Thanks to the movie's muted tone, and its minimalist score of discreet, sighing strings, the scene in which Abby waylays an unsuspecting passerby in a dark tunnel is just as much of a shock here as it was in the Swedish film. As is the famous scene from the original movie, set in a school swimming pool, in which Kenny and his fellow bullies finally get theirs, in a spectacular way.

Reeves injects some fresh tension into the story by way of a new character—a suspicious cop played by Elias Koteas—and a nail-biting new sequence in which an attempted carjacking of an intended victim goes terribly wrong. Like Tomas Alfredson, the first film's director, he doesn't venture all the way into the black depths of the 2004 Swedish novel on which both movies are based—the book's elements of pedophilia and child mutilation would never play on film. Fortunately, the story offers much more to work with, and Reeves, like Alfredson before him, makes the most of it.

The director has also been wise in his choice of leads. Moretz doesn't have the dark eeriness of Lina Leandersson, who played the girl in *Let the Right One In,* but she's a precociously skillful actress and she brings more relatable substance to the role. Similarly, Smit-McPhee, with his watchful eyes and wounded demeanor, adds more emotional layers to the boy than Kåre Hedebrant was able to do in the original.

The story, of course—an intimate examination of young love and loneliness, and of a deep yearning that can never be quenched (or so it seems)—retains its mesmerizing appeal. Anyone unfamiliar with the

Swedish movie should find this one to be among the year's better pictures—certainly leagues ahead of anything to be found so far in the *Twilight* franchise. Those who *have* seen the earlier film, however, may feel that falling under the story's dark spell is a pleasure that's unrepeatable. At the end of this high-quality remake, so faithful in mood and structure to the original, and so sleekly crafted, they may be left wondering: what's the point? (October 2010)

Seven Psychos

The movies need maniacs, and Robert De Niro's Travis Bickle, Dennis Hopper's Frank Booth, Jack Nicholson's axe-wielding Jack Torrance, and Anthony Perkins's nail-biting Norman Bates can't do all the heavy lifting. Fortunately, this is a populous field.

John Davis Chandler, *The Young Savages* (1961): Chandler's soulless sneer lent a memorable chill to John Frankenheimer's teen gang-war film. Having watched his Arthur Reardon cackling dementedly as he tries to drown a little boy in a municipal swimming pool, we figure the case against him and some pals for killing a blind Puerto Rican kid should be open-and-shut. But Burt Lancaster, as an assistant New York district attorney, believes their crime has deeper socioeconomic roots—although Arthur's gleeful sadism seems beyond the claim of such earnest concern. Chandler had an unusual career: he subsequently made three movies with Sam Peckinpah and one with Clint Eastwood (*The Outlaw Josey Wales,* 1976). Then there was Chris Columbus's *Adventures in Babysitting*, in 1987, and the Madonna bomb *Body of Evidence,* in 1993. The actor died in 2010, but in *The Young Savages*, his whack-job charisma lives on.

Rudolph Klein-Rogge, *Metropolis* (1927): As the mad scientist Rotwang in Fritz Lang's silent classic, Klein-Rogge, outfitted with a black-gloved mechanical hand, created an archetype—the character was echoed in Peter Sellers's performance as Dr. Strangelove thirty-seven years later and, most unexpectedly, in Nicolas Cage's soliloquy to his own artificial limb in the bakery scene in *Moonstruck* (1987). Klein-Rogge had already played the titular master criminal in Lang's *Dr. Mabuse: The Gambler* (1922) and also appeared in his two *Nibelungen* films (1924), even though the director had by then stolen away and married his wife, writer Thea von Harbou. The actor continued working with Lang, playing the sinister spymaster Haghi in *Spies* (1928) and returning to his popular earlier role in *The Testament of Dr. Mabuse* (1933). That was the end, though. With Hitler newly installed in power, Lang, of Jewish blood on his mother's side, divorced von Harbou—a Third Reich enthusiast—and soon lit out for Paris. Von Harbou and Klein-

★★★★★★★★★★★★★★★★★★★★★★★★★★★★★★

Rogge remained behind to work, sometimes together, under the Nazi regime.

Patty McCormack, *The Bad Seed* (1956): McCormack's Rhoda Penmark is the scariest pigtailed sociopath in screen history. Maxwell Anderson's stage adaptation of the William March novel was a big hit on Broadway, so McCormack and the rest of the main cast—including Nancy Kelly as Rhoda's hapless mother and Henry Jones as the maintenance man who has the little girl's number—were hired on for the movie version. In the era of Ozzie and Harriet, eight-year-old Rhoda was a jolt—a deviously pert little blonde whose sunshiny façade cloaked a gimlet-eyed monster, ready to murder anyone who crossed her. It's a performance that's still striking. McCormack won an Oscar nomination for it, but then soldiered on through years of films like *The Mini-Skirt Mob* (1968) and *Saturday the 14th Strikes Back* (1988) before turning up, seemingly out of nowhere, as Pat Nixon in the 2009 *Frost/Nixon*.

Walter McGinn, *The Parallax View* (1974): McGinn has one very quiet three-minute scene in Alan J. Pakula's paranoid political thriller, but it casts a dark spell over the whole movie. As Jack Younger, a recruiter for the Parallax Corporation—a shadowy international assassination bureau—he pays a visit to Warren Beatty's Joe Frady, a newspaper reporter working undercover on a story about a mysterious series of murders. Frady is living in a bleak rented room posing as a violent antisocial headcase who can't hold down a job. Younger informs him that Parallax happens to be looking for "unusual personalities." Then, with whispery expertise, he begins probing and manipulating Joe's feigned hostility and frustration: "Has it ever crossed your mind that maybe it's everybody *else's* problem they don't get along with *you?*" By the time Frady moves on to take the official Parallax test—a famously disturbing film montage—McGinn is essentially gone from the picture. You never forget him, though.

Joshua Miller, *Near Dark* (1987): One year after his emergence in the grim *River's Edge*, twelve-year-old Miller brought his dyspeptic glower to Kathryn Bigelow's innovative vampire flick. As the "kid" in a bloodsucker "family" roaming the Southwest in an RV with blacked-out windows,

Miller's gore-crusted Homer smokes, gambles, packs a gun, and—frozen forever on the cusp of adolescence—yearns mightily to get laid. ("You have any idea what it's like to be a big man on the inside and a small man on the outside?") Coming upon a little girl at a motel soda machine late one night, he trembles at the possibility of finally scratching that itch. It's one of the most arresting sequences in a movie that's not short on bold moments.

Benoît Poelvoorde, *Man Bites Dog* (1992): In this blackest of black comedies, Poelvoorde is Ben, a giddy serial killer leading around a three-man video crew to chronicle his depredations. He's pretentiously cultivated ("Gaudí—a very organic style") and a total pro at his chosen trade. Weighting down a corpse for disposal in a river, he notes, requires precise ballast: "Three times body weight for an average adult . . . but for children and midgets it's different." Sweet-talking his crew into the apartment of an old woman, he pulls a gun to do her in, but then just shouts at her, triggering a heart attack. ("Easier on the neighbors," he says.) This Belgian movie, a student project shot in raw black and white, is both appalling (especially a nasty rape scene in which the crew members enthusiastically join in) and electrifyingly funny. You find yourself choking on the laughter. You keep choking, but you're still laughing. Rated NC-17, for reasons that are very soon clear.

Michael Rooker, *Henry: Portrait of a Serial Killer* (1986): In his movie debut, Rooker's dead-eyed menace as a notorious serial killer is genuinely frightening. The real Henry Lee Lucas, who confessed to killing hundreds of people, had a ghastly MO: driving aimlessly around the country in the late 1970s and early 1980s, Lucas and his loathsome pal Ottis Toole (played here with flamboyant depravity by Tom Towles) would pick victims at random, killing them for no reason and thus depriving investigators of a consistent motive to track. John McNaugton's film version of this dismal tale, shot mostly in Chicago, has a low-budget squalor that's disturbing in itself; and his staging of one scene—a brutal sexual attack on a suburban family captured on a video camera the killers have brought along—is unforgettably horrific. By the time the movie ends, with Henry

★★★★★★★★★★★★★★★★★★★★★★★★★★★★★★

depositing a large suitcase by the side of a road, we feel as if our soul has
frozen over. The real Henry recanted most of his hundreds of confessions,
and police came to agree they were in fact mostly lies. McNaughton's
film, however, grounded in Rooker's icy performance, suggests very dark
possibilities.

★★★★★★★★★★★★★★★★★★★★★★★★★★★★★★

THE TORTURE NEVER STOPS

n a blighted land beyond the border of even the goriest horror films lies the dark valley of torture porn—a genre devoted to torment, agony, and sanguinary shenanigans of the most deplorable sort. We can thank exploitation entrepreneur Herschell Gordon Lewis for dragging this sort of thing out of the shadows and into the nation's drive-ins—the title of his dreadful first effort, the 1963 Blood Feast, is a concise summation of all that was to follow. Latter-day torture porn auteurs like Eli Roth play this stuff for idiot kicks, just the way old Herschell did. The difference today is that fans of the form tend to look at it as depraved comedy, which is a little disturbing. Who goes to see these movies? I'm afraid I do. But only so you don't have to.

The Human Centipede (First Sequence)

Bughouse

Is there any place left that torture porn won't go? Not now. *The Human Centipede (First Sequence)*, an abominable curiosity by Dutch writer-director Tom Six, takes the dismal genre in an entomological direction that few could have expected and fewer still might have wished. The picture has already won awards in the usual places (Screamfest, Austin Fantastic Fest), and now here it is for the delectation of . . . well, of people you probably wouldn't want to get to know too well.

The opening sequence is a parody of the torture-porn form. Two American girls, Lindsay (Ashley C. Williams) and Jenny (Ashlynn Yennie), passing through Germany on a European vacation, set out in search of a hot nightclub and wind up lost in the woods on a dark and rainy night. They come upon a house, ring the bell, and are beckoned inside by the cadaverous inhabitant, Dr. Heiter (Dieter Laser). They don't appear to notice the big framed photographs of grotesquely conjoined creatures hanging on the walls, although they are a bit creeped out when the doctor grimly informs them, "I don't like human beings." Before they can think too deeply about this, however, they find themselves waking up in a drug haze in Heiter's basement operating room, strapped down and soon joined by a third victim, a Japanese man named Katuro (Akihiro Kitamura). With this captive audience in place, Heiter begins to explain what's coming next.

There's no delicate way to put this. Heiter intends to create a human centipede, in three segments. The unfortunate Katuro will be in the lead, with the two girls following behind, each of their faces sutured to . . . well, let's just say the centipede's human components are to be connected through their gastric systems. There's also some surgical kneecapping and brief tooth yanking involved, but in this dreadful context those are minor indignities.

The picture is skilfully shot, on hi-def video, and there are even occasional twitches of humor. (A grave marker on the doctor's property bears the German words for "My beloved three-dog.") It must also be admitted that Dr. Heiter is one of the more memorable mad scientists in recent horror history. (The ranting Laser, with his puttylike complexion and razor-slash mouth, seems genuinely deranged.) And the movie's intentions are appropriately modest: it seeks only to be disgusting—to be an instant cult film, in other words—and in this it easily succeeds.

But there's something especially foul about this picture. I don't believe I've ever felt more pity for actors than I did for Williams and Yennie, who spend most of the movie in positions of appalling degradation (wordless, of course, and in one case topless, too). The sight of hapless performers submitting themselves to such humiliation lends *The Human Centipede* a documentary hatefulness that makes it even more repellent.

The movie leaves us wondering: *now* is there any place left that torture porn won't go? The director plans to shoot a *Centipede* sequel this summer, so I guess we (or someone far outside our circle of acquaintance) will soon see. (April 2010)

Hostel: Part II

Gore Gore Girls

Despite all the "torture porn" invective heaped upon last year's *Hostel*, none of the horrors that director Eli Roth depicts in either that movie or its just-released sequel, *Hostel: Part II*, is really new. Roth's slashings, beheadings, and jokey castrations knowingly echo the innovations of the Italian slashmaster school: Dario Argento, Joe D'Amato,

Lucio Fulci, all those guys. In his new film, Roth has even made room for a, shall we say, juicy cameo by *Cannibal Holocaust* director Ruggero Deodato.

This sort of fanboy preening can be irksome (see Quentin Tarantino's half of *Grindhouse*). But Roth brings such exuberance to his arterial tributes that you can't help but applaud his spirit. And *Hostel II* differs from its predecessor in significant ways. There's not quite as much nudity in the new film, which is of course too bad; but it's a funnier picture, with a more interesting story.

This time out, the people in highly anticipated peril are three young women: rich girl Beth (Lauren German), carnal firecracker Whitney (Bijou Phillips), and doomed geekette Lorna (*Welcome to the Dollhouse* icon Heather Matarazzo). On vacation in Rome, they're approached by a mysterious beauty named Axelle (Euro fashion model Vera Jordanova), who advises them that the Eternal City is nothing compared to the wonders of Slovakia, where she knows, as do we, of a happening hostel. The three girls nitwittedly agree to accompany her there, and are soon headed east on a train that's also transporting a herd of subhuman thugs, with whom they naturally make an unwanted acquaintance. Roth starts tightening the screws here with malignant expertise.

Arriving at the hostel, the three Americans are greeted by everybody's favorite Slovakian desk clerk (Milda Jedi Havlas). They hand over their passports and he hands them their keys. Then he scurries down to the basement, photocopies their passport pictures, and e-mails them out to homicidal maniacs worldwide, along with the announcement that bidding is now open. The winners of this lethal auction turn out to be two other Americans, a well-heeled stud named Todd (Richard Burgi) and his shlubby bud, Stuart (Roger Bart). Soon they, too, are on their way to exciting Slovakia.

After reporting in to their hotel, Todd and Stuart are escorted to the familiar *Hostel* murder factory and issued a pair of black leather butcher aprons and an assortment of drills, knives, chain saws, and what have you. They get right to work. Amid the ensuing mayhem, only one scene, I think, completely qualifies as torture porn. It's a repulsive interlude in which the suspended Lorna is tormented with a scythe by a naked woman who lies beneath her, bathing in her blood. ("Mrs. Bathory," the woman's called—one of Roth's little gore-lore jokes.) The other abuses on view—skull sawing, face munching, ear needling—although staged with brio, will hardly be new to fans of cinematic excruciation. Even the requisite genital severing is played for laughs. And then there's the amusing scene in which Todd manages to only half kill one girl, and the management quickly peddles her off to another demented client at a discount.)

Like every other sequel these days, the conclusion of this one offers the tantalizing possibility of yet another one. In this case, however, the setup actually is intriguing, and a sequel might, from some viewpoints, be worthwhile. Most moviegoers, however, would no doubt find this picture to be a deplorable exercise. Who would want to see such stuff? Well, at the screening I attended, Roth himself was on hand, introducing the film with a triumphal bray: "Are you ready for some fucked-up shit!" The response, from a large contingent of the crowd, was a gleeful chorus of bleats and cheers. Fanboys—what're you gonna do with 'em? (June 2007)

Captivity

Blood Simple

I suppose this sorry horror flick might have started out as torture porn. That was certainly the promise conveyed by those bondage billboards that caused such a ruckus in Los Angeles earlier this year. The billboards were classic PR hype, of course, like the launch party held for the picture a couple of weeks ago, which, according to *The New York Times* (!), was supposed to feature cage fighting, porn girls, and "live torture rooms." I'm kind of sorry I missed that. There have also been "rumors" that *Captivity*, which was filmed two years ago, had to be extensively reshot—really, *really* extensively—to qualify for an R rating. Love it.

Not since the 1950s has exploitation pump priming been so shameless. For this we can apparently thank Courtney Solomon, the head of After Dark Films, a quickie horror operation now nestled wetly beneath the wing of the more respectable Lionsgate Films. Solomon is clearly a man who knows what he wants. The question is, does anybody else want it?

Captivity was made by a real director, Roland Joffé, who back in the 1980s was nominated for Oscars for movies like *The Killing Fields* and *The Mission*. So the picture has a certain visual sophistication. And it's fashioned around a story from the legendarily feverish mind of Larry Cohen, the man behind such one-of-a-kind 1970s schlock as *It's Alive* and *God Told Me To*. So it has a certain sort of *top this!* pulp dementia.

What it doesn't have is a story strong enough to stifle a viewer's increasingly frequent yawns. In fact, this is the story: Elisha Cuthbert gets kidnapped by a big fat guy in a black hood who drags her to his house of horrors to menace her with guns, knives, and pliers, and pour body-part smoothies down her throat, until the end of the movie arrives after way too long and she escapes.

The picture isn't scary, or even disgusting, really; it's oppressive— dark and unpleasant in a depressingly unimaginative way. I'd lament Cuthbert's taste in film projects, except that . . . well, for one thing, she's already starred in the pointless *House of Wax* remake; and secondly, nobody's gonna *see* this thing.

After Dark's next picture is a werewolf film called *Skinwalkers*. There's said to be some "buzz" around it. Wonder where it's coming from? (July 2007)

I Know Who Killed Me

And Why

It's been a bad tabloid week for Lindsay Lohan, but this gothic fever dream of a movie probably won't make it much worse. By the admittedly undaunting standards of slasher-flick chicks past, Lohan's not bad. It's the director here who could probably use some rehab.

Lohan plays a hard-bitten stripper named Dakota. She has an unusual approach to her job: while all around her in the club where she works waitresses and fellow ecdysiasts writhe and totter about toplessly, Dakota never removes any key items of clothing. And since Lohan appears in these scenes to be on the edge of a coma—dull-eyed and lackadaisical—her stripping interludes may be the most unerotic ever filmed.

The actress also plays a second character, a good girl named Aubrey, who has been abducted by a bloodthirsty fiend of the inexplicable variety (he just does what he does, shut up). The movie is much gorier than the widely reviled *Captivity,* and possibly even more sadistic, although that's a fine line. We get to watch Aubrey being tortured in extended close-ups: skin ripped off, limbs amputated, that sort of thing. It's pretty vile. But the intended impact of these scenes is considerably dulled by the movie's underlit murkiness and its near total lack of energy and momentum, and we find our minds wandering from the blood sport on-screen to contemplate the picture's abundant technical deficiencies.

The script, by first-timer Jeffrey Hammond, flirts with incoherence and often embraces it in a full-body hug. Are Dakota and Aubrey connected in some way? Guess. But are they twins? Their DNA is identical, but Aubrey's mom is pretty sure she gave birth to just one baby. Wouldn't she know? Dakota grabs a Mac and logs on to About.com, where she's directed to "stigmata." Could this be the answer? By the time we're invited to wonder, we've forgotten the question.

The real star of this baffling show is, as I say, the director, Chris Sivertson. I confess a lack of familiarity with his previous work, although a little research suggests that it's been concentrated in video. In any case, he's clearly a man of overheated ambition, and the imagery he's concocted here sails so far above the usual gore-movie conventions that it leaves you with a crick in your neck.

There's a heavy-handed color motif throughout the film—something aqua blue seems to turn up in every other scene: blue roses, blue coffins, blue gloves; the killer even does some of his dissecting with what looks like a big blue icicle. There's a guy with a huge wriggling tattoo over his heart and a rip in his skin from which an eyeball peers out. There's an avalanche of flashbacks to various other uninteresting parts of the story, and there are long, puzzling pans through sinister woods and down along gently burbling brooks. And Sivertson gets extra credit for including an amputee sex scene—although it's not as twisted as it sounds, and since Lohan once again remains mostly clothed, it doesn't even qualify as hot.

I won't embarrass the other actors in the movie by naming them. Why Lohan thought it was worth stinting on her rehab schedule last year to make this picture is more mystifying than anything Dakota and Aubrey get up to. Her career could take a hit only if anybody goes to see this thing. For her, that may be the only good news of the week. (July 2007)

Funny Games

Last Laughs

Life sucks. We're born in pain, schooled by torment, and shadowed throughout by a bleak, inescapable fate. There is no God, no love, no mercy, and anyone who thinks otherwise is clearly not in on the cruel joke.

That's how the director Michael Haneke seems to see things, anyway. His icy and borderline-unwatchable new movie, *Funny Games* (an English-language remake of his own 1997 German film of the same name), pushes this point of view about as far as it can go. It opens with a well-to-do couple, Ann and George (Naomi Watts and Tim Roth), and their twelve-year-old son, Georgie (Devon Gearhart), driving through the far leafy reaches of eastern Long Island on the way to their big, gated vacation home. Their house is one of several widely spaced around a placid bay, and en route they pull over to call out a greeting to a pair of neighbors who are standing on the lawn of their own country estate. Standing with this couple are two young men in what look like tennis whites. The neighbors are acting oddly, and Ann and George, mildly puzzled, continue on to their nearby home.

A short time later, after Ann and George have settled in, the husband from the neighboring house appears at their gate accompanied by one of the young men they saw him with earlier. The kid tells George his name is Paul (Michael Pitt), and we notice that along with his white tennis outfit, he's also wearing white gloves. The neighbor seems ill at ease in Paul's presence. Having made this fateful introduction to George, he and Paul leave.

Before long, the other young man Ann and George saw with the neighbors appears on the porch. His name is Peter (Brady Corbet), and he too is wearing white gloves. He tells Ann he's come to borrow some eggs; the woman in the neighboring house has run out. Peter is enormously polite. His request for eggs seems simple enough, but it becomes oddly complicated. Then Paul turns up again. He too is ornately gracious. Ann, by now creeped out, wants both of these characters gone from her house. They feign puzzlement at her sudden hostility. They grow angry; they won't leave. When George and his son come in from the dock, where they've been rigging the family sailboat, terrible things begin to happen. Followed by much worse things.

Eventually, Peter and Paul tell the family that they've come to play a game. They bet that by the end of the next twelve hours, Ann and George and their son will all be dead. Presumably, the couple themselves will want to bet otherwise. Turning directly to the camera, Paul addresses us, the viewers. He knows we're on Ann and George's side, he says. Not that it matters. (Haneke doesn't overwork the old fourth-wall thing, so it's still unsettling later on, when, at an especially portentous juncture, with hopelessness thick in the air, Paul turns to us once again. "What do you think?" he asks, with a small, chilling smirk. "Don't you want a full-length movie, with plausible plot developments?" Too bad if we do.)

There is of course nothing funny about the games this picture plays. Although it's drenched in country sunlight at the outset, the movie has a black heart. The director slowly dismantles our expectations for a story of this sort—that the besieged family will escape, that justice and virtue will prevail. Whenever respite seems imminent, the menace suddenly mutates. "Level two," Paul announces, at one especially dispiriting point.

The film is like a torture-porn movie, but with the torture and humiliation staged offscreen, out of our view. Haneke's characteristically unmoving camera parks in front of the action with a numb impartiality, taking in the two captors' inhuman perversity but then blinking away whenever mayhem actually erupts. We hear howls of anguish, but what we see is Paul prowling the family's kitchen in search of a snack. We listen as Paul and his partner hound Ann to strip off her clothes in front of everybody, but the camera never leaves her half-crazed face as she does. Real fans of pain and debasement may feel cheated.

Haneke's perverse narrative strategy has the unintended effect of undermining his purpose in making the picture. In the movie's production notes, the director says he decided to remake his original film with an English-speaking cast because he believed Americans needed to see it. He disapproves of the sort of American movies in which violence and degradation are paraded across the screen for desensitized audiences to savor. The man is a Euro-art-house moralist of a familiar sort. But in carefully pulling away from the loathsome goings-on in his story, he loses all opportunity for moral illumination. We would have to *see* the awful things that are happening in order to be unsettled by the conflict between feelings of arousal and shame. The movie that Haneke has made is thus uninstructive in this regard.

What it is, instead, is a new kind of monster movie—a horror film with an awful new intimacy. The actors are all fine, and Naomi Watts (also one of the film's executive producers) gives a harrowing, fearless performance. But the picture derives a lot of its dark power from Michael Pitt's zero-degree portrayal of emotional dislocation. With his cold insect gaze and his inexplicable hostility, he's a disturbing presence. We're never told who he really is, or what he and his twisted sidekick want (they're not robbers; they seem like particularly soulless preppies). It's only slowly that we realize where they've come from, and only at the dismal end that we know where they're going next. By then, like the movie's other characters, we've abandoned all hope. (March 2008)

FUNTIME

Dying is easy," someone or another famously said. "Comedy is hard." Not as hard, however, as sitting through an alleged comedy that's just not funny. Is any other movie genre as reliant on good writing? Without a sharp script, an attempted film comedy will wither on the screen. The labored setups, wafer-thin characters, and hoary T & A wisecracks of so many purportedly funny pictures of our time are dismaying—although not, of course, to that youthful component of the audience that will be experiencing these threadbare elements for the first time. Which is as it should be. The rest of us, however, are inordinately grateful whenever an even halfway well-written, artfully acted, and inventively directed comedy comes along—as, thankfully, they sometimes still do. ·

Adventureland

Good Together

*A*dventureland isn't a message movie, but one of the messages it nevertheless imparts is this: no matter how long you spend at an amusement park trying to toss a wooden ring around the neck of a bottle, you're never going to win the "giant-ass panda" that is the top prize for doing so, because the game is rigged. And there's a more important auxiliary message: with sufficient boldness, the panda *can* be yours. I'd like to think that feat needn't require possession of a weapon, as it does in this sparkling comedy, and I believe the characters would like to think so, too. Mainly, you just gotta have heart.

The movie is a big step up for its two stars, Jesse Eisenberg and Kristen Stewart. He plays James Brennan, a young man whose plan for spending the postcollege summer of 1987 in Europe before starting grad school at Columbia in the fall collapses after his parents suffer a serious financial setback. He is thus suddenly stuck at home in small-town Pennsylvania, where he's compelled to take a job at Adventureland, the tacky local amusement park, a place where dreams go to die. Here he meets Stewart's character, Em, an NYU student who's passing the summer with her remarried dad and his insufferable new wife. Em is also carrying on an icky after-hours affair with the park's married maintenance man, Connell (Ryan Reynolds), a failed musician on the other side of thirty whose sole claim to distinction is having once "jammed with Lou Reed" (as if Lou Reed were in the habit of jamming with anyone). James is an unusual type for a movie of this sort: not just brainy, but smart—he's anything but a slacker. Em is even smarter in certain ways: she knows things James may never know—things she's coming to wish she didn't know herself.

Director Greg Mottola's last film, *Superbad*, was a pure product of the Judd Apatow laugh factory—a raucous exercise in arrested male development. *Adventureland* bears no resemblance to that movie; it's set in traditional youth-flick country, but it strikes out for more interesting territory. In a picture that was more reliant on cliché (fortunately, Mottola also wrote the script), Em might be set up as an unattainable prize to be cutely won by James, whose hyperverbal intelligence keeps him out of synch with the workaday world. (His mind has a mind of its own.) But *he* doesn't buy into this dork stereotype—why should he? He simply perseveres. And Em doesn't see James as some sort of heaven-sent chance to regain the innocence she's lost in her squalid trysts with Connell; the movie doesn't pretend innocence can be regained. Em needs a new direction in life, and James just might be going her way. Nothing in the movie is overdetermined, and nothing about the characters rings false.

Eisenberg, with his skittery earnestness, and Stewart, a dream girl with unexpected depths, are a perfect match in these roles. And the other main characters are portrayed with similar invention as they go about their silly duties among the park's bumper cars and Tilt-A-Whirls. The gangly Russian-lit major Joel (Martin Starr), a career-schmo in the making, brings a prickly deadpan woe to his scenes. (Explaining the bent hoops that preclude anyone winning a basketball-based game, he laments a "criminal use of the laws of perspective.") And park hottie Lisa P (Margarita Levieva) vividly embodies the disco life force of the period, if not much else. (When James, acknowledging the tragic lack of fabulousness that Lisa instantly perceives in him, tells her, "I guess my legend precedes me," she says, "What?") Also on hand are the park's whacked-out owners, played by Bill Hader and the invaluable Kristen Wiig (who always seems besieged by the daffy non sequiturs crackling through her head). But the most affecting character is Reynolds's Connell—a man whose tatty hookups with each season's park ingénues (carried out in the basement of his mom's house, his lone refuge from his wife) are emblems of the downward trajectory of his life. He's not a bad guy, but he knows he's not much good, either; and Reynolds, here muting his romantic star power, captures Connell's despondence with gentle precision.

Apart from the consistently funny lines and situations that flow through the movie, there's a perceptive appreciation of the part that music plays in people's lives. The year may be 1987, but the hits of that day—by Bruce Hornsby, Wang Chung, or Starship, say—are never name-checked. (Falco's 1985 "Rock Me Amadeus" pumps through the park's sound system, but it drives everybody nuts.) The music that James and Em and their friends favor comes from a place beyond the pop charts—we hear them enthusing over Big Star, Brian Eno, and the Velvet Underground. (Lou Reed's work is referenced throughout the film, and the scene in which we see James sadly knocking back drinks in a bar while the Velvets' "Pale Blue Eyes" plays on the jukebox has the glow of magical recontextualization.)

James and Em aren't youth-movie clichés; they're people we immediately know without having to have them explained. They may contemplate the possibility of catching Judas Priest at the local arena, but secretly they'd just as soon snuggle down with a copy of Eno's "Here Come the Warm Jets." And we understand. Because here they come. (April 2009)

Zombieland

Road Kill

Zombieland may be the first undead road-trip movie. The picture is light and breezy; it has a jaunty spirit. It's funny beyond the call of genre and—the cool part, of course—wonderfully disgusting.

The premise has a classic low-budget simplicity. A nationwide zombie plague has turned the country into a wasteland of stumbling gut munchers (although they can move pretty fast when they want to). Only a few uninfected human outriders remain, following ten simple rules to stay alive. One of these is "Beware of bathrooms" (zombies like to crawl up on you under toilet-stall doors). Another—which should be retroactively posted inside every monster movie of the last sixty years—is: "Check the backseat!"

The scattered plague survivors make their way through the national wreckage under adopted hometown monikers. One of these twitchy characters, a gun-happy hayseed called Tallahassee (Woody Harrelson), reluctantly joins forces with a chattery college nerd called Columbus (Jesse Eisenberg). Tallahassee has a van full of guns and ammo and a great enthusiasm for using them. After some introductory fiend-swatting and blowing away a bunch of fat junk-food zombies in a convenience store, he and Columbus encounter a pair of sisters called Wichita (Emma Stone) and Little Rock (Abigail Breslin). These two claim to be scared and helpless, but not for long. The girls turn out to be scam artists, and they quickly relieve the guys of their weapons and their wheels. The boys find another van, though, filled with even bigger guns, and they give chase. Before long, they track down the girls, a truce is called, and all four of them set off for California, where Wichita says there's an amusement park called Pacific Playland, outside of L.A., that's entirely zombie-free. Sure.

The movie dives with relish into the bloody splatter and crunch that make zombie flicks fun. These zombies aren't just run-of-the-mill flesh rippers—they crack bones and suck marrow. And along with being wasted by shotguns and clubbed to death for real by baseball bats, they're also dispatched in some inventive new ways—crushed flat by a falling piano, whacked like a golf ball by a big, pendulous amusement park ride. The picture gets maximum bang for its low-budget buck.

Stone and Breslin are as appealing as always, and Eisenberg plays his usual jittery-dweeb persona for solid laughs. But it's Harrelson who motors the film, mowing down zombies with demented glee, peppering the mayhem with addled one-liners (recalling the death of his young son: "I haven't cried like that since *Titanic*"), and generally doing whatever it takes to pump up the hilarity. The man is an unstoppable comedy machine.

The movie hits a wall about three-quarters of the way through, when the story runs out of places to go. And an interlude involving Bill Murray, playing himself, feels like a buddy favor (the comic, an old Harrelson costar, was making a movie around Atlanta at the same time this film was shooting), and it's nowhere near as funny as you'd expect. The nutty stuff is really prime, though. And any movie that gives us a zombified carnival clown—bulb-nosed, fright-wigged, dripping blood and hostility—and beats him to the ground with a giant midway mallet can be forgiven an awful lot. (October 2009)

The Devil Wears Prada

Fashion Victims

Can a simple pair of sandals actually be worth $900 just because they bear the name of Jimmy Choo? How about an $1,100 handbag by Marc Jacobs? Or a $4,000 cocktail dress by Valentino? In the world of high fashion, these are rhetorical questions. The answers are yes, definitely yes, and "I'll take two, please."

The Devil Wears Prada, a movie starring Meryl Streep in one of her wickedest comic performances, casts a knowing eye on the international couture business through the lens of its U.S. bible, *Vogue* magazine, and that publication's famously feared editor, Anna Wintour. Or . . . no, that's not exactly right. Actually, the magazine is called *Runway* here, and its editor, played by Streep, is named Miranda Priestly. These adjustments were made by author Lauren Weisberger in the best-selling 2003 novel on which the movie is based. Weisberger has been coyly insistent about denying that her book is modeled on *Vogue* or Wintour. But since she spent nearly a year working *at Vogue* as an assistant *to* Wintour, that assertion has been dismissed, especially in Fashionville, with a lip-licking smirk.

The story concerns a young woman named Andy Sachs (Anne Hathaway), a freshly minted college graduate who has moved to Manhattan to pursue a career as a journalist. The job market is ferociously competitive, as always, and she winds up at the editorial offices of

Runway—an alternate universe peopled by impossibly willowy women clacking around the halls in designer high heels—to interview for a slave-level assistant position. It's a desperate move: Andy knows nothing about fashion, has never read the magazine, and therefore has never heard of Miranda Priestly. She somehow gets hired, though, and soon learns.

Miranda's arrival at the office each morning is an occasion for gut-clenching panic among her employees. Tossing back her mane of silver-gray hair as she exits the elevator, she sails into the office lobbing little grenades of demand and desire at every staffer she passes: "Get me Isaac." "Where's that piece of paper I had in my hand yesterday?" "Get me that little table I like in that store on Madison." Requests for clarification are icily swatted away: "Please bore someone else with your questions."

Andy is completely at sea. Although any character played by Anne Hathaway must unavoidably be pretty in a fairly unimprovable way, around the *Runway* offices, Andy's a dog. She's still wearing her sensible little skirts and sweaters from college, and she clearly hasn't yet made the leap to $300 haircuts. Her fellow workers are openly contemptuous. "Who is that sad little person?" asks Nigel (Stanley Tucci), the magazine's effete photo chief. "Are we doing a before-and-after piece I don't know about?" Andy's immediate superior, an intensely snooty English girl named Emily (Emily Blunt), fears that Andy's lack of fabulousness will reflect badly on her—and possibly result in Miranda not taking Emily along to the big spring fashion shows in Paris. "If you lose Paris for me," she hisses, "I will search every Blimpie's in the tristate area till I find you."

Andy never had a "weight problem" until she arrived at *Runway*, land of the sticklike glamazons. Nigel, taking pity, counsels her in dress sizes. "Two is the new four," he says. "Zero is the new two." Andy tells him she's actually a size six. "Six," he says, "is the new fourteen." But he kindly decides to come to her rescue, pulling together fabulous new outfits for her from the photo-shoot wardrobe closet. Before long she's a full-fledged fashionista, resplendent in loan-out Chanels and Manolos and looking very little like the serious journalist she once wanted to be. The boyfriend she lives with, Nate (Adrian Grenier), a chef in a downtown restaurant, can feel her slipping away from him. And indeed, when a slick, smarmy magazine writer named Christian (Simon Baker) starts hitting on her, Andy feels the unaccustomed stirring of erotic temptation.

The movie captures New York in all of its media-lashed uproar, from the teeming streets and shops of SoHo to the money thickets of TriBeCa and the chic eateries of the Meatpacking District. And Paris in the spring, with its rain-slicked side streets and twinkling tree lights, has rarely looked more gorgeous. But the most dazzling presence in the film is Streep's Miranda Priestly. She's a woman of boundless self-absorption—the world is her backdrop but not her concern. And she manages to impose her monumental ego on her frazzled underlings around the clock, even when she's out of town. (Calling in to the office from some faraway airport, she fumes about the fact that her flight has been canceled. "Some absurd weather problem," she says, as a hurricane batters the departure-lounge windows. "Call Donatella—get her jet.")

It would be easy to trash this abrasive character, but the director, David Frankel, a *Sex and the City* veteran, and the screenwriter, Aline Brosh McKenna, are too smart to take that tack. And in one scene, during a *Runway* staff meeting, they allow Miranda to state her own case, explaining to Andy the rarely appreciated utility of high fashion: how this season's unaffordable designer styles will be knocked off into next season's high-end retail offerings, which will then blossom democratically the following season in shopping malls across the country. "In fact," Miranda says, taking in Andy's humble collegiate cardigan, "you're wearing a sweater that was selected for you by the people in this room." It's the movie's most penetrating fashion statement. (June 2006)

Julie & Julia

Half-baked

Julie & Julia is one-half of a great biopic. In portraying Julia Child—the effervescent chef and author whose four decades of TV cooking shows made her an intimate presence in millions of American homes—Meryl Streep gives a performance that's virtually an act of reincarnation. One of the film's most striking moments is an early scene in which Julia, not yet a cook, and her husband Paul (Stanley Tucci) are having dinner in a Paris restaurant, and Paul asks his wife what it is she most likes to do. Happily chewing a forkful of food, Julia tosses her head and blurts out, "Eat!" That's all. But Streep's careful twining of gestures and expressions—breezy, ebullient, half-dotty—is so precisely Julian that a smile of delight is hard to suppress.

Streep's accomplishment is remarkable because Julia Child—an American original—seems so far beyond the reach of nonsatirical depiction. She was a towering Californian (six feet, two inches tall) who joined the OSS (precursor to the CIA) during World War II, working for the agency in both Washington, D.C., and China (as an intelligence researcher, not a spy, in her account). At age thirty-four (still a virgin, she blithely noted), she married Paul Child, a U.S. Foreign Service officer. In 1949, he was assigned to Paris, and it was there that Julia had her first French meal—a simple filet of sole with butter and lemon that changed her life.

Immediately impassioned, she started learning French and enrolled in Le Cordon Bleu, the celebrated (and overrated, she said) Paris cooking school. Soon she connected with two Frenchwomen, Simone Beck and Louisette Bertholle, who were attempting to write a book about French cooking for Americans. Julia joined them, and over the next eight years, as she moved with Paul to Marseilles, Bonn, Oslo, and finally back across the Atlantic to settle in Cambridge, Massachusetts, she and her two partners continued working on the book by mail.

Their final manuscript was a collection of more than five hundred recipes—each one meticulously researched and translated, and repeatedly tested by Julia—that would eventually run to 720 printed pages. More than one publisher shied away from a specialized book of this size, especially since it was commonly assumed at the time that American cooks—meaning American women, for the most part—were quite happy with canned soups and packaged mixes and had no interest in classical cooking techniques. Julia Child's breakthrough perception was how wrong this assumption was. The book she created with Beck and Bertholle, published in 1961 as *Mastering the Art of French Cooking,* was an immediate success and is now in its forty-ninth printing.

Two years later, a Boston PBS station offered Julia her own cooking show. *The French Chef* started out as a low-budget black-and-white production that showcased not only the star's culinary expertise but also her cheery knack for on-camera improvisation. In one famous incident, while frying a large potato pancake, she lifted the pan to flip the thing and—*whoops*—slopped a good part of it onto the stovetop. "That didn't go very well," she muttered, scooping the clumps back into the pan. "But you can always pick it up. And if you're alone in the kitchen, who is going to see?" (A persistent urban legend has Julia dropping a whole roasted chicken or lamb haunch on the floor in one show and lifting it back onto the serving plate. According to Snopes.com, the killjoy website, there's no taped evidence that this ever happened.)

The potato-pancake incident makes it into *Julie & Julia*, along with much else from Child's memoir, *My Life in France,* which was assembled from letters and memories by an admiring grandnephew, Alex Prud'homme, and published in 2006, two years after Child's death. As in the book, a prominent theme in the movie is Paul and Julia's extraordinary mutual devotion. Paul, a paragon among husbands, it seems, offered Julia unflagging encouragement and assistance (in the early days of the TV show, he washed the pots). Streep and Tucci, last paired in *The Devil Wears Prada,* have a natural chemistry that brings this grand relationship—a rare perfect match—to full, glowing life.

Unfortunately, *Julie & Julia* isn't entirely about Julia Child. It was writer-director Nora Ephron's cute idea to pair the story told in *My Life in France* with another one adapted from a 2005 book called *Julie & Julia: My Year of Cooking Dangerously,* by Julie Powell. In 2002, Powell, a thirtyish New Yorker stuck in a dead-end office job, began a yearlong Salon blog in which she undertook to cook every recipe in *Mastering the Art of French Cooking.* The blog became popular, and the book deal followed. In the film, Powell is fetchingly portrayed by Amy Adams, and there are some amusing moments as she slogs her way through Child's daunting tome. (Tapping away at her laptop, Julie tells her online audience, "We are, I am sorry to say, entering aspics.")

But Powell's story is an emaciated thing compared to Julia's. She, too, has a husband (played by Chris Messina), but his support only extends so far, and at one point he leaves her. (In a second book called *Cleaving,* Powell recounts an extramarital affair.) More important, though, the contrast between Julia Child's accomplishment and Julie Powell's—which could pass for an accomplishment only in the blog world—deflates the movie like a failed soufflé. Child created a book (several, in fact) and a public persona that were unique in their time; she removed the intimidation from French cuisine and made it a possibility for home cooks. (She also inspired many a future celebrity chef.) Powell simply slipstreamed behind her. And so Powell's story, a modest online entertainment, is a wobbly element in a movie that might have been better had it concentrated fully on its most fascinating subject. (August 2009)

Hancock

Stuporman

John Hancock (Will Smith) is a new kind of superhero. He's a mess. One night in Miami, after a mugging, he woke up in a hospital with no money, no ID, and not a clue who he was. When a nurse asked for his John Hancock on a form, he gave it to her—"John Hancock"—and then kept the name for his own. That was eighty years ago. Today, Hancock is an L.A. street drunk with a mean disposition and some offbeat abilities. He can fly, for one thing. And he can pick up a car with one hand and stop a speeding locomotive with his outstretched fist. Also, as he tells his new friend Ray Embrey (Jason Bateman), "I don't age."

Hancock works the slickest twist on the superhero movie since *Unbreakable.* In that M. Night Shyamalan film, the nature of the narrative subterfuge evolved slowly, through an accretion of odd details and sudden iconic images. In *Hancock,* the plot twist is sudden and startling—it comes winging in out of left field and it transforms the picture. Unfortunately, it also forces the movie into an ending that makes not even a tiny bit of sense. Everything that comes before that, though, earns our retrospective forgiveness.

Ray meets Hancock when the shabby superhero saves him from being flattened by a train. He already knows who Hancock is, of course; everybody does. When he's not passed out on the street in a nest of empty bourbon bottles, Hancock spends his time flying around town fighting crime and saving people's lives. Everybody hates him, though, because with all his good deeds he does a lot of damage. Every time he comes soaring down out of the sky, he tears up fifty feet of neighborhood asphalt in landing. When he tosses a beached whale back into the ocean—hurling it like a big blubbery discus—it lands on a passing yacht. Lawsuits are piling up. TV host Nancy Grace is calling for his scalp. There's a warrant out for Hancock's arrest (as if any jail could hold him).

Ray, a PR guy who's too good-hearted for his own good, knows just what Hancock needs: an image makeover. He takes him home for dinner, where Ray's young son (Jae Head) is thrilled, but his wife (Charlize Theron) is repelled by Hancock's surly lack of social skills . . . and maybe something else. Ray advises his new client to turn himself in to the police and do some voluntary jail time. Hancock reluctantly agrees. With the sourpuss superhero behind bars, the L.A. crime rate shoots up 30 percent, and soon, at the sheriff's request, Hancock is back on the crime-fighting beat, now togged out in a neat black-leather superhero costume (Ray's idea) and doing his best to be polite to people (it's hard).

The first half of the movie is very funny, as we watch Hancock grumping at the citizenry (to a staring old lady: "I'll break my foot off in your ass, woman") and butting ahead of some cute kids lined up at an ice-cream truck. (He just extinguished a burning building; he needs to cool down; why doesn't anybody understand?) And the big plot turnaround, which comes about halfway through the picture, arises in a sky-high battle chase that trashes property values all over town. From this point on, though, the movie's tone shifts radically. It grows darker and more earthbound, and at the end it stretches toward tragedy—which eludes its grasp. (The plot point on which it depends—let's say it concerns the importance of nearness and distance—is glaringly self-contradictory.)

But *Hancock* is still a lot of fun. Will Smith remains one of the most likable of movie stars, and he's a master of offhand sarcasm. Risking his box-office rep on such wild material as this is admirably audacious. Jason Bateman is used mainly for his amiable sweetness, and his character begins to fade in the darker second half of the picture. But Charlize Theron, radiant as always, demonstrates unexpected comedy skills.

Despite its heavy complement of expensive digital effects, the movie doesn't feel like a holiday blockbuster (it's only about ninety minutes long). It looks raw and grainy (it might have benefited from a little more visual stylization), and director Peter Berg is way too fond of 360-degree camera whirling. But the story is inventive and the script is filled with crisp, snappy dialogue, for which writers Vy Vincent Ngo and Vince Gilligan deserve a fee boost for their next feature. They could also use a talking-to about that ending, though. (July 2008)

Juno

Girl Most Likely

*J*uno is a comedy about teenagers (among other things), but it's not a "teen comedy." There's no hierarchy of geeks and snoots and clueless 'rents, no arsenal of desperate sex jokes. You come away from the film feeling grateful and happy, and scrambling for superlatives to shower on the subversive snugglebug Ellen Page, who gives a bust-out performance in the title role.

Page plays Juno MacGuff, a sixteen-year-old suburban nonconformist. One day she takes the first-time-sex plunge with her pal Paulie Bleeker (the eloquently impassive Michael Cera) and, as bad luck would have it, becomes pregnant. Her repairman dad (J. K. Simmons) and stepmom Bren (Allison Janney) are of course taken aback when she breaks the news ("I was hoping she was expelled, or into hard drugs," says Bren), but then they rally 'round. A visit to an abortion clinic proves offputting (handing her a blank form, the receptionist says, "We need to know about every score and every sore"). So Juno decides to have the baby and then give it up for adoption, maybe to "a woman with a bum ovary, or a couple of nice lesbos."

She eventually connects with a childless couple named Mark and Vanessa Loring, and if this were a standard teen comedy, they would surely be the objects of merciless potshotting. Their home is huge, their taste in clothes and furnishings leans heavily toward beige, and they drink things like ginseng coolers. But the movie doesn't blow these two off as soulless yuppies. Instead, it shows us that Mark (Jason Bateman), a failed rock musician now crowding forty, who makes a plush living scoring commercials, feels like a sellout. And Vanessa (Jennifer Garner), a good-hearted career woman longing for maternal fulfillment, is tired of biding her time till Mark outgrows his rock-star fantasy. ("If I have to wait for you to be Kurt Cobain," she tells him, "I'm never gonna be a mother.")

Juno bonds with both of them, keeping Vanessa updated on the baby-to-be with ultrasound photos and swapping music with Mark. (He thinks the greatest record ever made is Sonic Youth's version of "Superstar"; she worships at the shrine of Iggy Pop.) Then, as Juno's belly blimps out ("I'm a planet!"), something unexpected happens. And then something else. And then romance blooms in a not-entirely-predictable quarter. The movie ends with the sweetest final shot since *Little Miss Sunshine*.

First-time screenwriter Diablo Cody—cult blogstress, fledgling memoirist, and one-time stripper—is a formidably funny woman. True, the first part of the movie, in which priceless retorts erupt like explosions in a wisecrack factory, feels a little self-consciously clever. But the lines are so sharp, there's little basis for complaint. There are also slightly creepy overtones in some parts of the film. But as the story deepens—and at the same time grows funnier—you know Cody can probably write her own ticket to whatever Hollywood destination she may have in mind next.

Director Jason Reitman knows just what to do with this material: he has given the picture a fresh, cheery visual style, and he never milks the laughs. The actors are first-rate, too, especially Bateman as a wilting hunk beset by midlife confusion and the invaluable Simmons (*Daily Bugle* editor J. Jonah Jameson in the *Spider-Man* movies), hereby nominated for big-screen dad of the year. Also notable is the movie's soundtrack, a procession of just-right songs by Kimya Dawson, Cat Power, Buddy Holly, and Belle and Sebastian, among others.

Ellen Page was already extraordinary two years ago in *Hard Candy*. Now she's twenty years old, but could still pass for twelve, and her poised accomplishment is even more striking. Traipsing through the movie in her ragamuffin duds, preceded everywhere by a huge prosthetic belly and snapping off killer quips like gum bubbles, she turns what might have been a really good comedy into a great one. In fact, a classic. (December 2007)

Hot Fuzz

Lawn Order

Sergeant Nicholas Angel has a problem, one I think we've all had. He's way too good at his job. As a top London cop, Angel (Simon Pegg) is fearsomely expert in all of the butt-kicker arts, from judo to weaponry to precision jaw clenching. He's an unstoppable law enforcement machine, with an arrest record that's 400 percent higher than anyone else's. Naturally, his brother officers hate him—he's making them look bad. "You can't be the *sheriff* of London," says his condescending boss (Bill Nighy), before breaking the news that Angel is to be reassigned to a new post in the faraway, leafy tranquility of Sandford, "the safest village in the country."

Angel is a professional, so he dutifully relocates. As expected, Sandford, with its cobbled town square and smothering coziness, is no place for a seasoned lawman—its most felonious resident is a renegade swan. But Angel is determined to find some crime to stop. Soon he's rousting beer-sodden teens from the local pub and busting a chubby drunk named Danny Butterman (Nick Frost), who turns out to be a local cop himself, thanks to his dotty dad (Jim Broadbent), the chief of police.

Inevitably, Danny and Angel are soon teamed as partners. Danny, an action-movie buff who venerates the peerless *Point Break,* is thrilled—to Danny, Angel is the personification of big-city cop action, a fantasy world in which bullets crowd the air like high-caliber locusts and the favored mode of public transport is the car chase. Angel advises Danny to banish such thoughts; amid gathering clouds of despair, he has pretty much banished them himself.

But as he begins training his outsider's eye more closely on the Sandford scene, an unsettling pattern begins to emerge. True, there hasn't been a murder recorded in the town for twenty years. But there's been a curious abundance of *deaths*—most recently the skull-pulverizing elimination of a troublesome journalist who happened to be standing in exactly the wrong spot one night when a large chunk of building came crashing down on him. "Have you ever wondered," Angel asks his sleepwalking colleagues, "why the crime rate is so low, and yet the accident rate is so *high?*"

No, they haven't. Nor have they paid much attention to the town's grinningly sinister supermarket magnate (Timothy Dalton), who says things like, "I'm sure if we bashed your head in, all sorts of secrets might come tumbling out." Or the local Neighborhood Watch group that likes to don dark robes for its late-night meetings and is determined to win an upcoming "Best Village" competition by any means necessary. There's also an old geezer with a barn full of guns—although he's actually okay: his lethal weaponry comes in handy when a hooded slasher starts stalking the town, at which point it becomes clear that only Angel and Danny have the gumption to stop him.

Director Edgar Wright and his pals Pegg (who cowrote the script) and Frost bring the same affectionate touch to this winning action satire that they applied to their first film, the left-field zombie hit, *Shaun of the Dead. Hot Fuzz* doesn't have quite the delectable fizz that the previous picture did, and it's a little too long. But it's consistently funny—there are few passages that pass by without a complement of laughs. (Appalled at one point by the villagers' abominable behavior, Angel berates them with straight-arrow indignation: "You should be ashamed, calling yourselves 'The Community That Cares'!")

Wright is especially adept at shorthand montage, and his tight editing gives the movie the comic punch of good blackout skits. Best of all, though, he and his partners don't use their deep knowledge of old action movies in an overbearingly pedantic way. They satirize the knuckle-headed conventions of those old films—the *Die Hard* and *Bad Boys* and *Beverly Hills Cop* pictures—because they were dumb then and they're lovably dumb now. But what the director and his two stars really enjoy about those movies, and what they capture most rousingly, is their exuberance—the uncomplicated fun they provided. It's even funnier in this silly new context. If there's anything more mindlessly exhilarating than seeing a gang of louts mowed down with a hail of bullets, it's seeing it done in a quaint village square. (Not to mention the special joy of seeing a little old lady taken out with a flying face kick.)

Like *Shaun of the Dead*, *Hot Fuzz* is distinguished by the affection of its parody. This is not the work of hyper-referencing film geeks; it's a movie that finds no shame in being purely enjoyable. (April 2007)

Up in the Air

First Class

U p in the Air, the new Jason Reitman movie, is difficult to pin down. It's not really a romantic comedy, although it is very funny and romance is one of its subjects. And it's not exactly a drama, either, although it pokes around in some dark corners of contemporary life. The picture is really one of a kind.

George Clooney, in one of his most subtle performances, plays Ryan Bingham, corporate executioner. Ryan spends his life flying around the country at the behest of downsizing companies that hire him to break the bad news to the employees they're laying off. It's an awful job, but Ryan loves the life. He loves the anonymous luxe of his business hotel suites, his VIP car rental accounts, the first-class airport lounges and the astronomical amounts of frequent-flier miles he racks up. Who needs friends when there are always fellow passengers to talk to up in the air? Who needs a romantic relationship when transient sex abounds? Who even needs a home? (Asked on a flight where he's from, Ryan says, "I'm from here.")

But then two women enter Ryan's life and soon have him reconsidering all that. The first is Alex Goran (Vera Farmiga, terrific once again).

Alex is a corporate road warrior, too, and transient, no-strings sex is one of her specialties. ("Think of me as yourself," she tells Ryan, "with a vagina.") Ryan likes Alex, and soon they're slotting on-the-fly hookups into their complicated itineraries. Before long, Ryan starts to *really* like Alex. Now what?

The second woman on the scene is a perky young bean counter named Natalie Keener (Anna Kendrick of the *Twilight* movies). Natalie is a new hire at Ryan's company, and she has brought with her a big idea: instead of paying to fly guys like Ryan around the country to lower the boom on discarded employees, why not just conduct these firings over the Internet, via iChat, right from the company's Omaha headquarters?

Ryan hates this idea. Apart from the threat it poses to his high-flying lifestyle, he feels it lacks the human touch. After all, this is a delicate business: "We take people at their most fragile and we set them adrift." But Ryan's boss, the suavely heartless Craig Gregory (Jason Bateman), is excited by Natalie's plan. Since she has never actually fired anyone, though, he tells Ryan to take her out on the road for one last go-round and show her how it's done.

So he does. First he teaches Natalie how to travel. Never check luggage, for one thing—a carry-on wheelie is the way to go. (Ryan is all about bare essentials.) Also, always get in line behind Asians at the airport security checkpoint—they pack light and move through quickly. The hardest lesson Natalie learns is how to face a person she's never met before and will never see again and tell them they're losing their job. These scenes are piercingly affecting because the people we see being sacked are nonactors—they're people who really were recently fired from longtime jobs at the time the movie was made, and they're reliving their responses. (Reitman recruited them through newspaper ads in Detroit and St. Louis. As he says in the film's production notes, "We got so many submissions, it was heartbreaking.")

Natalie, for her part, tries to get Ryan to see the emptiness of his worldview. How can he never want to get married, have a home and kids? She might as well be speaking Venusian. (Ryan has a sideline giving motivational speeches to business groups, in which he says things like, "Relationships are the heaviest components in your life. You don't need to carry all that weight.") The man is hopeless. Or is he?

The movie is based on a book by Walter Kirn; Sheldon Turner did an early draft of the script, then Reitman went to work on it himself. This is only his third feature (after *Thank You for Smoking* and *Juno*), but he's already adept at populist filmmaking, a director whose supple comic touch recalls golden age auteurs like Preston Sturges and Frank Capra. The characters here keep peeling away layers of personality— they keep evolving—and we're never sure what they'll do next. (The movie is full of surprises.) Will they do the right thing? In such an uncertain world, do they even know what that would be? (December 2009)

Youth in Revolt

Good Boy Makes Bad

As every nice guy knows, girls have an inexplicable thing for bad boys. Which is bad news for Nick Twisp (Michael Cera), who unfortunately couldn't be nicer. Nick is sixteen years old and a budding sophisticate whose tastes—shared by no one in his circle of acquaintances—run to Frank Sinatra records and old Fellini movies. He's also a virgin whose knowledge of sex consists entirely of hearsay. He longs to score, ideally with a girl whose tastes run to Frank Sinatra records and old Fellini movies.

But there's no one like that in sight. And meanwhile, everyone around Nick seems to be scoring like mad, even his divorced parents. His mom (Jean Smart), with whom he lives, is currently filling the vacancy in her love life with a beardy schlub named Jerry (Zach Galifianakis); and his dad (Steve Buscemi) is shacked up with a twenty-five-year-old cupcake named Lacey (Ari Graynor). Nick is *so* ready to join the scoring multitudes, if only he could figure out how.

As we see, *Youth in Revolt,* which is adapted from a comic novel by C. D. Payne, has the usual hallmarks of a Michael Cera movie. This time out, though, Cera opens up his familiar whimsical-nerd character, inserts a grenade (well, a small grenade), and pulls the pin. The result illuminates new facets of his subtle talent and suggests new directions in which he might take it.

Nick naturally meets the girl of his dreams. Her name is Sheeni (Portia Doubleday), and not only is she mind-foggingly cute, she's also a fledgling Francophile who's partial to the films of Jean-Paul Belmondo and the 1960s song stylings of Serge Gainsbourg. Sheeni responds to Nick's nice-guy qualities, but wishes he were a little more . . . well, bad—like Belmondo in *Breathless.* This would seem to be a deal killer, but Nick is determined. He conjures up from his subconscious an alter ego called François—a haughty Euro stud in aviator shades, with a caterpillary mustache and an ever-present hand-rolled cigarette pasted to his lip. François teaches Nick all about being bad—from spitting on the carpet to blowing stuff up. In the process, he takes over the picture.

Having overcome his nice-guy handicap, Nick must now attempt to interpose himself between Sheeni and her quasi boyfriend, the dauntingly hunky Trent (Jonathan Bradford Wright). François is happy to help. So when Sheeni's parents send her off to a snooty boarding school—where Trent also happens to be a student—Nick and François (both played by Cera, of course, with fluid expertise) set off in pursuit. Sheeni wanted bad? Nick brings it.

The movie has some delectably droll scenes—spiked with Cera's gift for the sour throwaway quip—and some wild lines. (François's suggestion for a studly come-on: "I'm going to wrap your legs around my head and wear you like the crown you are!") There are also tasty cameos by Fred Willard and Ray Liotta (as a scummy cop, what else?), and brief, zesty performances by Justin Long (as Sheeni's 'shroom-swacked brother) and Rooney Mara (as her frankly slutty roommate). Does Nick finally get the girl? That's hard to say, actually. But when Sheeni looks at him and says, "Kiss me, you wienie," you know anything's possible. (January 2010)

The Other Guys

Idiots Delight

*T*he Other Guys is that rare thing, a goofball summer buddy comedy that actually delivers. The movie is a return to form for Will Ferrell, who finally reins in the idiot frenzy he's so often deployed in the past (most recently in last year's dismal *Land of the Lost*) and—an added blessing—shows no skin, either. It's also a breakthrough for Mark Wahlberg, who dipped a toe into the comedy waters of *Date Night*, but here makes a sizable splash. Wahlberg isn't an all-out clown in the Ferrell style, but his careful restraint in this picture—his comic simmering and his lag-timed reactions—is funny in a different way.

The stars play Allen Gamble and Terry Hoitz, two New York City police detectives stuck in the paper-pushing backwaters of their department while a pair of more charismatic cops (Dwayne Johnson and Samuel L. Jackson in fleeting cameos) get all the action, and the headlines. Allen (Ferrell) is a forensic accountant—he loves paperwork. His partner Hoitz (Wahlberg) hates it—but his career was sidelined after he accidentally shot Yankees star Derek Jeter one night. ("You shoulda shot A-Rod," another cop snipes.) Then these two stumble onto a big Wall Street financial scam—a Ponzi scheme being run by an English investment mogul named Ershon (Steve Coogan). If Allen and Terry can crack this case, career resuscitation will surely follow.

This thicket of financial shenanigans is the movie's most strained element—it's essentially a platform for the filmmakers to lecture the audience about the evils of capitalism. (Addressing a business gathering, Ershon cackles, "Live for excess—it is the American way.") As always, though, this rote Hollywood moralizing sits awkwardly in a big-budget film, especially one starring a man who reportedly makes $20 million a picture.

The high-finance plot is in any case a distraction that's generally obscured by the laugh bombs going off all around it. Allen is endlessly castigated by his fellow cops as an overgrown sissy (drives a Prius, loves the Little River Band), but he's also, inexplicably, a major chick magnet. (Taking Terry to his home, he warns that his wife is something of a dog: "She's a big old broad." Then she turns out to be played by the definitively undoglike Eva Mendes.) He has also written a downloadable app called Faceback—scan in the back of someone's head and it shows you the face. The script, by director Adam McKay and Chris Henchy, also provides some nifty business for the boys' boss, Chief Mauch (Michael Keaton), who moonlights as a salesclerk at Bed, Bath & Beyond and is prone to converse in TLC lyrics (a joke that's milked a little too much). It's good to have Keaton back in the comedy big time; he's been away too long.

The movie is a full-throated parody of the urban action genre: many cars crash, many bullets fly, and a whole lot of stuff blows up. But even the pandemonium has a comic shape. (The sequence in which a helicopter attack is repelled by a blizzard of golf balls is explosively funny.) And the ricocheting one-liners rise above even the most clamorous mayhem. When Terry erupts in frustration over being a desk-job drone— "I'm a peacock! You gotta let me fly!"—the movie earns the highest possible praise for this sort of project: it's truly ridiculous. (August 2010)

Brüno

Celebrity Holocaust

*B*rüno is both a confirmation of Sacha Baron Cohen's comic gift and a proof of its limitations. The movie is less irritating than *Borat,* his last exercise in guerrilla humiliation. Here, instead of ridiculing blameless Romanian peasants and unsuspecting everyday Americans, Cohen takes aim at a more deserving target—the great puffed-up world of modern celebrity. Early on, we see the star at a Milan fashion show, interviewing a real-life model about her job. "It's really hard, isn't it?" he asks, deviously sympathetic. When she responds, "It's *very* hard," you wish the movie had focused exclusively on the international fabulatti.

But then we'd be deprived of Cohen's mega-tasteless physical comedy. His character this time out, as even blameless Romanian peasants must know by now (to their relief), is Brüno, the flamboyantly gay host of an Austrian TV fashion program called *Funkyzeit*. Brüno is as much fashion victim as fashion arbiter (witness his tulip-yellow lederhosen). But he's the master of his sexual domain, as we see in an athletic session with a diminutive boy toy in which he makes alarming use of everything from champagne bottles to DustBusters to enema equipment—a sequence that ventures far beyond the usual confines of an R rating. (There's also a talking penis later on—a real one. Not really *talking*, but . . . well, you have to see it.)

The movie's structure—"plot" isn't really the word—involves Brüno screwing up and getting fired from his TV job. ("For ze second time in a century," he says, "ze world has turned on Austria's greatest man.") So he flies off to L.A., reasonably assuming it to be his kind of town. There he acquires an agent (a colorless character), who secures him a part as an extra on the TV show *Medium* (a meandering sequence). Then he visits an "anal bleaching salon"—mainly so he can deliver a bitchy comment about Salma Hayek.

These segments, and another one involving a puzzled karate instructor, are surprisingly flat. Other scenes—especially an overnight camping trip with three decidedly heterosexual hunters and an interlude in which Brüno undergoes army basic training—feel staged. And Cohen's trademark yokel baiting, while still sometimes funny (and rather courageous in a he-man wrestling match that devolves into gay fondling and an eruption of bottle-tossing audience fury), is no longer as fresh as it was in *Borat*. (A looming concern for Cohen would have to be that he's now too well known to continue getting away with this incognito act.) Most pitifully, Brüno's pants-dropping assault on mild-mannered congressman Ron Paul returns Cohen's shtick to its wretched *Candid Camera* roots.

But Brüno's visit to Israel—where he attempts to bring Jews and Palestinians together but confuses Hamas with hummus—is prime stuff. And when Cohen trains his savage eye on celebrities, his aim is invariably true. It's a shame that an elaborately rude interview with La Toya Jackson was cut from the film following Michael Jackson's death. But we still have Brüno returning from an African sojourn with that most prized of celebrity accessories, a black baby; and then defending his adoptive fatherhood before an irate black audience on a bogus talk show.

Best of all, perhaps, is the movie's conclusion, in which Brüno is joined in a recording studio by the likes of Bono, Sting, Slash, and Elton John to record a faux charity single of the "We Are the World" variety. (The song's title is "Dove of Peace.") The stars are complicit hipsters, secure in the knowledge that they're actually in on the joke. Which is the part of the joke they're actually not in on. (July 2009)

THE LAND THAT LAUGHS FORGOT

B ad comedies are of two kinds. One is lifeless, inert—becalmed by lame conception and awkward execution. This sort of bad comedy, essentially harmless, leaves you feeling peevish and cheated—still hungry for the laughs that were never delivered. Really bad comedies, on the other hand, can leave you questioning the meaning of life. Think of the following not just as reviews but as warnings.

MacGruber

Saturday Night Jive

One approaches any movie based on a *Saturday Night Live* skit with basement-level expectations. Still, the new *MacGruber* manages to disappoint. The only interesting thing about the picture is that, with a little tweaking, it might actually have been turned into a serviceable parody of a 1980s-style action flick: bullets fly, stuff blows up, doorway-size heavies lend menace, and it's all been rendered with a knowing fondness for the form by cinematographer Brandon Trost (who also shot *Crank: High Voltage*). But too early on, comedy begins cropping up, and it's all subbasement from there on out.

SNL enthusiasts will know that the skits this picture seeks to inflate are riffs on the 1980s TV show *MacGyver,* the protagonist of which was a gun-shy secret agent capable of combining the unlikeliest oddments—a cuff link, a crayon, and a cantaloupe, say—into useful tools in stressful situations. The skits mine laughs from the manic incompetence of their special agent, MacGruber (played both there and here by Will Forte), and from the explosions he inevitably fails to abort. The movie attempts to do the same, but after maybe twenty minutes of Forte's frantic, one-note mugging, it's left with nowhere else to go—and there's still more than an hour of this thing to sit through.

The story has MacGruber, long thought dead, being tracked down to the remote monastery where he has holed up by his former commander, Colonel Faith (Powers Boothe). The colonel has a new assignment for him: stopping MacGruber's old adversary, Dieter Von Cunthe (Val Kilmer), from wreaking havoc with a nuclear warhead he's stolen. Since Von Cunthe is the man who blew up MacGruber's wife ten years earlier, the legendary agent agrees to take a shot. To this end, he assembles an A team of special-ops brutes (all played by professional wrestlers), who are suddenly disbanded when the van into which he's packed them (what else?) blows up. Desperate for replacements, MacGruber recruits an old colleague, Vicki St. Elmo (Kristen Wiig), and a whippersnapper army lieutenant called Piper (Ryan Phillippe). Wiig remains a master of the throwaway mumble, but some of the lines she's handed here should have been thrown away before they reached her; and Phillippe, for his part, is employed as a wooden straight man whose only function is to endure (along with us) Forte's endless pop-eyed verbal conniptions.

Bad taste is supposed to be a badge of honor in a movie like this, but really, is there anyone left to offend? The nonstop barrage of F words and whatnot unleashed in this film lost any ability to shock long ago; and while the name Cunthe was no doubt good for a giggle around the writers' table, in its twentieth repetition here it tests the limits of tedium. There's also more poop humor than one might have thought strictly necessary. In fact, the movie has something of an anal fixation: one of MacGruber's diversionary tactics is to stick a stalk of celery between his thighs so that it wiggles out between his bare buttocks; and he's curiously prone to offer up his nether region for rough use by men from whom he seeks favors.

The picture also suffers from a lack of comic precision. At one point, we see Von Cunthe painting a picture using a topless fat old woman as a model. This has the shape of a gag—but what is it? Von Cunthe's art hobby comes out of nowhere and immediately returns there, and we're left with nothing in the way of amusement beyond an old woman's degradation. Presumably, this seemed funny during the scripting sessions, too.

MacGruber painfully demonstrates the inadvisability of attempting to stretch a one-minute TV sketch into a ninety-minute movie—especially when the lead character is nothing more than an assemblage of overamped and decreasingly funny wisecracks. *SNL* has been pounding the MacGruber character for more than three years now; could anyone really have thought there was a single drop of humor left to be wrung from it? Or an audience desperate enough for laughs to want more? (May 2010)

Land of the Lost

Into the Mild

Many a 1970s kid thrilled to the cheesy TV series *Land of the Lost*, and some of them, it appears, grew up to run movie studios. That might explain why this decrepit property has now been turned into a movie. The picture is a CGI adventure comedy with a mild line in PG-13 laughs, a surprising lack of fresh adventure (did the filmmakers chop up an early print of *Journey to the Center of the Earth* and snort it?), and very little in the way of digital dinosaurs and whatnot that hasn't stampeded past us many times before. It's worth noting that two of the movie's funnier scenes—one involving a giant mosquito and the other a confrontation with Matt Lauer on the *Today* show—can be seen for free in the trailer. Just a thought.

The plot is a thing of standard-issue silliness. Will Ferrell, in his familiar arrogant-dork mode, is Dr. Rick Marshall, an expert in "quantum paleontology" and inventor of a "tachyon amplifier" that allows its operator to travel "sideways in time." Rick is an idiot, of course, but he does have a champion—a pretty young English scientist named Holly Cantrell (Anna Friel), who pops up out of nowhere with the news that she has proved Rick's tachyon theory to be true. Before you can say "weak plot device," she and Rick are off to the desert in search of a time portal to a parallel dimension. I'm pretty sure that's what's going on. Anyway, they find this portal at a roadside amusement park run by a small-time wisecracker named Will Stanton (Danny McBride). Soon the three of them are barreling over a waterfall and down into the Land of Computer Generation, where rampaging behemoths, swooping pterodactyls, and bubble-eyed lizard men conspire to justify the movie's large budget.

Rick and company soon acquire a fourth companion, a hairy young

Neanderthal named Cha-Ka (Jorma Taccone), the movie's most amus-ing character. Cha-Ka doesn't speak English, of course; but Holly, be-ing a scientist and all, understands his native gibberish, and even his penchant for good-natured bosom fondling. (Bosom ownership may have been the chief qualification in casting Friel's largely decorative character. Too bad the only bosoms actually bared here belong, inevi-tably, to Will Ferrell.) Before long the group encounters an alien scien-tist called Enik (John Boylan), who warns them about the Zarn—an evil entity who's plotting to conquer Earth with his lizard warriors and can only be stopped by Rick's tachyon thing. Need I continue?

There are some good bits. A gag about Mesozoic walnuts is a little strained in its setup, but Ferrell's panicky dance through a pit full of hatching pterodactyl eggs is a cute nod to the *Alien* movies, and the conversion of a giant crustacean into instant hors d'oeuvres is pretty inspired. Some key scenes are limply shaped, though: when Ferrell wanders into the group's jungle camp playing a banjo, it's distractingly pointless—why's he playing a banjo? (And why, since he's not *really* playing it, is he playing it left-handed? Camera logistics shouldn't draw such attention.)

It's a little dismaying to hear a man as funny as Will Ferrell give forth with witless exclamations like "Captain Kirk's nipples!" But Fer-rell seems to be expending a lot of his career in this sort of schlock-buster trash. What's more distressing is watching Danny McBride, an actor with a fierce comic edge, biding his time through this lackluster film. True, he does get the movie's funniest line: coming upon a primi-tive jungle temple built around what looks like a towering Lucite obe-lisk, McBride cocks a brow and says, "Maybe this is where our ancient ancestors hosted the Latin Grammys." It's downhill from there, though. (June 2009)

Year One

Time Warped

Remember *Land of the Lost*? The Will Ferrell movie? Came out two weeks ago? Right, that one. Do you think there's still room in the tank to which that picture was instantly consigned for the new *Year One*, another prehistoricky gagfest with not a single gray cell in its tiny noggin? The movie was directed by Harold Ramis, who once gave us *Groundhog Day*; and it numbers among its producers the raunch king Judd Apatow. That might seem a match made in comedy heaven, and you might expect the picture to kill. But it overkills, in an altogether underwhelming way. Even with the customary complement of Apatow veterans on hand—Paul Rudd and Bill Hader wander through, as does Ramis himself—the movie tuckers us out.

The stars, Jack Black and Michael Cera, play themselves, essentially: Jack's a leering cutup, Michael's a sensitive dweeb. Their characters are Zed and Oh, proto-dork members of a tribe of hunter-gatherers back in . . . well, not the Year One, exactly—not by any reckoning I know of. Let's just say back in the primitive, prewheel days of our planet. Zed and Oh long to lie with two tribal hotties, Maya (June Diane Raphael) and Eema (super-cute Juno Temple). But the girls rebuff them as losers, as does everyone else in their jungle encampment, so they soon set out on their own to discover what lies beyond the mountains encircling their little world.

What they find turns out to be the Land of Biblical Times. Zed and Oh first come upon the squabbling brothers Cain (David Cross) and Abel (Rudd), and after the former cheerily dispatches the latter (and then claims it was an accident), the guys get to meet Cain's sister Lilith (Eden Riegel), who's quite a hottie herself, although, alas, a lesbian. Zed and Oh get sold into slavery and reunite with Maya and Eema, who've suffered a similar fate. A detachment of Roman soldiers rides in on chariots. The boys escape and next come upon Abraham (Hank Azaria), the Old Testament personage, who's about to sacrifice his son Isaac (Christopher Mintz-Plasse). Zed and Oh intervene, and the grateful Isaac volunteers to lead them to another destination, the notorious city of Sodom ("where the sinners are winners," he enthuses). In Sodom they encounter a blubbery high priest (Oliver Platt in lipstick, mascara, and an overabundance of fake chest hair) and discover that a virgin competition is under way for a rain-making sacrifice. There's also an enlightened princess (Olivia Wilde), a palace eunuch (Black's Tenacious D partner Kyle Gass), a gaudy bacchanal (rather mild, actually), a dungeon, a stoning (with two stones), a "Holy of Holies" and much, much more—stuff just keeps piling up.

The movie's basic joke is that most of the characters speak in a wisecracking modern vernacular. If only comedy were so easy. Very occasionally this conceit pays off, as when Azaria's Abraham, a crusader for universal circumcision, insists that "it's gonna be a very sleek look—this is gonna catch on!" More often, though, we get droopy witticisms like, "You know what's the best thing about Sodom? The sodomy." And the picture's desperate, teen-baiting assemblage of fart jokes, dick jokes, poop-nibbling and (a new one, possibly) urine inhalation are a dreary reminder that no matter how far removed the setting's supposed to be, the land of lame Hollywood japery is always near at hand. (June 2009)

The Dukes of Hazzard

Crashing Bumpkins

If you're a devoted fan of the old *Dukes of Hazzard* TV series . . . well, I probably don't know you. But you'll likely want to see this movie just to find out how much of a travesty it might be of your beloved show. I'm not sure how you'd go about travestying a cornpone wheeze like

Dukes, but possibly you'll lament the fact that the late Waylon Jennings isn't around to narrate and sing his *Dukes* theme song, "Good Ol' Boys." (The song does get sung, though, by Waylon's ol' pard', Willie Nelson; that's something, I guess.) And quite possibly you'll resent the fact that the character of Luke Duke is now played by the guy from *Jackass.* I feel for you.

Fans of Jessica Simpson might also be wanting to see how she does in the old Catherine Bach role of sexy Daisy Duke. She does fine, as far as it goes. Admirers should be advised, though, that there's not all that much of her *in* this movie. Oh, her cleavage goes cruising by from time to time, and she does bust out a bikini briefly. But Daisy is really a peripheral character here. Just so you know.

The *Dukes of Hazzard* TV series ran on CBS from 1979 to 1985 and then joined the army of the undead in syndication, where it has lurched about ever since. The movie, like the series, is set in fictitious Hazzard County, Georgia, and celebrates the exploits of two hell-raisin' cousins, Luke and Bo Duke (gamely played by Johnny Knoxville and Seann William Scott), who are "as restless as two cats thrown into a swimmin' hole." Tearing around the county in their 1969 Dodge Charger, known as the General Lee, the boys run moonshine for their Uncle Jesse (Willie Nelson again, here a font of backwoodsy one-liners) and do their best to evade the bumbling county sheriff, Roscoe P. Coltrane (M. C. Gainey). Roscoe is the dim-bulb stooge of corrupt county commissioner Boss Hogg (Burt Reynolds), a man who's said to be "as crooked as a hillbilly's smile." And Hogg sure do hate them Duke boys.

The plot concerns Hogg's scheme to buy up all the land in Hazzard County and sell it to strip-miners. The Dukes aren't about to let this happen. That's the plot. Along the way, we see lots of cars flying through the air (a big deal in the old TV series, apparently, but by this late date *we've seen it,* thank you) and one so-so bar fight. (Which got me wondering: if there are bars in or near Hazzard County where you can get legally snockered, why is there a need for bootleg likker?) We also get to see Bo and Luke impersonate a pair of Japanese engineers, which is about as hilarious as it sounds. And we get to hear one cracker wit ask, in regard to Daisy, "Do you shuck her corn?" Which is right up there with Daisy herself, in a moment of vehicular distress, saying, "I think something bounced up into my undercarriage."

I don't know what fans of the old *Dukes of Hazzard* TV show are going to make of all this; or, heaven knows, fans of Jessica Simpson. Fans of neither might surely wonder what they're doing watching this movie. But then they won't be, will they? (August 2005)

Talladega Nights: The Ballad of Ricky Bobby

Running on Empty

This loud, dumb, funny-impaired comedy has a message for NAS-CAR racing fans, and possibly for Red State residents generally. The message is: you're idiots. This was also the message of *Anchorman: The Legend of Ron Burgundy,* Will Ferrell's last collaboration with his old *Saturday Night Live* associate, writer-turned-director Adam McKay. But in *Anchorman,* the message was directed at a class of people—self-important local-TV personalities—whom we know to actually be idiots. *Talladega Nights* takes aim at something more amorphous, a "redneck" cultural stereotype that feels dated. The film's satirical sights aren't set a whole lot higher than the level of an old *Dukes of Hazzard* episode.

Ferrell is Ricky Bobby, a stock-car star with the IQ of a hubcap, making him just a little bit brighter than his best friend, a brother moron named Cal Naughton Jr. (John C. Reilly). Ricky has grown rich on endorsements (the movie is a fiesta of corporate product placement). He has a hot blond wife (Leslie Bibb) who chews gum at the dinner table, and he's the proud father of two snotty kids, one named Walker, the other (what else?) Texas Ranger.

When a racetrack crackup leaves Ricky unhurt but unhinged (he's convinced that he's on fire and spends many mirthless moments leaping about the field in his Jockey shorts), his career tanks, and he's reduced to delivering pizzas for a living. Meanwhile, Cal takes up with

Ricky's wife and soon marries her. (Their wedding, we're told, featured a Styx cover band and a "nacho fountain.") Worst of all, Ricky's place at the top of the NASCAR heap is taken over by a gay French Formula One racing champion named Jean Girard (Sacha Baron Cohen, channeling the cheek-sucking delivery of Mike Myers's Dr. Evil to modest comical effect).

As was the case with *Anchorman,* this skeletal tale has been infused with dialogue that appears in large part to have been improvised. Improvisation is often thought to be a guarantee of fresh comedy, but obviously this can't always be the case. Here, the worst misfires are, as usual, rounded up into a blooper reel at the end of the movie, with the actors cracking themselves up in time-honored, tedious fashion. But these blown gags don't seem a lot less funny than some of the bits that actually made it into the film. There's a strained barroom squabble about the virtues of pancakes versus crepes, for example, that runs out of comedic steam well before it reaches its mild payoff. And there's a bizarre Reilly monologue about posing for *Playgirl* magazine that emerges out of nowhere. Jean Girard, whose gay-guy attributes reduce the locals to speechless gawking (what a buncha hicks), is pictured at the wheel of his speeding car sipping espresso at one point (he has to pour it over the chin guard of his helmet straight onto his face), and at another point reading a book by Camus. One-liners fizzle left and right. When a character is told, "There's no smoking in here," he replies, "It's okay, I'm a volunteer fireman."

The movie's execution is as crude as its concept. The picture was shot by Oliver Wood, probably best known for his skillful work on *The Bourne Identity* and *The Bourne Supremacy.* But *Talladega Nights* unfolds in a sunny glare, and with its casual staging and awkwardly blocked shots, it might almost be a behind-the-scenes NASCAR documentary. (At the other extreme, some of its indoor scenes seem to be taking place on a dimly lit back porch.)

Will Ferrell is a funny guy—is there anyone who does broad, beady-eyed, lovable-knucklehead comedy better? But he shines brightest in the company of comedic equals like Paul Rudd, Steve Carell, and Seth Rogen, who provided him such solid support in *Anchorman.* As the one true zany in *Talladega Nights,* he's left holding his shtick, and it feels heavy. (August 2006)

Semi-Pro

Benchwarmer

Even if the basketball-related bear-wrestling scene in this new Will Ferrell comedy weren't the only basketball-related bear-wrestling scene in movie history, which it almost certainly is, it would more than likely still be the *dumbest* such basketball-related bear-wrestling scene. That it's not the dumbest scene in the picture may suggest all you need to know about *Semi-Pro.* Not even Ferrell, spinning his comic wheels here, can save this film.

There are two sorts of people who might find the movie to be something more than a waste of overpriced popcorn. One would be basketball nuts. The story is set in Michigan in 1976, the last year of the American Basketball Association, a low-rent league that operated in the shadow of the more prestigious National Basketball Association. Here, the NBA is about to take over the ABA and has decreed that only the four best ABA teams will be kept going; the rest will be disbanded. Jackie Moon (Ferrell), owner and manager of the (fictitious) Flint Tropics, is determined that his team will be among the survivors. To this end, he brings in an NBA castoff named Monix (Woody Harrelson), who proves to be no help at all. Worse yet, Jackie's top player, Clarence (Andre Benjamin, of Outkast), is itching to split for the NBA himself.

Another possible audience for the movie would be people who find anything to do with the 1970s hilarious by definition. For them, chuckles may abound, because the picture is overstuffed with period referents—the usual fat ties, batwing collars, dorky headbands, and powder blue leisurewear. But we've seen all of this before, and we've seen it in a better Will Ferrell movie—the 2004 *Anchorman: The Legend of Ron Burgundy.* However, Ron Burgundy was a comic exaggeration of a recognizable cultural type: a slick, self-satisfied, small-market newscaster. Jackie Moon has no such real-world root—he's just a construct on which to hang gags. And the gags are strained. What reason could there be for making Jackie a failed pop singer (his one hit was a dance inanity called "Love Me Sexy") other than the opportunity it allows the filmmakers to yank a laugh by showing us that he's installed a giant disco ball over the team's home court? And what reason could there be *at all* for having Jackie decide that a clever psych-out against an opposing team would be to have his own players hit the court wearing eye shadow?

The cast is surprisingly game for all of this, especially Jackie Earle Haley, who puts in a few woozy appearances as a brain-fried stoner fan. But the picture's tone is hopelessly muddled. We're apparently meant to be moved by the waning of the ABA—yet another shard of eccentric Americana tinkling off into history. But the halfhearted attempt at pathos sits awkwardly alongside Ferrell's trademark nitwit shtick (there's a puking sequence that goes on about two weeks longer than it should). And as social satire, the picture feels tired. People have been laughing at the 1970s since . . . well, since the 1970s. Comedically speaking, Ferrell has sucked that decade dry. Maybe it's time to move on. I hear the 1990s are still free. (February 2008)

Zack and Miri Make a Porno

Boffo

Zack and Miri Make a Porno, the new Kevin Smith movie, is about a guy and a girl—lifelong friends, now platonic roommates—who are flat broke and swamped with unpaid bills. Although they've never had sex together ("It would be like fucking my brother," says Miri), they decide to make a porn film to get out of debt.

The picture has a knockabout charm, thanks to the actors; but its premise is flawed. Zack and Miri have been spy-cammed walking around in their underwear (and less) by two nosy kids, who post the results on YouTube. Zack decides that a homemade porn film could profitably exploit this sudden Internet stardom. Well, maybe. But since Zack and Miri have to tap out their friends for funds just to shoot the movie, where will they subsequently get the money to produce and promote the necessary DVDs?

Another plot defect is a function of the picture's casting. Since Zack is played by the famously cuddly Seth Rogen, and Miri by the lovable Elizabeth Banks, and since both of their characters complain at length (and of course hypergraphically) about how incredibly horny they are, it's hard to accept that they haven't already given in to the obvious solution—however quasi-incestuous it might seem—and had sex together off-camera before taking the even more daunting step of having it on-camera.

There's a larger problem, too. While Smith's 1994 *Clerks* was a milestone in the sweet-and-salacious comedy genre that's since been polished to blockbuster perfection by Judd Apatow, at this point *Zack and Miri*—which features several actors from Apatow's movies (Rogen and Banks were both in *The 40-Year-Old Virgin*)—seems like an attempted Apatow picture that doesn't quite make the grade. The movie does have some funny, very Smithian moments. But his generally crotch-centric humor, without the wild situations and verbal pizzazz of the Apatow films, seems like little more than a string of "dirty" jokes—which in turn seems a little dated.

Still, Rogen and Banks have an easy chemistry, and their big on-camera sex scene (which is nongraphic) has a sweet romantic warmth. They also get strong support from Craig Robinson (the club doorman in Apatow's *Knocked Up*) as a friend who has shelled out to become a "producer" of the film and who deludedly anticipates a cash avalanche. ("I'm gonna be *Oprah*-rich!") Smith's longtime foil Jason Mewes is on hand as a studly recruit, and so are two actual porn stars—the long-retired Traci Lords, as Bubbles, the continuity girl (who shows no skin); and the still-active and winningly perky Katie Morgan (who shows lots, including a pair of hugely fake breasts). There's also a surprise appearance by two well-known actors playing a gay couple at a high school reunion, and they're so unexpected, and so into their roles, that they walk away with the scene.

But apart from a freewheeling interlude in which Zack and his friends lounge around trying to think up a good, punny title for their porno (*Edward Penis Hands? Lawrence of the Labia?*), the jokes with which the picture is crammed are too predictably crass and dudish, and after a while they drag the movie down. Can Smith ever outgrow this sort of rote, depleted raunch? Or is he on his way to becoming a punch line himself? (October 2008)

Cop Out

Misfire

The bad news about *Cop Out,* some will probably think, is that Kevin Smith didn't write it. He did direct it, but that's part of the bad news, too. The good news? There is no good news.

The movie is an uncalled-for attempt to resurrect the buddy-cop film genre of the 1980s. As you'll recall, those action comedies mined their laughs from the antics of a pair of ill-matched crime fighters, one of them a somewhat straight arrow (Danny Glover, say, or Nick Nolte), the other a complete loon (Mel Gibson, for example, or Eddie Murphy). *Cop Out* botches this concept. Its two detectives, Jimmy Monroe (Bruce Willis) and Paul Hodges (Tracy Morgan), are starved of the spicy banter these films require by the limp script, which was concocted before Smith was hired on by TV guys Robb and Mark Cullen. And since Willis is so oddly inscrutable here—he has the animated presence of a man waiting for a traffic light to change—the picture must rely for its yocks on Morgan, the sort of noisy comic who's in your face and over the top and then down behind your back yanking at your pants. In a desperate mood, the filmmakers might try to sell this movie as satire. But satire is supposed to be smart. *Cop Out,* among other things, offers us the sight of a detective on a stakeout disguised as a giant cell phone.

Because of their predictably unorthodox methods, Monroe and Hodges are little loved by their superiors. In fact, they've both just been suspended, without pay. This is especially bad news for Monroe, who needs to come up with $48,000 to pay for his daughter's wedding, which will otherwise be gloatingly funded by her snotty stepfather (Jason Lee). Monroe's only salable asset is a rare baseball card, a treasured boyhood gift from his father. But just as he's about to make a big-bucks deal for it at a memorabilia shop, two robbers burst in and loudly Taser Monroe, loudly rip off his card, and loudly make their getaway. Hodges is standing right outside the shop window, but he doesn't notice any of this because . . . he's making a phone call.

The boys soon find themselves in league with Seann William Scott, giving the movie's only live-wire performance as a burglar whose professional calling card is taking a dump in the houses he loots. (This is not a movie that shies away from poop humor.) There's also a showdown with a Mexican drug-gang boss (Guillermo Diaz), a trash-talking eleven-year-old, a by-the-book car chase (action isn't the director's natural métier), and some labored hottie interaction (with Ana de la Reguera, far too classy for these proceedings).

There are lots of old-movie references, as you'd expect, and even a couple of knock-knock jokes, which you probably wouldn't. The picture has no comic rhythm and no action style. It sits on the screen imploring you to take an interest, when your interest lies elsewhere—back by the exit. (February 2010)

Drillbit Taylor

Mild Thing

Contrary to what you might expect, given the participation of such grossmeisters as producer Judd Apatow and writers Seth Rogen and Kristofor Brown (a *Beavis and Butt-head* veteran), the new Owen Wilson movie *Drillbit Taylor* is as sweet and smooth as a bowl of pudding. That it's not a lot more memorable than that isn't something one wants to grouse about in these foul times, but your reviewer is compelled to be candid.

The picture is pleasantly formulaic; you can sit back and watch its unsurprising plot unfold with only an occasional impulse to check your watch. The story's vintage familiarity may have something to do with its origin in a twenty-year-old unproduced film treatment by 1980s teen-flick king John Hughes. Three high school freshmen, tormented by a pair of troglodyte bullies, advertise on the Internet for a bodyguard to be their proxy butt-kicker. Lovable Owen Wilson is the guy they unwisely end up hiring. That's basically it. The kids bear more than a passing resemblance to the teen trio in that earlier Apatow-Rogen production, *Superbad*: one's a gangly geek (Nate Hartley), one's an over-weight wiseacre (Troy Gentile), and the third is a militant dweeb (David Dorfman). What's missing this time around is the mow-'em-down raunch of that previous movie. (*Superbad* was rated R; this one's PG-13.) There are a few pro forma pubic amusements, things like that, but they're undistressingly mild and entirely familiar.

In Hughes's original story, apparently, the bodyguard the kids hired was a battle-hardened mercenary—an actual butt-kicker. Rogen and Brown have tweaked this character into a nonviolent army deserter whose butt-kicking bona fides are nonexistent. It's a custom-fit role for Wilson, whose stoned charm and soulful glow are never less than likable. (And he does get off a few good lines. Deflecting praise for an unexpected heroic act, he says, "It's like when a mother lifts an automobile off her child.") But Wilson's comic amiability is most effective in a context of seething loutishness (as was provided by Vince Vaughn in *Wedding Crashers,* for instance). Here there's nothing swinish for him to counterbalance; he's beset on all sides by niceness.

Plausibility is an optional ingredient in this sort of movie; the writers here have not opted for it, and director Steven Brill (*Without a Paddle*) is content to play it their way. So we're asked to buy the proposition that the homeless Drillbit (the name's a very small joke I'll not spoil) soaps up in the nude every morning at an unenclosed public shower on a sunny L.A. beach. We're also invited to accept the over-the-top behavior of the two bullies (played by Josh Peck and the alarmingly maniacal Alex Frost), whose vile depredations—which involve automotive attacks, vicious beatings, and even some business with a samurai sword—surely wouldn't go unbusted in or around a school as upscale as the one depicted here. Then there's Drillbit's attempt to protect his teen employers by infiltrating the school as a substitute teacher, an uninspired plot contrivance—as is the flimsy romantic subplot involving Drillbit and a love-starved English teacher, played by Leslie Mann.

Drillbit Taylor doesn't necessarily suggest that the avant vulgarity in which Apatow and Rogen have so successfully specialized in the past is played out. For one thing, a picture merely produced by Apatow, like *The TV Set* or *Kicking & Screaming,* is a different thing from a picture he has also directed, like *Knocked Up* or *The 40-Year-Old Virgin.* But *Drillbit* does demonstrate one thing: when the appeal of a comic style depends crucially on a conflation of the sweet and the scabrous, sanitizing it in order to reach the lucrative PG-13 audience is a self-crippling move. This movie's upcoming lukewarm box-office performance should be a caution. Three words, in other words: the Farrelly brothers. (March 2008)

I Now Pronounce You Chuck & Larry

Dire Straights

This tolerance lecture trying to pass as a funny movie brings us the news that—brace yourself—gay men are *actually okay*. In fact, they're just like other people. Except for the gay thing. Which normal guys—uh, make that *other* guys—can easily get past if they'll just grow some sensitivity. And there's a bonus, other guys: playing gay can get you a ringside seat as Jessica Biel strips down to her underwear. Who knew?

The movie is annoying on several levels, and it's a shock to learn that Alexander Payne and Jim Taylor, who've scripted such wonderful pictures as *Sideways* and *Election,* had a hand (along with many others, over many years) in writing this one. It might've been cooked up at a comedy keg party.

Chuck (Adam Sandler) and Larry (Kevin James) are Brooklyn firefighters and best friends. Larry is a widower with two young kids. When he tries to make them the beneficiaries of his life insurance policy, he's told it can't be done unless he remarries. With no female prospects immediately at hand, Larry decides to apply for one of those "domestic partner" deals that are only available to gay people. And who better to ask to pose as his partner than Chuck?

Chuck is of course the unlikeliest possible candidate for this role. He's not just straight; he's ragingly heterosexual. He orders porn and condoms by the case and can't really tamp his erotic fires unless he beds several women at once. (Preferably women in tiny little shrink-wrap outfits that invite the camera to zoom in on their nether assets when Chuck orders them to bend down real low.)

Nevertheless, after some perfunctory reluctance, Chuck agrees to help Larry out by becoming his "gay" partner. They consult a civil rights lawyer named Alex (Biel), who tells them the most convincing way to pull off this charade would be to actually get married. So they drive up to Canada, that beacon of enlightenment in these matters, and seek out a wedding chapel. Here we are confronted with one of the most deplorable performances in recent memory. The chapel owner who'll be tying Chuck and Larry's knot is a caricature of a Japanese man straight out of burlesque—bowl haircut, slightly bucked teeth, epicanthic eye folds that appear to be attached with library paste—and he's played by *Rob Schneider.* ("Do you have the ling?" he asks Chuck.) This appalling impersonation is one step away from black-face minstrelsy, and it's mystifying how a major studio (that would be Universal Pictures) found it to be just fine.

The story stumbles along boobishly, and as Chuck struggles to control his titanic libido in the presence of Alex, who's adopted him as a girl-talk confidante, a number of gay characters naturally crop up. But in order to differentiate them from the straight characters, they're all depicted as prancing queens—among them a gay shop clerk portrayed by Dave Matthews (!) with a smoldering sissy pout and madly rolling eyes. Even the one he-man closet case in the film (Ving Rhames) goes all limp-of-wrist the moment he comes out. It's the kind of movie in which, when a firehouse shower-room scene comes up, you just know somebody's going to drop the soap.

Director Dennis Dugan (*The Benchwarmers*) keeps this wretched exercise moving along, for what that's worth; and because the picture was shot by Dean Semler (*Apocalypto*), it looks better than it has any right to. Sandler and James put a lot of energy into their performances, but to little effect. The movie is impossibly conflicted: the guy-centric wisecrackery by which it seeks to convey its alleged message is part of the problem it pretends to address. While inviting us to laugh at fat people and unattractive older women along the way, the movie purports to chronicle the indignities to which gay people are subjected. Naturally, the usual suspects—Boy Scout leaders, Little League baseball groups, homophobic evangelicals—come in for ritual head slaps. But at a key moment toward the end, when a chaste kiss between Chuck and Larry would seem to be required, the picture cravenly chickens out—none of that stuff here, thank you. (It's as if Sacha Baron Cohen had never bestrode the box office.) The movie is a numbskull insult to gay people. Just on the basis of the mirthless trailer, however, they'll probably ignore it. One doubts they'll be alone. (May 2008)

OTHER WORLDS

f we date it from Georges Méliès's 1902 A Trip to the Moon, *the science-fiction genre is nearly as old as the movies themselves. Over the course of its many decades it has produced some of the medium's most indelible imagery, from the false Maria of Fritz Lang's* Metropolis *and the resplendent Deco futurism of William Cameron Menzies's* Things to Come *to the strange new worlds and wonders of Alien, Dune, and* The Matrix. *Even the most impoverished schlock of the 1950s is now remembered with indulgent fondness, extending the commercial life of pictures with guys in cheap gorilla suits trying to pass as aliens into the age of home video. Does any other genre offer such boundless opportunities for speculative flight? Sci-fi continues to provide some of our most thrillingly imaginative movies. And, of course, some of the most soulless junk as well.*

Moon

The Dark Side

Making a sci-fi outer-space movie for $5 million has to be like trying to build a palace on pocket change. English director Duncan Jones has managed it, though. *Moon,* his first feature, a blend of miniature models, deftly applied CGI, meticulous production design and a singular performance by Sam Rockwell, takes—or returns—cinematic science fiction to some interesting places.

Rockwell plays Sam Bell, an employee of Lunar Industries, a company engaged in mining helium-3 on the far side of the moon for use in energy production back on Earth. After three years of isolation at the moon base, monitoring the Lunar machinery, Sam will soon be rotating back home, where his wife and daughter are waiting for him. It's been lonely duty: The live-communication satellite intended to serve the base has been broken forever, and so his only contact with his family has been via videotaped messages. He does have company of a sort: a soft-spoken, boxlike robot called Gerty—a tangible manifestation of the base computer system. Gerty appears to mean well (whatever that might mean), but he—it—is still a machine (with the voice of Kevin Spacey).

As his time winds down, Sam feels his health starting to falter; in fact, he feels like he's falling apart. While driving out on the desolate lunar surface to investigate an odd occurrence, he steers his rover into a gully and . . . well, he must have passed out. But when he wakes up, he's back inside the base—convalescing, according to Gerty. How did he get here? And who's the new guy he sees walking around? He looks like Sam himself. In fact, as it turns out, he *is*. A support team in a company ship is on its way to take Sam (or Sam 1, as we can call him) back to Earth, and now, more than ever, he feels it can't get here soon enough.

The look of the movie inevitably echoes earlier landmarks of the deep-space genre. The scenes set in the placid interior of the moon base, where Sam has little to do besides work out on a running machine, recall the bland crew areas of the interstellar ship in *2001: A Space Odyssey;* but the exterior sequences, with Sam's grubby rover bumping along over the vast lunar plain of dust and rock, echo the grittier world of *Alien.*

As impressive as the film's design is, it's the picture's emotional core that lends it a resonance that's been uncommon in this sort of film for many years. What is the toll taken by total isolation from the rest of humankind? Who are we—and what is our value—if we're also someone else? Will Sam ever make it home, and if he does, what will home now be like? Rockwell, often acting opposite himself (and occasionally a lookalike, Robin Chalk), is impressively resourceful in capturing his character's physical and spiritual disintegration—and his mounting desperation as the Lunar Industries retirement plan slowly becomes clear.

Jones, who devised the story (which was turned into a script by first-time screenwriter Nathan Parker), came up through TV commercials and video games; but the movie has none of the rote clamor that such a background might seem to threaten. (In this way it's reminiscent of *The Man Who Fell to Earth,* a similarly temperate fantasy in which Jones's father, David Bowie, starred more than thirty years ago.) By focusing on the human element throughout the film, and launching the story into a new dimension at the end, the director has avoided that most common of extraterrestrial traps: getting lost in space. (June 2009)

The Invasion

Bomb Away

The most interesting thing about *The Invasion* is its backstory. The German director Oliver Hirschbiegel, best known here for his grim, Oscar-nominated Hitler movie, *Downfall,* seemed an odd choice to helm a remake of a sci-fi story that had already been done to a turn in at least two of three previous films (including, of course, Don Siegel's 1956 original). Hirschbiegel's version, shot in 2005, was found wanting by producer Joel Silver, who called in his friends the Wachowski brothers to do some uncredited rewriting and summoned their directorial protégé James McTeigue (*V for Vendetta*) to do extensive reshooting, including a ludicrously ill-considered new ending.

The picture *is* creepy, effectively distilling the paranoia engendered by an invisible alien invasion that's turning the populace into dead-eyed pod people (although the actual pods of Siegel's film, which spawned that term, have been discarded here). There are some disturbing new details, too: when the extraterrestrial spores start spreading from the debris of a space shuttle crash, for instance, the government is suspiciously prompt in producing a vaccine with which to begin compulsory inoculations of every citizen.

Mainly, though, *The Invasion* is a humdrum squandering of its two stars, Nicole Kidman and Daniel Craig, who in any event have no chemistry. (Not that they need any: early on, Kidman's character, a psychiatrist named Carol Bennell, announces that a romantic relationship with Craig's Dr. Ben Driscoll isn't in the cards, and that's that.) The movie has been assembled with daffy abandon (it *opens* with a flashforward); and some scenes, not surprisingly, seem ill-matched to the rest of the picture. After a bit of dutiful exposition in the beginning, the film devolves into a chase flick, with Carol and her little boy (Jackson

Bond) in endless flight from neo-pod pursuers, led by her newly weird ex-husband (Jeremy Northam). There's also quite a bit more car crashing than one might normally wish to endure in this sort of picture.

Apart from a few effective jolts (like Carol's ominous encounter with a late-night census taker), the movie is flat and uninvolving. Veronica Cartwright, who appeared in Philip Kaufman's 1978 *Body Snatchers* remake, turns up here to deliver a meandering plaint about her newly sinister husband, and to re-create Kevin McCarthy's frantic alarm-sounding scene from the Siegel movie (which McCarthy himself reprised in the Kaufman film). And Jeffrey Wright, another worthy actor wasted, is on hand solely to explain everything to us (the nature of the alien spores, the search for an antidote, and so on).

Kidman has rarely given such a shuttered performance—she actually seems to be ticked off about being involved in this listless debacle (the reshoots must have been a pain). And Craig, who's not around that much, always seems to be on his way somewhere else—a better movie, perhaps. Oh, Lord, we think, in mounting exasperation—if only we could go with him. (August 2007)

Cloverfield

Trampled Underfoot

*C*loverfield is a nifty update of the 1950s schlock monster movie, and it's mercifully unadulterated by delusions of contemporary relevance or nitwit nudge-wink irony. The picture is what it is: a group of people whose chances of survival wouldn't appear to be much of a betting matter encounter a rampaging behemoth from who knows where and spend the rest of the film trying not to attract its sustained interest. It's a movie that aspires only to be scary, and it largely succeeds.

That it's also more subversive than such primordial schlock-fi predecessors as *Them!* and *It Came from Beneath the Sea* and especially the 1956 *Godzilla, King of the Monsters!* is a credit to the pulp expertise of the filmmakers. Director Matt Reeves, writer Drew Goddard, and cinematographer Michael Bonvillain—all veterans of one or another of producer J. J. Abrams's popular TV series *Lost, Alias,* and *Felicity*— have brought a fresh modern spirit to the project. The movie appears to have been shot entirely by handheld, consumer-grade video camcorders. (A certain amount of illusion is involved here, though: the scenes are skillfully lit, and there was, after all, a cinematographer in residence.) The roiling instability of the images creates a sense of chaos that's realistically unsettling. Something awful is clearly going on—we can hear the screams and the explosions (the soundtrack is earthquake-loud)—but because the camera work is so chaotic, we can never quite see what it is. Until, as they say, it's too late.

The story is simple, as it should be. The picture opens at a loft party in the New York yuppie precinct of TriBeCa, where everybody is young and hot and sloshed. It's a going-away bash for Rob Hawkins (Michael Stahl-David), who's making a career move to Tokyo, and it's being documented by his buffoonish buddy, Hud (T. J. Miller), through whose shaky-cam lens we meet the rest of the cast: Rob's brother Jason (Mike Vogel); the beautiful Beth (Odette Yustman), with whom Rob recently had a one-night stand; and a pair of ancillary babes played by the gorgeous Jessica Lucas and the droll, dark-eyed Lizzie Caplan.

It's unfortunate that this opening sequence goes on for twenty minutes (nearly a quarter of the film's runtime). It's too long, and it gives us too much time to become annoyed by the partygoers' abrasive bonhomie, and to wish that a colossal prehistoric lizard of some sort would stomp onto the scene and squash most of them like sand fleas. Fortunately, our patience will soon be rewarded.

When all hell suddenly breaks loose in the streets outside, Rob and his friends race up to the roof to see what's happening. Here we encounter the movie's most audacious visual strategy. Amid the seismic tremors, thunderous explosions and strange, terrible howling, we see collapsing buildings crowned with flames and, before long, standing walls of dust and debris billowing through the narrow streets. It's the familiar, horrific imagery of 9/11, and it might have been a dreadful miscalculation. But the buildings don't specifically suggest the long-gone Twin Towers, and the raging pandemonium on view can be plausibly read as the work of . . . whatever that bellowing, skyscraper-size thing is that—thanks to the incompetent amateur cameraman—we see only distantly.

A monster is a monster, pretty much (unless you're working with a *Lord of the Rings*-level effects budget—*Cloverfield* reportedly cost a modest $30 million to make). The monster here is entirely adequate; but the real terror is provided by the scrabbling creatures it rains down on the city—hideous, dog-size, flesh-rending crabosaurs capable of scuttling across ceilings and battering down doors. Because of their ground-level menace, these are more intimate horrors, and their fierce assaults are electrifying. Monster Number One may get the big set-piece scenes—splintering the Brooklyn Bridge with the slam of a single humongous tentacle, for instance—but these ferocious little brutes are even more appalling.

Is it believable that Rob, after getting a cell phone call from Beth, who's trapped uptown and grievously wounded, would set off into the tumult with his pals to rescue her? Of course it is. How else would we see this earnest little band get whittled down, one doomed member at a time? Or discover that the army has arrived in force with an ominous last-ditch plan called Hammer Down, in case things get really out of hand in Manhattan? This is the stuff we want from a cheap monster movie—it may be the only stuff we want from one, really—and as always, we'll go along with just about any pretext to get it.

Naturally, we wonder about the monster—why is he so peeved? Nuclear testing? Environmental despoliation? In the movies of the 1950s, these things would have been explained at narcotizing length. Here, nothing is explained. The creature is wreaking havoc, take it or leave it. And when the artfully devised ending arrives, we can admire the plot preparation that has gone into it. It may not be a conclusion that would have played in the old days—in fact, back then it would surely have been papered over with cheerier prospects. Today, though, when even more gruesome real-life frights are only a click away on the Internet, this dismal denouement seems just about right. (January 2008)

Terminator Salvation

Metalheads

A lot of hard work has gone into *Terminator Salvation,* the fourth installment of the time-shuffling robot-war series and the first since the 2003 *Terminator 3: Rise of the Machines* detoured the franchise into the realm of unintentional hilarity. Unlike the past films, this new one is set in the future—the one from which android assassin Arnold Schwarzenegger was dispatched a quarter-century ago to travel back to 1984 and terminate Sarah Connor, the soon-to-be mother of John Connor, who, in the future from which Arnold was dispatched, had grown up to be the leader of the human resistance forces battling the metallic minions of Skynet, the sentient computer entity that had taken over the world. Oh, and also to put a stop to Kyle Reese, who had likewise beamed in from the future for the purpose of becoming John Connor's father. Is your head starting to hurt again?

Joseph McGinty Nichol, the director who boldly continues to call himself "McG" (a childhood nickname, he says), has staged a few memorable scenes here. There's a gigantic Skynet aircraft swooping down on a bridge filled with fleeing humans; and a leap from a helicopter into a storm-tossed ocean far below to rendezvous with a rebel submarine; and—in the movie's most alarming image—a disembodied Terminator spinal column thrashing around on a lab gurney while its human captors struggle to hold it down.

But *Salvation* is crippled by tired-franchise syndrome. There's not one character in it as memorable as that original Arnoldian Terminator, or the shape-shifting T-1000 model that brought new menace to the 1991 *Terminator 2: Judgment Day.* Instead, what we have here is just a whole bunch of beady-red-eyed Terminators—although some of them are the size of small buildings (or, dare I say, Transformers), and at least one, if I'm not mistaken, is accessorized with a dashing ban-dana wrapped around its metal brow. The Terminators battle the hu-man rebels—nominally commanded by General Ashdown (sci-fi vet Michael Ironside), who directs his forces from the safety of that sub-marine, but effectively led, out in the Terminator wastelands, by the courageous John Connor (Christian Bale).

It's odd that Bale, a good actor, is so uncharismatic here—especially in comparison to a new character named Marcus, who's played by the effortlessly charismatic Sam Worthington. (Worthington was appar-ently recommended to McG by James Cameron, director of the first two *Terminator* films, who had cast the Australian actor as the lead in his long-brewing 3-D epic, *Avatar.*) Also notable is the talented Anton Yelchin as Kyle Reese. And Moon Bloodgood brings some emotional dimension to the role of Blair Williams, the movie's requisite butt-kick girl. The rest of the cast is a blur, though. Helena Bonham Carter, in weird-lady mode, has some brief moments as a bald Skynet doctor (she's afflicted with cancer). Bryce Dallas Howard barely registers as Connor's pregnant wife, Kate. And it's hard to work out what the wonderful Jane Alexander is doing in this picture. (Playing the leader of a combat-shy anti-Terminator faction—but really, why?)

Given its setting, in the middle of a worldwide robot conflagration, the movie also suffers from inevitable longueurs, which can best be sum-marized as: bang-bang-bang; pow, pow; fireball, fireball; ka-boom! The color is usually leached down to the dismal blues and grays familiar from other sci-fi hellholes, some of which—especially the *Mad Max* films and, again, *Transformers*—are clear influences. The picture lacks con-ceptual flair—we really have seen most of this stuff before—and you kind of wish the producers would acknowledge the futility of their un-dertaking and put this tired series back in its box for good. (Especially now that the far superior Fox TV series, *Terminator: The Sarah Connor Chronicles*, has—coincidentally?—just been canceled.) No such luck, though: *Terminator 5* is already in the pipeline. Do you feel an even big-ger headache coming on? (May 2009)

The Adjustment Bureau

Off with His Hat

Does the fate of the world hang on the chance meeting in a men's room of an aspiring politician and a saucy ballerina? Yes. Well, maybe. Anyway, it does in *The Adjustment Bureau*. The movie is based on what I'd say was a hurried reading of an old Philip K. Dick short story called *Adjustment Team*. Dick's story featured a talking dog. Watching the movie, I missed that dog. He could've been fun. But this is a film in which fun is not overabundant.

Fortunately, it does have Matt Damon, keen and likable as always, and Emily Blunt, to whom sauciness is second nature. They go well together; they have chemistry. He's David Norris. He was running for the New York State Senate before an embarrassing incident from his college days surfaced (dredged up by the damn *New York Post*, naturally) and scuttled his campaign. She's Elise Sellas, modern-dance star on the rise, and just moments after meeting in that men's room (please don't ask), she and David are wrapped in a full-face embrace. Then she has to run off. Can David find her again?

It's going to be difficult. David is being shadowed by a quartet of slick-looking guys in gray hats, gray suits, gray ties, gray overcoats—wherever it is they're from, gray is clearly the new black. Their job, for reasons mysterious at first, is to keep David and Elise apart. They're pretty good at it, but not infallible. David keeps giving them the slip and getting back together with Elise. When David goes to work one day, he finds everybody in his corporate offices frozen in midmotion and the hat guys going over them in a garage-mechanic kind of way. They're doing a "recalibration," it seems. "We are the people who make sure things happen according to plan," says one of them, a fellow named Richardson (John

Slattery, of *Mad Men*). "You've just seen behind the curtain you're not even supposed to know exists."

The plan to which Richardson alludes—or the Plan, actually—is the work of an unseen eminence called the Chairman. In olden Hollywood days, this would have been code for God and the hat guys would have been angels. God being a nonstarter in movie land at the moment, however, this person is just the Chairman, looking down on Manhattan from his own corporate headquarters in another part of town. And the hat guys aren't angels. Or probably not. Take it or leave it. (Right-wing cultural-conspiracy enthusiasts will note with dismay that David is, for no relevant reason, a solar-energy proponent, and they'll no doubt have a good grumble at the cameo appearances put in here by people like James Carville, Wolf Blitzer, Jon Stewart, and even one actual deity, New York's mayor, Michael Bloomberg.)

David has a covert ally on the hat team, it turns out—a man with the very earthbound name of Harry Mitchell (Anthony Mackie). Harry lets David in on several hat secrets, among them the locations of magical doors that serve as shortcuts for him and his colleagues to make their way around the city. (Open one door and you're in Yankee Stadium. Open another and you're on Ellis Island. I didn't notice a door into Per Se, with dinner and drinks comped, but it's something they might look into.)

Before long, the David-and-Elise situation starts getting out of hand—there's just no keeping these two apart. So the hat men have to call in an enforcer, a gent named Thompson. Thompson is cold, haughty, and sonorous—which is to say, he's played by Terence Stamp. He lets David in on another secret, one concerning David's future, which is all mapped out. All he has to do is never see Elise again. This is a tough call. Will David tell Thompson to stuff it? Will he opt instead for true love? Let's move along.

The trailer for *The Adjustment Bureau* makes the movie seem like a gripping sci-fi thriller. If only. What we have here basically is the old story about free will versus predestination—not a brain-twister of the first freshness. Writer-director George Nolfi might have been better advised to embrace the sci-fi side of the tale and to whip up some much-needed cheap thrills. As it is, the picture has no tension because the hat squad has no real menace. Its only ability is to prevent Matt Damon from attaining vast political power. In some quarters, that might be looked upon as a good thing. (March 2011)

District 9

The Uninvited

District 9 seems an oddly misguided sci-fi movie. Where are the Hasbro toy tie-ins? The skeletons of ancient TV series? There's not even a comic-book connection. What is wrong with this picture?

Actually, the movie is based on . . . what's the term? Ah, yes: an original idea. It's a good one, too. The film does have aliens, but they're not the traditional galactic marauders. These unexceptional extraterrestrials were just cruising along over South Africa some twenty-odd years ago when their huge spaceship suddenly conked out in the sky above Johannesburg, where it's still parked. The humans below managed to ferry the passengers down—more than a million of them—but then were stuck with the problem of what to do with these unwanted interlopers. Assimilation was out of the question—the creatures resembled big weird crustaceans with a snoutful of wriggling worms, and their native tongue sounded like a flock of ducks being eaten alive. They did have some interesting technology—especially in the weapons department—but it was biomechanical and could only be operated by beings with alien DNA. Bummer.

The locals loathed these outlanders instantly—they were ugly, disgusting, definitively alien. And so ever since, the uninvited guests—reviled as "prawns"—have been confined in a trash-pit shantytown called District 9, where they live in abject squalor, foraging among the garbage heaps for sustenance (they favor cat food, raw meat, and rubber) and dreaming of someday, somehow, returning home. As the story begins, the government, bowing to public demand, has enlisted the operatives of a sinister munitions outfit called Multi-National United (MNU) to begin rounding up the District 9 populace for relocation to a faraway concentration camp, festooned with welcoming wreaths of barbed wire, where they'll no longer fan the resentment of the master species.

The movie obviously stirs thoughts of the old South African apartheid system (as well as American racial segregation and the Nazi genocide), but it's not an alien-rights lecture—there's no noble message being pounded home. *District 9* is an action movie with a full payload of bullets, blood, and much that's more wonderfully worse. The director, Neill Blomkamp, has a striking sci-fi vision. A South African now residing in Vancouver, Blomkamp became such a hot commodity directing music videos and TV commercials that he came to the attention of Peter Jackson, the noted New Zealand Ring-lord. Jackson recruited Blomkamp to direct a movie based on the Halo video games. When that project fell through, he took an interest in a six-minute short Blomkamp had made called *Alive in Jo'burg* and suggested that they (and Blomkamp's writing partner, Terri Tatchell) beef it up into a feature film. The result is *District 9*.

Blomkamp has given the picture a distinctive look. The aliens—worked up by Jackson's Weta Digital workshop, the Tiffany's of high-end fantasy fabrication—aren't deployed as expensive showpiece creations, to be paraded through for our techno-delectation. They're seamlessly embedded in the movie's scruffy visual texture—an urgent whirl of zoom and blur and general handheld instability. The movie was shot without a script (there was only a storyline; the dialogue was improvised), and it looks less like a standard sci-fi feature than it does a low-budget documentary about an impossible subject.

The picture also gets an infusion of antsy energy from its lead performance by Sharlto Copley, who plays Wikus Van De Merwe, the bumbling government functionary who's been put in charge of the alien relocation program. Copley, a South African writer and producer, isn't an actor (or wasn't—he is now). But he's just right, in an odd way, as a dim-bulb bureaucrat caught up in a . . . let's say a transformative experience. In rousting aliens out of their miserable shacks, Wikus comes across a canister of nasty-looking black gunk which, klutz that he is, he inadvertently gets on his face. As the hideous effect of this contamination becomes visible (it's really icky), he finds himself on the run from brutal MNU operatives and a vicious Nigerian gang boss and falling in league with an alien called (in a resonant slave-name touch) Christopher Johnson (Jason Cope). Christopher says he can heal Wikus, but he needs the black gunk—which also has a secret alien use. Unfortunately, the stuff has been removed to a creepy lab at MNU headquarters—a place where unspeakable experiments are conducted. When Wikus and Christopher finally arrive there, things get wild, and a lot gooier.

The movie's own DNA is an amalgam of many earlier films, among them *Independence Day*, *E.T.* (Christopher has an ugly-cute little CGI kid) and the 1955 Hammer classic, *The Creeping Unknown*. But Blomkamp has a gift for raw action, and like Jackson himself, back in his *Meet the Feebles* days, he's happy to home in on the most gruesome imagery. Can Wikus be saved? In the normal run of sci-fi movies, the answer would be preordained. Here, though, it's . . . well, worth seeing for yourself. (August 2009)

Sky Captain and the World of Tomorrow

Neverland

Sky Captain and the World of Tomorrow is an impressive technical achievement, a movie in which everything except the actors has been created on computers: digital "sets," digital "locations." It's a misty vision of a future that never happened, and strictly on an eyeball level, it's entrancing. Therein, unfortunately, lies a problem, although not a crippling one.

The story, set in 1939, is mixmaster pulp. It opens with a spectacular, snow-lashed overhead shot of a gargantuan dirigible—the *Hindenburg III*—tying up at the top of New York's Empire State Building. (Something similar was apparently attempted around that time, unsuccessfully, on two separate occasions.) Down on the ground, we learn that some of the world's great scientists are inexplicably disappearing, and that Polly Perkins (Gwyneth Paltrow), a plucky reporter for the *New York Chronicle*, is on the case. She meets at Radio City Music Hall one night with Dr. Walter Jennings (Trevor Baxter), a famous and now-frightened scientist who's convinced he'll be the next to go. Jennings tells Polly he was once a member of a secret scientific unit outside of Berlin, where he did "terrible things." Now, Jennings says, "He's coming for me—Totenkopf."

While we're taking this in, a fleet of giant flying robots comes crashing down out of the sky and crunching through the city streets on metal feet the size of Greyhound buses. We see a cop on a pay phone calling for reinforcements. We see retro-impressionistic radio waves beaming out from a control tower. Then we see leather-jacketed Jude Law responding to this signal from the cockpit of his high-flying fighter plane. "This is Sky Captain," he says. "I'm on my way!"

The daredevil Sky Captain's real name is Joe Sullivan, and he and Polly have a history. Three years before, in the war-torn Chinese city of Nanjing, they'd been an item. But then, in a snit of some sort, she sabotaged his plane, which resulted in his being held captive for six months in a "Manchurian slave camp." Polly did this, we later learn, because she thought Joe was cheating on her—which, it turns out, he was, with Naval Air Captain Francesca "Franky" Cook (Angelina Jolie), the beautiful, one-eyed commander of an all-female amphibious fighter squadron.

Anyway, the attack of the robots appears to be going on worldwide. While Joe executes some wild, robot-dodging swoops through the canyons of Manhattan, his sidekick and gadget master, Dex Dearborn (Giovanni Ribisi), is back at their home base on a remote tropical island, testing a new ray gun and contemplating his moments-ago discovery that the robots appear to be controlled by a strange, low-frequency radio signal. Hmm.

Things get complicated pretty quickly—too quickly, in fact, to keep precise track of in one viewing. Dr. Jennings reappears to give Polly a pair of critically important metal cylinders, but dies before he can tell her what they're for. There's an assault by a swarm of giant mechanical birds, and also by a herd of tentacle-armed combat robots controlled from afar by a mysterious, black-hooded Asian woman—a deadly ninja in the employ of the evil and even more mysterious Dr. Totenkopf. The robot signals are discovered to be emanating from "Shambala"—the legendary Shangri-la—so Joe and Polly set off in his plane for Nepal. At one point, running out of fuel, Joe has to radio his old inamorata, Franky, who guides them to safety on a mobile landing strip that's perched—gorgeously—high up in the clouds. (Looking like a Third Reich S & M pinup in her tight gray uniform, peaked officer's cap, and snug black eye patch, Franky runs her lone orb over Polly and says, "Nice to meet the competition.")

Dr. Totenkopf is of course a madman who wants to destroy the world. The how and why of his plan to do so, however, are interesting—this is a cleverly plotted tale. In fact, *Sky Captain* would seem to have everything anyone could ask of a period action-adventure romance. It's certainly a triumph for first-time writer-director Kerry Conran, a film-school-trained computer-animation specialist who spent six years working on the movie. (He started out with a reportedly dazzling six-minute version that he'd created entirely on his home computer.) Jude Law and Gwyneth Paltrow contribute muted star power, and it's fun to count the references to old comics and movie serials and great 1930s sci-fi and fantasy films like *Things to Come* and *Lost Horizon*, not to mention echoes of the Indiana Jones pictures. (When Polly says, "You know what a careful girl I am," you can't help but recall Indy himself uttering virtually the same words as he suited up for his own Himalayan adventure in *Raiders of the Lost Ark*.)

As I say, it's a movie that pretty much has it all. And yet its sweep and spirit are undermined in a way that's familiar from other, much more expensive CGI extravaganzas. The very thing that makes the picture so arresting—the sumptuous artistry of its digital images—tends to muffle your wonderment. When Indiana Jones and the nightclub singer Willie Scott went hurtling out a window in the opening of *Temple of Doom*, then plummeted through a succession of rain-soaked awnings to land in a car down below, you goggled in amazement at that great stunt: How on earth did they do it? When the huge dirigible ties up at the top of the Empire State Building in the beginning of *Sky Captain*, that's pretty amazing, too, but in a different way. You don't wonder how they did it; you know: they did it with computers. The fun of this synthetic picture is real, but the bloodlessness of the process drains our amazement. (September 2004)

The Day the Earth Stood Still

Wasted Space

I like Keanu Reeves myself—he has a unique star presence. But the nobody-home screen persona his detractors grouse about cannot be denied in *The Day the Earth Stood Still*, a boldly mediocre remake of the 1951 sci-fi saucer-man movie. Here, Reeves never cracks a smile, hikes an eyebrow, or, for all we can tell, draws breath. There may be puddles of spilled beer more expressive.

Not that his role allows for a lot of latitude in this regard. Reeves plays Klaatu, the interstellar emissary from somewhere or other who's come to Earth to . . . well, more about that in a moment. Klaatu touches down in New York's Central Park, not in a standard spaceship like the one in the original movie, but in a big shiny silver ball that looks like nothing so much as a giant Christmas tree ornament. He has brought along a towering robot bodyguard called Gort, who's only marginally less gregarious than his deadpan master. They're welcomed by the traditional contingent of itchy-fingered soldiers and goggling scientists, among them astrobiologist Helen Benson (Jennifer Connelly). As Helen approaches the ornament with a gesture of welcome for Klaatu, one of the soldiers naturally shoots him, and the wounded visitor is quickly spirited away to a military lab for inspection and interrogation. As if any such puny human installation could contain him.

Klaatu has not come alone—other alien arrivals are being reported around the world. The secretary of defense (Kathy Bates) is upset about a military satellite that's gone missing. ("They know everything about us now!") But the head scientist on the case (Jon Hamm, of *Mad Men*) is more concerned about Helen. (Although not *too* concerned; this is a movie that rates zero on the sexy meter.) Meanwhile, Helen's pouty stepson, Jacob (Jaden Smith, son of Will), is entirely focused on being a supercute plot annoyance.

But what does this Klaatu fellow *want,* exactly? In the 1951 movie, he'd come to warn us to cut it out with the atomic weapons or our planet would have to be vaporized for the good of the universe. His message now, however, is more up to date: "I came to save the Earth," he says. "This planet is dying. The human race is killing it." Great—an intergalactic Al Gore. The solution, he says, isn't to death-ray our dying orb but to terminate its messy populace. Talk about Earth First.

Klaatu announces that the countdown to annihilation has already begun. To ensure that a mistake isn't being made, though, he decides to have one last consultation with a fellow alien, Mr. Wu (James Hong), who has lived as a deep-cover mole in the wilds of New Jersey for the last seventy years. (That they meet in a McDonald's and converse in crafty subtitles, is one of the loopiest parts of the picture.) Wu confirms that the locals are a hopeless lot ("and they won't change"), yet he kind of likes them anyway. Also weighing in on the wait-a-minute side of the argument is an academic named Barnhardt (John Cleese in a sad cardigan), who's won a Nobel Prize for his work in "biological altruism" (a very Pythonian name for an actual subject of scientific inquiry). Barnhardt urges some cutting of slack for the human race, and Klaatu—after tamping down an infestation of ravenous, globe-gobbling CGI—decides that a second chance may well be in order. But, he warns, "It would come at a price to you and your way of life." His new human friends—with visions of Priuses dancing in their heads, no doubt—reply with a message straight from the heart of Hollywood: "We'll try!"

It should be noted that at no point in this very silly movie does the Earth actually stand still. You may need to reboot your brain on the way out of it, though. (December 2008)

THE HIT FACTORY

While a bad big movie can be depressing, as noted earlier, a good one, bringing to bear both epic scale, top talents, and of course blimploads of money, can be uniquely exciting. The success of such films often derives from iconic characters, visionary directors, and famous actors cast in uncharacteristic roles. Of course, even a movie that meets one or another of these criteria can also be flawed, and in some cases very bad. But because such films are often critic-proof, they can also pay off— the perfectly dreadful Sex and the City 2 had such a firmly locked-in audience that it managed an international gross of nearly $300 million. But when one of these box-office monsters has been executed at the highest levels of craft—as was the case with The Dark Knight, which after many subsequent viewings I've come to see as one of the grandest of genre films—it deserves every penny of the multimillions it goes on to make.

The Dark Knight

Ledgerdemain

There's an electrifying moment early on in *The Dark Knight* that involves a demented villain, a troublesome thug, and an everyday writing device. It's over in an instant—a sudden jolt—but from that point on, the Joker, as alarmingly incarnated by the late Heath Ledger, has our undivided attention.

This is a considerable feat, given how crowded the movie is with Other Stuff: a love triangle, a second supervillain (third, if you count the brief encore by Cillian Murphy's Scarecrow—out on a day pass from Arkham Asylum, presumably), angry mobsters, doomed clowns, an intricate financial rip-off, a side trip to Hong Kong, and, of course, wall-to-wall, floor-to-ceiling, sea-to-shining-sea pyro-automotive mayhem.

The Dark Knight is even more ambitious than its predecessor, the 2005 *Batman Begins*. Director Christopher Nolan lingers over roaring flames and flying rubble as if he had only lately discovered them. (Maybe he figured they'd seem fresher down at the tender end of the movie's target demographic.) The rest of the picture is briskly edited, but Nolan's delight in nonstop detonation helps push it up to the two-and-a-half-hour mark, and then over it. Fortunately, whenever the Joker appears, with his crumbling pancaked face, seaweed hair, and giddy malevolence, things always perk up.

As the movie begins, Batman (Christian Bale) is in ill repute among the citizens of Gotham, who now curse him as an out-of-control vigilante. Meanwhile, the municipal criminal element, led by Salvatore Maroni (Eric Roberts, an even less persuasive Italian mob boss than Tom Wilkinson was in the last picture), has problems of its own: somebody has hoovered millions in ill-gotten gains out of the syndicate's secret bank accounts. Then there's the crusading new district attorney,

Harvey Dent (Aaron Eckhart), a straight arrow who's just as committed to thug-busting as Batman is, but equally opposed to the hooded crime fighter's corner-cutting butt-kickery. Batman, for his part, welcomes Dent's arrival on the scene—what with all the burgher bad-mouthing lately, he's seriously considering retirement. On the other hand, Bruce Wayne, the man beneath those bat ears, can't help noticing that Harvey is also making moves on the girl of Wayne's dreams, assistant DA Rachel Dawes (Maggie Gyllenhaal, in for Katie Holmes).

The would-be mastermind who's ripping off the mob is a rogue mogul named Lau (Chin Han), who's inconveniently located in Hong Kong. Batman and the Joker both want this guy (the mobsters, idiots all, think the Joker is working for *them*); but it's Batman who goes the extra ten thousand miles to make the collar. Was this trip worth the sizable chunk of production budget it undoubtedly cost? Maybe. There's a glorious shot of the globetrotting superhero perched high above the gleaming city, and when he dives down into the night and his cape wings snap open and he begins sailing around among the skyscrapers, you smile at the elegant beauty of the imagery. Then, following a ferocious bullet ballet at Lau's corporate headquarters, there's a spectacular airborne getaway that justifies whatever amount it cost to stage.

In fact, few directors can whip up action with such mad gusto as Nolan. His set-piece 18-wheeler truck somersault, already familiar from the trailer, may be a first; but the smaller-scaled shot in which Batman guns his armored motorcycle (okay, "Bat-Pod") halfway up a wall and flips it to reverse direction is pretty slick, too. And the long chase through Chicago's multilevel streets—a riot of careening trucks, plummeting helicopters, and thundering bazookas—is a virtuoso demonstration of choreographed pandemonium.

Amid all this, however, the story of Harvey Dent—one of the more complex characters in the Batman universe—feels oddly truncated. As anyone eager to see *The Dark Knight* will probably know, Dent suffers a gruesome injury that leaves half of his face looking like something that might be found hanging from a hook in a meat locker. It also cleaves his personality, turning him into the tragically conflicted Two-Face, a semivillain who determines his every significant action—for good or for evil—with the flip of a coin. Aaron Eckhart's heroic jaw and beaming blondness make for an appealing predisaster Dent, although his slide into madness has a rote dementia. In the comics, Two-Face, who's been around almost from the beginning of the saga, keeps coming back to instill further worry in his costumed adversary (in fact, Dent is still around today). In this retooled film franchise, however . . . well, let's say that probably won't be happening.

As in the first movie, Bale does his most personable work as Bruce Wayne. Bantering with his suave armorer, Lucius Fox (Morgan Freeman), and his loyal butler, Alfred (Michael Caine), or languidly disporting himself on a yacht filled with twittering ballerinas, Bale the actor seems actually to be having the fun that the troubled Wayne character can only pretend to. Once he slips into Batman's cape and cowl and trademark glower, though, he's boxed in; and the weirdly choked growl with which he voices his lines seems weirder than ever—he sounds as if he were speaking from the bottom of a frog pond.

This enables Ledger to take over the movie. His performance as the Joker bristles with unexpected twitches and tones, and it lightens the movie's thick, operatic texture. The character as written has an odd flaw: although he's supposed to be an improvisational maniac ("Do I look like a man with a plan?"), his murderous schemes—especially one involving two ferries filled with terrified passengers—are in fact carefully worked out in advance. But Ledger plays him as a wild card anyway, and he's scary and funny and fascinating. Whatever the movie's shortcomings (an attempt to raise FISA-style objections to an altogether nifty eavesdropping stunt is pretty lame), Ledger barrels past them. Eerily, at the end of this film, his Joker is set up for a return engagement in the next one. "I think you and I will be doing this forever," he tells Batman. If only. (July 2008)

Avatar

Pass the Kool-Aid

James Cameron's *Avatar* is the most amazing . . . no, wait: the most staggeringly amazing, jaw-droppingly triple-awesome unbelievable movie ever made. That's the feeling among the reviewers aggregated at Rotten Tomatoes, anyway. I quote:

"An overwhelming feast of visual artistry unlike anything you have ever seen before."

"Much more than a film. It's a prescribed cinematic experience."

"An entertainment to be not just seen but absorbed on a molecular level."

"Cameron has achieved no less than a rebirth of cinema."

"Make sure you can say you were there when the future of cinema began."

What, are we all fanboys now? Or just unpaid studio publicists? *Avatar* without question represents a new high point in motion-capture technology—the digital technique whereby the movements of human actors are used as the armature for animating fanciful characters. (Peter Jackson's Gollum in the *Lord of the Rings* films was the breakthrough in this area.) And the movie offers deep 3-D panoramas of computer-generated imagery that really are stunning. (For the first two hours, anyway—at which point there are still forty-some minutes left to go.)

But all of this expensive tech has been put at the service of a story so triflingly generic you wonder why anyone would bother to tell it. Briefly: paraplegic ex-Marine Jake Sully (Sam Worthington) gets selected to participate in the Avatar program, a military-industrial project designed to plunder the natural resources of the faraway planet of Pandora. Of particular interest is a mineral called "unobtainium" (yes, really), which could be the solution to the apparently eternal energy crisis back on Earth. Unfortunately, Pandora's populace, the Na'vi—who are bright blue and ten feet tall, with long, whippy tails—inhabits a vast field of this stuff, and they don't want to move. The humans are of two minds about this problem. Dr. Grace Augustine (Sigourney Weaver), who heads the science team to which Jake has been assigned, wants to befriend the Na'vi and negotiate with them. To this end, "avatars" have been created— Na'vi-like figures fabricated out of human and Na'vi DNA that can be remotely powered by human "drivers" in the base headquarters and sent out among the natives to make friends and learn their language and their charmingly primitive ways.

Over on the evil side, meanwhile, the project's snarling security chief, Miles Quaritch (Stephen Lang), and resident corporate greedhead Parker Selfridge (Giovanni Ribisi) would just as soon exterminate the Na'vi ("fly-bitten savages who live in trees," as Selfridge puts it) and seize their land. To this end, Quaritch secretly recruits Jake to bring back useful military intel from his nice-making science explorations among these creatures. Jake is okay with this at first, until he really gets to know the locals—especially a Na'vi princess called Neytiri (Zoe Saldana). So the plot boils down to this: can Jake win Neytiri's heart (or whatever she has in there) and foil his fellow humans' plan for corporate conquest? Even a Na'vi might guess the answer to that.

Fortunately, Cameron is a great action director. And there's a lot to look at here: the luminescent glow of the jungle in which the Na'vi live, the ancient Tree of Souls with which they commune, a spectacular range of mountains hanging high in the sky up above Pandora. There's also a lot going on. The director and his battalion of digital technicians have cooked up a fantastical bestiary of Pandoran creatures—hammerhead rhinos; dog-fighting battle dragons; and, in one virtuoso sequence, a vicious six-legged thingy that chases Jake through the jungle and off the edge of a cliff. The meticulous detail in which these alien fauna have been rendered, and the complexity with which they're arrayed within the film's exotic environments, are undeniable marvels of moviemaking art.

Unfortunately, whenever the action lets up and we're returned to the piddling story, the picture sags. It's also laced with political instruction of a most familiar sort. Cameron, who's now fifty-five, is a self-acknowledged aging hippie, and his boomer worldview is strictly by the numbers. Quaritch and Selfridge are evil Americans despoiling the Na'vi's idyllic planet in exactly the same way that the humans have (we're told) trashed their own native orb. The invaders are armed with deplorable corporate technology (an odd animosity in a major-studio movie that reportedly cost more than $300 million to make), and they speak the familiar—and in this context rather anachronistic—language of contemporary American warmongering. ("We will fight terror with terror!" "It's some kind of shock-and-awe campaign!")

The Na'vi, on the other hand, with their bows and arrows and long braided hair, are stand-ins for every spiritually astute and ecologically conscientious indigenous population ever ground down under the heel of rampaging Western imperialism. They appear to have no warlike impulses themselves, and they live in complete harmony with their environment. (They even talk to trees.) Why, the movie asks, as if the thought were new, can't *we* be more like *them*?

The central question that *Avatar* poses, however, is whether expensively advanced filmmaking technology is enough in itself to carry a whole film. The story here is a simpleminded mash-up of every old cowboys-and-Indians and jungle-adventure movie of the 1930s and 1940s. And while Saldana manages to project shadings of emotion through her digital carapace, and Worthington and Joel David Moore (as a friendly biologist) bring nice-guy appeal to their roles, the characters are blandly conceived. We watch them go about their business advancing the predictable plot and uttering Cameron's sometimes clunky dialogue ("The sky people have sent us a message!" "This land is our land!"), and we wonder when the battle dragons will come swooping back in to break the tedium. In the story, the machines don't win, of course; but in the tech-centric scheme of the movie, they conquer all. (December 2009)

Sex and the City 2

Lost Girls

S ex and the City 2 is a ghastly mess, a stake in the heart of the stylish TV series that ran from 1998 to 2004. This second *SATC* movie is misconceived on every level. Consider:

1. After opening with the usual helicopter footage of New York sky-scrapers (*Look, there's the Chrysler Building!*), this very long picture decamps for what seems like half an hour to a gay wedding in Connecticut, complete with glittery male choir and a Liza Min-nelli (!) dance number, which nearly sinks the film on its own. It then decamps even farther to Abu Dhabi, of all places, where there's no sex and, for the story's purposes, no city either. This is where most of the movie takes place.

2. Whereas the old TV series pioneered a new female candor about sex and relationships, this movie gives ample screen time to a busty young nanny who's shown cavorting with kids in a park while her breasts leap around inside her blouse with a life of their own. Later we see her chest accidentally sprayed with water, which turns that scene into a one-girl wet T-shirt contest.

3. To balance things out, we also meet a group of young hunks at a swimming pool and are given close-up crotch shots of their bulging Speedos. Later there's a hunky Danish architect and a lingering close-up of *his* crotch in all of its protruding tumes-cence. This character has naturally caught the eye of our gal Samantha (Kim Cattrall), still ravenously randy at the age of fifty-two. She asks his name. It's Richard Spirtz. She decides to just call him Dick.

4. The writing, which was one of the glories of the TV series, sharp and pungent, is here abysmally juvenile. Samantha, upon learning that a World Cup soccer team has arrived on the scene: "Did they bring their balls?" And later, spotting a hot guy in the desert: "Lawrence of my labia!" At one point someone actually says, "Abu Dhabi do!"

No movie this boldly brainless should be set in an Islamic city—even one purportedly as Westernized as Abu Dhabi (which actually refused permission for the filmmakers to shoot there, forcing them to fake it in Morocco). After Samantha, who's been recruited to do PR for a local luxury hotel, arrives on the scene with her pals Carrie (Sarah Jessica Parker), Charlotte (Kristin Davis), and Miranda (Cynthia Nixon), we soon see them swanning around in their usual wildly inappropriate clothing (they seem to don garish new outfits every five minutes) and—in one of the film's many preposterous sequences—breaking out in a karaoke rendition of "I Am Woman" at a hotel nightclub while the other women in the audience—some of them Arab—cheer and sing along.

Since the position of women in traditional Islamic societies is famously, shall we say, constricted, there are issues to be dealt with here that are beyond the grasp of bubbleheaded comedy. Miranda grows momentarily irate at the sight of so many Arab women wearing face-covering *niqabs*, but she can only respond with a feminist cliché: "Some men really don't like strong women!" (As if she and these women were victims of the same oppression.) We also note that upon checking into the hotel, Charlotte drops her married name, Goldenblatt, in favor of her more goyish maiden name. This issue, too, is quickly shooed away.

Why writer-director Michael Patrick King felt compelled to take the *SATC* girls out of glamorous Manhattan and deposit them in the arid Middle East is baffling. The sleek elegance of their native turf was always part of the old series's fun. Abu Dhabi, with its golden domes and gaudy chandeliers and $22,000-a-night hotel suites, makes Miami look like Geneva by comparison. And Carrie and company are no longer footloose thirty-somethings in the American city of dreams.

They're now forty-somethings (and more, in the case of the loudly menopausal Samantha), and most of them are married and feeling stifled. The high spirits that once drew us to them are long gone. Possibly King realized that the franchise was near-dead anyway, and awaited only the coup de grâce. This movie should provide it. (May 2010)

Sherlock Holmes

Action Man

Director Guy Ritchie calls his new movie *Sherlock Holmes*, but surely he jests. The title of this picture should be changed immediately to *Robert Downey Jr.* Ritchie's revisionist take on "the world's greatest consulting detective" may be a good thing, in a way (Downey is always entertaining), but it's not so good in several other ways.

Holmes purists will be taken aback by how little the movie derives from the classic tales—the four novels and dozens of short stories that Arthur Conan Doyle began publishing in 1887. Doyle's Sherlock was a supercilious egghead with only occasional use for firearms and virtually none at all for women. Downey's rendition of the celebrated sleuth—whom he plays with ripe, fruity intonations that intermittently suggest an English accent—is an action man, a disheveled bohemian who packs a revolver, gets shirtless in a bare-knuckle boxing pit, and has a definite eye for the ladies.

Well, one lady. Doyle's Holmes was chastely obsessed with the mysterious adventuress Irene Adler, the only person who ever outfoxed him. Here, played by Rachel McAdams, Adler is the hot love of Holmes's life. Then there's Dr. Watson, Holmes's Boswell, the chronicler of most of his adventures. In the books, Watson is an affable muddler; in the movie, played with great good humor by Jude Law, he's as much of a roughneck crime fighter as Downey's Sherlock. There *are* some wisps of vintage Holmes lore nestled around the edges of the story (the bored detective idly shooting holes in the wall of his room, a passing reference to Watson's war experience in Afghanistan), and a few jokey riffs (Holmes smokes a pipe here, but it's pointedly *not* a fat, curvy meerschaum; and when he whips out a magnifying glass, it's but a wee small thing). In every other respect, though, this is a whole new Holmes world.

The story is also a departure. Sherlock's adversary this time out is the newly invented Lord Blackwood (Mark Strong), an adept of the dark arts who is conniving to bring down the British government and install a satanic new order. At the film's beginning we find Holmes and Watson intervening in one of Blackwood's occult rituals, which involves a torch-lit basement, a crowd of hooded devotees, and a young woman stretched out on a sacrificial altar. Blackwood is arrested, tried for practicing black magic, and dispatched on the gallows. In a matter of mere movie moments, though, he's back from the dead and up to no good again.

Can Holmes somehow stop this supernatural blackguard? Can he lure Watson away from dallying with his own lady love (Kelly Reilly) to provide backup? And what about Irene Adler? She claims to want to help, but then we learn that she's actually in the employ of a sinister "professor." (Guess who, Holmes fans.) We never really see this character, but then his only purpose in the proceedings is to set up the sequel.

Soon Holmes and Watson are beset by louts, and there's much chasing about and brawling in shipyards, slaughterhouses, and other grotty locales. This being a Ritchie film, some of the action is incoherent (as is some of the plot—I spent half the movie trying to figure out who the "ginger midget" was). And while Downey and Law are a crack team and bring a lot of personality to the picture, they're frequently eclipsed by the overload of commotion.

Ritchie's pandering to the action audience (an agenda no doubt reinforced by knock-'em-dead producer Joel Silver) strips Holmes's world of its style. The director and his production designer, Sarah Greenwood, have taken pains to conjure the dark cobbled streets and plush interiors of Victorian London, and as shot by Philippe Rousselot, this is often a great-looking movie. But the gracious restraint of earlier Holmes films has been displaced by the familiar, overamped frenzy of our own cinematic age—appropriate for a Downey film, and inevitable for a

Ritchie project, but as an addendum to the Holmes canon, a bit of a mystery. (December 2009)

Inception

Dream Warriors

Are they handing out joints at the box office for *Inception*? That would make the movie considerably more fun. Christopher Nolan's latest is a terrific-looking picture that bounds around the globe from Paris to Tangiers to Tokyo (among places that actually exist) in the wake of a freelance dream thief named Dom Cobb (Leonardo DiCaprio). Cobb's specialty is infiltrating the dreams of corporate big shots and extracting their most valuable secrets. His latest assignment, however, is a little different—a Japanese industrialist named Saito (Ken Watanabe) has hired him to *implant* an idea in someone's head that will allow Saito to take over a rival titan's business empire. Cobb's reward for achieving this goal: an end to his exile from the United States, where he's currently a wanted man, and a yearned-for reunion with his two children.

Right here you may wonder why anyone in search of secret information would break into someone's dreams, which are so often distortions of waking life, rather than their memories, which could be more precise recollections. But Cobb is not a memory man, so . . . whatever.

Gearing up for his mission, Cobb assembles an A-team of dream-work specialists. There's an "architect" named Ariadne (Ellen Page), whose job is to structure dreams; a "forger" named Eames (Tom Hardy), who can pass for any other person in a dreamworld; and a "chemist" named Yusuf (Dileep Rao), whose drug concoctions allow penetration not only into dreams, or into dreams within dreams, but into dreams within dreams *within* dreams. There's also a fixer named Arthur (Joseph Gordon-Levitt), whose purpose is to handle details and look sharp in skinny suits.

As we see, the movie all but nudges us to notice that some of these characters' names refer to celebrated figures outside the story. But this is sometimes cute to no apparent purpose. An industrial heir named Robert Fischer (Cillian Murphy) offers no indication of a chess master's cunning; and since there's already one architect on the team, why name another character Eames (unless a strained filmmaking reference is intended)? Then there's Cobb's estranged wife, Mal (Marion Cotillard), who haunts his dreams and does her best to screw up his every plan: as her name unnecessarily denotes, she be bad. And what about Dom Cobb himself? Is his unlikely moniker meant to suggest *Dummkopf*? That would seem counterintuitive.

Many of the movie's effects and digital manipulations are spectacularly imaginative, especially a sequence of weightless action in a rotating hotel corridor, the unexpected arrival of a huge train in a scene without tracks, and the startling sight of a long boulevard peeling up off the ground and rising to double over on itself. These eye-popping amazements are much appreciated in a story that goes on and on for two and a half hours, with Cobb and his team flashing back and forth disconnectedly from one dream level to another, occasionally touching down in reality (whatever that is). Each of the dream invaders carries a "totem," an everyday, real-world tchotchke that tips them off as to whether or not they are in fact in a dream, either their own or someone else's. As the dream levels and their far-flung locales piled up and intermingled—a collapsing Japanese mansion, a bullet-pocked snowscape, an exploding Parisian street—I wished I had a totem myself to keep track of what was going on.

Unlike Nolan's clever 2000 film, *Memento*, which was a devilishly complex mystery, *Inception* is essentially a complicated heist flick—there is no mystery to ponder and penetrate. Cobb's goal is clear from the beginning; we spend the rest of the movie attempting to parse its many confusions as he attains it. Nolan says he spent ten years obsessing over this story (the script is only the second one he has written on his own), which may explain its central problem. Despite its technical brilliance and its fine cast (Hardy is clearly a star, and DiCaprio brings an emotional depth to the tale that is nowhere else in evidence), the picture is a puzzle palace with far too many rooms. The director himself may have gotten lost in it. (July 2010)

Taken

No More Mister Nice Guy

A few years back, the French director Pierre Morel made a movie called *District B13*—an action flick so compact and focused it felt like an actual kick in the head. I'm sure there was a storyline, but I can't be bothered to recall it. The picture was pure kinetic frenzy, a modest classic.

Now, Morel has been given a much larger budget and yet come up with a movie that seems somehow smaller. Bryan Mills, the hero of *Taken* is a merciless killing machine—would we have it any other way? But he's a *sensitive* merciless killing machine—sensitive, in fact, to the point of pining whininess. I suppose it's a good thing that Mills is played by Liam Neeson, that master of manly emotion; but even he can't hold together such an awkwardly bifurcated character.

Mills is a retired spy whose black-ops career wrecked his marriage and made him very sad. His ex-wife, a bitch from hell named Lenore (Famke Janssen in a barely written role) was no great loss, but he rues the estrangement of his daughter, Kim (Maggie Grace), now seventeen. We get to rue this right along with him for longer than we might wish as he mopes among her childhood snapshots and browses for a cute birthday present to give her. No kicks in the head here; not even a gift-shop jostle. Finally, though, Kim herself shifts the plot into gear when she asks Dad to allow her to spend a summer vacation in Paris, with a girlfriend. Mills is reluctant. He knows the world is a dangerous place—he spent his spy career helping to make it that way. But he relents, and soon Kim and her friend are en route to Paris, where—just as Mills figured!—the two girls are immediately abducted by a gang of

Albanian sex-slave traffickers. Quicker than you can say "merciless killing machine," Mills has hopped on a plane himself, and the chase is afoot. Excellent.

The action gets under way as soon as Mills arrives in Paris. Tipped by an old spook colleague, he makes his way to a red-light district, busts up a skuzzy bordello, rescues one of the drugged sex slaves therein, cures her of her forced drug addiction with a hotel-room transfusion, and quickly gets a line on Kim. By this early point, Mills has already greased seven scumbags and put three more in the hospital. Next, he lays hands on one of the Albanian goons and hooks him up to an electrical generator. ("We used to outsource this sort of thing," he says, by way of banter.) Then he shoots somebody's wife to make a point and moves on to the main event—a sex-slave auction at a grand Paris mansion. Here he not only catches sight of Kim, but learns that some fat Arab is willing to pay half a million dollars for the pleasure of her company. (This struck me as a bit much: Maggie Grace is pretty and all, but come on.)

The action continues at a raging pace, and Morel, who started out as a cinematographer, knows how to put us right in the middle of it. A lot of the liveliest stuff—the close-quarters bone cracking and the Seine-side automotive melee—is fundamentally Bourne again. But even thrills of such a second freshness are hardly boring, and Liam Neeson, who's now fifty-six but used to be a boxer, acquits himself with savage grace. Some would no doubt object to most of the vile guys in the picture being, shall we say, not in the mainstream of Western civilization—but is it not for such people that movies like *Hotel for Dogs* are made? With no more Nazis to provide shorthand villainy, what's a shameless action director (and his equally shameless writer-producer partner, Luc Besson) to do?

What finally tanks this movie is the character at the center of it. Bryan Mills is such a wet sock in the early scenes, mooning on and on over his little girl, that we can't quite track his sudden switch into terminator mode. And his Mr. Softy side continues putting in appearances after that, and becomes a considerable distraction, not to say a major annoyance. Couldn't somebody, like, terminate *him*? (January 2009)

Unknown

Liam Neeson on the Run

Berlin is no longer the entertaining cesspool of espionage and political intrigue that it was when Cold War operatives like George Smiley and Harry Palmer skulked its shadowy streets. But in the new movie *Unknown*, the once-divided metropolis provides a sufficiently sinister environment for Martin Harris, a visiting American who's as dangerously out of his element as Joseph Cotton's Holly Martins was in the postwar Vienna of *The Third Man*. Although let me apologize in advance for mentioning that movie in the vicinity of this one.

Harris (Liam Neeson), a world-famous Chicago botanist, has just flown in to Berlin to attend an international biotech conference with his sleek blond wife, Elizabeth (January Jones). Arriving at their deluxe hotel, he realizes that his briefcase—idiotically containing his passport and all other forms of identification—has been left behind at the airport. Without saying a word to Elizabeth, who's already checking in, he hops in a taxi to go back and reclaim it. As you'd hope, everything that could possibly go wrong now begins to do so.

The movie has a Hitchcockian complement of plot twists and fakeouts. (If only it also had Hitchcock.) En route to the airport, there's a traffic pileup, and Harris's taxi goes sailing off a bridge into the River Spree. His cabbie, a Bosnian immigrant named Gina (Diane Kruger, possibly the least Balkan of actresses), pulls her unconscious passenger out of the water to safety, then disappears. Four days later Harris awakes from a coma in a hospital, where a doctor natters on about memory loss and disorientation. There's a television in the room, on which Harris sees a news report about the big biotech conference, and a shot of the hotel into which he has still failed to check. Fleeing the hospital, he goes there, spots his wife in a salon and approaches her. She greets him with the words, "Do I know you?" Then she introduces her husband, the world-famous botanist Martin Harris, who looks for all the world like Aidan Quinn. The real Harris implores the hotel security chief to look him up online, which he does—and pulls up a photo of, yes, Aidan Quinn. (How this might have been arranged we can leave to the puzzlement of anyone who's ever done Internet research.)

Now things get really hectic. Harris finds himself being stalked by a vicious assassin (grim-lipped Olivier Schneider). Fortuitously, he makes a connection with a crusty investigator, a former East German spy named Jürgen (Bruno Ganz), who believes Harris's wild story. Then Gina the cabbie re-enters the picture; she sort of believes Harris, too. Unbelievably, she also allows this virtual stranger to crash in her tiny apartment. But not for long—very soon they're on the run, pursued by killers for reasons Harris can't begin to fathom. Also arriving in the story are an Arab prince (Mido Hamada), who funds biotech projects; a pioneering German scientist named Bressler (Sebastian Koch, of *The Lives of Others*); and a heinous plot, a mysterious book code, an international murder bureau, a ticking bomb, and identity games that really do keep you guessing (but not, alas, as long as they should). As a final complication, there's Harris's longtime friend Rodney Cole (Frank Langella), who arrives toward the end to make himself useful and, let's say, fails to do so.

Spanish director Jaume Collet-Serra (whose 2009 *Orphan* was a fine little horror flick) keeps all of this moving along at a snappy pace. Even the bad-guy beat-downs and the inevitable car chase through the icy streets of Berlin are rousingly staged, as such things go; and an assault in the hospital has a nice compact nastiness. Plot holes are a minor distraction in this sort of film (the preposterous ending here is more of a problem); but what really keeps the movie from being a solid genre gem is its star. Neeson's expertise at projecting inner turbulence and delicate emotional shadings overbalances this pulpy tale; and as has been the case in some previous films (even *Taken*, I'd say), his air of earnest contemplation grows dull. More surprising than any of the other rub-outs on view is the way it smothers the movie. (February 2011)

Five Child Actors You Don't Want to Shoot

*A*n unobjectionable child actor must neither squeak (Shirley Temple), peeve (Jake Lloyd in *The Phantom Menace*), or stupefy (Michael Stephenson in the epically dreadful *Troll 2*). It is also best that the underage thespian not set the adorability bar so high that no ordinary kid can ever attain it, thus instilling a lifelong resentment of the offending paragon (the otherwise estimable Freddie Bartholomew). A good child actor should first of all be a good actor, with a unique presence that's undeniable, even in a being of such diminutive proportions. Cuteness is almost always in attendance as well, but is not entirely the point.

Jennifer Connelly, *Once Upon a Time in America* (1984): Who can forget the scene? In 1920s New York, Connelly's twelve-year-old Deborah Gelly, practicing her ballet pirouettes in a tenement grocery storeroom of improbably vast dimensions (this *is* a Sergio Leone film), realizes that a young admirer is secretly observing her. The awareness brings a subtle glow of pleasure to her dark eyes, and she summons him from the shadows. Sitting him down, she admits a reciprocal affection; but because he has set himself on a path to criminality, she quietly informs him that she can never be his. Who can forget the heartbreak, up on the screen and inside the theater? Making her movie debut, Connelly's precocious combination of angelic serenity and clear-eyed, womanly assessment is ravishing. She has given many fine performances over the years—in *Requiem for a Dream, A Beautiful Mind, Little Children*—but none more beguiling than this one.

Tatum O'Neal, *Paper Moon* (1973): Depression-era con man Moses Pray (Ryan O'Neal) meets his larcenous match in nine-year-old orphan Addie Loggins. Ryan was never the most interesting of actors, but his daughter, making her movie debut, was a true star, imbuing Addie with a very funny deadpan calculation that won her an Oscar against some stiff

★★★★★★★★★★★★★★★★★★★★★★★★★★★★★★★

competition. (Linda Blair was nominated that year for *The Exorcist*, Candy Clark for *American Graffiti*, and Madeline Kahn for her costarring role in *Paper Moon*.) Tatum and her dad were subsequently teamed in another Peter Bogdanovich film, *Nickelodeon* (1976), and she has found regular work over the years in pictures ranging from *The Bad News Bears* (1976) to *The Runaways* (2010). Along the way, she dated Michael Jackson, married tennis hothead John McEnroe, had some tabloid drug adventures, and in 2004 published an autobiography that cast her father in a most unflattering light. Less complicated and no doubt happier days for both of them are preserved in *Paper Moon*.

Haley Joel Osment, *A.I.: Artificial Intelligence* (2001): Osment was a child actor who could easily have coasted on pure cuddly cuteness, but never did. He was already a marvel at the age of ten, holding the screen through emotionally complex scenes opposite Bruce Willis in *The Sixth Sense* (1999). But Spielberg's *A.I.* was a triumph. The movie was too long, and its intentions were garbled, but Osment—playing a synthetically created boy abandoned by the family that had acquired him as if he were a pet that had outworn its welcome—gave a masterfully structured performance. He broke your heart without making any detectable attempt to do so. Now twenty-two, he has yet to find another project so worthy of his remarkable gifts. He'll clearly be ready when one comes along.

Natalie Portman, *The Professional* (1994): Like Jennifer Connelly and Tatum O'Neal, Portman brought a charge of star power to her first screen appearance. As the suddenly orphaned twelve-year-old Mathilda, she's taken under the wing—or, more precisely, inserts herself there—of the expatriate "cleaner" Léon (Jean Reno). "You mean you're a hit man?" Mathilda asks, in a wide-eyed whisper; then, with a perfectly calculated brow lift: "Cool." Portman already knew how to underplay funny lines (provided by writer-director Luc Besson), and she hit some weighty emotional marks, too. (Mathilda's family had just been wiped out by some very persistent killers.) It would be seventeen years before she finally won an Oscar, but at least the possibility of her doing so was clear from the beginning.

Martin Stephens, *Village of the Damned* (1960): We'll never know how good an actor Stephens might have become. He attained a lasting fame for his iconic presence as the platinum-haired, laser-eyed, not-of-this-earth kid in this film, which was based on a John Wyndham novel and directed by the unnecessarily prolific Wolf Rilla. The following year, Stephens was given more to work with as the eerie child driving his new governess (Deborah Kerr) crazy in *The Innocents*, a movie derived from Henry James and cowritten by Truman Capote. The eleven-year-old actor gave a performance of some accomplishment; but after twelve movies, he was growing bored. He did two more, then quit the business for university studies, and eventually became and remained an architect. Lesser actors have taken decades longer to come to a similarly reasonable decision.

NEVER-ENDING STORIES

Establishing a movie franchise is the holy grail of Hollywood film-making. When a franchise works the way it's supposed to, the initial picture locks in a huge audience that keeps coming back for future sequels—even when, as was the case with the Matrix movies, the sequels are woefully unworthy of the classic original that launched them. What's the secret of a successful franchise? It's certainly not the generative material. Who ever would have thought that a movie based on an amusement-park ride could be a worthy endeavor—until the first Pirates of the Caribbean rocked the box office? Nothing is "never ending," of course, and franchises like the Harry Potter and Twilight movies are limited by the number of the books on which they're based. But let us also note that the Bond franchise, still going strong (or at least going profitably) after nearly fifty years, will soon, as this is written, be spawning its twenty-third installment, far outnumbering Ian Fleming's ancient source novels. Which suggests that Captain Jack Sparrow, too, can sail on as far as the tides of audience allegiance will take him.

Pirates of the Caribbean: At World's End

Lost at Sea

I love pirate movies, and like just about everybody else, I loved the first *Pirates of the Caribbean*. Not only did it honor the best elements of the classic swashbucklers—the romantic dash of Errol Flynn, the athletic pizzazz of Burt Lancaster, the timeless *Arghh* of Robert Newton—it also introduced something new: Johnny Depp's fey, funny, heavily mascara'd and entirely Keith Richards–like Captain Jack Sparrow. This marvelous character turned what was already a good buccaneer picture into a great one.

A lot of people didn't care for the second *Pirates of the Caribbean*. They thought it too long—which it was. Still, there was some wonderful stuff in it: the rousing sword fight atop the rolling mill wheel, the tentacle-headed Davy Jones, the towering squid-monster called the Kraken. If *Pirates 2* was a lesser gem than the first movie, well, I thought, maybe it would seem worthier after the story reached its conclusion in the third and final film in the series, *Pirates of the Caribbean: At World's End*. As a fan, I could hardly wait.

And so, as a fan, it pains me to report that *Pirates 3* is an overstuffed and lumbering disappointment. The picture is almost half an hour longer than the first film (it runs nearly three hours), and you can feel every unnecessary minute dragging by like endless anchor chain. The movie is thronged with characters new and old—so many that none of them has room to shine. And the plot has spun completely out of control.

All of the original characters are back, of course: Captain Jack; his sly rival, Barbossa (Geoffrey Rush); the slightly tiresome young lovers Will (Orlando Bloom) and Elizabeth (Keira Knightly); Elizabeth's ex-swain, Norrington (Jack Davenport); Jack's loyal bo'sun, Gibbs (Kevin R. McNally); the comic-relief swabbies Pintel (Lee Arenberg) and Ragetti (Mackenzie Crook); and Barbossa's undead monkey (this time packing heat). Also on hand, from the second film, are Davy Jones (Bill Nighy); Will's heavily barnacled dad, Bootstrap Bill (Stellan Skarsgård, still a glum presence); the snotty Lord Cutler Beckett (Tom Hollander); and black-lipped voodoo girl Tia Dalma (Naomie Harris). There's also a boatload of fresh characters, among them a Chinese pirate lord named Sao Feng (Chow Yun-Fat, energetically overacting); a grizzled "Keeper of the Code," who turns out to be Jack's dad (Keith Richards, in an agreeably brief appearance); and an international array of new pirates. It's a very crowded picture.

The plot is a confusing brew of conflict, betrayal, and whatever. Cutler Beckett now has possession of Davy Jones's disembodied heart, and thus of Jones himself and his scary ship, the *Flying Dutchman,* and its crustaceous crew. Beckett wants to wipe out piracy worldwide. Barbossa is determined to foil this plan and arranges a summit meeting of the world's pirate lords in Singapore under the auspices of Sao Feng—who turns out to be holding Will prisoner in a tub of water. Elizabeth, now a feisty pirate herself, is also in attendance, and—having developed tender feelings for Jack Sparrow in the last movie—now has very mixed feelings about reencountering Will (who is hardly encouraged by her assurance that "once we find Jack, everything will be all right"). As for Jack himself, last seen stepping boldly into the maw of the hideous Kraken, he's now confined (at the beginning of the picture) in the vast white hereafter of Davy Jones's Locker, along with a gang of other, identical Jacks, none of them getting along.

Everybody has an agenda. Davy Jones pines for an old love, the sea goddess Calypso. (We see him seated at his wheezing pipe organ, wiping away a tear with a stray tentacle.) Will doesn't care about the endangered future of piracy; he just wants to save his father. But that would mean losing Elizabeth. But then she might not mind being lost. And in any case, Will's father doesn't want to be saved. There's quite a bit of business with the "Brethren Court" at Shipwreck Cove, and with Jack's crazy compass, and oh, so much more. Davy Jones's still-beating heart is still being fumbled around, too. And there's also the conflicted Norrington, who . . . well, I could go on. And on.

There's so much going on, and so many characters going on with it, that the first half of the movie is leaden with talk and very lean on action. And given that the talented Ted Elliott and Terry Rossio once again wrote the script, it's remarkable how little lively dialogue there is in the film—nothing on the order of such great earlier lines as "Welcome to the Caribbean!" or "Hide the rum!" (Depp is especially short-changed by this lack of colorful gab; and since he has little room here to work up humorous new wrinkles in his now familiar character, we miss him even when he's on-screen.)

The director, Gore Verbinski, remains a virtuoso of huge set-piece sequences. One in particular here—in which an enormous whirlpool opens up in the midst of a furious sea battle—is a marvel of visionary CGI. There's also a scene involving a flotilla of scurrying crabs carrying a ship across a desolate waste that's unlike anything I believe I've seen before. And there's no shortage of lovely scenic effects. (One shot, of a pirate ship slipping through still waters sprinkled with reflections of the star-filled sky above, is particularly entrancing.) But another elaborate digital effect—pumping up one of the characters into a looming giant—is remarkably cheesy. And even the most imaginative of these technical exertions are drained of impact by the lack of a clear story they might have adorned.

This movie does not prompt feelings of eager anticipation for the next sequel. It's an overeventful and underinteresting epic that leaves you feeling numb and puzzled—rather the way you might have felt after staggering out of the second *Matrix* film. What's next: *Pirates of the Caribbean: Revolutions*? (May 2007)

Ocean's Thirteen

Stargazing

The best thing about the latter-day *Ocean's* movies is how immeasurably better they are than the original *Ocean's Eleven*, a 1960 Rat Pack souvenir that is now virtually unwatchable. That film presented Frank Sinatra and his drinking cronies (Dean Martin, Peter Lawford, Sammy Davis Jr., and so on) as the incarnation of wisecracking hipness. What they really were, though, in the parlance of the period, was "swingers," a rather less-cool thing. The movie got over on the strength of the stars' showbiz charisma, which was real; but their Vegasoid swanning—even in a story that was *set* in Vegas—is now leadenly dated.

No doubt audiences forty years in the future will look back upon Steven Soderbergh's three *Ocean's* movies and their stars (George Clooney, Brad Pitt, Matt Damon, and so on) as irretrievably mired in their own period, too. But the species of contemporary hipness in which these actors trade seems (to us, at least) less grating than the Pack product. Flashes of winking self-regard sometimes flicker through, but for the most part the stars underplay their celebrated fabulosity. It helps that Clooney and Pitt, especially, can own the screen just by walking into a scene. Unfortunately, with the arrival of *Ocean's Thirteen*, the spectacle of A-list salaries on parade is beginning to seem insufficient to sustain the series much longer. Especially since the films' disregard for the intricacies of good heist-flick plotting is now unignorable.

In this new installment, a Vegas casino magnate named Willie Bank (Al Pacino) is about to open his latest high-roller hotel—a project he's pulled together by swindling Reuben Tishkoff (Elliott Gould), a longtime pack mate of Danny Ocean (Clooney). Deeply steamed, Danny calls together his crew—Pitt, Damon, Don Cheadle, Carl Reiner, Bernie

Mac, the gang's all here—to sabotage Bank's big opening. Doing this will require several unlikely things: creating a fake earthquake by burrowing underneath Bank's hotel; fomenting labor unrest at a factory in Mexico as a cover for the installation of radio-control doohickeys in a whole shipment's worth of casino dice; and altogether too, too much more.

In an effective caper movie—*Rififi*, let's say, or the nail-biting *Day of the Jackal*—a viewer's pleasure lies in being presented with a series of seemingly insurmountable obstacles and then being shown precisely how they are surmounted. In *Ocean's Thirteen,* that bottom-line requirement is ignored. The team's genius tech expert, Roman Nagel (Eddie Izzard), is suitably skeptical of Danny's plan. "You're analog players in a digital world," he wisely cracks. But he's being kind. This scheme was hatched in another world altogether, one in which the laws of probability have been placed on hold. The picture resembles one of the dreadful latter-day Bond movies, the kind in which the villain is headquartered in an Arctic ice castle or something.

Which isn't to say there's not a lot of action here—there's plenty. And it looks great because Soderbergh once again shot the film himself (under his "Peter Andrews" pseudonym). There are some witty ideas, too. (Willie Bank hires his restaurant waitresses as "models who serve," so that if they gain weight he can fire them without breaking any labor laws.) And some of the running gags still pay off. (The team's Asian acrobat, played by Shaobo Qin, continues to spout nothing but Chinese, which nobody else can speak; but they continue to understand him anyway.) And the scriptwriters, Brian Koppelman and David Levien, provide some fine breezy dialogue. (There's a funny scene in which Willie's sexy aide-de-camp, played by Ellen Barkin, is coming on to Matt Damon with a fine wine. "Château d'Yquem?" she purrs. "As long as it's not '73," he gasps.) But then we get a twilight interlude of humid reminiscence in which Clooney and Pitt meditate on the old Vegas of the Sinatra days, when a casino on the Strip was still a magical place. "They built them a lot smaller back then," says Clooney. "They seemed pretty big," says Pitt. Neither of these guys had even been born in 1960.

Ocean's Thirteen is a polished professional product of considerable charm—an unobjectionably entertaining movie. But the silliness in this one is more flagrant than in the previous films, and so the picture has the narrative heft of a cream éclair. Three desserts may be enough. (June 2007)

Harry Potter and the Half-Blood Prince

Snogwarts

*H*arry Potter and the Half-Blood Prince is one of the darkest of the Potter books, so it's no surprise that the movie version is the darkest of the films to date. What is surprising—and I say this as someone who loves the books and has loved the movies up to this point—is how sluggish the new picture is. It gets under way with a limp scene set in a train-station café—a trivial flirtation between Harry, now sixteen, and an admiring waitress—and proceeds in surges and sags for the next two and a half hours. There are some marvelous scenes, beautiful images, wonderful moments—it isn't a "bad" movie, really. But it lacks the dynamic sweep of the pictures that preceded it.

Every fan knows the story: darkness is descending on Hogwarts and all of the wizarding world. Voldemort's Death Eaters are on the attack, and have even crossed over into the unsuspecting Muggle domain. The Dark Lord (Ralph Fiennes) has tasked Draco Malfoy (Tom Felton, newly prominent) with an especially evil mission. Albus Dumbledore (Michael Gambon) is in mortal danger, as, of course, is Harry (Daniel Radcliffe). And the deliciously malevolent Professor Snape (Alan Rickman) appears to be up to even more in the way of no-good than usual. In addition, there's a Horcrux crisis. (Need it be said that this isn't the place for first-timers to attempt to enter the Potter universe?)

J. K. Rowling's book is more than 650 pages long; compression was obviously requisite and no doubt tricky. Still, Potterphiles may wonder why some key plot elements have been shortchanged while others, less crucial, have been played up. We're told, for example, that Snape has finally been put in charge of the school's Defense Against the Dark Arts course (at last!). But why do we not see him teaching a class—one with Harry in it? (This is kind of important.) And some illuminating Horcrux detail gets lost in the consolidation of the story's Pensieve episodes. Then there's the fierce struggle, radically truncated here, that results in the death of a major character—a loss that passes with a curious minimum of emotional emphasis.

On the other hand, a subsidiary theme in the book—the hormonal rumpus among the Hogwarts kids now that they're in their midteens—has been inflated to an extent that suggests crass demographic pandering on the part of director David Yates and writer Steve Kloves. Ron Weasley (Rupert Grint) is being stalked by Gryffindor hottie Lavender Brown (Jessie Cave), much to the dismay of Hermione Granger (Emma Watson), who, as we've learned in earlier installments, now has eyes for Ron herself. Hermione, meanwhile, has been romantically targeted by Quidditch lug Cormac McLaggen (Freddie Stroma). And Harry is finally getting tight with Ginny Weasley (Bonnie Wright), Ron's sister. There is thus a lot of snogging going on—rather more than necessary to make the point. Although it does produce one of the picture's loveliest shots—a long, winding camera move up and around a Hogwarts tower, gliding slowly past Ron and Lavender in midembrace and then continuing its ascent to settle on Draco, on a high balcony, brooding darkly in the gathering night.

There's one significant new character on hand: Professor Horace Slughorn (Jim Broadbent), a former Potions teacher who years ago numbered among his students Tom Riddle—the embryonic Voldemort. (Riddle's childhood incarnation is played by Ralph Fiennes's nephew, the unsettlingly sinister Hero Fiennes Tiffin.) Slughorn has been in hiding from the Death Eaters, but Dumbledore lures him back to his old job and assigns Harry to get close to him in order to plumb his memory for desperately needed information. Nobody does avuncular muddling better than Broadbent; still, compared to previous guest wackos in the series, like Kenneth Branagh's Gilderoy Lockhart and Brendan Gleeson's Mad-Eye Moody, Horace lacks a vital fizz. The vivacity gap is further widened by the absence of dastardly Lucius Malfoy (currently confined to the Azkaban wizard prison) and Voldemort himself (who'll be back, of course). And some of the most beloved Potter characters get only token face time: Professors Lupin (David Thewlis) and McGonagall (Maggie Smith); the imposing Hagrid (Robbie Coltrane); the cranky Filch (David Bradley); and the wily Weasley twins, Fred and George (James and Oliver Phelps). By the time the gloriously spacey Luna Lovegood (Evanna Lynch) pops into a shot wearing some sort of giant lion hat on her head, we're so starved for whimsy that we want to hug her (and not let her go).

The film's production design, once again by Stuart Craig, is as intoxicatingly detailed as ever. And the sequence in which Dumbledore steers Harry by boat across a dark underground lake to a small island, where they're attacked by a throng of hideous, Gollum-like Inferi, is as uncannily beautiful as any episode in the cinematic Potter world. But as in several other passages of the film, the color is drained so far down into a spectral blue that it sometimes verges on murk. And while there's a sufficiency of the action magic familiar from earlier films—wizard duels and such—the element of magical enchantment that's always distinguished the series appears to have been mislaid. "Wands out, Harry," Dumbledore says at the beginning. By the time you reach the movie's ominous conclusion, you may wish that someone had given the picture itself one final wand-over before sending it out into the canon. (July 2009)

Harry Potter and the Deathly Hallows: Part I

Lost in the Dark

There are teenagers today who have lived their entire lives in the age of Harry Potter. J. K. Rowling's first book in the Potter series was published in Britain in 1997, and made it to the movies in 2001. The novels have sold hundreds of millions of copies worldwide; the pictures have grossed more than $5 billion and spun off all manner of shelf-clogging merch. (I myself am in possession of a Harry Potter clock, a number of adorable Potter figurines, and of course a replica of the young wizard's mighty wand—all promotional freebies, I hasten to add.)

But the literary Potter saga came to an end three years ago, with the publication of the very dark *Harry Potter and the Deathly Hallows.* So with the conclusion of the tale no longer in doubt, the movies have been reduced to playing catch-up, going through the familiar motions on their way to a culmination that's already well known. I thought last year's *Harry Potter and the Half-Blood Prince,* with its destabilizing fixation on teen hormonal stirrings, was the least interesting of the films to that point. However, the new *Harry Potter and the Deathly Hallows: Part 1,* with its clotted talkiness and abundant longueurs, now supplants it.

The decision to split Rowling's final book into two movies (*Part 2* will arrive next July—in 3-D, inevitably) was perhaps understandable: There are an awful lot of plot strands to be wrapped up. But the longest of the Potter books, *Order of the Phoenix,* somehow fit into a single film. And since whole sequences of this new movie cry out for trimming, or even elimination, one wonders if *Deathly Hallows* couldn't somehow have been condensed in similar fashion. No doubt Warner Bros. is reluctant to hurry the end of this fabulously profitable franchise; but the result is that *Part 1,* after two and a half lackluster hours, comes to an abrupt and thoroughly unsatisfying halt.

The original enchantments of the *Potter* series—the kids in their spruce black boarding-school robes; the wonderfully eccentric teachers; the grand premises of Hogwarts, with its shifting staircases and multitudes of hovering candles—have pretty much fallen away here. Hogwarts itself doesn't even put in an appearance; and while we do get a herd of iconic characters from the past—among them Hagrid (Robby Coltrane), Snape (Alan Rickman), Mad-Eye Moody (Brendan Gleeson), even the now-dead Dumbledore (Michael Gambon)—most of them are doing cameo duty and are quickly hustled back offstage. The focus now is unsparingly on Harry (Daniel Radcliffe) and his loyal mates Hermione (Emma Watson) and Ron (Rupert Grint) as they flee the resurgent Lord Voldemort (Ralph Fiennes) in search of the Horcruxes that can bring about his downfall.

This is not an entirely good thing. Apart from seeming just a little old for their roles at this point (especially Grint, a burly twenty-one at the time of filming), the three leads don't really have the expressive heft (or the dialogue that would facilitate it) to hold this long movie together; and so some of the many meandering conversational scenes are sadly awkward. Worse yet, they take place in some exceedingly dull locales—there's a *lot* of mooning about in forests and tents—and you can almost feel the young actors itching to move on to the final installment of the series and bring their decade-long labors to an end.

There are some moving interludes (like Harry's visit to Godric's Hollow and the cemetery where his parents are buried) and some funny ones, too (the transformation, via Polyjuice Potion, of a group of characters into identical Harry doppelgängers is wittily staged); and there's a delicate animated sequence that is the movie's most charming adornment. Naturally there's some impressive CGI, too—particularly a mad chase through the night sky with Harry and Hagrid swooping down on their flying motorcycle into a London tunnel teeming with traffic. But the movie is generally slow and morose, and, in the end, beyond the redemption of even the snazziest technology.

Which is to say that the magic seems to have flown, at least temporarily, from this once-captivating series. David Yates, who also directed the underwhelming *Half-Blood Prince*, may bring things to a stirring conclusion with the final picture, who knows. On the basis of this one, though, longtime fans have some cause to worry. (November 2010)

Twilight

Teen Anemia

The movie version of *Twilight* is a considerable improvement over the windy bestseller on which it's based. The first half of author Stephenie Meyer's vampire romance is a heaving sea of puppy-love gush. After a couple hundred pages of plucky Bella Swan and her super-cute bloodsucker boyfriend, Edward Cullen, endlessly expressing their adoration ("His beauty lit up the kitchen," "Just give me a minute to restart my heart"), I was sure I felt a coma coming on. Fortunately, Meyer does get down to narrative action in the second half, and it's not bad, as these things go. But it's a long book, and a long slog.

To convert this woozy tale into a movie, screenwriter Melissa Rosenberg (who is more productively employed on the excellent *Dexter* TV series) wisely approached the novel with a machete, whacking out several acres of godawful lovebird jabber and moving the cool stuff—mainly a trio of vicious vampire interlopers—to the fore. This allowed the director, Catherine Hardwicke (*Thirteen*), and her editor, Nancy Richardson, to step in and give the story a desperately needed kick in its saggy pants. Unfortunately, all the snappy pacing and swooping camera movement in the world can't finesse the novel's sillier conceits; and bringing some of them into sharp focus only makes them seem a lot sillier.

The movie, like the book, has the approximate structure of a 1950s rock-a-teen B movie, the kind in which a good girl falls for the leader of a bad motorcycle gang to the horror of her family and friends, who just don't understand how *sweet* he really is. Here, the good girl is Bella (Kristen Stewart), who has moved to the rainy little town of Forks, Washington, to live with her divorced dad, Charlie (Billy Burke), the local police chief. In the cafeteria at her new high school one day, she sees a table full of weird siblings who all look like they've had their faces pounded into a flour bin. These are the Cullens, and one of them, the strange-but-yummy Edward (Robert Pattinson) is staring at Bella from beneath his gel-stiffened pompadour with a look of wild alarm. What is his *problem*?

Bella and Edward butt heads for about a minute before he starts saving her life with some very mysterious abilities; then she starts looking at him in a new way. Adding up his endearing oddities—extreme goth-guy pallor, serious hypothermia—she realizes that he's a vampire. But she doesn't care. "I'm not afraid of you," she tells him. "I'm only afraid of losing you." Before long, they're off to the woods, where they coo in the trees and nuzzle in the grass amid fat, dewy mushrooms and dreamy acoustic-guitar noodlings on the soundtrack. Edward takes Bella to his home, out in the middle of nowhere, to meet the family. His dad (Peter Facinelli) has a sort of dead-Liberace vibe, but he's real nice, and with the exception of one sister, Rosalie (Nikki Reed), who has obvious anger-management problems, the whole clan is very . . . well, warm isn't the word, but they like Bella a lot. *Her* dad isn't quite so enthusiastic, but hey—kids: what're you gonna do? He gives his okay for Edward to take Bella to the prom. They have a swell time. But then the interloping vampire trio swoops back in and tries to wreck everything. (A sequel is of course preordained.)

The phenomenal popularity of *Twilight,* the novel, is no mystery. It doesn't simply update the vampire genre for the modern teen market—Lord knows, that's been done. What it does is strip vampires of their dark erotic threat and present them as chaste, untroubling love objects for young teen girls. (Bella and Edward are supposed to be seventeen, but they don't act that way; Bella's never even had a date.) There's not a whisper of sex in the book, and none in the movie—which is problematic. Pattinson, an appealing presence in the fourth *Harry Potter* film, has been directed here to smolder in such an outlandishly sultry manner that you wonder why he never displays any carnal interest in Bella. Is he gay? (That might have been interesting, actually.) And it doesn't help that he and his vampire brothers have been so heavily caked with face powder and overloaded with hair product that they look like a troupe of mimes.

It's the pretty Stewart who holds the movie together, infusing the largely passive character of Bella with glimmers of spirit and determination. She's solidly matched by Reed (who cowrote and starred in *Thirteen*) and by Ashley Greene, who plays Edward's other sister, the clairvoyant Alice, as a cheery punkette. And I kind of wish the movie had more of Jackson Rathbone, who plays Edward's brother, Jasper, with a weird, demented intensity.

Certain elements of *Twilight* were doomed to fail on film. Vampire baseball, for instance, was already a tough sell in the novel; here, with all its leaping and zooming around, it looks like a special-ed Quidditch match. And one of Meyer's more curious inventions—vampires who don't shrivel in the sun, but sparkle instead—is a bizarre thing to behold. When Edward soaks up some rays and goes all glittery, he looks like he just stumbled home from an all-night rave.

These attempted additions to the vampire canon seem all the more lusterless in light of the many more effective genre staples that have been cast aside: no coffins, no bat transformations or crucifix panics, no silver phobia. There's a very brief dream scene in which we see Edward bent over Bella's neck and then rising up with the traditional rivulet of blood running down his chin. It's a fleeting reminder of how much dumb fun is missing from this oddly neutered neo-horror movie, and how little is being offered in its place. In *Twilight*, the only characters drained dry are the vampires themselves. (November 2008)

The Twilight Saga: New Moon

Eclipse

In *New Moon,* an unexpected character joins the *Twilight* family of nuzzly teen creatures. It's the Invisible Man. Not far into the picture, the undead Edward Cullen (Robert Pattinson) fades out of the action for a bit and is replaced by wolf boy Jacob Black (Taylor Lautner). Edward eventually returns, but he never really *comes back.* Last year's sensitive hunk, with his pasty face and mopey demeanor, is no match for this year's actual hunk; and the more vibrant Jacob—who's also madly muscular—romps off with the picture.

It's a silly picture, of course: given the series' source material—Stephenie Meyer's blathery teen novels—what else could it be? But thanks to Lautner and newly recruited director Chris Weitz, *New Moon* is a notable improvement over *Twilight.* There's not quite so much moony young-adult yearning (although Lord knows there's enough of it), and there's a little more action; and with cheery Anna Kendrick and Ashley Greene back on board, and Michael Sheen (really!) camping it up as some sort of lord of the vampires, the movie approaches the outskirts of liveliness. It never *gets* there—no surprise—and if the picture were at least fifteen minutes shorter maybe that wouldn't matter so much. In any case, fans surely won't care.

The story is once again nominally centered on Bella Swan, now eighteen and once again played by Kristen Stewart, an actress of real talent who's once again wasted in this wooden role. Bella is still hot—no, that's not the word; "warm," maybe—for Edward and wants him to turn her into a vampire, too, so they can be together for, like, ever. Edward, up to his rouged lips in gooey emotional torment, refuses to do this, and after much po-faced dithering, he informs her that he's going away and that she'll never see him again. This struck me as an excellent development, but Bella is distraught.

Enter Jacob, the young werewolf, who wastes little time in stripping off his shirt, which stays off for much of the rest of the film. In a giddy mood, Bella buys a pair of junked-out motorcycles so that she and Jacob can spend time together repairing them. Soon they're flirting, sort of, and Bella tells Jacob that she really needs him—although not in the way he might think. Whatever that might mean is unclear. She is, after all, still carrying a torch—well, maybe a lighter—for Edward, who keeps popping up in ghosty little inserts to prove that he's . . . still in the picture, so to speak.

The amusingly ashen Cullen family is also on hand again, with clairvoyant Alice (Greene) clocking the most screen time. Bella's interchangeable school friends put in occasional appearances, too, with best pal Jessica (Kendrick) bringing spurts of welcome energy to her few scenes. And lurking in the woods around the town of Forks are the outlaw vampires Laurent (Edi Gathegi) and Victoria (Rachelle Lefevre), still more interesting than most of the rest of the movie's characters, although Jacob and his werewolf clan—all similarly hunky and similarly shirtless—do have their CGI-assisted feral moments.

But then the story drags us back to Edward, who's decided to kill himself. (An odd plan for a guy who's already dead.) To do this, he has relocated to Italy to petition the Volturi—vampire royalty—to put him out of his endless friggin' misery. Bella gets word of this and flies off to Italy, too. There's much yakking in the royal court, presided over by the mincing Aro (Sheen) and attended by a fearsome bloodsucker named Jane (Dakota Fanning). Around about here, Pattinson gets to bare his own chest—a bad idea in a movie that also features Taylor Lautner—and we notice that while his face is heavily pancaked, his torso is of a normal human hue. Whatever, I suppose.

The movie ends—just stops, really—with a question. I assume it'll be answered in the next *Twilight* film, *Eclipse*. That one's due out next year. No rush. (November 2009)

The Twilight Saga: Eclipse

Vampires Wanted

Eclipse may be as good as the *Twilight* films are going to get. The main actors have settled comfortably into their roles in this third installment of the franchise: Jackson Rathbone, Nikki Reed, and Ashley Greene, the more interesting of the home-team vampires, have a welcome new prominence, and Robert Pattinson even has a scene in which he displays a twinge of character development. The movie also has some actual action—a big vampires-versus-vampires-versus-werewolves battle sequence at the end of the picture.

However, having imposed something like narrative clarity on the story, new director David Slade is still stuck with the story—which, deriving as it does from the paceless goop of Stephenie Meyer's books and having been wrestled into a script by Melissa Rosenberg, is a threadbare quilt of preteen romantic clichés padded out unconscionably with long character flashbacks and rambling dialogue that's deader than any of the vampires in attendance.

We begin where the last movie left off, with chaste young lovers Bella Swan (Kristen Stewart) and Edward Cullen (Pattinson) nuzzling in a sunlit flowery field. She's reading him poetry. He's glistening a bit, as the *Twilight* vampires ridiculously do whenever they're out and about in the daytime. He asks her to marry him. "Change me," she replies—meaning, turn her into a vampire, too. He doesn't want to do this. But we already know that, and we wish he'd just get over it and get it over *with*, because we've been through this monotonous routine before, and we know lots more of it lies ahead.

Bella's dad (Billy Burke) doesn't like her hanging out with Edward so much. Why can't she spend more time with the other kids, like that nice Jacob Black (Taylor Lautner)? Jacob, of course, as we also know, is a member of the local werewolf clan, and he's in love with Bella, too. Possibly in vain, though. "I don't feel that for you," she says. "I don't buy it," he snaps. Then he tries to kiss her, and she punches him in the face. (Given Jacob's superiority to Edward in the liveliness department, we can only assume she must be mad.)

You could count the minutes Lautner doesn't spend topless in this picture on the hands of a cartoon character. ("Doesn't he own a shirt?" says Edward, deploying one of the movie's several self-aware wisecracks.) This is an understandable strategy on the part of the filmmakers, since Lautner, a formidable physical specimen and a mildly appealing presence, does most of his acting with his abs. (True, he hasn't been given a lot to work with by the script, but who here has?)

Jacob and Edward's territorial sniping over Bella continues even after the need arises for both of their families to band together against an attack by the rogue vampire Victoria (now played by Bryce Dallas Howard) and her army of "newborns"—vampires who've only recently been turned. Here we puzzle once again at Stephenie Meyer's indifference to traditional vampire lore—to the basic characteristics that make these creatures fun. Apart from the fact that her bloodsuckers can walk around in the sunlight and have no fangs, we're now informed that newborns are the most powerful of all vampires because they still have traces of human blood running through their veins. Traditionally— logically—the most ancient vampires are the most powerful. And anyway, don't most vampires have human blood coursing through them? Isn't human blood what they *live on?* The contending vampire contingents in this movie could as easily be rival biker gangs or feuding hillbilly families with little adjustment required in the story.

This brings us once again to the sex question. There comes a scene where Bella and Edward are canoodling on a bed, and she asks him— begs him, actually—to have sex with her. But after a quick montage of button fumbling, Edward backs away. "Believe me, I want to," he says. "I just want to be married to you first." Then he says, "I'm from a different era." If I had to guess, I'd say that era was the 1950s, when cinematic sex, if it happened to rear its troublesome head, was consummated off-screen, following a tasteful fade-out. In the *Twilight* films, carnal closure isn't even implied. No one's saying that Bella and Edward should get naked, in the manner of HBO's immeasurably superior *True Blood* series. But their dinky cuddling and cooing has not even a faint erotic charge. It's like a pizza without pepperoni—all cheese.

Just as our patience with this picture is about to collapse—following mini origin stories for two of the Cullens, and a meandering campfire chat with the tribal elders of the Black clan, and a scene in a tent with Bella, Edward, and Jacob that may still be going on, for all I know—we finally get the big battle between the local vampires and werewolves and Victoria's invading army of newborns. The werewolves are meticulously animated CGI (although as usual in *Twilight* land we wonder how guys in pants can transform into pantsless wolves and then transform back again to guys in pants). But the battle itself is oddly earthbound—the two groups of antagonists simply charge across a field at each other and collide. There's lots of thrashing and gnashing and flying through the air, but what this smackdown summit of vampires and werewolves boils down to is a big street rumble.

The people behind the *Twilight* films clearly feel that fans will sit through anything that brings the books they love to the screen. I wonder how long that'll hold true, though. Could this really be as good as the series is going to get? Without ever getting good? (June 2010)

THE HOLLYWOOD VERSION

There's something particularly irritating about the phenomenon of wealthy filmmakers—actors, screenwriters, directors—presuming to deliver political instruction to the people who pay to see their pictures. Cultural conservatives are always complaining about this, and about the predictable lockstep liberalism of planet Hollywood. And no matter where you stand on the political continuum, it's hard to deny that they have a point.

Redacted

Casualty of War

What is there left to say about the Hollywood assumption that Americans are too dumb to realize that war is hell, that the war in Iraq is particularly troubling, and that only moral instruction from, well, Hollywood can bring a benighted nation to its senses? Moviegoers have already signaled their disdain. Three recent antiwar pictures that reflect the film colony's imperious self-regard—*In the Valley of Elah*, *Rendition*, and *Lions for Lambs*—have been quickly fitted with box-office body bags. Soon they'll be joined by *Redacted*, the talky, torpid, borderline-hysterical new movie by Brian De Palma.

The picture's conceptual incoherence is clear at the outset, when we're told that it was "inspired by an incident widely reported to have happened in Iraq." What can this possibly mean? The atrocity at the center of *Redacted* isn't some sort of rumor; it's a well-established fact. In March of 2006, in a village south of Baghdad, five U.S. Army soldiers broke into the home of an Iraqi family; some of them murdered the mother and father and their five-year-old daughter, then gang-raped their fourteen-year-old daughter, shot her in the head, and set the house afire. (The blaze was apparently an attempt to make the attack look like the work of terrorist insurgents.)

The movie's implication is that such horrors are common, but that they're covered up by the military and the craven mainstream media. This is possible, of course. But the contention is unpersuasive in this particular case, since all five of the soldiers involved were arrested and charged, and three have been tried and sentenced to 90, 100 and 110 years in prison—information the movie declines to convey. The alleged ringleader of the group, Pfc. Steven D. Green, had been discharged from the U.S. Army before the crime was reported by another soldier three months after it happened. Green is now scheduled to be tried in a federal court in Kentucky, and prosecutors are reportedly seeking the death penalty. Green is a high school dropout with a record of drug and alcohol problems that was disregarded by the army when he enlisted; he had already been identified as having "homicidal ideations" while serving in Iraq, and he was discharged after sixteen months because of an "antisocial personality disorder." The army's alarmingly lax recruiting standards are an important issue, but De Palma—convinced that it's the unjust war itself that turns young soldiers into monsters, not the problems they bring with them into the service—doesn't address it.

The director is a skilled filmmaker who seems to have fallen on hard times. His last big hit was the 1996 *Mission: Impossible*; his previous movie, *The Black Dahlia*, an L.A. period piece shot mainly in Bulgaria, bombed. This picture was commissioned by HDNet chief Mark Cuban, who wondered if the director would be interested in shooting on video. He was. All kinds of video, actually: *Redacted* is a mosaic of faux footage harvested from the film's ubiquitous GI vidcams and blogs, terrorist and antiwar websites, military surveillance cameras, even a French TV documentary (also faux, of course).

Unfortunately, this jumble of wandering narrative focus and flat visual tones leaves De Palma—a man who knows where to put a real movie camera and how to move it around—in a creative straitjacket for much of the picture. There are some startling bursts of action (and the tightly edited rape scene is appalling without being exploitative), but they're enclosed by static stretches of aimless barracks japery, drinking, and card-playing, especially in the film's first half. Tedium sets in quickly. And the necessity to tell the story through supposedly "found" footage leads to some awkward improbabilities. When we see one of the soldiers warning another not to breathe a word to anyone about the murders, we wonder why he's chosen to impart this admonition while standing in front of a surveillance camera.

The little-known actors here are competent, but they're used mainly to embody war movie clichés: one character is quiet and bookish, another smart and personable, another an amiable jester. The two really bad guys are cartoons, one of them a standard-issue brutal slob, the other—the Green character—a nasty drunk. (We know he's extra-rotten because at one point we see him sprawled on a chair that's draped with a Confederate flag—in the terms of Hollywood iconography, he may as well have the Number of the Beast tattooed on his forehead.)

De Palma's use of an abominable crime as a signifier of U.S. conduct in Iraq is a gross insult to American soldiers who've never done such things—which is to say, the overwhelming majority of them. But the director thinks he's courageously lobbing a truth grenade into the cultural conflict over the Iraq War, and no doubt he's hoping that any attendant controversy will help sell tickets. Recently, he's been trumpeting his own victimization by the great media-military war machine: because the movie's distributor insisted on masking the faces in a collage of real-life bloody bodies at the end of the film, De Palma claims that his own movie has been "redacted." It seems not to have occurred to him that the families of those dead people might resent his use of their identifiable corpses to score a facile political point.

"People will be arguing over this film," De Palma said, hopefully, in an interview with Sky News last spring. Maybe they will. First they'll have to want to sit through it, though. (November 2007)

Green Zone

The Bourne Insufficiency

It's only been seven years since the United States led a multinational invasion of Iraq that deposed the dictator Saddam Hussein but then failed to find the weapons of mass destruction that (among other things) had prompted our visit. It was a period rich in intrigue and contending characters—the Western intelligence hotshots, the Republican Guards and Ba'ath loyalists, the scheming weasels like Ahmed Chalabi. Who could forget?

Well, anyone could. And so *Green Zone*, the new movie by director Paul Greengrass, may be hard for some viewers to digest. Because not only does the picture restir that chunky political stew; it thickens it with fiction. And Greengrass, who forged a powerful action style out of handheld camera work in the second and third *Bourne* movies (among other films), here goes totally over to the shaky-cam side. There's not one stable shot in the whole movie—even a scene with two guys talking at a table is filmed as if there were a riot going on. So, what with all the whip pans and night blurs and general visual chaos, it can be difficult, even if you remember the real-life players, to work out who the elusive General Al Rawi is supposed to be; or the Pentagon spookmaster who's so chummy with that *Wall Street Journal* reporter; or the money-funneling CIA agent, who turns out to be—in a Hollywood movie!—one of the good guys.

Films that undertake to deal with America's Middle East incursions—*Rendition, Redacted, Lions for Lambs, In the Valley of Elah*—have a dismal box-office history; even the Oscar-winning *Hurt Locker* hasn't sold a lot of tickets. So this picture, which reunites Greengrass with *Bourne* star Matt Damon, is being hopefully marketed as a straight-on action pic—*Bourne 4*. Which, believe me, it isn't.

Damon plays Chief Warrant Officer Roy Miller, leader of an army team that's scouring Baghdad for those stashes of WMD—and coming up empty-handed. Miller is beginning to suspect that the intelligence fueling this search is wrong, maybe fabricated. Pentagon fixer Clark Poundstone (Greg Kinnear, in full sleaze) suggests that he shut up. But CIA station head Martin Brown (Brendan Gleeson, indelibly Irish) knows Miller is on to something. On the other hand, *Journal* reporter Lawrie Dayne (Amy Ryan) remains convinced the intel is genuine, because she knows its provenance—a super-secret source with the code name Magellan, to whose debriefings she has conveniently been made privy.

Here the movie elbows us with its political bent. Dayne is clearly meant to represent Judith Miller, the reporter who actually was snookered into promoting the WMD story line in her internationally influential newspaper. But Miller didn't file (or cofile) her anonymously sourced reports for *The Wall Street Journal.* The paper she wrote for was *The New York Times,* which was ultimately compelled to express regret for publishing several dispatches on which she had worked. It's also a little odd that the most vicious character in the movie is a U.S. Special Forces officer named Briggs (Jason Isaacs with a bandido mustache), while the fugitive Al Rawi (Igal Naor), the man who holds the key to the WMD puzzle, is considerably more sympathetic—even though, as one of Saddam's top generals, he was presumably complicit in the yearslong regime of torture, rape, and mass murder that the dictator inflicted on his own people.

But the political underpinnings of the Iraq War are murky enough to accommodate any number of interpretations. What sinks *Green Zone*—which was "inspired by" a book by former *Washington Post* Baghdad bureau chief Rajiv Chandrasekaran—is its insufficiency as a moviegoing experience. It's an action movie if it's anything (who would thrill to its rehash of recent history?), but it's an action movie with no sense of adventure. The *Bourne* pictures swept us off to places like Paris, Berlin, Madrid, and Goa; they also had romantic interest. This film, unavoidably, is confined to the dusty rubble of Baghdad (re-created largely in Morocco); and Dayne, its lone female character, is a cold emotional cipher. Damon is as hardy a presence as always, and the other main actors are equally okay (especially Khalid Abdalla as a conflicted Iraqi called Freddy). But the story feels tired, and we can see why the movie's release was delayed for so long. It may soldier on to DVD more quickly than expected. (March 2010)

The Day After Tomorrow

We're All Gonna Die

The Day After Tomorrow, director Roland Emmerich's new global-warming disaster tutorial, is crammed with the sort of head-slamming special effects that could only be improved upon by taking all the money it cost to create them and handing it out at the door.

There's a cleverly conceived wolf-pack chase sequence the likes of which I don't believe I've seen before.

There are impressive digitized close-ups of a vast Antarctic ice shelf cracking off into the sea.

There are hailstones the size of bocce balls pelting down on Tokyo, and monster waves swelling up out of the sea and engulfing the Statue of Liberty. Oh, and the Sydney Opera House, too. (This is a disaster movie in which the disaster really gets around.)

There are tornadoes prowling Los Angeles like great, howling predators, sucking up the Hollywood sign whole, and then, in a body blow to the already ailing music industry, ripping apart the iconic Capitol Records building. There are also enormous floods and hurricanes, and all sorts of motorized transport hurtling through the air. In one crowd-pleasing moment, a yammering TV newsman gets flattened by flying debris.

You set your brain on idle and settle in to let all this computerized chaos wash over you, and then you notice something. Something unbelievable. It's the plot. This is the plot:

Global warming is melting the polar ice caps. This in turn is screwing up the Gulf Stream, which in turn is affecting the icy stratosphere way up above us, sucking it down into the balmier troposphere in which we humans have long whiled away our days, ignoring the fevered exhortations of environmental zealots to trade in our SUVs for Rollerblades and start heating our homes with aromatherapy candles in order to avoid the climatological calamity that is—oops—now upon us.

Bad things begin to happen very quickly. Temperatures start dropping ten degrees every second. Endless snow piles up into drifts hundreds of feet deep. Cities flood and abandoned ships drift through canals that once were streets. People die by the millions. In just days, a new ice age has begun. Very worrisome!

Among those doing the worrying are paleo-climatologist Jack Hall (Dennis Quaid), who early on strives to convince the government that something really, really awful is about to happen. Unfortunately, he has to make this case to the president of the United States—a clueless boob—and his hard-nosed vice president, who has shadowy agendas of his own, none of which would likely involve trading in an SUV.

It's transparently clear whom these two characters are meant to represent; the VP even bears a passing resemblance to Dick Cheney. But the president, for some odd reason, looks for all the world, not like George W. Bush but like Al Gore. Either this casting choice represents some sort of political wish fulfillment for the director or it's an odd nod to Al, who has now joined the leftist agitation group MoveOn in proclaiming the release of *The Day After Tomorrow* an excellent opportunity for people like themselves to "raise consciousness" about things like this that haven't happened yet. Either way, it's sort of strange.

But back to Jack. He has a seventeen-year-old son, Sam (Jake Gyllenhaal), who's visiting New York with some friends. When the weather starts getting scary, Jack swears to Sam, by phone, that he'll come to Manhattan to get him and bring him back home. New York is about two hundred miles from Washington, D.C., and, as you might think would be made clear by looking out the window, the East Coast is being buried by the worst snowstorm in . . . well, a couple thousand years, maybe.

But Jack is unfazed. He and two hardy colleagues set off in what one hopes is a seriously all-terrain vehicle. For shelter in the midst of this subzero weather riot, they bring along a smallish yellow tent, which we're asked to believe does the trick. Their ride dies about forty miles outside of New York. Although the apocalyptic onslaught of snow and slashing wind is, if anything, even more brutal than when he started out, Jack decides to walk the rest of the way. In what seems a curiously short time, he arrives in Manhattan. All of this, if it need be said, is hilariously implausible.

Meanwhile, in the grand, now-unthronged halls of the New York Public Library, where they've taken refuge from the fast-rising flood waters, Sam and his friends have been having implausible adventures of their own. To keep warm, they've been burning rare books. The room they're huddled in is a large, wood-paneled space filled with tables and chairs and other things that would burn longer and give off more heat, but . . . they're burning books. Earlier, we've been told that these are ultra-bright students. Clearly.

More stuff happens. One of the students has developed a septic infection in a leg wound sustained earlier, and Sam leads a few of his friends out into the icy urban ruin in what would seem an unpromising search for penicillin. Luckily, a crewless Russian freighter that drifted in from the harbor has gone aground in front of the library, and the intrepid little band scrambles aboard. They find the ship's infirmary stocked with medications, but all the pill bottles are of course labeled in Russian. Except for one. One is labeled "penicillin." How fortunate.

None of this would matter much if *The Day After Tomorrow* were a standard-issue disaster movie. But it's not. The conceit of the film is that it's a message movie. But given the hooting improbabilities of the end-of-the-world plot, one can't help but wonder about the science that's said to underpin the message.

Serious people can disagree about the extent and the importance of global warming. Scientists certainly do. And some of them have already weighed in on *The Day After Tomorrow*. In *USA Today*, Patrick J. Michaels, a research professor of environmental sciences at the University of Virginia, said of the film's various meteorological catastrophes, "Each one of these phenomena is physically impossible." The stratosphere will change places with the troposphere, Michaels said, "when all three laws of thermodynamics are repealed." He also pointed out that according to MIT oceanographer Carl Wunsch, in a letter published in the April 8 issue of *Nature* magazine, the only way to create the sort of Gulf Stream collapse fantasized in the film would be "either to turn off the wind system, or to stop the Earth's rotation, or both." According to Wunsch, Michaels says, the chance of such an occurrence happening "any time soon—within tens of millions of years—has a probability of little more than zero."

Engaged laymen have been equally derisive. Gregg Easterbrook, a senior editor at *The New Republic,* and a man who takes global warming seriously, earlier this month described the doomsday scenario presented in *The Day After Tomorrow* as "preposterous" and derided the movie's "imbecile-caliber 'science.'"

And where did this "science" come from? Well, it's worth noting that *The Day After Tomorrow* was "suggested in part" by a book called *The Coming Global Superstorm,* by Art Bell and Whitley Strieber. Art Bell is a UFO buff who hosts a syndicated radio show devoted to the paranormal. Whitley Strieber is the author of a best-selling 1987 book about his many encounters with space aliens. The title of the book is *Communion.* Its subtitle: *A True Story.* (May 2004)

Sicko

Heavily Doctored

Michael Moore may see himself as working in the tradition of such left-wing muckrakers of the last century as Lincoln Steffens and Upton Sinclair—crusaders against political and corporate corruption, the proverbial men who made a difference. In his new movie, *Sicko,* Moore focuses on the U.S. health-care industry—a juicy target—and he casts a harsh light on some of its failures.

There's a man who mangled two of his fingers with a power saw and learned that it would cost $12,000 to save one of them, but $60,000 to save the other. He had no health insurance and could only scrape together enough money to salvage the $12,000 finger.

There's a woman whose husband was prescribed new drugs to combat his cancer but couldn't get their insurance company to pay for them because the drugs were experimental. Her husband died.

Then there's a woman who made an emergency trip to a hospital for treatment and subsequently learned her insurance company wouldn't pay for the ambulance that took her there—because it hadn't been "pre-approved." And there's a middle-aged couple—a man, who suffered three heart attacks, and his wife, who developed cancer—who were bankrupted by the cost of copayments and other expenses not covered by their insurance and have now been forced to move into a cramped room in the home of their resentful son. There's also a seventy-nine-year-old man who has to continue working a menial job because Medicare won't cover the cost of all the medications he needs.

Moore does a real service in bringing these stories to light—some of them are horrifying, and then infuriating. One giant health-maintenance organization, Kaiser Permanente, is so persuasively lambasted in the movie that, on the basis of what we're told, we want to burst into the company's executive suites and make a mass citizen's arrest. This is the sort of thing good muckrakers are supposed to do.

Unfortunately, Moore is also a con man of a very brazen sort, and never more so than in this film. His cherry-picked facts, manipulative interviews (with lingering close-ups of distraught people breaking down in tears), and blithe assertions (how does he know eighteen thousand people will die this year because they have no health insurance?) are so stacked that you can feel his whole argument listing to the left as the picture unspools. The American health-care system is surely in need of reform. Some 47 million people are said to be uninsured (although many are only temporarily so, being either in between jobs or young enough not to feel a pressing need for health insurance). There are a number of proposals as to what might be done to correct this situation. Moore has no use for any of them, save one.

As a proud socialist, the director appears to feel that there are few problems in life that can't be solved by government regulation. (That would be the same government that's already given us the U.S. Postal Service and the Department of Motor Vehicles.) In the case of health care, though, Americans have never been keen on socialized medicine. In 1993, when one of Moore's heroes, Hillary Clinton (he actually blurts out the term "sexy!" in describing her in the movie), tried to create a government-controlled health-care system, her failed attempt to do so helped deliver the U.S. Senate and House of Representatives into Republican control for the next dozen years. Moore still looks upon Clinton's plan as a grand idea, one that Americans, being not very bright, unwisely rejected. (He may be having second thoughts about Hillary herself, though: In the movie he heavily emphasizes the fact that, among politicians, she accepts the second-largest amount of political money from the health-care industry.)

The problem with American health care, Moore argues, is that people are charged money to avail themselves of it. In other countries, like Canada, France, and Britain, health systems are far superior—and they're free. He takes us to these countries to see a few clean, efficient hospitals, where treatment is quick and caring; and to meet a few doctors who are delighted with their government-regulated salaries; and to listen to patients express a beaming happiness with their socialized health system. It sounds great. As one patient in a British hospital run by the country's National Health Service says, "No one pays. It's all on the NHS. It's not America."

That last statement is even truer than you'd know from watching *Sicko*. In the case of Canada—which Moore, like many other political activists, holds up as a utopian ideal of benevolent health-care regulation—a very different picture is conveyed by a short 2005 documentary called *Dead Meat*, by Stuart Browning and Blaine Greenberg. These two filmmakers talked to a number of Canadians of a kind that Moore's movie would have you believe don't exist:

A fifty-two-year-old woman in Calgary recalls being in severe need of joint-replacement surgery after the cartilage in her knee wore out. She was put on a wait list and wound up waiting sixteen months for the surgery. Her pain was so excruciating, she says, that she was prescribed large doses of Oxycontin and soon became addicted. After finally getting her operation, she was put on another wait list—this time for drug rehab.

A man tells about his mother waiting two years for life-saving cancer surgery—and then twice having her surgical appointments canceled. She was still waiting when she died.

A man in critical need of neck surgery plays a voice mail message from a doctor he'd contacted: "As of today," the message says, "it's a two-year wait list to see me for an initial consultation." Later, when the man and his wife both needed hip-replacement surgery and grew exasperated after spending two years on a waiting list, they finally mortgaged their home and flew to Belgium to have the operations done there, with no more waiting.

Rick Baker, the owner of a Toronto company called Timely Medical Alternatives, specializes in transporting Canadians who don't want to wait for medical care to Buffalo, New York, two hours away, where they don't have to. Baker's business is apparently thriving.

And Dr. Brian Day, now the president of the Canadian Medical Association, talks about the bizarre distortions created by a law that prohibits Canadians from paying for even urgently needed medical treatments, or from buying private health insurance. "It's legal to buy health insurance for your pets," Day says, "but illegal to buy health insurance for yourself." (Even more pointedly, Day was quoted in *The Wall Street Journal* this week as saying, "This is a country in which dogs can get a hip replacement in under a week and in which humans can wait two to three years.")

Actually, this aspect of the Canadian health-care system is changing. In 2005, the Canadian Supreme Court ruled in favor of a man who had filed suit in Quebec over being kept on an interminable waiting list for treatment. In striking down the government health-care monopoly in that province, Chief Justice Beverley McLachlin said, "Access to a waiting list is not access to health care." Now a similar suit has been filed in Ontario.

What's the problem with government health systems? Moore's movie doesn't ask that question, although it does unintentionally provide an answer. When governments attempt to regulate the balance between a limited supply of health care and an unlimited demand for it they're inevitably forced to ration treatment. This is certainly the situation in

Britain. Writing in the *Chicago Tribune* this week, Helen Evans, a twenty-year veteran of the country's National Health Service and now the director of a London-based group called Nurses for Reform, said that nearly 1 million Britons are currently on waiting lists for medical care—and another 200,000 are waiting to get *on* waiting lists. Evans also says the NHS cancels about 100,000 operations each year because of shortages of various sorts. Last March, the BBC reported on the results of a Healthcare Commission poll of 128,000 NHS workers: two-thirds of them said they "would not be happy" to be patients in their own hospitals. James Christopher, the film critic of *The Times* of London, thinks he knows why. After marveling at Moore's rosy view of the British health-care system in *Sicko*, Christopher wrote, "What he hasn't done is lie in a corridor all night at the Royal Free [Hospital] watching his severed toe disintegrate in a plastic cup of melted ice. I have." Last month, the Associated Press reported that Gordon Brown—just installed this week as Britain's new prime minister—had promised to inaugurate "sweeping domestic reforms" to, among other things, "improve health care."

Moore's most ardent enthusiasm is reserved for the French health-care system, which he portrays as the crowning glory of a Gallic lifestyle far superior to our own. The French! They work only thirty-five hours a week, by law. They get at least five weeks' vacation every year. Their health care is free, and they can take an unlimited number of sick days. It is here that Moore shoots himself in the foot. He introduces us to a young man who's reached the end of three months of paid sick leave and is asked by his doctor if he feels ready to return to work. No, not yet, he says. So the doctor prescribes him another three months of paid leave—and the young man immediately decamps for the South of France, where we see him lounging on the sunny Riviera, chatting up babes and generally enjoying what would be for most people a very expensive vacation. Moore apparently expects us to witness this dumbfounding spectacle and ask why we can't have such a great health-care system, too. I think a more common response would be, how can any country afford such economic insanity?

As it turns out, France can't. In 2004, French health minister Philippe Douste-Blazy told a government commission, "Our health system has gone mad. Profound reforms are urgent." Agence France-Presse recently reported that the French health-care system is running a deficit of $2.7 billion. And in the French presidential election in May, voters in surprising numbers rejected the Socialist candidate, Ségolène Royal, who had promised actually to raise some health benefits, and elected instead the center-right politician Nicolas Sarkozy, who, according to Agence France-Presse again, "plans to move fast to overhaul the economy, with the deficit-ridden health care system a primary target." Possibly Sarkozy should first consult with Michael Moore. After all, the tax-fueled French health-care system may be expensive, but at least it's "free."

Having driven his bring-on-government-health-care argument into a ditch outside of Paris, Moore next pilots it right off a cliff and into the Caribbean during the final stop on his tour: Cuba. Here it must also be said that the director performs a tangible service. He rounds up a group of 9/11 rescue workers—firefighters and selfless volunteers—who risked their lives and ruined their health in the aftermath of the New York terrorist attacks. These people—there's no other way of putting it—have been screwed, mainly by the politicians who were at such photo-op pains to praise them at the time. (This makes Moore's faith in government medical compassion seem all the more puzzling.) Their lives have been devastated—wracked by chronic illnesses, some can no longer hold down jobs and none can afford to buy the various expensive medicines they need. Moore should be thanked for bringing their plight before a large audience.

However, there's never a moment when we doubt that he's also using these people as props in his film, and as talking points in his agenda. Renting some boats, he leads them all off to Cuba. Upon arrival they stop briefly outside the American military enclave on Guantánamo Bay so that Moore can have himself filmed begging, through a bullhorn, for some of the free, top-notch medical care that's currently being lavished on the detainees there. Having no luck, he then moves on to Castro land.

Fidel Castro's island dictatorship, now in its fortieth year of being listed as a human-rights violator by Amnesty International, is here depicted as a balmy paradise not unlike the Iraq of Saddam Hussein that Moore showed us in his earlier film, *Fahrenheit 9/11*. He and his charges make their way—their prearranged way, if it need be said—to a state-of-the-art hospital where they receive a photogenically warm welcome. In a voice-over, Moore, shown beaming at his little band of visitors, says he told the Cuban doctors to "give them the same care they'd give Cuban citizens." Then he adds, dramatically: "And they did."

If Moore really believes this, he may be a greater fool than even his most feverish detractors claim him to be. Nevertheless, medical care *is* provided to the visiting Americans, and it is indeed excellent. Cuba is in fact the site of some fine medical facilities (surprising in a country that, as Ricardo Alonso-Zaldivar noted in the *Los Angeles Times* last month, "imprisoned a doctor in the late 1990s for speaking out against government failure to respond to an epidemic of a mosquito-borne virus"). What Moore doesn't mention is the flourishing Cuban industry of "health tourism"—a system in which foreigners (including multimillionaire film directors and, of course, government bigwigs) who are willing to pay non-Cuban cash for anything from brain surgery to dental work can purchase a level of treatment that's unavailable to the majority of Cubans with no hard currency at their disposal. The Cuban American National Foundation (admittedly a group with no love for the Castro regime) calls this "medical apartheid." And in a 2004 article in Canada's *National Post*, writer Isabel Vincent quoted a dissident Cuban neurosurgeon, Doctor Hilda Molina, as saying, "Cubans should be treated the same as foreigners. Cubans have less rights in their own country than foreigners who visit here."

As the Caribbean sun sank down on Moore's breathtakingly meretricious movie, I couldn't help recalling that when Fidel Castro became gravely ill last year, he didn't put himself in the hands of a Cuban surgeon. No. Instead, he had a specialist flown in—from Spain. (June 2007)

Capitalism: A Love Story

Money Jungle

In his new movie, *Capitalism: A Love Story*, Michael Moore casts a fiery eye at the U.S. financial system—a rich and appalling subject at the moment—and comes, alas, to the usual loopy conclusion: hateful capitalism is dead; time now for government to step in and take charge. This mad idea has worked out so badly so many times in the past (has it not been just twenty years since Soviet communism collapsed?) that one is always baffled to see it exhumed as a cutting-edge nostrum. So I'm not a Mike fan.

And yet there's a section of this picture, very well edited and fueled by raw fury, that made me want to rise up and cheer. Or rise up and throw stuff, actually. It's the section in which Moore focuses on the current economic collapse—the heedless Wall Street financial machinations, the unconscionable corporate bailouts, the rampant political scumbaggery. Naturally, George W. Bush, the man who unleashed the flood of taxpayer money into the hands of incompetent finance weasels, takes some well-deserved lumps here (to the predictable accompaniment of out-of-context file footage showing him doing silly things). But then, to his credit, Moore trains his guns on the other side of the political aisle and starts whaling on some equally deserving Democrats: the Fannie Mae–shielding Barney Frank; the Countrywide-coddling Christopher Dodd; and the egregious Timothy Geithner, brazen tax dodger and now—somehow!—secretary of the Treasury.

Moore also clearly illustrates the revolving door between the executive suites of high finance and the halls of government. The name of Goldman Sachs, the big investment banking firm, crops up *a lot* here. And while in another part of the picture the director lapses into predictable Obama adoration, here he pointedly notes that Goldman Sachs was the biggest corporate contributor to Barack Obama's presidential campaign.

This is rousing stuff. Unfortunately, it has nothing to do with the legal and financial system called capitalism. What it does have to do with is corruption. And no matter how loudly businessmen and politicians may proclaim their reverence for free markets, once corrupted, they're no longer capitalists.

The rest of the picture suffers from Moore's usual mixture of populist demagoguery and tear-jerking sentimentality. We're shown several families who are being evicted from their homes—by the same banks that are simultaneously hoovering money out of the federal treasury. Some of these scenes are heartbreaking. But they'd be more compelling if Moore let us know *why* these people are being kicked out into the street. Presumably, they couldn't make their mortgage payments. Did they yield to the lure of government-mandated easy credit and re-finance their mortgages in order to refinance their lifestyles—and then get caught short? Or were they genuinely snookered? (Moore is convinced that one of these families, the Hackers, was robbed, and he says he's hired a lawyer to get to the bottom of their case.)

Then there's the deplorable story from Wilkes-Barre, Pennsylvania, in which a private company, PA Child Care LLC, was hired to run a pair of juvenile-detention facilities and kept them filled by paying more than $2 million to two local judges, who obligingly remanded hundreds of kids—many found guilty, without benefit of lawyers, of the most piddling offenses—into extended custody. But again, this has nothing to do with capitalism. The judges and the company were flagrantly corrupt; both judges have been removed from the bench and are now facing a sizable if not sufficient number of years in jail.

There's lots more, some of it riveting, some of it bordering on vaudeville. Moore once again labors to hold the movie's sprawling elements together with his familiar lovable-schlub persona—part homespun Marxist, part wisecracking provincial—and the look of sly mock baf-flement on his face as first a Wall Street executive and then a Harvard professor try (and fail) to explain the mystery of derivatives is one of the more entertaining episodes in the film.

Moore has taken a lot of stick in the media following the New York premiere of his movie last week, and no wonder—one needed hip boots to wade through all the hypocrisy on display. The premiere was held, first of all, at Lincoln Center, the uptown high-culture temple, every square foot of which appears to have its own corporate sponsor. (There's even a Bank of New York Box Office.) Outside the theater where the picture was to be shown, stylishly attired people milled around the Morgan Stanley lobby sipping champagne and murmuring about the length of the lines in which they were being obliged to stand for their free VIP tickets. The premiere was sponsored by *Esquire*, one of the many bibles of yearning upward mobility, and the magazine also threw the after-party, which was held in an ultra-luxe SoHo penthouse stocked with free drinks, tasty high-end tidbits, and apparently even a hot tub equipped with cute rent-a-babes. (I'm afraid I missed the afterparty. Well, skipped it.)

Moore dismisses critical carping about this sort of thing by claiming it's just an unavoidable shoal in the sea of irony he's forced to navigate for professional purposes. I don't know who he thinks he's kidding. Actually, he's kidding himself. Consider: hardworking filmmaker delivers new movie to a studio for distribution; deals are struck, promotion is planned. No one is coerced, no one is cheated—it's a textbook demonstration of voluntary economic behavior. Can Moore really not recognize what's going on here? Can he somehow not see? It's capitalism. The real thing. (October 2009)

REAL DEALS

The fundamental requirement of movies is that they move, and the earliest motion pictures did little more than that. The Lumière brothers' first films, made in 1895 and running less than a minute in length, showed factory workers walking, two blacksmiths laboring at a forge, three men and a horse standing in a field. Robert Flaherty opened up this documentary form with his groundbreaking 1922 film, Nanook of the North. Flaherty documented the harsh life of an Inuit family in the Canadian Arctic, but he also imposed a narrative structure on his footage (and staged some scenes, too). On such muddied waters was the feature-length documentary launched. Nobody expects totally unbiased reportage from nonfiction films anymore, of course (or from the evening news, for that matter). But documentaries with a point of view can be every bit as instructive as those pretending to an impossible objectivity, and are usually a lot more entertaining. And so today's documentary scene is one of the most fertile of filmmaking arenas, a place of happily proliferating styles and techniques, boundlessly free in the range of its concerns.

Exit Through the Gift Shop

Art Damage

In his lengthy career as an international man of mystery, the English street artist who calls himself Banksy has evolved from a teenage spray-bomb guerrilla in his hometown of Bristol in the early 1990s to a worldwide art presence whose arresting works—stencils, silk screens, and sculptural provocations—are auctioned off at places like Sotheby's for prices sometimes in excess of half a million dollars. He never shows his face, but he seems to be always *in* our face, installing his hit-and-run pieces in locations as far afield as Israel, Australia, even Disneyland. Some of his works have graced the hallowed walls of the Louvre in Paris and the Tate Britain gallery in London—but only because he snuck in and hung them there himself. And who could forget his salting of U.K. record stores with reconfigured copies of a 2006 Paris Hilton album—the dead-on-arrival *Paris*—with such newly added tracks as "Why Am I Famous?" and "What Am I For?" (The CD inside, all-instrumental, was recorded by Danger Mouse.)

Banksy is both a penetrating conceptual artist and a serious-minded joker, and with the release of his wild new documentary, *Exit Through the Gift Shop*, you have to wonder how much longer he can remain an art-world phantom.

The film has a unique structure. It started out as a project by Thierry Guetta, a peculiar Frenchman living in Los Angeles, where he ran a vintage-clothing shop selling shamelessly overpriced apparel to the sort of well-to-do hipsters who were happy to pay for it. This, we later realize, was useful preparation for his subsequent art-world adventures.

Guetta was also an obsessive videographer, training a cheap mini-cam on virtually everything in sight, from the contents of his fridge to—more tellingly—his own face as reflected in mirrors. On a trip to Paris, he was introduced to the world of street art by his cousin, an eminence in the scene known as Invader. Soon, Invader was taking Guetta along to shoot low-rez footage of him and other street artists in action. Returning home to L.A., Guetta connected with the well-known street-art entrepreneur Shepard Fairey (the man who created the famous "Hope" poster for the Obama presidential campaign). Before long, the little documentarian had infiltrated the L.A. street-art scene, his pain-in-the-ass qualities outweighed by his usefulness as a lookout and willingness to do risky things in order to document the artists' nocturnal sorties.

In 2006, Banksy quietly arrived in Los Angeles to mount a warehouse exhibition called Barely Legal. In need of an assistant, he contacted Fairey, who recommended Guetta—who couldn't believe his luck. The exhibition was extravagantly successful—thirty thousand people turned out, among them Jude Law, Christina Aguilera, and Brad Pitt and Angelina Jolie, who purchased some pieces. Guetta, having gone deep into hock to pursue his filming activities, was inspired by the amounts of money being made by an artist other than himself. Soon he persuaded Banksy to become the focus of the long-fermenting documentary he kept yammering about. Banksy agreed, as long as he was shot from behind and only his hands were ever shown. "Maybe I needed to trust somebody," the artist says, in rueful retrospect.

In fact, Banksy says quite a bit in this film. His voice—actually the voice of actor Rhys Ifans—is electronically obscured, and his face hidden in deep shadow; but his mordant observations set the tone for the whole strange story being told.

After eight years of obsessive shooting and editing, Guetta finally brought a rough cut of his documentary to England for Banksy's evaluation. The film was an incoherent mess. "It was at that point," Banksy says, "that I realized Thierry was not a filmmaker, and maybe he was just someone with a mental problem with a camera." The art star told his acolyte to forget filmmaking and return to L.A. and start doing his own art. As for his dismal footage, Banksy would hold on to that. *Exit Through the Gift Shop* is the result of this inspired switcheroo. What started out as a documentary about an artist and a scene has been turned into a documentary about the oddball filmmaker—and about the evergreen gullibility of the art world itself.

On returning to Los Angeles, Guetta created his first work—an image of himself holding a camera—which he stenciled onto walls all over the city. This gave him instant cultural presence. The rest of his oeuvre—silk screens of Michael Jackson in a blond wig, a series of spray-bomb cans bearing the Campbell's soup logo—was heavily derivative of Andy Warhol, among other already heavily derivative artists. Nevertheless, Guetta—now calling himself "Mr. Brainwash"—decided to mount a huge exhibition of his work (most of it fabricated by other hands). He asked his former mentor to provide a promotional blurb, and Banksy responded with: "He's a force of nature, he's a phenomenon. And I don't mean that in a good way." Local media seized on this celebrity endorsement, however ambiguous, and very quickly turned Guetta into a star himself.

The exhibition was a near-disaster and might have collapsed entirely had Banksy not dispatched some knowledgeable colleagues to help organize it. (Contemplating Guetta's own organizational style, one assistant here says, "He's just kind of retarded.") Far from being humbled by the modest extent of his talent, Guetta began tagging his works with Banksy-level sale prices. Who, we wonder as we watch, would pay such astonishing sums for this stuff? Who would pay anything at all?

The joke, of course, is on us in the end. And the picture, thick with revealing detail and astonishing developments that pile up on each other like a succession of train wrecks, leaves us with much to ponder—not least the unstoppable Thierry Guetta. "I always used to encourage everyone to make art," Banksy says from the shadows. "I don't do that so much anymore." (April 2010)

The Nomi Song

Wild Thing

The Nomi Song, director Andrew Horn's fascinating documentary about the late New Wave singer and art object Klaus Nomi, gives off a rich whiff of the New York punk bohemia of the late 1970s and early 1980s. There it all is: the skinny ties, the spazzy New Wave dancing, the packed little tables at Max's Kansas City. There's the bar at CBGB, with Talking Heads bassist Tina Weymouth and Blondie's Chris Stein and Debbie Harry all high and happy in some long-ago late-night revel. And then—it's still a jolt—there's Klaus Nomi, with his piercing falsetto, his warbly junk-pop arias, and his brittle Martian-kabuki persona, floating forth through thick billows of stage fog as strobe lights erupt all around him. What on earth, you still wonder, after all these years, is *that*?

The movie doesn't answer this question. There doesn't seem to be an answer. "Klaus Nomi" was an entirely artificial construct put together by a lonely young German named Klaus Sperber. When it was complete, Sperber disappeared into it and never again emerged.

What *The Nomi Song* does provide is the pungent recollections of old colleagues, like the photographer Michael Halsband. ("People thought he was from another planet. *He* thought he was from another planet.") And there's the vivid context of rare club footage, some of it pried out of personal archives. The portrait the film pieces together is of a man isolated within the hollow shell of trendy "avant-garde" fame, and so lonely he's reduced to prowling the Hudson River piers in search of sexual connection. (Klaus Nomi made the cover of Japanese *Vogue* while Klaus Sperber was servicing truck drivers in West Side parking lots.)

He had hoped for much more. He was a true, if untrained,

countertenor—the upper range of his voice could hit your ears like an ice pick, but it could also be quite beautiful. He'd grown up enthralled by opera singers, especially the celebrated Maria Callas, and back in Berlin he would offer up a cappella tributes to the great diva in local gay bars. In the mid-1970s, he moved to New York, and there worked the traditional assortment of lowly jobs while waiting for his time to come. Surprisingly, it did, sort of.

Klaus Nomi made his first significant New York club appearance, slotted in among a cast of kooky musicians, good-natured strippers, and other downtown cutups, in a "New Wave Vaudeville Show" mounted by the singer and actress Ann Magnuson. Eventually he acquired a backup band and astounded audiences wherever he appeared with his unwinking mixture of classical arias by Saint-Saëns and Purcell and less exalted works by the likes of Donna Summer, Chubby Checker, and Lou Christie. (His keening rendition of "Lightning Strikes" might have been his greatest hit, had he ever had one.) But with his pop-eyed stare and black-lipped pout and a wardrobe that ran to vinyl capes and ironic tuxedos with huge, mesalike shoulders, Nomi had to seem like a one-note joke to most people—the ultimate novelty act.

Novel he certainly was, but not entirely extraterrestrial. His lipsticked-robot demeanor owed much to the German synth band Kraftwerk (and to *Cabaret*); and of course David Bowie had softened up the pop market for alien androgyny years before. In fact, at the end of 1979, Nomi got a call from Bowie, who'd been booked to play *Saturday Night Live*. He wanted Nomi to appear with him and sing backup on three songs. Here it was: the big time. Bowie, looking to reclaim the cutting edge he had dulled during his soul-pop years, wore a dress. Nomi came as he was. The show was a sensation, and Bowie said he'd stay in touch. As a Nomi associate says in the film, though, "We never heard from him again."

The brief Bowie association didn't do as much for Nomi as he'd hoped. He finally scored a record deal, but it was with the French division of RCA. (His only two studio albums were released in 1982.) And he was still compelled to do rent-paying gigs. (Opening up for Twisted Sister at a concert in New Jersey was an especially dismal one.) Meanwhile,

his health was failing: His voice was losing its power, and he was growing strangely weak. He was in the hospital developing skin lesions when
he heard the news about a new "gay cancer" that was both incurable and
fatal. The disease was so new, and so terrifying, that most of his friends
were afraid to go see him one last time. They never said good-bye.

"The party was over," says painter Kenny Scharf, looking back on
those last, pre-AIDS days of freewheeling gay sex. Klaus Nomi was the
first semi-well-known figure on the New York scene to make that terrible exit. Really famous, like really happy, was something he never got
to be. (February 2005)

Tyson

Iron Man

Picture a professional boxer punching you in the head. Pretend you
survive. Now picture the same guy continuing to punch you in the
head for the next twenty years.

From 1985, when he won his first pro bout with a first-round knockout, to 2005, when he suddenly quit the fight business midway through
a humiliating beat-down by opponent Kevin McBride, Mike Tyson absorbed that sort of punishment on a continual basis. You can see the result in *Tyson*, a stunning new documentary by director James Toback.
The former heavyweight champ, now forty-two, fills the screen, adrift in
amiable confusion ("I met the president of Chechnya, I met the president
of Istanbul") and veering off into private worlds where he hears voices
he can't quiet. Now, looking back over his outlandish career, he says,
"Everything was totally cryptic to me."

What makes the picture so enthralling are the moments when Tyson's interior fog clears and he enters a state of unexpected clarity and
insight, revealing a rough poetic soul. ("Money is like paper blood," he

says, in his surprisingly high-pitched, lisping voice. "You need it to live.") As Toback observed after an early screening of this film a few months back, "He has these different selves, in a sort of Whitmanesque sense— he contains multitudes."

They're all on display here, sometimes all at once; because Toback, working with the editor Aaron Yanes, has created a new documentary form. Apart from the archival fight footage of "Iron Mike" destroying one contender after another, the picture is constructed entirely from thirty hours of interviews the director conducted with Tyson over the course of a week and then cooked down, over the course of a year, into a ninety-minute film. Toback turns this static footage into a thrilling experience by crowding the screen with multiple panels of interview segments, weaving sound and image together to create a sense of Tyson talking among his selves. It's a dazzling effect.

The ex-champ has done things in his life that many people might never forgive—chief among them the rape of an eighteen-year-old black beauty queen in an Indianapolis hotel room in 1991, for which Tyson served three years in prison. He's still furious about what he insists was a wrongful conviction in that case: "I may have took advantage of a woman before," he says bitterly, "but I never took advantage of *her*." On the other hand, he's candid about his inclinations. "I want a strong woman," he says at one point, "and then I want to dominate them sexually."

An appalling childhood in one of the worst precincts of Brooklyn provides some context for his brutality. A fat kid with asthma and glasses (and that lisp), he began getting into street fights early. There were many arrests, and at the age of twelve, he took his first trip to a juvenile correctional facility, where he encountered some familiar neighborhood faces. "It was like a class reunion," he says. "I started going there on a often basis." It was in juvie that his talent for boxing was noticed, and his life began to gather meaning. At fourteen, he competed at the Junior Olympics, where he knocked out another kid in eight seconds. In 1986, at the age of twenty, he became the youngest heavyweight champion on record. Life got good, but then bad, and then much worse.

At his peak, Tyson was world famous and blindingly successful. He didn't earn millions of dollars; he earned *hundreds* of millions. But he got sloppy. He signed on with the notorious promoter Don King. ("So many leeches," Tyson says. "That was my downfall.") He got lax about training and started losing fights. There was an ugly divorce from TV sitcom star Robin Givens ("I felt like half of a person"), and the famous ear-biting match with Evander Holyfield, which cost him his boxing license. And then the prison stretch, too.

In *Tyson*, we meet a man who has fallen from the heights down into a hole. The money's all gone now ($300 million is the estimate—the champ didn't keep meticulous records), and many people still see him as little more than an animal. But Toback, a longtime friend (he cast Tyson in his 1999 movie *Black and White*), enlarges the frame to show us more of the picture. And we see that after all the years of rage and calamity, Iron Mike appears to have found some kind of lonely peace. Viewing the completed film for the first time, he told Toback, "It's like a Greek tragedy, except I'm the subject." (April 2009)

Inside Deep Throat

Gimme Some Skin

*D*eep *Throat* brought hardcore pornography out of the scum swamps in which it had traditionally festered and ushered it into the everyday world. So successful was the movie in doing this that today, not only is porn of every sort available instantly to all who seek it, it's also available—suddenly, startlingly, right there on a computer screen—to those who don't. In this regard, the modern porn industry is as evangelical, in its way, as the religious groups that revile it.

Inside Deep Throat, a sad and funny new documentary by Fenton Bailey and Randy Barbato, takes us back to June of 1972, when *Deep Throat* opened without fanfare at a theater in New York's Times Square. Up until that point, sex on film had been the illicit province of short, squalid "stag" reels and "loops." *Deep Throat* was something new. The movie had been shot in Miami Beach the previous January, over the course of six days, by a stag-film entrepreneur named Gerard Damiano. Its star was a twenty-three-year-old loop veteran called Linda Lovelace, whose then-exotic sexual specialty gave the picture its name. Her costar was an awful but nevertheless aspiring twenty-four-year-old actor working under the adopted moniker Harry Reems. The picture cost about $25,000 to make; Damiano had raised the money from certain flush associates, men with names like "Butchie" and "Joe the Whale." Lovelace received $1,200 for her impressive efforts; Reems strutted away with two hundred and fifty bucks.

Deep Throat was an immediate sensation. Unlike the short black-and-white 8-millimeter loops of the past, the movie was shot on 35-millimeter color film, and it ran a little over an hour. It also had a story line (or at least a beginning and an end), and some wheezy laughs, too. It was a low-grade comedy. New York municipal authorities, clueless as always, rushed in to give the picture a huge publicity boost by shutting it down, and then shutting it down again, and again. This attracted the attention of celebrities and intellectuals—the kind of people who normally wouldn't have been caught within skulking distance of a stag movie but could fearlessly enjoy the same arousing experience in the guise of adventurous hipsters. There they all were, in the papers, on the news, lining up to see *Deep Throat*. They also rallied around the picture as a First Amendment issue, which of course it was, and Lovelace and Reems began popping up on TV talk shows discussing the free-speech aspect of their work. (The documentary contains a clip of the sweet but hapless Lovelace telling a reporter, "The last person who started censorship was Adolf Hitler, and look what happened there.")

When *Deep Throat* began pulling in spectacular amounts of money, Damiano says, the mob cut him out of the profit picture and began marketing the movie directly to theaters around the country on a cash basis. This may have led in some cases to the sort of Better Business Bureau infractions usually memorialized in headlines like "Theater Goes Up in Flames" and "Owner Washes Up on Shore." Despite unrelenting official hostility, however, *Deep Throat* got seen. It's impossible to say how much money the film has made over the last thirty-three years, but some estimates put the total as high as $600 million. That's more than any of the *Lord of the Rings* movies has earned in this country, more than any of the *Star Wars* movies, and is almost exactly the amount taken in here to date by *Titanic*, the highest-grossing Hollywood movie of all time.

Deep Throat didn't enrich its stars. Linda Lovelace went on to a life of drugs and destitution, claiming in later years that she'd been forced to perform in the movie at gunpoint. (No one else remembered it that way.) She died, penniless, in 2002. Harry Reems made several more porn films before spiraling down into alcoholism and vagrancy. He was at one point reduced to panhandling for spare change on the Sunset Strip in Los Angeles. Eventually he sobered up, though, got born again, and today, as we see in the documentary, is a very cheerful Realtor in Park City, Utah. As for Gerard Damiano, he continued churning out sex movies into the mid-1990s. He's now an old man living in Florida with his gold medallions and his white toupee, and he says he never saw a penny from the most profitable porn film of all time.

Deep Throat was banned in twenty-three states, and in 1975, infuriated federal prosecutors, in the service of a Republican administration, tried, but ultimately failed, to put away virtually everyone involved with the movie on conspiracy charges. It was too late to stem the porno tide, though. In 1977, home video arrived, a whole new venue for sex movies, free from government prohibition. And glimmering on the horizon was the Internet, the ultimate pornotopia. Today, rock musicians routinely consort with porn starlets, and hot outfits that might've been lifted straight out of a vintage skin flick can often be seen on thirteen-year-old girls, emulating the sleazy-hip styles of their favorite pop stars. Porn is so thoroughly dispersed in the cultural mainstream that such secondary effects have become almost invisible.

There may be changes in the wind, though. In Washington, posturing congressmen continue their crusade for media "decency," and clamor ever more loudly to extend government control over the fading broadcast media into the uninhibited precincts of cable TV. Significant segments of the population cheer them on. Sensing a cultural shift, perhaps, Arrow Productions, the company that currently owns *Deep Throat* and is about to reissue the movie on DVD, is being very shrewd. The picture will be released in two versions. One will be full-X, but the other will be trimmed to qualify for an R rating. Imagine. That'll leave . . . what? The plot? The jokes? The afterglow? (February 2005)

American Swing

The Sultan of Sex

By the mid-1970s, the hippie "free love" ethos of the 1960s had seeped out into the suburbs. Suddenly there were "swingers": men in the most alarming period finery—disco chains, gull-wing collars, crotch-strangling bell-bottom trousers—and the women who loved them (who loved many of them, in fact, sometimes all at once). These people would gather on weekends to form flesh piles at one another's homes. They had their own rites and recognition signals, their own publications. Finally, one of these plebian hedonists, a burly New York meat wholesaler named Larry Levenson, decided the time had come to take swinging public. Well, heterosexual swinging, that is—the gay bathhouse scene was already in full rut. So in 1977 Levenson rented a hotel basement on the Upper West Side of Manhattan that had once housed a famous gay pleasure dome called the Continental Baths (where Bette Midler launched her career, backed by Barry Manilow in a bath towel) and turned it into Plato's Retreat, America's first straight public sex club. For better and then, later, for worse, things would never again be the same.

American Swing, an evocative new documentary by filmmaker Mathew Kaufman and journalist Jon Hart, captures the Plato's period in all its pungent glory. Over the course of three and a half years, the directors managed to assemble an archive of raw footage shot inside the club. We see the fabled orgy room (wall-to-wall mattresses), the proletarian buffet ("disgusting," one regular recalls), and the appalling pool, a chlorine soup thickened with the by-products of aquatic coupling. ("It was like chemical warfare," says porn-tabloid publisher Al Goldstein, an habitué.) There's a lot of skin on view, of course, and some actual sex, too (the picture isn't rated). But the editing, by Keith Reamer (his real name, I'd like to think), is remarkably artful—we see enough to realize what's going on, but not enough to shift us into ogling mode. The picture doesn't feel like a porn film—not one the porn moguls of today would bother distributing, anyway.

Levenson seems sincerely to have believed that swinging was a grassroots "movement" that promoted "social *and* sexual intercourse," as he says here in an old TV interview. Unlike the snootily exclusive Studio 54, Plato's had no velvet-rope ritual at the door. No one was turned away for being too fat, too plain, or (Lord knows) too hairy. Couples (and single women) of all kinds were welcome, and from the exurbs of Long Island and New Jersey, and even farther out of town, they flocked. Celebrities of the day put in appearances, too, and visiting stars like Richard Dreyfuss and Sammy Davis Jr. are name-checked by a talkative array of Plato's veterans, ranging from showbiz hyphenates Buck Henry and Melvin Van Peebles to *Cosmopolitan* editor Helen Gurley Brown, former New York mayor Ed Koch, a smattering of actual porn stars, and an erotic specialist called Danny the Wonder Pony. Their recollections are refreshingly unvarnished. Feminist sex-book author Betty Dodson remembers "the smell and the sweat" of the club. Another woman recalls contracting a major infestation of crab lice there. Another says, "It completely killed your idea of romance."

It was in any case a party that had to end. There was the AIDS virus, for one thing, first identified in 1981, the year after Levenson moved Plato's to a new midtown location. But there was also a substantial flaw in the concept of swinging. Levenson and other enthusiasts saw multi-partner social sex as a way to accommodate men's longing for sexual variety within the context of marriage or romantic commitment. As long as a man and a woman had sex with other people while in each other's presence (or at least with each other's knowledge), then it was "just sex," with no emotional complications. This would seem to be a fundamental misreading of the human heart. Levenson's own relationship with a longtime girlfriend and fellow swinger—a woman identified only as Mary in the film—was ruptured when she became romantically involved with another man, who may have been responsible for a beating that put Levenson in the hospital at one point. (Mary suffered a mental breakdown and was later institutionalized.) Next, the "King of Swing," as Levenson didn't mind being called, was busted for tax evasion and sent to prison for nearly three years. In his absence, the club went downhill, and by the time he returned, business was so meager that prostitutes had to be hired to fill in the dwindling crowds. In 1985, with AIDS a full-fledged plague, Plato's Retreat was closed down by the City of New York. Levenson was reduced to driving a taxi to sustain a newly acquired crack habit. He died in 1999, following heart surgery. Today, the site where Plato's Retreat once did business is a parking garage.

American Swing is bawdy fun, and unexpectedly poignant. It's oddly touching to hear surviving Plato's swingers, now middle-aged, looking back on their lubricious youth. Would they do it again? Betty Dodson, who did it all, says, "I'm an old lady with no regrets." (March 2009)

End of the Century

Punked Out

To the short list of great rock documentaries—*Don't Look Back*, *The Kids Are Alright*, *The Decline of Western Civilization*, a few others—can now be added *End of the Century: The Story of the Ramones*, which is currently in limited release and worth tracking down if you're a fan, even if it involves airfare.

If the Ramones hadn't been such a terrific band, if their songs hadn't been so transporting and their style so unendingly influential, their commercial neglect wouldn't have been so heartbreaking. But they were, and they were, and it was, and heartbreak courses through this movie like a cold, subterranean stream.

End of the Century, a yearslong labor by filmmakers Michael Gramaglia and Jim Fields, lays out the Ramones' story through extensive interviews and rousing back-in-the-day concert footage. Four glue-sniffing mooks from suburban Forest Hills, Queens, decide to form a band in 1974. First they have to learn to play some instruments, which they sorta do. (In the film, guitarist Johnny Ramone says that a Manhattan group, the proto-punk New York Dolls, had demonstrated for him "how great you could be with limited musicianship.") They record their first album in 1976. It contains fourteen tracks; its total running time is less than thirty minutes. The songs' subject matter is eccentric, drawn from singer Joey Ramone's adventures in mental institutions and bassist Dee Dee Ramone's exploits scoring drug money as a teenage male prostitute. The group's idea of a love song is "I Don't Wanna Walk Around with You." The album barely charts, then disappears.

But the Ramones are sudden stars at a Bowery wino dive called CBGB, along with other young bands like Television and Blondie; and when they fly to London to play a club called the Roundhouse in the summer of 1976, they spark a loud-and-fast musical explosion among the local dole-queue youth, leaving new groups like the Sex Pistols and the Clash sprouting in their wake—bands whose colorful snottiness and media-ready anti–fashion sense would soon eclipse the New York musical originals who inspired them.

The Ramones' first four albums are punk-rock keystones, but they didn't get played on the radio and they didn't sell. Desperate for a hit, the band agreed in 1979 to put themselves in the hands of producer Phil Spector, the teen-pop king of the early 1960s, then languishing and hungry for a hit himself. But their union was ill-fated. The recording of the band's fifth studio album, *End of the Century,* was complicated by Spector's heavy drinking, drug gobbling, and well-known fondness for firearms. Obsessed with the ringing guitar chord that opens the song "Rock & Roll High School," Spector—according to New

York producer Ed Stasium, who was present at the sessions and who recalls them in the film—insisted on playing the snippet of sound back for the band a total of 160 times. This, according to legend, took something like twelve hours. Johnny—an abrasive person himself, by his own admission—finally walked out. In the movie, still disgusted, he dismisses Spector as "a little man with lifts in his shoes, a wig on top of his head, and four guns."

End of the Century only reached number 44 on the *Billboard* album chart. Statistically, it was the Ramones' biggest hit, but it was a bitter disappointment. In the movie, Johnny says he saw the writing on the wall. "At that point, I knew, I finally accepted, that we wouldn't sell any records. That's it. Just try to maintain our career and keep making money. This is a job, let's do the best we can do. . . . This is your spot in life."

The Ramones made their living on the road, and Johnny kept them out there, touring the world relentlessly, for twenty years. They were miserable—not least because Johnny, a hard-nosed political conservative, ran the band like a drill sergeant. (When Dee Dee once blew a note onstage, Johnny punched him in the head afterward.) Even more problematic was the fact that Joey's onetime girlfriend had left him in the early 1980s to take up with (and later marry) Johnny. Because of this, the two men essentially stopped speaking to each other for the rest of the band's career—despite the fact that they spent much of their lives cooped up in tour vans together. (Joey memorialized this romantic betrayal, as he saw it, by writing a song called "The KKK Took My Baby Away.")

By 1995, the Ramones had had it. They titled their final album *Adios Amigos* and played their final show (gig number 2,262, to be exact) in Los Angeles, oddly enough, on August 6, 1996. After the show, Johnny says in the film, "I just went and changed my clothes and walked out. . . . Maybe I said, 'See you later.'" Joey, whose health had always been delicate, began a long battle with lymphatic cancer. But even when the singer lay dying in a New York hospital in 2001, Johnny stubbornly refused to call him. "If I didn't like someone," he says in the movie's most chilling moment, "I wouldn't want them callin' me up if I was dyin'. I wouldn't want them to have any regrets for not talking to me—I'm happy that they didn't talk to me. . . . That's how it goes."

The Ramones were often portrayed—even portrayed themselves—as punk-rock idiot savants, clueless geeks who happened to stumble upon a formula for creating art out of the most disreputable materials: heavy-metal power chords and bubblegum-pop melodies. But in *End of the Century*, we see them as they really are (or, in the case of the late Joey and Dee Dee, as they were): inspired amateurs whose enthusiasm outshone their technical shortcomings, and who thereby inspired a whole genera-tion of similarly unsophisticated younger bands. Best of all, we see them onstage at their peak, in rare footage from the 1970s and early 1980s, playing their music at full roar. (Says Dee Dee at one gig, "We could blow this place apart if we wanted to.")

Was the Ramones' timeless music worth all the heartache the band went through to create and sustain it? For us, sure. For them? That's a still-open question. (September 2004)

My Date with Drew

Love Bomb

Three years ago, Brian Herzlinger was a shlubby twenty-seven-year-old East Coast film-school grad who had relocated to Los Angeles to be near the movie biz but was failing to become in any way a part of it. He was broke and unemployed and yet—for reasons that offer no re-ward to close inquiry—strangely optimistic. When he suddenly won $1,100 as a contestant on a TV game show, he decided to use the money to make a movie—a documentary about his near-lifelong obsession with Drew Barrymore, and his determination to score a "date" with her.

Enabling him in this venture were two film-school classmates who had also made the trek west, Brett Winn and Jon Gunn. Setting out from square one, they realized that the first thing they would need to make Herzlinger's movie would be a camera. Fortuitously, they found they could pick up a nifty digital-video model from Circuit City, which was advertising a no-questions-asked thirty-day return policy. This would give the fledgling documentarians nearly a month to make their film with just enough time left at the end to take the camera back as unsatisfactory and retrieve their money. Someday, Circuit City will have to answer for this.

The result of Herzlinger's quest is *My Date with Drew*, a labor of something sort of like love, I suppose. As is the case with all movie stars, Drew Barrymore proves very hard to contact. Poking around among their own acquaintances, the three filmmakers obtain the name of a limo driver they hope might know something, but he's not a lot of help. They secure an audience with Barrymore's first cousin, but she turns out never actually to have met her celebrated relative. They pay a visit to the premises of Drew's "facialist," where we get to watch Herzlinger having blackheads extracted from his mug. They arrange a meeting with the remarkably smarmy Eric Roberts, who apparently has enough free time to play along with this sort of thing. (Roberts tells Herzlinger he's a pudding of a man and needs to get buff, then rolls up a sleeve to offer his own baseball-size muscle as an aesthetic ideal.) They also rope in longtime punch line Corey Feldman—a guy with even more free time on his hands than Roberts, unsurprisingly—and solicit his advice, which proves to be useful mainly for purposes of plumping up the film with even the most dubious sort of celebrity presence.

Throughout all of this, the person we learn the most about, neverendingly, is Brian Herzlinger. He exults in the camera's solicitous, unquestioning gaze, chattering away about his various inadequacies (too much body hair, too little cool) and wielding them like a verbal bludgeon to disarm anyone who might find this quasi stalker to be less than engaging. The man is a militant nebbish. We see him pawing through his fanboy collection of movie memorabilia, still lovingly stored in his boyhood bedroom. (It of course includes a vintage certificate of membership in the Drew Barrymore fan club.) We see him staging a mock date in a restaurant with an actress he feels resembles Barrymore somewhat (well, at least as much as Corey Feldman does), and quipping to the waiter, "Merlot—that's the red one, right?" We see him calling his ex-girlfriend and asking, "What was your first impression of me?" Remarkably, it wasn't anything like ours.

In the end, after Herzlinger starts a Web site to publicize his date-with-Drew campaign, Barrymore herself finally gets wind of the project and, God bless her, finds it kind of sweet. A quick lunch is arranged by her intermediaries in the garden of a Manhattan restaurant, and when the actress arrives (announcing to Herzlinger that she's honored to be "a part of your journey"), her sweet, zesty presence gooses the film to life—at least for the ten minutes or so that she's actually in it. On the way out she tells Hertzlinger, "I'm very proud of you, even though I don't know you very well." And then she's gone. And that's it.

Brian Herzlinger may be a likable guy to his buddies, but there's way too much of him here. And while many film-festival viewers have reportedly found *My Date with Drew* to be irresistibly charming, it's hard to fathom the appeal of watching a grown man's pathetic infatuation with a famous person he's never previously met—and has no hope of ever getting to know—so relentlessly demonstrated. At one point in the picture, someone says of Herzlinger's quest, "The dumbing-down of America is complete." Let's at least hope it doesn't get much dumber than this movie. (August 2005)

We Live in Public

The Future Revisited

Josh Harris was an emotionally stunted computer nerd who came to New York City in 1984 with $900 in his pocket. He got into high-tech market research and made a pile of money. He pioneered chat rooms and then Web TV before it was really feasible (dial-up was a stumbling block). He surfed the big Internet wave, became a name player, and by the end of the 1990s was worth $80 million. How did he do this? And what ever happened to him?

He did it by inventing the future. Well, by inventing the way people would *live* in the future. Or so he thought. But would they? Do they?

We Live in Public, Ondi Timoner's new documentary about Harris, prompts a number of questions—about the future of privacy, the decay of intimacy, and technological totalitarianism—that keep twining around themselves. It's a maddening, mesmerizing film. Harris is a half-brilliant entrepreneur with no moral sense whatsoever. That he grew up in a loveless bubble—with emotionally absent parents, his only friend the living-room TV set, his real family the cast of *Gilligan's Island*—tells us a lot, if not everything, about the man, and about why he grew up to be so strange.

At the end of 1999, rolling in dough, Harris turned his eye toward bigger things than making money. He decided to ring in the new millennium with a monthlong techno-art happening he called "Quiet." This involved assembling about a hundred people—artists, musicians, other dot-com kids like himself—and installing them in an old building in downtown Manhattan that he had filled with more than a hundred video cameras, some stationary, some handheld and roving. There was a barrackslike "pod hotel"—essentially, rows of bunk beds with cameras affixed to record everything that went on in them. There was a big shower with see-through walls; the toilets had no walls at all. There were all kinds of great food, a 24/7 open bar, and, down in the basement, a firing range heavily stocked with weapons, many of them automatic. (You can hear the roar of machine guns in the background of the period interviews Timoner has dredged up here.) There were also drugs, of course, and lots of nudity, lots of sex, all of it obsessively documented by Harris's cameras. The food, the booze, the ammo were all free—Harris paid for everything. ("I spend money like it's sand through the fingers of time," he says.) The video footage, however, he kept for himself.

The atmosphere of creepiness that emanates from all of this thickens when we learn that every partygoer had to undergo an "interrogation" before gaining admission. These sessions, conducted by a stern note-taker, with a uniformed goon standing nearby, probed the subjects' fears and insecurities, their sexual practices, everything, with answers carefully jotted down in individual files. We see a bipolar man uneasily talking about the delusions from which he suffers and a girl instructed to demonstrate exactly how she sliced open her arm in a suicide attempt. (She breaks down in tears.) Harris is watching all this—everybody is watching, via video hookup—and at one point we see him consulting an on-the-scene psychiatrist, pressing him for suggestions about "any technique we can use to intimidate them—to break them, in essence."

According to one of the many cameramen who were on hand, "There was a tremendous fascist overtone to the whole thing." A woman adds, "It was absolutely a surveillance police state. Just by walking into the premises, you basically relinquished your rights." Harris saw it differently. "This is a perfect analogy of what the Internet will [become]," he said. "Everyone will have a camera and a monitor. . . . As time goes by, we're going to increasingly have our lives exposed. And we're gonna want that to happen."

In the end the police arrived, drawn by the sound of all the gunfire, and shut the party down. But Harris was just getting started. "With 'Quiet,'" he says, "I saw what surveillance could do to the human condition. The next step was to experiment on myself."

And so for the first time that anyone who knew him could remember, Harris acquired a girlfriend, a fresh-faced young woman named Tanya Corrin, whom he invited to join him in his next project. He called it "We Live in Public," and once again it involved lots of cameras and microphones, this time installed all around a large residential loft into which the new couple moved. There were cameras in the shower, the bathroom, the bedroom—no space was left unobserved. They were all wired together into a website that allowed a community of online voyeurs to observe what Josh and Tanya were up to at any hour of the day or night, and—this being all about interactivity—to offer streams of real-time text commentary about the lives these two people were living.

An iron law of human nature ensured that this sinister experiment would end badly. Tanya grew unhappy. ("I'm not gonna be your porn star," she shouts at one point.) Harris, possibly in an attempt to goose his Web hits, became abusive, pushing her around and bruising her. Finally, she left. Harris, who appears to be in denial about virtually everything in his life, responded with feigned nonchalance. "I couldn't wait to get rid of her," he claims. "Tanya was a pseudo girlfriend. I'd been trying to cast [that part], and she was perfect." He would soldier on: "I had to take living in public to the end because I'm a celebrity . . . there are people who watch." Unfortunately, observing Harris on his own—muttering to himself in the bathroom mirror or even taking a call on the toilet from a bank clerk telling him his account is empty (the big dot-com bubble had finally burst)—was remarkably uninteresting. When his audience dwindled to about ten people, he quit and left New York for a farm out in the middle of somewhere or other, where he fired off guns a lot and communed with the apple trees, which he felt could "sense my energy source."

Harris eventually attempted a comeback with another interactive website, but the new breed of younger moguls who might have financed it had no idea who he was, and they didn't. Then Harris disappeared.

So who is this man? Is he the guy we see in the film saying, "I'm an artist—one of the first great artists of the twenty-first century"? Or is he the guy telling us, "I'm sick. I'm mentally sick"? Timoner wants to make a case for Harris as a prophet ahead of his time—a man who foresaw the online-all-the-time world in which so many people now live. Maybe so. But he was hardly the first person to foresee the disquieting possibilities of modern communications technology. In his 1951 book, *The Mechanical Bride*, Marshall McLuhan suggested the manipulative allure of the dominant medium of his day: "Come on, kiddies. Buy a radio and feel free—to listen." But McLuhan gave this subject real thought; he stirred concern. Harris didn't care. The grave new world he saw coming seemed to get him off. Being an emotional nonentity himself, living in public may have been the only way he could really live at all.

At the end of this remarkable film, Timoner, who worked on it for ten years (and also worked on the "Quiet" project back in the day), tracks Harris down to the last place on Earth you'd expect to find him, far from the siren lure of digital media (and the even more insistent clamor of the many creditors he skipped out on). He has settled into real life at last and says he's there to stay. Let's hope so. (August 2009)

The Bridge

Last Looks

This ice-bath documentary—a visual record of the final moments of some of the twenty-four people who chose to end their lives with a leap from San Francisco's Golden Gate Bridge in 2004—leaves you feeling that perhaps hell is a little closer at hand than you'd previously imagined.

The Golden Gate, completed in 1937, is the second-longest suspension bridge in the country and reportedly the number one suicide destination in the world. After climbing the railing down onto the ledge that runs along the outer side of the structure, and then pushing off into the air, a jumper will fall for about four seconds before hitting the water 220 feet below, at a speed of 75 miles an hour. Few survive this experience. It's said that bridge authorities kept count of the number of suicides until 1995, when the total reached 1,000.

Eric Steel, a movie production executive who'd never actually made a movie, read about the Golden Gate's dark magnetism in a 2003 *New Yorker* article called "Jumpers," by Tad Friend. Fascinated, he flew to San Francisco, put together a video crew and gingerly extracted permits from the city to film the bridge every daylight hour, every day of the week, for one whole year. His setup was simple. One camera was locked down on a wide shot of the bridge, taking in its entire span; the other, equipped with an extreme long-range lens, was dedicated to zooming in on individuals in the constant stream of people walking across. (Steel says an overriding concern was to prevent suicide jumps whenever possible, and in some cases he and his crew did—we see loitering people being gently led away from the railing by cops. However, the telltale signs of an imminent leap—a suddenly shrugged-off backpack, a tossed wallet—happen so quickly that a jumper can be gone before a speed-dial call to the bridge police can even be placed.)

Steel's ninety-three-minute film is, among other things, one of the most beautiful movies yet shot with mini-DV cameras. The gorgeous picture postcard vistas of the great orange bridge, with pillowy white clouds tumbling by overhead and pelicans and windsurfers skimming the water down below, would be obscene, given the context, were the images not so hauntingly tempered by Alex Heffes's spare electro-acoustic score. Up close on the bridge, we see people strolling by, kids running around, lovers kissing. Then the camera homes in on a man pacing near the railing, talking into a cell phone. He's laughing. Then—it takes just seconds—he bends down to set the phone on the ground, mounts the railing, swings his legs over, crosses himself with his right hand, and jumps. The lack of drama is unnerving—there's no swelling music, no slick, manipulative montage. His life ends; the rest of life, passing by along the bridge, serenely continues.

Steel interviews the families and friends of the people we see plummeting into the water. Their comments have a terrible similarity:

"She was at the end of her rope."

"He felt his body was a prison. He felt trapped."

"Some days you think like that yourself. He thought about it every day."

We see a suicide note left behind: "I am fat, ugly, deaf, can't see, and I am tired."

A woman remembers a final phone call from a friend on his way to the bridge: "I just called to say good-bye," he tells her. "It's time."

Kevin Hines, now twenty-five, was driven toward the bridge by his severe bipolar disorder. He stood weeping near the railing for forty minutes, but nobody in the passing throng stopped to express concern. Finally a woman, a foreign tourist, approached and handed him a camera. She wanted him to take her picture. Bottoming out, Hines climbed down onto the ledge and jumped. Amazingly, he lived (although the impact of hitting the water rammed his shattered lumbar bones up into his internal organs). He remembers his last thoughts with an awful clarity: "The second my hands left the railing, I said, 'I don't wanna die.'"

Steel notes that the railing on the Golden Gate Bridge is only four feet high. But bridge officials have fought off calls for a more substantial suicide barrier for years, citing financial strain and aesthetic objections (even though both the Empire State Building and the Eiffel Tower have installed such barriers and no longer have a suicide problem). And so the bridge continues to exert its lethal allure to terminally troubled people across the country. In the movie, a woman recalls a close friend who, too poor to afford medication for his chronic depression, finally took the leap. It was so easy.

"I think the bridge has a false romanticism to it," she says, with extraordinary bitterness. "Maybe walking out there he had a romantic moment or two, or an hour. But hey, the water can't be fun." (October 2006)

Deliver Us from Evil

Monster Movie

Deliver Us from Evil is a documentary about depravity so gross, it leaves you infuriated that the men who enabled it have never been called to account. It's the story of a Roman Catholic priest, Oliver O'Grady, who for twenty years raped and sodomized scores of children who had been entrusted to his spiritual care—one of them a baby girl only nine months old. Whenever his predations started to become known, O'Grady was quietly transferred by the church's California hierarchy to another parish—and then another, and another. None of these congregations were informed about their new priest's proclivities, and they were thus unaware that they had officially been selected as a fresh source of victims for this ordained predator.

In a picture filled with astonishments, the most astonishing presence in *Deliver Us from Evil* is O'Grady himself, who appears on camera at length, admitting his crimes and even describing them, often with a disconnected smile on his lips and a rote twinkle in his eyes. A native of Ireland, he has the sort of ingratiating Gaelic charm that was once common in Hollywood movie priests—the kind who would warmly mentor wayward youths and attempt to guide them away from the path of delinquency. We understand why parents, and especially children, would like him. But as we watch this man liltingly recount his story, it becomes apparent who, or what, he really is.

"This will be the most honest confession of my life," O'Grady says at the beginning of the film. But his eerie detachment from his monstrous acts is chilling. He talks vaguely about "a major imbalance" in his life, about "these awful tendencies." As for his victims: "Basically, what I want to say to them is, it should not have happened." He is concerned about the damage he may have inflicted on the church, but not overly: "What we need to do as a church," he says, "is acknowledge our good days and our bad days." At one point, he pens a letter to be sent to some victims whose names he remembers, inviting them to meet with him for some hazy healing purpose. He's very keen on this, and he actually sends the letter out. "Godspeed," he says.

To represent O'Grady's many victims, director Amy Berg, a former CNN and CBS News producer, persuaded three of them—Nancy Sloan, Ann Jyono, and a man identified only as Adam M.—to appear in the film. They're now grown, but still emotionally hobbled by the horrors to which they were subjected. For them, in the beginning, O'Grady was simply the lovable "Father Ollie." Not for long, though. Looking back, Nancy says, "My last memory of Ollie is of severe pain, before blacking out." Ann, who's now thirty-nine, longs to marry and have children, but is unsure whether she'll ever be capable of doing so. The church has never offered her apology or condolence, and so, she says, "It's still not over." Adam remembers being delivered to a visit with O'Grady by his trusting parents and being told by the priest as he sodomized him, "Why would your parents bring you here if they didn't want you to do this?" Unsurprisingly, since his life has been emotionally stalled ever since, Adam remains fiercely embittered: "I get so angry just knowing that guy's alive."

Also still drawing breath, we note, is Cardinal Roger Mahony, O'Grady's former bishop in Stockton, California. O'Grady says he once told Mahony about what he calls "this awful problem that I had," and that it was Mahony—then in line to become the archbishop of Los Angeles, a position he now holds—who shuttled him around from parish to parish, thus tamping down, at least temporarily, one after another embarrassing pedophile-priest scandal. Mahony denies any knowledge of O'Grady's activities. (In courtroom-deposition footage from 1997, the cardinal says, "He was not a priest I would golf with, or have dinner with.") However, according to *The New York Times,* there are now more than five hundred civil suits related to sexual abuse by priests that are pending in Los Angeles County, some of them charging Mahony as being complicit in cover-ups. And William Hodgman, a deputy prosecutor in the Los Angeles District Attorney's office, which has long been trying to pry relevant records out of the archdiocese, told the *Times* he thinks O'Grady's statements in *Deliver Us from Evil* (in which Hodgman also appears) "will fuel ongoing consideration as to whether Cardinal Mahoney and others engaged in criminal activity."

Oliver O'Grady's twenty-year career as a child-molesting priest came to an end in 1993, when he was arrested for abusing two young boys. He was tried and convicted and sentenced to fourteen years in prison. He served only seven, and then was released and deported back to Ireland, where his sexual pathology once again went unannounced. He lives there today, roaming the streets in unsupervised freedom, supported by a church pension.

Rising up in lonely determination against O'Grady and his apparently proliferating ilk is a very different sort of priest named Father Tom Doyle, a scholar who has damaged his clerical career by becoming an advocate within the church for victims of sexual abuse by priests. Doyle says he once wrote a report predicting a "national crisis" over the issue, but that the report was buried by his superiors. He thinks that part of the problem is the Roman Catholic tradition of sexual celibacy for priests—a requirement he says has no basis either in the Bible or in canon law. (He amusingly notes what may have been the original motivation for the practice: unmarried priests, having no families to inherit their worldly goods, would leave them instead to the church.)

Since priests who attack children also debase the faith itself, the need for institutional reform of the sort called for by Doyle would seem urgent, especially considering the number of lawsuits piling up. But when Doyle leads O'Grady's three grown victims to Rome to petition the pope for simple acknowledgment of the wrongs done to them, they are turned away by Vatican guards. This reluctance by the Roman Catholic Church to confront such a serious problem sends a disturbing message—both to the Catholic faithful, who feel betrayed and abandoned, and to men like Oliver O'Grady, of whom there are presumably more than a few. Asked at one point what went through his mind when he found himself alone with a helpless child, O'Grady says, "This was an opportunity to be sexual with him. Because God knows when I'd get to do it again." (October 2006)

Until the Light Takes Us

Dead Boys

My favorite Norwegian black-metal story, well known by now to connoisseurs of the demented, is the one about the singer called—prophetically, as it turned out—Dead. Per Yngve Ohlin was his sane-world name, and he fronted the influential black-metal band Mayhem. One day in the spring of 1991, at a house the group shared not far from Oslo, Dead blew his brains out with a shotgun. ("Excuse all the blood," his suicide note politely read.) His body was discovered by the band's guitarist, Euronymous. He realized the police would have to be called, but before doing so, he scurried out to buy a cheap camera, returned to the house, arranged the death scene a little more arrestingly—the shotgun carefully positioned next to the corpse, with its frontal lobe still slopping out of the cranium—and snapped some pictures. He also gathered up a number of skull shards, which he later fashioned into souvenir necklaces for friends of the deceased. But that's not the really good part. The really good part is that one of those photos turned up a few years later as the cover art on a Mayhem bootleg called *Dawn of the Black Hearts*. And that record is still in print—I just found a copy online, signed by the band's drummer ("Hellhammer," what else), retailing for $356. Dead may have lost his looks, but he still moves units.

The world is overstocked with flamboyantly wasted rock stars and heavily strapped rappers, but few of them can hold a guttering candle to the ghoul-boy nutters of Norwegian black metal. Theirs is a tale splattered with murder and church-burning rampages, perfumed with rumors of cannibalism and devil worship, and marinated in a rich broth of violent homo-anxiety and neo-Wagnerian nationalist mysticism. (Sons of Odin, and all that.) For those with no painful personal experience of these things, it's a hoot.

The NBM story has been told before, beginning with the 1998 Feral Press book *Lords of Chaos*. Now it's been reprised by two first-time American filmmakers, Aaron Aites and Audrey Ewell, in a documentary called *Until the Light Takes Us*. Aites and Ewell get points for moving to Norway for two years to suss out the scene before starting to shoot. And no doubt they were working with a budget that even Ed Wood might've found restrictive. Still, their doc, with its awkwardly staged interviews and episodic meandering, is likely to play best for viewers with at least a little prior knowledge of the subject.

Black metal, the Nordic offspring of 1980s death metal, apparently came together as a scene around an Oslo record shop called Helvete in the early 1990s. The shop was run by the aforementioned Euronymous, who also operated a record label on the premises called Deathlike Silence Productions. Among the new-school metalheads drawn to the store was a fresh-faced Tolkien fan named Varg Vikernes, soon to become famous—and then infamous—as a one-man black-metal band called Burzum. Euronymous signed Vikernes to his label, but their relationship came to an unhappy end one night when Vikernes showed up at Euronymous's apartment and stabbed him in the head—fatally, as you might imagine. Vikernes—already a person of interest to police in connection with an ongoing series of arson attacks on dozens of medieval wooden churches—was sentenced to twenty-one years in prison for the murder.

The movie is anchored by jailhouse interviews with Vikernes and rambling interludes with another black-metal star, Gylve Nagell, of the band Darkthrone. The Nagell segments, which wander all over the place, expose the directors' central weakness, which is editing. The Vikernes interviews compel more attention. Here we have a talented musician whose rosy-cheeked smile never slips as he reviles Christianity and all of its works, takes barely veiled potshots at Jews, and describes with eerie nonchalance the bloody murder of Euronymous, which he committed at the age of twenty. (Vikernes was paroled earlier this year, after sixteen years in prison.)

The rest of the movie is a potpourri. There's a startling scene in which the very odd Satyricon drummer Frost makes a performance-art appearance at a gallery in Milan, Italy, in which he furiously stabs a sofa and then—after slicing up his own neck and arms—proceeds to bleed all over it. There's also a story, framed by newspaper headlines, about a young black-metal musician who murdered an older gay man for no reason. (It's followed by a shot of two other black-metal musos laughing appreciatively.) And there's a curious cameo by the American alt-film director Harmony Korine, whom we see cavorting around another art gallery in black-metal makeup and a yellow fright wig. (Korine slotted a Burzum song into the soundtrack of his 1997 film, *Gummo*.)

In its erratic framing and dodgy sound, the movie is as low-tech as black metal itself. (Vikernes says that at his first recording session, he demanded that the engineer provide him with the very worst microphone available.) But the directors are admirably disinclined to sensationalize a subject that's already plenty gaudy. And they get you interested in the music, some of which, if you can believe, rewards further investigation. (December 2009)

Cool It

Some Really Inconvenient Truths

The world is not coming to an end. I know: *shocker!* And yet there are still people who feel this to be so. These climate alarmists—whose tribe has somewhat dwindled of late—believe the seas will all too soon rise twenty feet and submerge our cities; that the noble polar bear is on the very cusp of extinction; that our planet, in sum, is hurtling toward a fiery doom.

The Danish environmentalist Bjørn Lomborg is not one of these people. True, he does believe that global warming exists, and that human beings are at least partly responsible, and that something must be done. But in his two contrarian books, *The Skeptical Environmentalist* (published in English in 2001) and *Cool It* (2007), Lomborg argues that the strategies employed over the last two decades—the dodgy ecological horror stories, the vast siphonings of taxpayer money into the clamorous movement—are outdated and ineffectual. Like the late free-market sage Julian Simon, whose writing launched his own journey away from alarmism, Lomborg believes that human ingenuity is the key to planetary improvement. And now, in Ondi Timoner's provocative new documentary, also called *Cool It*, he travels the world to make that case in a most persuasive way.

The alarmist community's objections to Lomborg—apart from his sunny, upbeat plausibility, which must surely rankle—often concern his academic bona fides. Although his focus is on economics, statistics, and cost-benefit analyses, his PhD, they point out, is actually in political science. So, like, what could *he* know? In fact, Danish scientists were so angered by *The Skeptical Environmentalist* that they complained to the Danish Committees on Scientific Dishonesty (*paging Mr. Galileo!*), which ruled that the book's conclusions were in fact "dishonest," but that, in effect, Lomborg was too ignorant to realize it. (This decision was subsequently dismissed, rather curtly, by higher Danish scientific authorities.)

In the film, Lomborg deals with this episode forthrightly. He also allows a generous amount of screen time to Stanford University environmental biologist Stephen Schneider, one of his most hostile antagonists. ("This guy needs to be taken down," Schneider says.) And he does this without bringing up Schneider's role in helping to trigger the long-building backlash against ecological alarmism with his famous remark in a 1989 magazine interview that "we have to offer up scary scenarios, make simplified, dramatic statements, and make little mention of any doubts we might have"—a foreshadowing of last year's Climategate e-mail leaks.

In addition, Lomborg credits *An Inconvenient Truth*, the Al Gore movie, with helping to raise awareness of global warming, although with dubious assertions. For example, the polar bear population, Lomborg says, has actually increased since the 1960s and is now most endangered by Arctic hunters, who shoot between three hundred and five hundred of the animals every year. Gore's prediction of a twenty-foot rise in sea levels was wildly overwrought, and in any case, Lomborg observes, "Sea levels in the last century rose one foot—did anyone notice?" He also says that, while global warming *is* a serious concern, we should bear in mind that human beings manage to thrive both on the equator and at the frozen poles: "People can adapt to climate, which is always changing."

Lomborg believes that the world climate summits held in Rio, Kyoto, and Copenhagen over the last eighteen years have been futile, because no country—especially such rising powerhouses as China and India, just now emerging into prosperity—will agree to cold-cock its economy in order to join the sketchy Western global-warming crusade. And he claims that since the $250 billion the European Union spends every year to combat warming will ultimately reduce temperatures by only 0.01 percent, that money would be better channeled into worldwide battles against malaria and AIDS—diseases that are killing people *right now*—and into funding new climate technology.

Traveling through Europe, the United States, and Africa, Lomborg consults with several eminent scientists, like physicist Freeman Dyson, who says that the computer climate-simulation models upon which so much ecological alarmism relies "do not begin to describe the real world we live in." And he points out the promise of wave power, seaborne windmills, algae-based fuel, and a prospective nuclear technology that could lead to the creation of nuclear reactors that run on nuclear *waste*. He also brings in Benjamin Franklin, whose observation that an Icelandic volcano eruption in 1783 had caused an abnormally severe winter in Europe suggests, Lomborg says, that artificial volcanoes could be employed to cool the Earth today.

A considerable part of Lomborg's appeal lies in his rejection of dogmatic certitude. In his search for concrete solutions, he never presents himself as an infallible authority, and he appears to welcome detractors. When the pugnacious Professor Schneider died last summer, before the picture's completion, Lomborg must have felt the loss of a useful critic: *Cool It* is dedicated to Schneider's memory. (November 2010)

Restrepo

The War That Won't End

Can there be an upside to war? Possibly. In a new documentary by veteran combat journalists Tim Hetherington and Sebastian Junger, we find ourselves on patrol with a company of U.S. soldiers in the Korengal Valley, one of the bloodiest corners of the ongoing Afghan conflict. It's the spring of 2007, and the men have just weathered a heavy firefight. One of them emerges from it jacked up and exultant. "That was fun!" he says. "You can't get a better high. Once you get shot at . . . you can't top that."

The film vividly captures the dust and blood and sheer drudgery of war. The unit has been assigned to build a new forward outpost right up against the edge of Taliban territory—build it from scratch, with picks and shovels, amid continual potshots from the enemy in the surrounding mountains. The Taliban come so close they can be heard talking to one another. But the American soldiers work straight through the night, and make a good start. They never complain. They christen the new base Restrepo Outpost, after a departed comrade, Juan "Doc" Restrepo, who recently took two bullets in the neck and bled out on the medevac helicopter. They talk about their departed friend a lot, and we see footage of him goofing around on the flight that brought the men over here from a base in Italy. Like them, he was very young.

Still sleepless, they set out on patrol. They pass through battered villages, stopping occasionally to interrogate suspicious-looking locals. ("You got pretty clean hands for a goatherder.") They meet with village elders and promise to "flood" the area with money and medical supplies if the villagers will only help fight the resurgent enemy. But the people caught in the middle of this conflict have defeat written on their faces. One man tells the company's captain, through an interpreter, "If we let you know about Taliban, then we will get killed." Alternatively, of course, this man could *be* Taliban. As was the case in the Vietnam War forty-odd years ago, in which the United States fought another indigenous enemy that didn't wear uniforms, it's impossible to know.

The company moves on. Intermittently, the crackle of gunfire flares up, and the camera jostles wildly in keeping up with the GIs as they hit the ground and crawl through the dirt. One of them gets hit, shot dead. One of his friends briefly breaks down in tears. Another soldier tries to comfort him: "It was quick," he says.

The unit comes to another village. This one has been chewed up by missile fire from the U.S. Army attack helicopters whirling overhead. Five civilians have been killed, more wounded. Inside one house we see women, children, even a baby wet with blood. This is the face of collateral damage.

Somewhere there's a grand plan for this war, a political scenario devised by a regiment of office warriors back in Washington. But the soldiers here don't talk about it. All they know is that there's an enemy their country is fighting, and their job is to kill him. They're tough and brave, and they're good at it. They casually discuss the fact that they may well die here, but that's not what concerns them most. What concerns each of them most is the possibility that one of their fellow soldiers may die—one of their pals, the only family they have in this hostile place.

The movie follows this company through 2008, when the men completed their fifteen-month deployment and were being flown back to Italy. What we don't see is the aftermath. This past April, having alienated the local populace, the army withdrew the last of its troops from the Korengal Valley. Earlier this month, the Afghan conflict, which began directly after 9/11, became the longest war in U.S. history. More than a thousand U.S. soldiers have died in it. Last December, President Obama announced his intention to send thirty thousand more troops to Afghanistan, bringing the total number of U.S. forces in-country to a hundred thousand. But at the same time, he also announced that he'll begin pulling them out again next year. The president has since wobbled on that commitment. Still, it's hard to imagine the Taliban not feeling that victory in this long war is now mainly a waiting game.

The directors, Hetherington and Junger, acknowledge that they are men of the political left. We don't know what editing decisions they've made, but the footage we see unavoidably recalls the disturbing images that emerged out of Vietnam, and ultimately turned America against that war. *Restrepo* is the answer to a question that will surely continue to be asked. (June 2010)

Client 9: The Rise and Fall of Eliot Spitzer

Hooked

The fall of New York Governor Eliot Spitzer in 2008 provided a smorgasbord of schadenfreude on which his many detractors were delighted to feast. Spitzer, who had reveled in busting a big prostitution ring in 2004, when he was the state's showboating attorney general, was himself driven from office by a call-girl scandal in which he figured as "Client 9," a man who paid thousands of dollars an hour to engage high-end "escorts"—and, more deliciously yet, kept his socks on while being serviced by them. Following the ritual farewell press conference with his humiliated wife by his side, Spitzer slunk off into shamed seclusion while his most famous sex rental, one Ashley Dupré, became a talk-show fixture, a MySpace sensation, and an "advice" columnist for the *New York Post*. What was not to love about all of this?

Well, it *is* hard to have much sympathy for Spitzer, an abrasive political climber. But Alex Gibney's new documentary, *Client 9: The Rise and Fall of Eliot Spitzer*, does him—and us—the service of situating his transgressions within the sordid political context in which they occurred. It's not a pretty picture.

Upon becoming attorney general in 1998, Spitzer announced a crusade against white-collar crime, especially as rife, he claimed, on Wall Street. He boldly targeted bankers and traders and the previously untouchable solons of such firms as Merrill Lynch and American International Group (AIG, later a recipient of huge Bush administration bailouts). These were dangerous people to irritate, but Spitzer gloried in his new renown as the "Sheriff of Wall Street." "My job," he said, "is to change the system." As if.

Moving on to the political cesspool of Albany to become governor in 2006, Spitzer, a liberal Democrat, immediately butted heads with the state's silver-haired Senate majority leader, Joseph Bruno, a powerful Republican. At one point, in a scandal dubbed Troopergate, Spitzer engaged state police to keep records of Bruno's comings and goings. Bruno was angered but unintimidated. In Gibney's film he says he told Spitzer to his face, "I been threatened by hoods and thugs all my life. You're an amateur."

Then began the fall. That same year, Spitzer started patronizing the Emperors Club, an online escort service that provided "the girlfriend experience"—classy prostitutes whose fees ranged up to $5,500 a night. As he explains in the film, sitting uncomfortably through a Gibney interview, Spitzer turned to call girls as a preferable alternative to becoming involved in an extramarital romantic affair. He prepaid for his assignations with money orders—more than $100,000 worth over the course of two years. His bank began to take notice, and, as required, reported the heavy activity on his account to the IRS. Soon the FBI moved in and set up wiretaps. Somehow, *The New York Times* got wind of the feds' findings and went to press with them. Spitzer was nailed.

Gibney, who previously charted corporate corruption with *Enron: The Smartest Guys in the Room*, makes a persuasive case that government Republicans, in collusion with vengeful Wall Street titans (presumably not liberal Democrats), conspired to bring Spitzer down in the most embarrassing possible way. His antagonists are presented as fairly scary guys, especially former AIG boss Hank Greenberg, onetime New York Stock Exchange director Kenneth Langone, and the flamboyant lobbyist and fixer Roger Stone (himself a devotee of strippers and swingers' clubs). Gibney makes Spitzer seem prescient about the high-finance scammery that would soon lead to a national economic meltdown. And he brings in some unusual talking heads to provide commentary, to varying effect: Cecil Suwall, a giggly young woman who was CEO of the Emperors Club, is the film's most winning presence; but hiring an actress to mouth the transcribed words of one of the company's escorts—a Spitzer favorite called Angelina here—has a dodgy feel. And why he thought it necessary to solicit the thoughts of Karen Finley, the faded erotic performance artist of the 1990s, is anybody's guess.

The most pressing question the film elicits, though, is why the government should still be allowed to use anti-prostitution laws to harass citizens who are doing no one (or in Spitzer's case, no one beyond themselves) any harm. Eliot Spitzer was never charged with any crime, but he was taken down anyway. It's hard to say how much he'll be missed. ("He was gonna be our first Jewish president," a friend muses wistfully.) But judging by his current embarrassing gig as a CNN talk-show host, missing is what he'll continue to be from the cutthroat political action in which he once made his name—which is now, and possibly forever, mud. (November 2010)

Overnight

The Ego Has Landed

Considering how many self-important jerks one meets in life, it's strange how rarely you get to see one of them crash and burn. The great gratification of the new film *Overnight* is that it preserves such a comeuppance in the form of a documentary—which is to say that the world-class flameout it depicts actually happened, to an actual jerk. His name is Troy Duffy, a would-be genius who moved from Boston to Los Angeles to pursue his twin dreams of selling a script he'd written for a movie he wanted to direct, called *The Boondock Saints* and, at the same time, scoring a record deal for his band, the Brood, in which he played guitar. The movie begins in the spring of 1997. The twenty-eight-year-old Duffy is working as a bartender at a West Hollywood tavern called J. Sloan's, but his script has been making the rounds, and Harvey Weinstein, the powerful cofounder of Miramax Pictures, has offered him a dream deal for a first-timer: $300,000 for the script, a $15 million budget to make the movie (on which he'll also have final cut), and a soundtrack side deal for the Brood with Maverick Records.

In an amazing instance of spontaneous inflation, Duffy's head immediately swells up to the size of a small planet, and he turns overnight into a raging blowhard. "Everybody knows this is the best fuckin' project in Hollywood," he rants to his cronies, in between chain-smoking cigarettes, knocking back drinks, and bad-mouthing anyone who comes to mind (Keanu Reeves: "a talentless fool"). And it doesn't help that Weinstein—the man who discovered Quentin Tarantino!—has publicly called Duffy "a unique, exciting new voice in American movies" or that the abrasive auteur has been written up in *USA Today* and *The Hollywood Reporter* and featured on the cover of *MovieMaker* magazine. With his own personal film crew in tow to document his rise into the heavens of cinematic legend, Duffy (who has unwisely signed away any control he might have had over the resulting footage) is launched on an ego trip from which he might never return. All of this before he's shot a single foot of film.

Then Harvey Weinstein stops taking his calls, and by the fall of 1997, Miramax has put *The Boondock Saints* into turnaround, meaning the project is up for grabs by any other studio that might want it. None does. And with production continually being pushed back, Maverick Records bails out of the soundtrack deal. (Duffy learns this when he tries to drop by the Maverick offices and is told he's not allowed in the building.) By now, the trade media are starting to look at the bartender-cum-director in a different light (headline: "Back Behind the Bar"). But then an independent production company picks up *The Boondock Saints*, and Duffy finds his movie back in play, although on a much-reduced budget. He finally manages to assemble a cast that includes Willem Dafoe, Scottish comic Billy Connolly, and porn star Ron Jeremy. Shooting begins in Duffy's hometown of Boston.

In addition to this cinematic resuscitation, the Brood has been offered a recording deal by Lava Records. This prompts the other members of the band, who have essentially been starving ever since they moved out to L.A. at Duffy's behest, to ask him to front them modest loans against the Lava advance money—not cash outright, just loans.

Duffy swats them away. "I don't believe you deserve a thing," he tells them. (One of the band members is his own brother.) Problems crop up quickly. Lava chief Jason Flom doesn't like what he's hearing from the Brood's initial sessions. But what does he know? In a meeting with the band, Duffy says that although Lava has put up a quarter-million dollars to make the album, "Look how Jewish they're being about it." In addition, it's been discovered that there's another band called the Brood—an all-girl group from Portland, Maine, that's been putting out records since 1992—and they won't sell the rights to their name. This doesn't sit well with Duffy. (According to *Overnight* codirector Tony Montana, he berated the rival Brood as "a bunch of talentless fuckin' dykes.") In the end, his band is compelled to release its album under another name—the Boondock Saints, what else? It sells a total of 690 copies. Lava quickly drops the band and the band quickly breaks up.

One of the sweetest sequences in the annals of payback is the one in which Duffy and his retinue travel to France in the spring of 1999 to screen the finished *Boondock Saints* for potential distributors at the Cannes Film Festival. Ensconced in semiswank digs on his talent agency's tab, Duffy swings wildly between his usual braggadocio ("I know I'm one of the best there is, and I'm gonna be *the* best") and—when distribution deals fail to materialize—clueless incomprehension. ("Where's the offer? What's going on?") The picture finally does get released—barely—in January of 2000. It plays for one week in five theaters, dies, and goes straight to video.

Wouldn't it be annoying if *The Boondock Saints* turned out to be a good movie, unjustly ignored? I recently picked it up on DVD (ten bucks) and can report that it's a film that almost certainly wouldn't exist if Quentin Tarantino hadn't made *Reservoir Dogs* and *Pulp Fiction* a decade ago. *Boondock* is a vigilante tale pitting two young Irish American men against all manner of urban scum. In hapless thrall to Tarantino, director Duffy cooks up offbeat forms of torment (a fat mobster gets his butt set on fire) and makes sure that somebody says "fuck" about every twenty seconds. Willem Dafoe, who appears not to have been given much in the way of direction, plays a gay FBI agent who listens to opera on his Discman while swanning around bloody crime scenes.

There's none of Tarantino's pop-cultural fizz to any of this, and none of his snappy way with dialogue. The movie opens with a beautiful color sequence shot in a Catholic church, but quickly begins to drift—you can feel the energy leaking out of it as it stumbles along. But if you stay with it . . . well, I don't know what would happen if you stayed with it. I couldn't. (November 2004)

AUTEURS

S ome directors are so successful, or at least celebrated, that their fans will flock to see any movie to which their name is appended. The incomparable John Huston maintained this status for more than forty years, to the very end of his career. Lesser auteurs—rising to fame as emblems of a time or a theme, but possibly little else—can wear out their welcome. And some, in my experience, were never all that welcome in the first place. Here we consider such famous surnames as Tarantino, Miike, Egoyan, Aronofsky, Weir, and the Coen brothers. Also the problematic Stone, the wobbly De Palma, the irritating Von Trier, and the sadly postgreat Allen.

Grindhouse

Fanboy Clubhouse

One of the unspoken pleasures of a fondness for exploitation movies was always the feeling that you were part of a cinephile underground—that when you dropped names like Sid Haig or *White Line Fever*, most people probably wouldn't know what you were talking about. But the illicit kick that these films once provided has long since evaporated. Insider appreciation started bleeding out into the mainstream in the early 1980s, with the publication of mass-market Z-movie bibles like Michael Weldon's *Psychotronic Encyclopedia of Film* and Danny Peary's *Cult Movies*; and by 1994, when Tim Burton released a major-studio biopic about the most celebrated bad director of such films, the cultists' clubhouse door was left dangling on its hinges. Ed Wood had left the building.

So there's an air of dated condescension wafting out of *Grindhouse*, the new fake double feature from exploitation fans Quentin Tarantino and Robert Rodriguez. The picture consists of two quickie-style movies—Rodriguez's *Planet Terror*, a spirited zombie flick, and Tarantino's excruciatingly dull *Death Proof*—intersected by a clutch of very funny fake trailers. The film purports to instruct us about what it was like to experience lovably bad exploitation movies back in the early 1970s, and so the footage has been digitally manhandled to give it a staticky, run-through-a-thousand-projectors look, complete with missing frames and even whole scenes; and many of the actors muster a period deadpan anti-charisma that's all too authentic.

But what was new about exploitation movies back then—their brassy determination to provide what couldn't be had from standard Hollywood fare, be it geysers of blood, hair-raising car crashes, or hot-for-the-time soft-core sex—is not new now. We've seen it all. And if there's any need for a cultural history lesson, as Tarantino, at least, appears to believe, we can easily go to the source—virtually all those old movies are available on DVD. Unfortunately, we can't watch them through the steamy windows of a car parked at the local drive-in thirty years ago, huffing beer or whatever and hollering at the screen during the inevitable long, talky interludes between bursts of the action we've really come to see. However much Tarantino may wish it were otherwise, you can't go back.

Rodriguez, to his credit, has no heavy pretensions in this regard; he just seems to be having fun. His *Planet Terror* may be a loving tribute to genre wonders like *Night of the Living Dead* or *The Quatermass Xperiment* or *Creature with the Atom Brain*, but it's also a whoopingly over-the-top monster bash, entertaining on its own terms. The plot is as perfunctory as you might hope: there's a sinister military base; a mysterious virus that's turning people into zombies (well, not *technically* zombies, but limb-rending, pus-dripping homicidal maniacs nonetheless); a bit of light cleavage-ogling (two cheers for Stacy Ferguson, of the Black Eyed Peas); and a brave-against-all-odds young couple, played by Rose McGowan and Freddy Rodriguez, who are damned if they'll succumb without a fight.

Planet Terror contains the only iconic image in *Grindhouse*: a shot of McGowan mowing down fiends with a machine gun that's been fitted onto the stump of her ripped-off leg. (She's extra-angry because the amputation has ruined her dream of becoming a stand-up comic.) The film also has a berserkoid sequence of a sort I've never seen before—a flailing testicle harvest that should provide some squirmy moments for half of the audience. (The other half can rear back in alarm at a scene in a subsequent trailer involving a girl doing splits on a trampoline and the sudden appearance of a butcher knife down below.) This is the true exploitation spirit—Rodriguez pushes things too far, and every time he does, we can't wait for him to do it again.

In *Death Proof*, on the other hand, Tarantino has re-created a completely unmourned aspect of the exploitation tradition. His film is nominally a tribute to old car-chase movies (he cites the 1971 *Vanishing Point* and the original, 1974 *Gone in 60 Seconds*), and the chasing and the crashing in it are suitably spectacular, in a very familiar way. But what he's mainly managed to replicate, with dismal precision, are the turgid stretches of low-energy talk-talk-talk that often becalmed those old pictures, and which are—surprise—every bit as boring now.

Kurt Russell, in full grizzly wheeze, plays a psycho movie stuntman called . . . Stuntman Mike. He roams the back roads of Texas offering high-speed thrills—and bloody deaths—to any young women unwise enough to hitch a lift with him or pass him in the fast lane. Among the women he encounters are some lively actresses, especially Rosario Dawson, Tracie Thoms, Sydney Tamiia Poitier, and real-life stuntwoman Zoë Bell. (Bell's wild ride atop the hood of a careening Dodge Challenger in the film's concluding chase scene is almost worth the tedious slog required to get to it.) Unfortunately, their characters are stranded in the shallows of some of Tarantino's droopiest dialogue. (This is not the Quent who brought a new kind of goosed-up verbal energy to pictures like *Reservoir Dogs* and *Pulp Fiction*.)

The women are up-to-date action chicks, and so along with the usual hard-nosed talk about men, they also engage in endless nattering about hot cars and of course other pop-culture concerns. They yammer on and on, in backseats and barrooms, while Tarantino, taking a cinematographer credit for the first time (he also acts in both films), pans around them in relentless circles. In some of these scenes, the restless camera work is the only thing really going on. Given Tarantino's proven gifts for writing and directing, his half of this movie, almost in its entirety, is baffling.

An important fact to be noted about *Grindhouse* is this: it's three hours and eleven minutes long. After sitting through the rousing Rodriguez feature that opens the film and the hilarious faux trailers that follow (courtesy of guest directors Eli Roth, Rob Zombie, and *Shaun of the Dead*'s Edgar Wright), one could be forgiven for not wanting to sit through a second picture, even a good one. And that, sad as it is for a Tarantino fan to say, isn't what's coming up next. (April 2007)

Inglourious Basterds

Long March

Quentin Tarantino is such a talented maker of films that you wonder when he's going to evolve into a complete filmmaker. Tarantino's new World War II movie, *Inglourious Basterds*, brings with it the director's usual avalanche of hermetic film-geek references: a character named Aldo Raine is a reference to the late Aldo Ray, star of the 1955 war movie *Battle Cry*; the name of another character, Hugo Stiglitz, is borrowed from a Mexican horror-film star. The subtlest of these allusions, though—possibly, anyway—involves two 1940s films by the French director Henri-Georges Clouzot. The title of one, *Le Corbeau*, is glimpsed here on a movie-theater marquee. A poster for the other, *L'Assassin Habite . . . au 21*, is seen on the wall in another shot. The star of both of those pictures was Pierre Fresnay, who also starred in Jean Renoir's World War I classic, *Grand Illusion*.

If such an oblique reference was intended, it serves as an inadvertent comment on the content of Tarantino's films. *Grand Illusion* is one of the most powerful of all war movies, and in its concern with the passage of time and the futility of war, one of the most humane. *Inglourious Basterds* deals neither with these things nor with such other mundane subjects as love, injustice, or loss. Tarantino's films are essays in cleverness, which relieves him of the burden of having to say anything meaningful about the human condition, even in a clever way. His multireferential jokiness worked brilliantly in the synthetic construct of *Pulp Fiction* fifteen years ago. But will he ever move on?

Tarantino's admirers might object that this is a wild comedy, not a serious-issues picture, and they're right. But great comedies, even the frothiest screwball classics, deal with actual people, or at least recognizable human types. Tarantino tends to deal only with his interests, which, even after all this time, are still limited mainly to movies.

Inglourious Basterds is an extended gag about Aldo Raine, a redneck army lieutenant (played by Brad Pitt) organizing a group of Jewish GIs to infiltrate German-occupied France for the purpose of killing Nazis. This premise at least has the virtue of moral clarity. And there's probably no point in being offended by Tarantino's turning World War II—a conflagration that consumed the lives of some 60 million people—into a giddy joke. The same has been said about the old TV series *Hogan's Heroes*—although that show did at least attempt to keep its distance from the war's hideous essence. Here we see Nazi soldiers firing their guns down through a farmhouse floor to exterminate a group of Jews who are hiding in the cellar. That the murdered Jews aren't actually seen allows the director to avoid any buzz-killing emotional charge.

One young Jewish woman escapes this slaughter. Her name is Shosanna (Mélanie Laurent), and when we next see her, three years later, she has made it to Paris, where she's managing—what else?—a movie theater. This being a Tarantino picture, it's relentlessly moviecentric. When the British high command decides to dispatch an officer to assist the Nazi-hunting Basterds, who've also arrived in Paris, he turns out to be a former movie critic, and he discourses for us on the Nazi takeover of Germany's legendary UFA film studio in Babelsberg (where this picture was partly shot). We're also given a barrowload of information about the flammability of old nitrate film stock. And movie scholars, if no one else, will register the presence of an actor playing Emil Jannings, the silent-film star who became a Nazi pet. (Jannings was also the first actor to win an Academy Award, in 1929, as you surely know.)

Along the way to Paris, we learn that Aldo Raine is half Apache, which is why he orders his men to bring back the scalp of every Nazi they kill. Can there be any other reason for this pointless plot quirk than the opportunity it offered Tarantino to insert a close-up of a knife hacking the scalp off a corpse? The movie's gore quota is further fulfilled by the director's pal, Eli Roth, playing a Basterd called "the Bear Jew," whose specialty is bashing in the skulls of captured Nazis with a baseball bat.

Raine and company have a special purpose in Paris. It has been learned that a new Nazi propaganda movie will be premiering there—at Shosanna's theater, in fact—and that Adolf Hitler and other top Nazis will be in attendance. The Basterds' assignment is to blow up the theater during the show. But Shosanna has a plan of her own for the big night. Can history be blithely rewritten? Of course. But to what purpose?

All of this said, the movie is beautifully photographed (by Robert Richardson, who also shot Tarantino's *Kill Bill* pictures). And it contains some wonderfully well constructed set-piece scenes—especially the opening farmhouse encounter that introduces the silky-scary SS colonel Hans Landa (Christoph Waltz); and later a chaotic shootout in a French pub. There's also some startling imagery: a shot of an ecstatic face rearing up on a screen amid engulfing flames is one of the most striking things Tarantino has ever come up with—it actually recalls some of the great old UFA silent films.

The actors seem to be having fun, too. Pitt's good-ole-boy impersonation is awfully broad, but he's such a star that he manages to make the character consistently entertaining. And Diane Kruger brings a vintage wartime glamour to the role of German movie actress (and secret British agent) Bridget von Hammersmark. The picture's one unforgettable performance, though, is by Waltz. His Hans Landa is a striking creation, all oily seduction and homicidal menace. In another context (a more serious movie, for instance), he'd be ghastly. Here the actor makes him mesmerizing, and Waltz owns every scene into which he sets foot. (He justly won the Best Actor award at the last Cannes Film Festival.)

How much of an audience *Inglourious Basterds* will be able to retain after its first week or two is an open question. The movie is two and a half hours long, and you may find your finger twitching in search of an unavailable delete button as the camera circles endlessly around overlong conversations or lingers for no reason on the dolloping of whipped cream onto a slice of strudel. There's more talk in the picture than there is action, and a lot of it is in subtitled French, German, and Italian. Tarantino is rightly esteemed for his sharp dialogue; but as was also the case with his last film, the dire *Death Proof*, there's too much of it here, and a lot of it's not as sharp as might have been hoped. *Inglourious Basterds* is not *Pulp Fiction*. It's not even a war movie, really. It's a movie about *other* war movies—a riot of references with no stabilizing core. Yet again. (August 2009)

Sukiyaki Western Django

Takeout

The most interesting thing about *Sukiyaki Western Django* is its high, if not especially fresh, concept: it's a samurai western. At least that conceit is clear enough to contemplate without losing your mind. The movie itself, which runs two hours, is something else.

Quentin Tarantino appears in the film as an actor, rarely a good thing. He isn't a *bad* actor, just an unconvincing one. This is why his movie manifestations are often greeted with ripples of fond laughter—no matter what role he may be attempting to play, he can only ever be one character: Quentin Tarantino. He's trapped in that famous face. And goofy line readings ("It goes a little sumpin' like dis," he says at one point here) compound the problem—they pull us out of the story. Although in this case, that's not an entirely bad thing.

Tarantino has no other connection with the picture (he's not a producer or a "presenter," for example), but it's saturated with his retro-blender sensibility. The Japanese director, Takashi Miike, is best known in this country for a pair of memorable shockers—the stylishly disturbing *Audition* and the pulverizing *Ichi the Killer*. Tarantino has been a vocal proponent of Miike's work for years, and Miike had a cameo role in Eli Roth's grisly *Hostel*, a movie of which Tarantino was an executive producer. Now here they are, together at last.

This was not a good idea, really. But then *Sukiyaki* is ill-advised in

several ways. To begin with, it's one of those preening film-geek "tributes" to an old B movie with which most people are, shall we say, not in-
timately familiar. (If they were, they might wonder why the geeks were
bothering to pay tribute to it instead of, say, coming up with an original
movie of their own.) In this case, the picture being saluted/plundered
is Sergio Corbucci's 1966 *Django*, a spaghetti western that cheerfully
ripped off Sergio Leone's 1964 spaghetti classic, *A Fistful of Dollars*,
which was already an adaptation of Akira Kurosawa's revered 1961 samurai epic, *Yojimbo*.

The story has a primordial familiarity: mysterious lone warrior wanders into corrupt village beset by contending gangs, plays them off
against each other, watches the body count mount till no one's left, then
wanders away again into the sunset. Miike relocates the action from an
Italian Wild West fantasyland back to feudal Japan, which was where
Kurosawa's film was set. Whether feudal Japan had Gatling guns, lip
studs, and dye-streaked hairstyles—or people saying things like "not
too shabby" and "keep it in your pants"—needn't distract us here, any
more than a sign at the side of a road that welcomes us to "Nevada." A
well-worn postmodern wackiness comes with this territory.

The picture is largely devoted to carnage, about which there's little
to say. Being generic, the story isn't especially involving (there's a chest
of gold at the root of whatever), and the endless shootouts, with their
bullet storms and blood rivers, aren't anything you haven't seen before.
The warring gangs—clans, actually—are distinguished by the colors
they wear, like medieval Crips and Bloods. The Genjis wear white,
which gives their leader (Yusuke Iseya), in his flowing white duster and
flamboyant chaps, an odd late-Elvis look. The Heikes are partial to red,
or just blood itself will do. (As a kooky aside, *their* leader, played by
Koichi Sato, has just discovered Shakespeare and insists that everyone
call him Henry VI.) The nameless gunman (Hideaki Ito) who's come to
upset all of these people's applecarts is heavily into black, and brooding. There's also a sort of vaudeville sheriff, played by Teruyuki Kagawa,
who contributes some of the most outrageous pop-eyed muggery
you're likely to see in a movie whose makers expect to be taken half
seriously.

This being a Miike film, however, there *is* some arresting imagery—a bank of fog pouring eerily through a forest, a blooming red and white rose with a fetus squirming at its center. And the opening scene is striking in its bold artificiality. It's set on a frankly fake high-plains homestead, under a lemony sun and a plainly painted sky, with what looks like a big cardboard mountain propped up in the distance. A man appears, wearing a cowboy hat and a serape, and proceeds to do some complicated things with a snake and an egg and a bullet. It's a great kickoff for a picture. Then, however, on closer inspection, the man turns out to be Tarantino, and inevitably we think, "Hey, it's Quent. What's he doing here?"

With the exception of Tarantino, whose serape character plays only a small part in the tale (although he also turns up later as a crusty old man in a wheelchair, about which the less said the better), the actors are all Japanese. However, they speak English—some quite well, but some with a clotted imprecision that's frequently impenetrable, especially amid all the machine guns, dynamite, and endlessly chattering six-shooters. There are two women in the cast (played by the lovely Yoshino Kimura and the sassier Kaori Momoi), but they're on hand mainly to be raped, ogled, and slapped around, although occasionally they, too, get to blow somebody away. One envies that opportunity. After what seemed like days of this overbearingly eccentric movie, I felt like turning a gun on myself. (August 2008)

Where the Truth Lies

Double Jeopardy

Director Atom Egoyan's hypnotic new movie is an examination of truth, identity, innocence, and murder. It's a mystery that becomes more and more mysterious as it moves along, and even at the end you may not be sure you've read all of it right. The leads—Kevin Bacon,

Colin Firth, and Alison Lohman—are extraordinarily good in ways they haven't been before, and they negotiate the film's graphic sex scenes with bold assurance. The picture is a classic film noir—it's suffused with seediness and unsavory secrets; but Egoyan has dragged the genre out of the shadows among which it was born and into the sparkling, almost stage-managed sunlight of Miami and Los Angeles, where the story's creepiness seems even more starkly perverse.

The movie opens in 1957, in Miami, where America's best-loved comedy team, Lanny Morris (Bacon) and Vince Collins (Firth) are hosting the Veteran's Day Polio Telethon—thirty-nine hours of crass mugging, corny songs, and witless wisecracks—which annually burnishes the image the two partners have crafted over many years in movies and nightclubs. Lanny is the obnoxious goofball of the act; Vince, an Englishman, contributes a redeeming touch of class. "His presence," Lanny says, in one of the film's rich stream of insinuating voice-overs, "gave America an excuse to like me." (The archetype here is clearly Dean Martin and Jerry Lewis.)

A little girl comes up onstage. Her own polio is in remission, thanks to Lanny and Vince's fundraising efforts, and she's adorably thankful. Lanny hugs her with tears streaming down his face. Nice guys, it seems—until we see Vince backstage beating another man bloody in a sudden fit of rage. Now we're not so sure.

The picture next jumps to 1972, and we learn that that telethon fifteen years earlier was the last time Lanny and Vince ever worked together; they haven't spoken to each other since. It seems that before the show began, the naked body of a dead college girl named Maureen (Rachel Blanchard) was found submerged in the bathtub of the luxury hotel suite the two comics were sharing. Police quickly concluded they weren't culpable and declared the girl's death a suicide. But Lanny and Vince were deeply shaken, and still are. And it's not entirely clear why.

We also meet Karen O'Connor (Lohman), the grateful little girl on the telethon stage, now all grown up. Karen is a fledgling journalist; she's written a few magazine cover stories, but she wants to make a bigger splash. Still fixated on her favorite comedy team, she sets out to secure their assistance in writing a book about them—a tell-all that will explain the reason for their breakup and finally reveal what actually happened the night that girl was found dead in their suite. She contacts Lanny about telling his side of the story but is informed that he's writing his own book (not to be published, we learn, until both he and Vince are dead). However, when Karen tracks down Vince, now living in seclusion in a swank, sterile home in the hills above L.A., she finds him more amenable—especially when she tells him that her publisher will pay him one million dollars if he'll come clean about everything. Vince agrees to work on the book with Karen. But first . . .

Well, it would be wrong to reveal too much of the film's intricate plot, and hard to do, anyway—it's a puzzle palace filled with locked rooms and dubious keys that stick at every turn. We're constantly having to revise our understanding of what's going on. The relationship between Lanny and Vince is an ever-shifting enigma, and when the deceased Maureen puts in a flashback appearance, even she turns out to be not what we expected.

Kevin Bacon, Colin Firth, and Alison Lohman might seem an oddly matched set of actors, but their performances mesh with remarkable finesse. Bacon, playing a showbiz slimeball, kitted out in garish, 1970s-style neck scarves and aggressively colorful tight trousers, still manages to suggest remnants of decency beneath the sleaze. Firth uses his characteristic inwardness to depict a man who may be unreadable even to himself. And Lohman, with her creamy complexion framed by luscious strawberry blond hair and photographed to look as if she's lit from within by a bundle of sunbeams, is the perfect incarnation of innocence waiting to be defiled. And, in this nasty little movie, not having to wait all that long. (October 2005)

Chloe

Curves Ahead

Chloe is a hot young prostitute with a deep dark side. Catherine, a middle-aged gynecologist, is unaware of this when she engages Chloe as an undercover temptress to bait her husband, David, a music professor she suspects of having affairs with his female students. Over the course of several liaisons with David, Chloe confirms Catherine's worst fears in graphic detail. This is disturbing news—although not nearly as disturbing as what's really going on.

Chloe is a sleek erotic mystery with unexpected twists. It's ideally cast—with Amanda Seyfried as Chloe, Julianne Moore as Catherine, and Liam Neeson as David—and its plot switches are triggered with a smooth calculation that might have won the Hitchcock seal of approval. Director Atom Egoyan usually writes his own extraordinary screenplays; here, though, he has opted for adaptation, of a 2003 movie called *Nathalie . . .*, by French director Anne Fontaine, and he has delegated the scripting to Erin Cressida Wilson, the writer of such strange films as *Secretary* and *Fur: An Imaginary Portrait of Diane Arbus*. The result is a small classic of murky desires and mixed signals, and of love gone really, really wrong.

It's difficult to say much about the movie without giving away its surprises. Egoyan has relocated Fontaine's story from Paris to Toronto, which is presented here as an urban jewel box of sparkling snowy streets and gleaming clubs and restaurants. Out for dinner one night with David and another couple, Catherine has an ambiguous restroom encounter with Chloe, a girl she's never met before. Returning to her table, she finds David and their friends embarked on a game called "spot the hooker." Catherine rolls her eyes—but then sees Chloe returning to her own table to join an older man who has "john" written all over him.

Later, alone at a bar, Catherine is again approached by Chloe; she buys the younger woman a drink and relates her suspicions about David's extramarital activities. "I want to find out," Catherine says, with a trace of desperation. Can Chloe be of service? "Most of my clients are married," she assures her. "He's not the client," says Catherine.

Chloe agrees to go to a café that David frequents and make herself noticeable, which is no problem. She reports back to Catherine that her husband did make a small pass, but they only talked. Her next meeting with David, at a mazelike botanical garden, goes considerably further. Then Catherine receives a text message from Chloe asking her to come to a room in a swank hotel. There she finds a bed in disarray, the remains of breakfast for two on a cart, and Chloe stepping naked from the shower. Here the movie's wild ride begins.

In bringing substance to the enigmatic character of Chloe, Seyfried gives her most impressive performance to date. She navigates a startling sex scene with unflinching assurance and radiates allure even in an opening voice-over, enumerating her skills as a paid companion: "I can become your first kiss, or a torn-out image from a *Playboy* magazine you saw when you were nine years old," she says. "And then I can disappear." We may never figure out what makes Chloe tick, but we can definitely hear her ticking.

Neeson and Moore are as expert as always. Neeson (who continued shooting this film after the sudden death of his wife, Natasha Richardson) exudes his usual masculine solidity, and he's a generous foil for Moore's Catherine, whose insecurities have begun to multiply as she ages beyond the youthful ideal to which she knows her husband is still drawn. Moore's talent for conveying complex emotional states with just a look or a subtly charged line reading is one of the movie's several satisfactions (along with Mychael Danna's rich score, which recalls the classic lushness of Franz Waxman and other golden age film composers).

But Seyfried emerges as the star of the picture. In playing a dangerous woman no one can ever really know, she manages to leave us feeling, at the end, that it's probably best that way. (March 2010)

The Wrestler

Death Match

Mickey Rourke has taken a lot of punishment over the years, most of it with a strange eagerness. In his movies of the 1980s, like *Diner, Angel Heart,* and *The Pope of Greenwich Village*, his whispery charisma made him one of the most riveting young actors of the day. Then, in the early 1990s, he left the business to become a low-rung professional boxer, which is where the punishment came in. Now, at the age of fifty-two, with a face so heavily repaired it suggests an Easter Island import, Rourke has found the role of a lifetime in Darren Aronofsky's *The Wrestler*, in which he plays a has-been grappler who has also taken a lot of punishment but can't stop coming back for more—punishment is his life. It's a fearless performance: Rourke himself may look lumpy and worked-over, but his charisma remains undented.

His character is Randy Robinson—"The Ram"—a star on the pro-wrestling circuit back in the 1980s. Twenty-five years later, he's still pulling on the tights and knocking back steroids, but the matches are sparse these days, and the money minimal—working a dead-end supermarket job on the side, he still can't make the rent in the dismal New Jersey trailer park where he lives. (Wintry New Jersey, with its bare trees and bleak flatlands, sets the picture's emotional tone throughout.) Wrestling has changed, too: now your opponents come at you with barbed wire and staple guns and rake dinner forks across your face. It's a young man's game, and Randy, with his bad back, hearing aid, and deteriorating ticker, is no longer young.

But wrestling is all he has. His daughter, Stephanie (Evan Rachel Wood), doesn't want to know him, since he bugged out on most of her childhood; and the only other woman he feels anything for is a stripper called Cassidy (Marisa Tomei), who's starting to fade herself. Randy's real home is the ring, even if it's just a makeshift affair in a school gym or a cheesy auditorium these days; and his only friends are other wrestlers: Lex Lethal, Tommy Rotten, the Necro Butcher—guys like that. The young up-and-comers remember him as the blond god of a thousand childhood wall posters, but the battered old vets he meets at tawdry memorabilia gatherings put a chill in his soul.

One day, Randy runs up against his own mortality, and a doctor tells him if he doesn't quit wrestling, he'll die. But a semi-big celebrity rematch has been scheduled, pitting him against his most famous opponent from back in the day, a bruiser called the Ayatollah (Ernest Miller—like the other ring rats here, an actual professional wrestler). "With a little luck," he tells Cassidy, "this could be my ticket back on top."

The movie is a demonstration of how much art can be made with very little money. (Even the complex ring scenes were shot with a pair of 16-millimeter cameras.) Aronofsky and his editor, Andrew Weisblum, keep the story coming right at you, fast and raw; and the director doesn't pull back from presenting the fight sequences as they would have to be: brutal, loud, and bloody. But there are also a few moments of piercing sweetness, especially the one in which Randy persuades Stephanie to take a walk with him on a deserted Jersey Shore boardwalk, and the two actors improvise an awkward waltz in an abandoned ballroom. There's also a funny scene in which Randy gets a day-job promotion to the deli counter (for which he's forced to don a humiliating hairnet) and turns it into a little performance amid the pesto pasta and the potato salad. (His audience is composed of actual patrons of the supermarket in which the scene was shot.) And Marisa Tomei is brave and heartbreaking as Cassidy, a woman whose own body, like Randy's, is fast approaching its use-by date. Cassidy is no longer having much luck finding takers for her lap dances, and the scene in which we see her gyrating around a stripper pole at the club, with her eyes registering the crowd's minimal appreciation, is crushingly sad.

But Rourke is the movie's central wonder. He plays Randy as a man with no future who won't give up on hope. "The world doesn't give a shit about me," he tells Cassidy backstage at a match. Gesturing toward the baffling world out beyond the arena walls, he says, "The only place I get hurt is out there." (December 2008)

The Black Dahlia

Pulp Fiction

Like the James Ellroy novel on which it's based, director Brian De Palma's *The Black Dahlia* is a fictionalized account of a famously grisly and still unsolved L.A. murder case. The victim was twenty-two-year-old Elizabeth Short, and her naked body was found in a weedy field on the morning of January 15, 1947. It had been severed at the waist and then apparently washed before the two halves of the corpse were transported from wherever it was that Short had been murdered. Her mouth had been slashed into a hideous rictus, and patches of skin were missing from other areas of her body. These are facts.

The movie additionally asserts that the cadaver had been drained of blood, and that the girl's viscera, including "her reproductive organs," had been removed. These are not facts. Nor is there any evidence for the picture's portrayal of Short as a dim-witted bisexual slut, an aspiring actress whose lack of talent was documented in a series of pathetic screen tests and whose only actual celluloid performance was in a short lesbian porn film.

These fabrications may not seem especially problematic at first, since *The Black Dahlia* is only glancingly concerned with Elizabeth Short's murder. Instead, its focus is on two LAPD detectives, Dwight "Bucky" Bleichert (Josh Hartnett) and Lee Blanchard (Aaron Eckhart). We don't meet this pair right away, because the movie opens, for some reason, in the midst of the Zoot Suit Riots of 1943, in which packs of U.S. soldiers and sailors roamed the streets of East L.A. beating up young Mexican pachucos, and local police reportedly followed along, arresting hundreds of the victims. These notorious clashes may deserve a movie of their own, but it's hard to grasp what they're doing in this one.

Our confusion deepens when we finally do meet Bucky and Lee, because at first they're not cops—they're amateur boxers. Lee is billed as Mr. Fire (he's a Benzedrine-stoked hothead); Bucky is Mr. Ice (a zingier handle than Mr. Inexpressive Mope). There's an elaborate arena bout in which these two bash away at each other for so long, we begin to wonder if we've wandered into a 1940s boxing movie. There's also some trivial business with Bucky's senile father, who has taken to shooting pigeons from his window and has to be put in an old-age home. Eventually, though, Bucky and Lee do morph into cops, complete with badges and gats, roomy period suits, and atmospheric tobacco habits. Are we about to get into the Dahlia case?

Not yet. First we have to meet Lee's girlfriend, Kay Lake (Scarlett Johansson). With her clingy sweaters and satin lounging outfits, Kay is a study in retro blond lusciousness. She's a reformed prostitute, once the property of a small-time pimp whom Lee cleverly sent to prison. Now the pimp is about to be released, and Kay is scared. Her boyfriend, Mr. Fire, is obscurely incensed. And Bucky is as puzzled as we are. For one thing, although Lee and Kay live together, Kay pointedly tells Bucky that they don't *sleep* together. (This intriguing wisp of information is never pursued.) Before long, the three of them become inseparable. They hang out around the house a lot, smoking and drinking and smoking some more, and when they go out to the movies, Kay sits between the two men and holds hands with both of them. This, too, remains unexplored.

The Black Dahlia appears at last in one of the movie's several stylishly constructed set-piece scenes—a crane shot that rises up from one street and across a rooftop to another street nearby, where, from high above, we see the body lying in the field. Given that the director is De Palma, the man who made the 1983 *Scarface* (if he had a boxing handle, it might be "Mr. Bloodbath"), you'd expect him to dive right down into this ghastly crime scene. But De Palma is oddly fastidious here; he doesn't push Elizabeth Short's mutilated corpse into our faces.

He does indulge his penchant for lurid kink, though. The fictitious porn film in which Elizabeth features (she's played by Mia Kirshner) is rendered with a knowing prurience. And when the murder investigation takes Bucky to a plush lesbian nightclub, it's a place so fabulously dissolute that the tuxedoed figure up onstage singing "Love for Sale," amid a bevy of writhing, tongue-kissing chorines, turns out to be k.d. lang.

We have plenty of time to savor these titillating details because the plot has left us far behind. There's a slumming rich girl named Madeleine (Hilary Swank), who's said to be a dead ringer for Elizabeth Short. (Unfortunately, Swank looks nothing like Mia Kirshner; here, she doesn't even much resemble Hilary Swank.) And there's her dreadful family: a moneybags dad (John Kavanagh) who admires Hitler; a pointlessly weird little sister (Rachel Miner); and a drunken, gibbering mother (Fiona Shaw, in the movie's worst performance). There's also a silly, sub-*Chinatown* plot thread involving a conspiracy to misuse rotten lumber from old silent-movie sets. But the picture's crowning lunacy comes at the end, when the Dahlia's killer is "revealed" in an extended sequence of such demented, squealing hysteria we want to avert our eyes in embarrassment for the actors.

De Palma is an expert technician, of course, and working with veteran cinematographer Vilmos Zsigmond, he creates some tour-de-force scenes (especially a shoot-out in a shadowy marble atrium). His attempted approximation of Los Angeles in the 1940s is also enterprising, considering that most of the movie was shot in Bulgaria. His stars, however, are a mixed proposition. Eckhart has a clenched intensity that's just right for a strong-arm cop; but when he's not on-screen, and Hartnett has to carry the action, the picture slumps—Hartnett is too mildly contemporary to be persuasive as a vintage tough guy. And Johansson's character is given little to do beyond smoking and posing (and inventing ever more challenging ways to do up her hair).

Despite the juicy tabloid material and the filmmaking talent involved, *The Black Dahlia* is a bloated and listless production. And it's a slog—it runs two hours, and it feels at least twenty minutes too long. There's also an unsavory aspect to the picture: it's repellent to watch a woman's agonizing death, even this many years after the fact, being wrapped in slanders and pumped up into entertainment. That the entertainment fails to be very entertaining makes it an even sorrier undertaking. Clearly, Elizabeth Short's abuse didn't end in 1947. (September 2006)

Antichrist

Artville

Lars Von Trier's *Antichrist* is a curious mash-up of torture porn and good old porn porn that underwhelms in both areas. Despite some wild gore touches that might draw gasps of admiration from Eli Roth, the picture is too preoccupied with Von Trier's dismal deep thoughts to exert the visceral grip an effective splatter flick requires. And despite a few graphic sex shots, the movie is arctically anti-erotic. What it most precisely evokes are the art-film pretensions of the early 1960s, when European auteurs could get away with a line like "acorns don't cry" and American aficionados were disinclined to complain. (Imagine how those old Resnais and Antonioni head-scratchers might have been enlivened by a few strategically placed insertion shots.) Still, the movie's beautiful and sometimes breathtaking imagery makes it difficult to dismiss.

You know you're in Artville when a film's only two characters are called He (Willem Dafoe) and She (Charlotte Gainsbourg). He is a psychotherapist; She is some kind of writer working on a book called *Gynocide,* which is about the torture and murder of women through the ages. In the opening sequence—a luminous weave of stylized water and snow imagery—we see the couple having sex in their apartment while, in another room, their young son totters from his crib and out to an open window, from which he falls to his death. The guilt-ridden mother is driven half-mad by this event; her mate views it more coolly—as a psychological trauma of a sort he's eminently qualified to treat. He suggests they decamp for their vacation cabin—Eden, they call it—which is way out in the woods somewhere. (The picture is arbitrarily set in Seattle; since the director numbers air travel among his phobias, it was actually shot in Germany.)

The cabin turns out to be a decrepit shack of a sort that might have been designed to propel a troubled individual over the edge. There's some alarming wildlife, too. Poking around in the brush, the husband comes upon a dead baby bird crawling with ants. (There ought to be a sign next to its little feathered corpse saying, "David Lynch was here.") And there's a startling shot involving a doe and a stillborn fawn that I doubt I'll be forgetting anytime soon. But then, unfortunately, there's a scene in which He happens upon a dead fox, with its guts spilling out onto the ground. The unfortunate part is that the fox suddenly lifts its head and *speaks*. It says, "Chaos reigns." And then, marking the point where the picture tips over into complete gaga absurdity, rain starts pouring down.

We haven't seen the last of these uncanny animals. Before their preposterous return, though, there's a lot of shouting and a lot of carnal grappling. The man becomes convinced that his wife's *Gynocide* project has led her to believe that women are inherently evil—that they deserve the abuse to which they're eternally subjected. She begs her partner to hit her; he complies. Then there's an extended and truly ridiculous sequence involving a power drill and a metal wheel that would fit seamlessly into one of the *Hostel* movies. On the other hand, there's also a close-up clitoridectomy—self-administered with a pair of rusty shears—that would be unlikely to find a home in any other movie of any kind anywhere ever. After a while it becomes impossible to respond to this picture; you just stare at it.

Antichrist contains fearless performances by Dafoe and Gainsbourg. And it was sleekly photographed by Anthony Dod Mantle, who also shot Von Trier's *Dogville* and *Manderlay*. But Mantle's expertise compounds the picture's oppressiveness. The director's visual design is so artily dank and claustrophobic the movie might as easily have been shot in a tool shed. Von Trier says the story came to him during a bout of deep, disabling depression, and after seeing it, we know how he must have felt.

Antichrist arrives on a wave of foaming notoriety. Von Trier premiered it at this year's Cannes Film Festival (where he also proclaimed himself "the best filmmaker in the world"). The picture's reception was explosive. I don't know if it's really true that four people fainted at the screening, but the general response was apparently one of outraged hostility. The picture was even awarded a special "anti-prize" for most misogynist movie.

And now here it is, opening in America—although what "opening" might mean for a film that's pugnaciously unrated (the death knell for newspaper advertising) remains to be seen. Von Trier is the sort of director who claims he makes movies for himself—who cares if anyone wants to see them? I don't think anybody buys this kind of line anymore (least of all his investors, you'd imagine), but it is in fact hard to envision how much of an audience there might be for this film. Or how many people there could possibly be who would ever sit through it twice. (October 2009)

No Country for Old Men

Fate Crimes

In *No Country for Old Men*, the chilly new Coen brothers film, the Spanish actor Javier Bardem is nightmarishly frightening as Anton Chigurh, a stone-faced hit man on the trail of $2 million that went missing after a drug deal collapsed in bullets and blood out on the West Texas plains. With his dead eyes and oddly unnerving 1970s haircut (David Soul with a dye job), Chigurh carries a tank of compressed air to power his slaughterhouse bolt gun, and he decides the fate of his more innocent victims with the toss of a coin. He could be death itself—silent, unfeeling, out there waiting to happen when you least expect him.

Llewelyn Moss (Josh Brolin) is the man who made off with the money. Moss was hunting antelope on the sunbaked flats when he came across the drug dealers' shot-up trucks parked amid their scattered corpses. He's a decent guy, but he and his young wife live in a ratty trailer park, and he wishes they didn't. So when he came across the bag of drug cash, he took it. This was a bigger mistake than he could have imagined.

Chigurh is being dutifully tracked by Sheriff Ed Tom Bell (Tommy Lee Jones), a mournful lawman old enough to remember real cowboys (the story is set in 1980); he no longer understands a world in which inexplicable creatures such as Chigurh exist. Meanwhile, both Chigurh and Moss are being stalked by Carson Wells (Woody Harrelson), a former federal agent turned bounty hunter, now employed by some very bad men.

No Country for Old Men has the narrative machinery of a chase movie—there's plenty of gunplay and considerable blood. But as the picture proceeds, we see that most of its characters are really being pursued not simply by cops or gunmen but by something larger and more implacable.

Writer-directors Joel and Ethan Coen have been meticulously faithful to Cormac McCarthy's 2005 novel, a book whose contemplation of inescapable fate is carried along on a mesmerizing procession of flat declarative sentences. The Coen brothers capture that meditative tone completely; and, collaborating once again with the great cinematographer Roger Deakins, they shape the parched, timeless Tex-Mex borderland into a character itself, a place where good and evil alike swelter under the sun and the prairie wind whistles by uncaring.

It's no surprise that Jones is perfectly cast as the superannuated Sheriff Bell—who better than this vividly wrinkled Texan to play the part? Brolin brings a tight-lipped tension to the role of Moss, a limited man in way over his head; and Harrelson gives one of his most engaging performances as Wells, a smiling pro delivering justice for hire but unable to comprehend the primordial justice that's bearing down on him. And the Scottish actress Kelly Macdonald builds a gathering strength into the part of Moss's sweet, supportive wife, Carla Jean, a woman too proud to plead, even for her life.

But it's Anton Chigurh—unsmiling, unstoppable—who dominates

the movie with the dark force of Bardem's characterization. "You should admit your situation," he balefully suggests, preparing to snuff out a life. "There will be more dignity in it." Announcing his presence to another victim, he says, "You know how this is gonna turn out, don't you?" Sheriff Bell believes that Chigurh is more than a simple lunatic—a plausible thought when we hear the killer tell yet another doomed soul, "If the road you followed brought you to this, what was the use of it?" The man metes out not just death but despair. Wells says he thinks Chigurh has principles nobody else understands. And probably never will. (November 2007)

Burn After Reading

Mixed Nuts

The Coen brothers are their own most daunting competition. Their new movie, *Burn After Reading*, can't really compete with such pole-axed classics as *O Brother, Where Art Thou?* or *Fargo*, but it's still a Coen brothers film—written, directed, and edited by, as usual—and so it's filled with warped dialogue and wonderfully mad performances.

The story is all quirks and comic tremors. It begins at CIA headquarters in Langley, Virginia, where Osborne Cox (John Malkovich), an intelligence analyst with a sideline in being perpetually pissed off, is getting the boot because of his drinking problem. Since he doesn't drink all *that* much (never at breakfast, for example), he's enormously pissed off about this. (When Malkovitch does one of his fury fits, his shaved head seems to swell and redden like a boil, making him look oddly like James Carville.) At loose ends, the discarded spook decides to write his memoirs, downloading some highly sensitive CIA files to stir his recollection. At this point, the movie happily loses its mind.

Cox's disk full of files winds up at a Hardbodies gym, where it falls into the clutches of two idiot employees named Chad Feldheimer (Brad

Pitt) and Linda Litzke (Frances McDormand). Chad, with his gum-chewing grin and his booty-shaking iPod addiction, really is an idiot. But Linda is a lost soul who's looking for love in all the wrong places—which is to say, on the Internet. She wants to reinvent herself and requires money for the multiple elective surgeries she feels are necessary to do so. ("I have gone just about as far as I can go with this body," she says.) Chad gets her excited about the disk of intel they've found; he wants to sell it back to Cox for big bucks. Linda gets the picture and is exultant: "We caught him with his thing caught in a big fat wringer, and we're in the driver's seat!" she crows. Unfortunately, when Chad makes a bumbling approach to Cox, the little troll listens for about ten seconds and then gets enormously pissed off.

Meanwhile, Cox's wife, Katie (Tilda Swinton), is having a long-running affair with a federal marshal named Harry Pfarrer (George Clooney). Katie's ready to dump her insufferable husband, and she wants Harry to do the same with his wife, Sandy (Elizabeth Marvel). How much Sandy might actually miss having Harry around is hard to say—in one of the movie's weirdest scenes, we see that Harry is a home hobbyist who's building a fantastical sex chair in their basement. Soon, Harry is driven to further philandering. He logs onto an Internet dating service and scores a hookup with—Linda Litzke. This is heartbreaking news for Ted Treffon (Richard Jenkins), the Hardbodies gym manager who is truly smitten with Linda and has already confided to her that before getting into the buffness industry, he spent fourteen years as a Greek Orthodox priest. (Linda's response: "That's a good job!")

Rebuffed by Cox, Chad and Linda decide to peddle their spyware at the Russian embassy. This quickly brings them to the attention of Cox's former overseers at the CIA. After checking out the bizarre situation, a mystified agent reports to his boss: "They all seem to be sleeping with each other." The boss (played by the sublimely droll J. K. Simmons) gives this a millisecond of thought and says, "Okay, no biggie. Report back to me when . . . I don't know, when it makes sense."

The cast couldn't be better. Clooney and Pitt are A-list morons, Malkovich is volcanically abusive, and Swinton, stiff with beady-eyed suspicion, is a perfect comic foil. The movie is hysterically funny in parts, and you keep waiting for it to really take off—to erupt into some totally new lunatic terrain. Who better than the Coens to do this? But the brothers don't seem to have been aiming for another masterpiece here; maybe they just wanted a little light refreshment after *No Country for Old Men*. But since just about every character in the film is an idiot of some sort—and one of the few sympathetic figures gets hacked to death with an axe—there's no one to relate to. All that's left are a lot of laughs. Which'll do, actually. (September 2008)

Whatever Works

Grumposaurus Rex

Whatever Works isn't a good Woody Allen movie, even by latter-day standards. It is, however, a surprisingly offensive Woody Allen movie, inviting us to sneer at benighted Southerners, idiot Christians, stupid kids and their hard-rock music—anything, in short, that wouldn't pass muster among the Big Apple sophisticates of whom the director is a longtime laureate.

Allen wrote the script more than thirty years ago, when he was making good movies like *Annie Hall* and *Manhattan*. Back then, his nebbish hostility had the fresh tang of underdog humor. Now he's wealthy and celebrated and seventy-three years old, and that youthful comic stance, transported into the present, just seems crabby and sour. And while casting Larry David as the film's lead character might sound like a masterstroke, it turns out to be an insurmountable problem. In his HBO series, *Curb Your Enthusiasm*, David is an inspired improviser and, in half-hour doses, an entertaining small-screen presence. He's not really an actor, though, and so here, confined to Allen's scripted dialogue, he seems wooden—you wait for him to bust out and soar, but he can't. He's just an amplifier for the director's vintage misanthropy, and he grinds you down.

David plays Boris Yellnikoff, a cantankerous physicist who has put his ex-wife and uptown life behind him and moved down to a seedy Chinatown apartment to cultivate his miserable worldview. In the opening scene, at a sidewalk café in the West Village, we see him wearying some friends with another installment of his round-the-clock rant about the rottenness of life—a "chamber of horrors" that "all comes to nothing." Then, in a long monologue delivered directly to the camera (in the Woodian manner of old), he tells us, unnecessarily, that "I'm not a likable guy" and that "this is not the feel-good movie of the year." We have been warned.

Boris's life takes an unexpected and entirely implausible turn when he encounters a young girl huddled on the pavement near his apartment. This is Melodie (Evan Rachel Wood at her sweetest), who has just arrived from Mississippi to pursue her fortunes in the big city. After some introductory insults about her intellectual inadequacy, Boris agrees to let this vagabond sunbeam come in and sleep on his sofa. In the days that follow, he berates her nonstop for her stupidity and her pathetic taste in music (she's never heard of Beethoven) and movies (or Fred Astaire). Nevertheless, within days, Melodie falls in love with this irascible benefactor, and before you know it, they've gotten married. (This self-flattering Allen plot device is as borderline-creepy now as it was thirty years ago, when the character played by seventeen-year-old Mariel Hemingway fell for the one played by the forty-three-year-old Woody himself. Now it's even more deluded: the scrawny, balding David is sixty-one; the dewy Wood is forty years younger.)

Before long, Melodie's mother, Marrieta (Patricia Clarkson), turns up, having tracked her daughter from Mississippi to Boris's dismal digs. (Exactly how she did this is unexplained.) Marietta is an evangelical Christian—a moron, in other words—but Boris and his hip New York friends quickly straighten her out, and before long she's smoking pot, sleeping around, and wearing a lot of black, just the way everybody should. When her estranged husband John (Ed Begley Jr.) arrives *chez* Boris a short time later, he, too, turns out to be a Bible-beating imbecile, but the big city cures him as well, the silly fellow.

Allen's cultural arrogance is breathtaking—especially in a man so out of touch he thinks a popular rock band would have a name like Anal Sphincter, and that the country's first black president "still can't get a cab in New York." When Melodie meets a young guy her own age (and delivers one of the film's few funny lines: "He's not a serial killer—at least he didn't mention it"), Boris launches into yet another tirade. Later, when she seriously reevaluates their relationship, he's more magnanimous: "Greatness isn't easy to live with," he allows, "even for someone of normal intelligence." Of course, someone of normal intelligence would never put up with this insufferable crank, even for a couple of hours. Lord knows it's hard for us. (June 2009)

The Way Back

Journeymen

If you're going to base a movie on an amazing true story, it would seem essential that the amazing story actually be true. This is unfortunately not the case with *The Way Back*. Not entirely, anyway. The picture is drawn from a 1956 book by Slawomir Rawicz, a Polish army officer who claimed to have escaped from a Soviet labor camp in 1940, along with six fellow prisoners, and to have walked four thousand miles to freedom through Mongolia and Tibet and over the Himalayas to British India. Subsequent research has indicated that, while Rawicz *was* a prisoner in a Siberian camp, he never took part in the hellacious trek his book describes. On the other hand, it does appear possible that another group of escapees did make this amazing journey, and that Rawicz, who died in 2004, might simply have been recounting their ordeal.

In the film's production notes, director Peter Weir acknowledges the ambiguous provenance of this tale; but he says that while Rawicz's book may not be completely true, it is probably accurate in its harrowing details, and in any case constitutes a great adventure. I think we can accept this reasoning. And the movie, which is very well made, has a number of things to recommend it. Working with cinematographer Russell Boyd (who also shot Weir's *Master and Commander* and *The Year of Living Dangerously*), the director leads us through some extraordinary environments, from the snow-blown forests of Siberia (actually Bulgaria) to the vast parched expanse of the Gobi Desert (actually Morocco). He also draws fine performances from the stars who portray three of the fugitives. The young English actor Jim Sturgess, playing Janusz, the Rawicz character, carries much of the film with unwavering confidence; Ed Harris, as an American caught up in the Soviet nightmare, is appropriately skeletal and emotionally conflicted; and Colin Farrell—stubbly, feral, and heavily tattooed—is surprisingly persuasive as an imprisoned Russian gangster the other fugitives bring along on their great escape, mainly because he owns a knife.

But the movie's tone is inescapably grim and grueling—at more than two hours in length it's an ordeal for the audience. And since we're told at the outset that four of the men do make it to India, suspense is minimal. What we have instead is a long procession of set-piece sequences of deprivation and duress. The opening passages in the Siberian camp are vividly horrific—we see prisoners worked literally to death felling trees and laboring in mines, with little clothing to protect them from the Arctic temperatures and even less food to sustain them. And once Janusz and his companions make their escape, in the middle of a furious blizzard, their desperation only increases. We see them cutting bark from trees for sustenance, eating worms and lizards, and sucking on cool stones and devouring snakes to alleviate their constant thirst. Fortunately, a runaway orphan named Lena (Saoirse Ronan, of *The Lovely Bones*) eventually joins the group on their journey, and her appearance briefly warms the story like a beam of sunlight, especially in her interaction with Harris's chilly American, who comes to see her as a surrogate daughter. (The lack of sexual menace when Lena arrives is a blessing, but the lack of even sexual tension seems odd. The director declines to explore the situation.)

Peter Weir is famous for his unhurried particularity in selecting projects: *Master and Commander*, his last film, was released in 2003; the one before that, *The Truman Show*, came out in 1998. His commitment to this story is admirable, as is his determination not to cheapen it with stock adventure-movie thrills. But the effect of so much unalloyed misery is exhausting. By the time Janusz and his three fellow survivors finally arrive in warm and welcoming India, our relief exceeds their own. (January 2011)

Wall Street: Money Never Sleeps

Bank Shot

I don't know about you, but I like my Oliver Stone straight up, with all the lunatic delusions writhing in my face. *JFK*, Ollie's 1991 fever dream about the Kennedy assassination, is the platinum standard here, I think. I haven't seen the 2003 *Comandante*, his mash note to Fidel Castro ("one of the Earth's wisest people"), but then not many have— HBO, which commissioned the doc, quickly dumped it. And I passed on last year's *South of the Border*, Stone's salute to Hugo Chavez ("the man is intoxicating"), and contented myself with watching news footage of the two of them swanning around the Venice Film Festival together in matching red ties.

Given his penchant for demented rich-lefty political blather, you'd expect Stone to approach the subject of the 2008 stock market meltdown with fangs bared. Oddly, though—possibly because of his pressing need for a hit—he hasn't done a full Ollie this time out. *Wall Street: Money Never Sleeps*, a sequel to his 1987 *Wall Street*, stops short of calling for the death of capitalism or a return to the comforting simplicity of a barter economy. Regrettably, this uncharacteristic restraint deprives us of the sort of what-the-fuck entertainment value that Stone can be so adept at providing. The film attempts both to tell a standard Hollywood love story and to stuff in all the details of the subprime mortgage mess around the edges. It's a pity the story flatlines, and in the end the details— too tangled for any movie to contain—bury the picture.

Michael Douglas, being irreplaceable, is back as Gordon Gekko. You'll recall that in the 1987 film, the Gekko character, with his slicked-back hair and strapping suspenders, provided not just the sartorial template for a real-world generation of Wall Street weasels but also a brazen battle cry: "Greed is good." (Adam Smith may still be weeping.) Now at large once again after eight years in prison on an insider-trading conviction, Gekko sniffs a new strain of financial malfeasance in the air. Biding his time till he can figure out a way to profit from it, he has published a book, called *Is Greed Good?* The titular question is of course rhetorical.

Gekko longs to reconcile with his estranged daughter, Winnie (Carey Mulligan), who runs an investigative news Web site presumably dedicated to taking down wheeler-dealers like her dad. And yet Winnie herself is romantically entwined with a young Wall Street investment wiz named Jake Moore (Shia LaBeouf). But Jake's okay—he's an anti-weasel, a specialist in funding virtuous new forms of alternative energy. Jake's beloved mentor is his aging boss, Lou Zabel (Frank Langella), who's presented as the last moral man on Wall Street (and possibly the most clueless: he says things like, "How do you make money on losses?"). When Lou's venerable firm is sacked by a hedge-fund snake named Bretton (Josh Brolin), Jake vows revenge. Fortunately, the wily Gekko is on hand to help out. (Sure.)

As the story marches resolutely toward the puddle of emotional mush into which it topples at the end, Stone has Gekko shovel in endless fiscal explication. There's the requisite stuff about bundled debt and evil bankers, but any film on this subject that presumes to explain the concept of moral hazard without even whispering the words "Fannie Mae" or "Freddie Mac" clearly has an agenda other than enlightenment. Cluttering things further are Stone's usual visual eccentricities, among them some alarmingly perky animated graphics (explaining fusion technology!). For bad measure, there's also a procession of celebrity cameos by Charlie Sheen (nudge, nudge), wing-haired *Vanity Fair* editor Graydon Carter, and, most distractingly, the director himself. Douglas, LaBeouf, and the heartily hissable Brolin give solid performances, and so does Susan Sarandon, in a few brief scenes as Jake's real-estate-flipping mom. But Langella is marooned in mopery, and the radiant Mulligan, so impressive in *An Education* and *Never Let Me Go*, is sunk in weepy tedium.

For those unintrigued by any of this, there's an inviting alternative. For less than the price of two tickets to this movie you could pick up a copy of *The Big Short*, Michael Lewis's fine book about the Great Crash of '08, which is both grippingly written and highly informative. Which is to say, it's entirely Ollie-free. (September 2010)

The Dying Game

The art of termination, so alarming in real life, is wholly enjoyable on-screen. But shooting, poisoning, blowing up—these things have all been done. To death, you might say. The search for new modes of liquidation goes ever on.

Bloodsucking Freaks (1976): Noted for its bare-butt-dartboard diversion, electro nipple torture, oral sex with a severed head (nine years before *Re-Animator*!) and brains sucked out of a cranium through a straw (twenty-one years before *Starship Troopers*!), this cheerfully dismal grindhouse item offers one lethal innovation that really is kind of brilliant—the scene in which a snotty New York theater critic is kicked to death onstage by a prima ballerina. Struggling playwrights of the world, this one's for you. Everyone else might just want to move along, though.

Shoot 'Em Up (2007): Veggie-loving tough guy Clive Owen, a master of nonstop mayhem, takes down one thug by ramming a large carrot deep into his eye. A method unique in my experience.

The Abominable Dr. Phibes (1971): As the titular madman in this AIP shock comedy, Vincent Price dispatches his enemies with swarms of bees, bats, rats, and locusts, not to mention a strangulating mechanical frog mask. All very witty. In the sequel, *Dr. Phibes Rises Again* (1972), the murderous medico expands his repertoire with an ear-piercing telephone, a scorpion chair, and a very hungry eagle. The following year Price starred in *Theatre of Blood*, an unrelated but similarly stylish film featuring a procession of Shakespeare-related torments, among them toy-poodle pie and the painful extraction of a pound of flesh. The many fans of this movie are still tormented by the fact that no sequel ensued; and *Phibes* admirers, tantalized by talk of a further installment, remain bummed that the series stopped at number two.

House of Wax (2005): A wholly unnecessary remake with one shining moment: Paris Hilton gets killed by a flying stake through the head. Only a movie, alas.

Kill Bill: Vol. 2 (2004): After two hours of teasing us with talk of the

★★★★★★★★★★★★★★★★★★★★★★★★★★★★★★★

legendarily lethal Five Point Palm Exploding Heart martial-arts technique, Tarantino finally has Uma Thurman demonstrate—and it's nothing: a tap, a twist, a look of dying surprise on David Carradine's face. A shameless fakeout, in other words. Pretty funny.

Machete (2010): At one pit stop along the highway of carnage here, titular avenger Danny Trejo rips open an attacker's stomach and yanks out his guts—good, good. Then he takes off with one end of the guy's intestines in his hand, leaving their owner wondering where this is going. A lesser auteur than Robert Rodriguez might have called a wrap here, but no. Holding tight to the long intestine, Trejo leaps through a window out into the air, swinging down and back to crash through another window on the floor below. Where the carnage, if it need be said, continues.

Demolition Man (1993): Sylvester Stallone and Wesley Snipes face off, at greater length than really necessary, in a "cryogenic prison," where inmates do their time in very cold storage. After much leaping about, Sly manages to soak Snipes with cryogenic stuff. Snipes turns to ice. Approaching the brittle bad guy, Stallone kicks off his head. It hits the floor, bounces, then shatters. I don't believe I've ever seen this before either, but I pine for the two hours I wasted getting to it.

Monty Python's The Meaning of Life (1983): Death by breath mint. You really have to see it.

BIG BANG BOOM

The least you can say about the modern action movie—with its crazed chases, clamorous battles, and endlessly blossoming explosions—is that it's never dull. Which is not to say it's always interesting. Action epics are among the hardiest omniplex staples—there's always a new young audience eager to gobble them up. And even the most uninspired action flick can at least be amusing, although often unintentionally.

Rambo

Fourth Blood

Twenty years after the last installment of this slaughterhouse saga, we find the hulking John Rambo (Sylvester Stallone, inhabiting the role for the fourth time) retired from the world's political frays and working in the jungles of Thailand as a riverboat captain and freelance reptile catcher for an onshore serpent circus, where the cobras and pythons he delivers are put through their snaky paces for the entertainment of whatever jungle tourists might, you know, happen by. This is a hilariously unlikely occupation, but it's a living, presumably. In any event, unlikeliness is the water in which this neo-Rambo enterprise wallows.

The plot, such as it is, is launched by the appearance of a Christian church group seeking Rambo's help in traveling upriver into neighboring Burma, where they intend to deliver medical help to the guerrillas who've been fighting the country's homicidal military junta for the last sixty years. Contemplating the little evangelical band, who just want to change the world for the better, Rambo's face morphs from a sneer into a snarl, thus exhausting his emotional range.

"You bringin' any weapons?" he asks the group's leader, a namby-pamby peacenik.

"Of course not!" the man responds.

Says Rambo: "You're not changin' anything."

But the group's lone female member (Julie Benz, the only unbutchered woman in the movie) pleads with him, and Rambo, regarding her in the curious way King Kong once contemplated a writhing sweetie clutched in his fist, finally agrees to put his river ferry at their service.

With this structural formality out of the way, the picture quickly descends into the familiar Rambo world of endless annihilation. Even in a cinematic age as murderous as our own, the movie is exceptionally violent. The explosions are red with gore and lumpy with flesh, and the limb severing and skull bashing are remarkably graphic. In its vintage *Dirty Harry*–style emotional strategy, the bad guys—the soldier-thugs of the Burmese government—are so irredeemably vile (when was the last time you saw a crying infant tossed into a fire?) that we lust to wipe them out before Rambo actually gets around to it.

Stallone, the movie's writer and director as well as star, doesn't really look his sixty-one years. Slicked with dark grease and glowering beneath a nest of stringy black hair, he's as ageless as a boulder and nearly as expressive. The picture was filmed in Thailand, and its rainy murk is as oppressive as its interminable brutality, which is monotonously undifferentiated—someone or other is always being blown up or hacked to pieces, and that's that. Stallone's indifference to plot and feeling and his unwavering commitment to carnage have the quality of obsession. We begin to wonder about his mental state. Not for long, though. (January 2008)

The Expendables

Blasts from the Past

*T*he Expendables isn't a parody of a 1980s action movie, you'll be relieved to hear. No, *The Expendables* actually *is* a 1980s action movie, its cast groaning with back-in-the-day authenticity. Sylvester Stallone, who also directed, leads a team of mercenaries that includes such vintage marquee names as Dolph Lundgren and Jet Li, with Bruce Willis and *Arnold Schwarzenegger* passing through in don't-blink cameos, Jason Statham adding whippersnapper appeal, and a real-life action man—ex-wrestler Steve Austin—playing a stone-cold character called (inevitably) Paine.

The picture opens with an appetizer of modern-day-pirate carnage in the Gulf of Aden before zipping back to the States for a quick breather at the boys' headquarters, a seedy tattoo shop run by retired teammate Mickey Rourke (peekabooing beneath stringy streaked hair, as usual, but also smoking a thoughtful pipe). After receiving a new assignment from a tight-lipped CIA agent (Willis), the lads relocate to Vilena, an island country so remote we never quite figure out where it's supposed to be. (The sequences were shot in Brazil.) Here we meet the plot: a corrupt general (David Zayas) is oppressing his people at the behest of a rogue, coke-dealing CIA agent (Eric Roberts, heavily armed with smirks and snarls), and their only opposition is the general's rebellious daughter (Giselle Itié).

This rickety narrative scaffolding is entirely sufficient to the movie's purposes, which are largely pyromaniacal. As in the old days, the focus here is on big sweaty men running in a crouch through fields of automatic-weapons fire, slapping wads of C4 explosive onto soon-to-be-smithereened buildings, and laying into their adversaries with knives, guns, fists, and whatever else may be at hand. Detonations are unending, and bodies pile up like cords of winter firewood.

Need it be said that women are extraneous to such testosteronic hubbub? An occasional ambient babe passes through the proceedings, but almost subliminally; and even the relationship between Stallone's character and the general's daughter turns out to be platonic. Plausibility is also a notional concern. Midway through the movie one character is rendered definitively deceased—but then he reappears again at the end with no explanation given. "He's back from the dead," says another character, and that's that.

This is all part of the retro fun, of course, as is the coy-dumb dialogue ("We'll die with you, just don't ask us to do it twice") provided by the script (which Stallone cowrote). The movie is a good-humored affair, and it delivers exactly what the action audience wants (or once wanted, anyway): maximum damage. In the production notes, the star emphasizes his avoidance of CGI in rendering the fiery mayhem, and he claims the actors did their own stunts (although in one furious beatdown scene in which he takes part, you have to wonder). This dedication to a faded action-flick ideal is rather touching, and you wonder how long Stallone, now sixty-four, can keep carrying the old-school flag. When he pops up unexpectedly in the midst of one of the film's many conflagrations, the general's daughter turns to him and says, "How are you here?" Says Sly: "I just am." Welcome back, champ. (August 2010)

District B13

Action Central

Imagine the most berserk bits of *Kung Fu Hustle*, the Indiana Jones films and *Ong-Bak: The Thai Warrior* all rolled into one big skull-flattening action movie. Now imagine it with subtitles. *Voilà*: *District B13*—a movie in French, it's true, but one that really speaks the international language of mayhem.

The story is set in 2010, in the grim *banlieues* outside of Paris—the gang-infested suburban housing projects so dangerous that police are disinclined to set foot or squad car anywhere inside them. Four years into the future, these grim districts have grown so ungovernable that the authorities have given up and sealed them off behind walls and barricades, leaving vicious drug lords and their private thug armies to wreak havoc within.

Only two men find this situation unacceptable and are willing to do something about it. One of them, Leïto (David Belle), born and raised in the nightmarish District B13, fights a daily battle to keep drugs and gangsters out of his apartment building. The other, Damien (Cyril Raffaelli), apparently the only cop in Paris not in cahoots with either the drug lords or corrupt city officials, still believes it's possible to tame the lawless district. When one of the worst of the gang chieftains, a man named Taha (Bibi Naceri), steals a nuclear weapon from a government ordnance truck—and kidnaps Leïto's sister, too—Damien and Leïto team up to kick a few hundred tons of bad-guy butt.

As with *Ong-Bak*, the beauty of *District B13* is in the meticulous planning that went into its elaborate action scenes and the refreshing lack of digital effects—the sometimes astonishing physical feats are real. (One stunt, in which Leïto leaps up from the floor and sails feet-first through a doortop transom that can't be much more than two feet high, is breathtaking.) Much of the credit for this must go to the movie's two leads. Cyril Raffaeli is a onetime circus acrobat, as well as a martial arts pro and a top French movie stuntman. David Belle, we're told, is the inventor of *parkour,* the "urban running" pastime that apparently facilitates an ability to go vaulting over the tops of cars and scampering up the sides of buildings. For the purposes of the movie, it helps that both of them are good-looking guys (Raffaeli could be a skinhead version of the late Jean-Paul Belmondo; Belle resembles the young Robert De Niro), and that their acting skills are more than adequate.

Working with these two appealing stars, and a large supporting cast filled with stuntmen, boxers, and every conceivable species of martial arts showoff, the first-time director, Pierre Morel (better known as a cinematographer—he shot last year's Jet Li epic, *Unleashed*), creates scenes of pure kinetic flow, with the action barreling forward in a torrent of bullets and flames and flying car parts. Morel is obviously a student of the form, and he's a talented one. So while the sequence in which Damien breaks out of the back of a speeding prison van, crawls up along the top of it, swings down into the cab, and cold-cocks the driver is clearly derived from *Raiders of the Lost Ark* and a hell-bent chase across multilevel rooftops unabashedly echoes *The Matrix*, they're still thrilling—and the thrills feel fresh.

District B13 could be the action movie to beat this year; we'll see if any other director comes close to equaling its delirious rush. The picture is eighty-five minutes long and it blows past you like a hurricane. (June 2006)

Eagle Eye

Flight Control

*E**agle Eye* is yet another action movie aimed at people unfamiliar with the wonders of CGI, whoever or however they may be. The story—a crumb of inspiration flicked off the lapel of executive producer Steven Spielberg some years back—is mildly intriguing, if hardly fresh. Stubbly slacker Jerry Shaw (Shia LaBeouf) checks out his undernourished ATM account one day and discovers that it suddenly contains $750,000. Proceeding on to his ratty apartment, he finds it stacked to the rafters with high-tech weaponry and serious explosives. His cell phone rings. A woman's voice tells him to run—the FBI is on the way. Jerry, slow on the uptake, is still processing this command when the FBI does in fact barge in. He's dragged off to headquarters, where an agent named Morgan (Billy Bob Thornton) says he knows Jerry's a terrorist. Jerry is given his requisite one phone call. When he picks up the receiver, he hears the mysterious woman's voice on the line again, informing him he's about to be busted out. You can see this sequence in the movie's trailer. But then you can see *most* of its better moments in the trailer.

Meanwhile, a divorced mom named Rachel (Michelle Monaghan) is putting her young son on a train to D.C., where he'll be playing the trumpet with his school band at some Kennedy Center wingding. (This later turns out to be relevant, in a strained way.) Soon, Rachel gets a call on *her* cell, with the same mystery woman telling her to get moving or her son's train will be derailed. Rachel gets moving.

Meanwhile (this is a movie with many meanwhiles—it seems to have been edited with a hand grenade), Jerry continues to receive travel instructions from the omniscient voice—on his cell phone, on the cell phone of *somebody sitting next to him,* on digital train station signs, and store window TV sets. Finally, he's told to hop into a nearby Porsche, and who should be driving it but—Rachel. *Vrooom!*

They bicker nonstop, of course, while the voice—which sounds like an overbearing dashboard GPS unit—keeps issuing perplexing commands. ("Get in the crate!" "Go to Macy's!") There are detours to Chicago and Indianapolis, through an unceasing storm of gunfire and explosions. Are there still people who'll goggle with delight at the sight of a jet plane chasing a car through a tunnel? Or even an out-of-control 18-wheeler doing somersaults down a street? And while I don't believe I've ever seen a bullet-strewn chase along a serpentine cargo conveyer belt, and I'm sure it was tricky to stage, it's nevertheless monotonous.

LaBeouf and Monaghan are good actors, of course, and you can feel the film's four screenwriters trying to shoehorn occasional nonexplosive moments into the script in which these two can develop their characters. (Rachel's ex was a bad dad; Jerry is estranged from *his* father; guess where this is going.) But no sooner do these few attempts to actually tell a story begin than another round of kabooming ensues, thunder drums rear up on the soundtrack, and the peculiar tedium of pyrotechnic overload envelops us once again.

This gives us time to ponder the plot's several improbabilities. Why, for example, have these two inconsequential individuals been chosen to foment a gynormous governmental meltdown when the all-powerful force that's pulling their strings could clearly do that fomenting itself? (The identity of this sinister agency will be intuited by Stanley Kubrick adepts long before its formal revelation, in much the same way that admirers of Alfred Hitchcock will instantly recognize the source of the movie's big Kennedy Center sequence.)

That director D. J. Caruso is a talented filmmaker was clear in his last picture, the compact thriller *Disturbia* (which also starred LaBeouf). Here, though, he seems to have lost his way amid the big bucks of a blockbuster budget, which is too bad. Hell-raising action is one of the many pleasures that movies can offer. *Eagle Eye* is a demonstration of why it usually shouldn't be the only one. (September 2008)

The Mechanic

Muscling Ahead

Jason Statham movies are often dismissed as brain-dead action trash. The delirious *Crank* and *Transporter* films would never be mistaken for one of the *Bourne* pictures, and the dreadful/hilarious *Death Race* couldn't even be mistaken for *Crank*. Still, Statham, who started out as an athlete (a member of the British national diving team), is a natural action star. His range as an actor is limited (soulful broods between the trademark butt-kickings), but his stubbly charisma holds the screen. And with *The Mechanic*, he's found a vehicle nicely suited to his narrow but nevertheless real talents.

The movie is a remake of a 1972 demi-classic that starred Charles Bronson. Screenwriter Richard Wenk has done a respectful take on Lewis John Carlino's original script (although he's changed the ending), and so once again we're swept up in the never-a-dull-moment life of Arthur Bishop (Statham in the Bronson role), a top hitman in the employ of a shadowy international assassination bureau. Arthur isn't your average thug. He's averse to just blowing people away, and instead carefully researches his targets and arranges their deaths to look like accidents. Between assignments, he repairs to his luxurious home on an island in a Louisiana bayou, where he chills to the sounds of Schubert piano trios and tinkers with a classic cherry red sports car (a possession of dubious utility on a mossy little island, but whatever).

After Arthur's mentor in the death business, Harry McKenna (Donald Sutherland), is murdered, Arthur finds himself saddled with Harry's alienated son, Steve (Ben Foster). Heretofore an aimless youth, Steve sees in Arthur's lively trade a lifestyle he'd like to have himself. Soon Arthur is tutoring him in the dark arts of termination, and before long they're performing hits together. When they realize that somebody is trying to terminate *them*, things get extra-lively.

English director Simon West (*Lara Croft: Tomb Raider*) stages action sequences with impeccable clarity. There's a long, complex chase-and-escape down the side of a building that never collapses into confusion, and a room-wrecking smackdown with a three-hundred-pound gay killer that might have left Jason Bourne himself a little winded. There are also some clever audience fake-outs (one involving a girl's hand and a garbage disposal) and some cute 1960s touches—a furious battle in a cramped bus salutes the famous train-fight scene in *From Russia with Love*, and the heavily reverb'd electric-guitar noodlings in Mark Isham's score are pure Morricone. A couple of women pass through the debris, but this boys-only world is not their natural habitat, however hard they try to adapt. (Coming on to the battered and bloody Steve after one fracas, a sultry bargirl purrs, "I wish someone would hurt *me* like that.")

Teaming Statham with a resourceful actor like Foster was a shrewd ploy. Foster's energetic characterization and his probing wit provide a focus for Statham's pensive stillness and afford it some resonance. Not that the older star is going soft or anything—the script sees to that. At one point, Arthur leaves a helpful note for another character. It says, "If you're reading this, you're dead." (January 2011)

ONE MORE TIME

There's nothing wrong, per se, with remaking an old movie. Mary Shelley's novel Frankenstein *was brought to the screen at least twice (in silent versions) before Universal's 1931 rendition, starring Boris Karloff, helped inaugurate the modern monster-movie era. Similarly, two screen versions of Dashiell Hammett's* The Maltese Falcon *were released before John Huston nailed the story with his classic 1941 film. And John Carpenter's 1982* The Thing *was an even scarier scary movie than the 1951 original he was remaking. Nevertheless, going to the well of old movies—or, more and more, old TV shows—is often a sign of creative exhaustion or terrible judgment. (Gus Van Sant's 1998 remake of Hitchcock's inimitable* Psycho *was one of the worst movie ideas of all time.) Proof, I think, follows.*

Friday the 13th

Slasher Crash

For a man so committed to the hockey mask as all-purpose evening wear, Jason Voorhees has amassed a lot of frequent-flier miles over the last three decades. Venturing forth from his rural base at Camp Crystal Lake, he's done Manhattan, explored outer space, even spent time in Hell. (But then who among those keeping track of his adventures hasn't?) Now, in the new *Friday the 13th*, he returns to his woodsy roots, casting an occasional backward glance to see if there's anyone left with an interest in tagging along.

The first thing to be said about this movie is that, despite its title, it is not a remake of the original *Friday the 13th*, which came out in 1980. Instead, the new film is yet another sort-of sequel—the eleventh, if you count the one in which Jason was heavily manipulated into hooking up with Freddy Krueger. Here, the big lug returns to his native boondocks to once more play Whac-A-Mole with a new generation of hot, horny, and touchingly dumb youths. The movie is so bereft of excitement, invention, or any of the qualities normally associated with minimally acceptable filmmaking that watching it becomes an exercise in wishing, with mounting excruciation, that it would end. (Spoiler alert: it finally does, kinda.)

The picture begins with a flashback to the original film, then leaps ahead into the present tense to bring on a new quintet of clueless teens—two hunks, two babes, and a nerd—who are wandering through the woods near Camp Crystal Lake in search of . . . oh, a patch of wild marijuana, whatever. Since the group includes two nuzzly couples, you wonder at first why there's a fifth wheel—until night falls and the nerd decides to wander off into the dark woods to look for that marijuana patch, at which point you wonder why on earth you wondered. Jason looms up, his signature machete in hand, and soon the flora is wet with flesh.

Next—well, "six weeks later"—another consignment of chattery knuckleheads arrives on the scene. They've come to party, and of course so has Jason. In familiar fashion, he begins picking them off one at a time: machete to the head, axe to the head, hand smack to the head (no, wait, that was me). As the bodies accumulate and the tedium swells, we bide our time waiting for the next requisite interlude of female nudity. Topless waterskiing enlivens one scene, and there's a long coital encounter that's made memorable by the featured actress, Julianna Guill, who was born to be naked, if nothing else.

The director, music-video veteran Marcus Nispel, numbers among his two previous feature credits the dismal *Texas Chainsaw Massacre* remake, which was also produced by the shameless Michael Bay. Since the original *Friday the 13th* is hardly a sacred text (it was a cheap rip of the 1978 *Halloween*, which seems in comparison a serene meditation on the varieties of cinematic surprise), one wonders why Nispel didn't trash it up and go for some fun. Instead, he's delivered a deadpan rehash of some of the hoariest slasher clichés. Even Jason seems a little bored by it all. The scariest thing in the movie is the threat of yet another sequel at the end. I'd suggest a return to outer space. Maybe deeper this time. (February 2009)

A Nightmare on Elm Street

Dead End

Given the advances in special-effects technology and the rise in audience blood thirst over the twenty-six years since the original *Nightmare on Elm Street* was released, you'd think the new remake would be ripping good fun. So it's odd how flat the movie is, and how rote its regurgitation of the familiar story. The young actors this time around are a colorless bunch (the 1984 film featured Johnny Depp and the memorable Heather Langenkamp); and in the role of the mock-horrible Freddy Krueger, Jackie Earle Haley can't really hold a claw to Robert Englund, the great cackler who played the part in the first picture. The movie's not bad; there's just nothing new in it. And the vintage teen-scream thrills, once so fresh, are now exceedingly stale.

The picture's by-the-numbers fright structure is established right at the beginning, as we see Dean Russell (a very brief appearance by Kellan Lutz, of the *Twilight* films) fending off dreams in the Springwood diner. "I *can* sleep," he tells his girlfriend, Kris (Katie Cassidy). "I just don't want to." Then—a knife-fingered glove flashes into view! Then—the diner goes dark and empty! Then . . . well, as I say, it's a very brief appearance.

Dean and Kris's high school classmate, Nancy (Rooney Mara, of *Youth in Revolt*), has been having strange dreams, too; and so has her would-be boyfriend, Quentin (Kyle Gallner, of *Jennifer's Body*). Soon, they discover that they and their friends have known each other much longer than they had previously thought—that as small children they'd all attended the Badham Day School together. Badham is long closed but still extant, decrepitly radiating bad vibes. What could have happened there? The parents in town all seem to know, but they're not talking. So it's left to Nancy and Quentin to start digging around, and before long they've discovered a suspiciously high mortality rate among the onetime tykes of Badham.

It turns out, as we well know, that Badham's former gardener, Fred Krueger, is at the root of the evil dreams. Krueger, now dead, was a child-murderer in the original film; here he's said to have been a child-molester—or was he? Quentin fears that the awful stories about Freddy that he and his friends told their parents—which drove them to set a fire that burned the man alive—might simply have been little-kid fibs. Which could be why Freddy, in search of beyond-the-grave revenge, is now haunting their teenage dreams, where he's ripping them apart with his razory claws. Who can stop him? Probably not Quentin—too sensitive (he wears a Joy Division T-shirt). That would leave . . .

It's all coming back, right? There's not one surprising development in this movie. Music-video king Samuel Bayer, making his first feature, dutifully replicates the iconic scenes from the first film: the clawed glove rising up out of Nancy's bubbly bathwater, the hysterical girl being flung about a room by the unseen Freddy's malignant force. But most of the "shocks" here are just cheap jolts, all supplied by Freddy in the most predictable way. Is that an empty mirror we see? A long dark road? Prepare for the sudden arrival of the legendary barbecued psychopath.

Haley appears to be playing Freddy as a cross between the child-molester he portrayed in *Little Children* and the wonderfully nutsoid Rorschach he gave us in *Watchmen*. He's too good for this role, and there's not much he can do with it. The character's ratty fedora and flame-broiled face are virtually unchanged from the first picture, but Freddy no longer has any good lines. (Well, there's one: explaining how a girl's pet dog wound up in a pool of blood, he says, with a clink of his claws, "I was just petting him.")

So Freddy is no longer the lovable wisecracker we once knew; and after a quarter-century and seven previous films in the original *Nightmare* series, he can no longer terrify us the way he once did, either. Which raises a key question: Why did the filmmakers feel the need to do such a formulaic remake? And why did they think anyone would feel a need to sit through it? (April 2010)

The Taking of Pelham 1 2 3

Stop Making Sense

I have a problem with *The Taking of Pelham 1 2 3*. It's the premise: four bad guys descend into the New York City subway system, hijack a train, hold the passengers hostage, and demand that the city bring a $10 million ransom down to the tunnel where the bad guys have parked their iron wheels. The problem, as I see it, is that there is *no way* these guys are going to get out of that tunnel and then out of the teeming metropolis above, where a legion of cops is waiting for them to come staggering up with their cash-stuffed duffel bags and attempt to hail a rush-hour taxi.

Pelham is director Tony Scott's steroidal remake of a well-regarded 1974 action movie, with a number of brainless new flourishes nailed on. John Travolta, who plays Ryder, the head hijacker, is fitted out with bandido mustache, diamond earring, a great big neck tattoo and, as we see in close-ups, a pricey Breitling wristwatch whose prominence must have helped ease the film's budget a bit. Ryder is a testy guy; we know this by the teeth-gnashing rants into which he constantly erupts (summoning fond memories of Travolta's immortal *Battlefield Earth*). He's on the phone with Walter Garber, a Metropolitan Transit Authority controller played by Denzel Washington with a paunch and a pair of mild-mannered glasses. Walter's actually a transit executive, but he's been demoted to control-room duty pending the results of a corruption investigation. (He allegedly took a bribe from a train manufacturer. In Japan. It's complicated, and blithely irrelevant.)

Ryder takes a liking to Garber and keeps him on the line. He wants the ransom money delivered in one hour or people will start dying. James Gandolfini, as the mayor of New York, breezes into the picture to contemplate this demand and quickly go along with it. John Turturro arrives on the scene as an MTA hostage negotiator (?) named Camonetti. He's trying to figure out who this Ryder guy is. And when the gabby Ryder tells Garber a ridiculous story about how he once picked up an "ass model" at a party and took her to Iceland, Camonetti suddenly knows—Ryder could only be a Wall Street stock wizard.

Our heads are already spinning as Scott cuts away to the sort of heavy-metal destruction he so famously favors. A police convoy is attempting to get the bags of cash to the scene but is having a helluva time: The cops keep crashing into taxis and spinning off highway overpasses down onto packed expressways, providing massive doses of Scottian boom-and-blaze, all of it egged on by an over-the-top soundtrack roar. (When Gandolfini says, "Why didn't we send a helicopter for the money?" he lifts the words right out of our gaping mouths.)

Our heads are now in our laps as we learn why Ryder has mounted this caper. It turns out he doesn't actually need the money—he still has a couple million dollars left over from an earlier stock swindle that sent him to prison. So why does he now feel he needs several million dollars more? You won't believe it. (No, really, you won't believe it.) As for Ryder's escape plan, it involves a secret subway platform under a well-known building and is utterly absurd.

The movie wastes a couple of good actors—chiefly Luis Guzmán, who gets minimal screen time as Travolta's chief henchman, an embittered ex-subway employee—and all but ignores a number of characters. (Ryder's other two heist associates, both hulking brutes, are on hand mainly to scowl and bleed.) There's plenty of action, conveyed in Scott's trademark jerky-cam swirl-and-blur style, but little to get excited about. You wonder why the picture was made (or, again, remade). At one of the film's many peerlessly silly points, Travolta tells Washington, "We all owe God a death." I nominate this movie. (June 2009)

The Amityville Horror

Monsters Inc.

This by-the-numbers boo machine of a movie achieves one small thing. It is the equal, in its oblivious imbecility, of both the book on which it's based (a 1977 bestseller by the late Jay Anson) and the 1974 hoax—I'm sorry, the "true story"—that the book purports to relate. It is also a series of feeble salutes to other, more original (and scarier) horror films. There's a mad dad with an axe. (Think *The Shining*.) There's an evil house and something about long-dead Indians. (Think *Poltergeist*.) There's even an exorcising priest. (Thinking time's up!)

It might be said that this *Amityville Horror* is better crafted, in a technical sense, than the hit 1979 movie of the same name, of which it is a costlier remake. But since that earlier *Amityville* was awful in *every* technical sense—even by the undemanding standards of AIP, the exploitation factory that produced it—such a thing is hardly worth saying.

But let's revisit the original, real-world tale. Among the few indisputable facts in the *Amityville* story are these. In the early morning hours of November 13, 1974, Ronald DeFeo Jr., an unstable, twenty-three-year-old heroin and firearms enthusiast, shot and killed both of his parents and his four siblings in the large house in which they all lived in Amityville, Long Island. One year later, rejecting an attempted insanity defense, a jury found DeFeo guilty of the killings, and a judge sentenced him to 150 years in prison, where he remains today.

It is also true that in December of 1975, less than a month after DeFeo's conviction, a recently married couple named George and Kathy Lutz moved into the Amityville house with Kathy's three young children from an earlier marriage. And that twenty-eight days later they moved back out, spinning a wild yarn about being driven away by ghostly visions, disembodied heads, blood-dripping faucets, strange oozy goo, a plague of flies, a demonic pig, and inexplicable bouts of levitation. (*The Exorcist*, that classic of otherworldly uplift, had been released two years earlier.)

Opinions about the Lutzes' story were divided from the beginning. People who had a sentimental attachment to facts and evidence found it preposterous; those who thought facts and evidence were overrated felt otherwise. For our present purpose, let's just note that Ronald DeFeo's lawyer, William Weber, later told the Associated Press that shortly after leaving the Amityville house, George Lutz approached him with a proposal to whip up a book about his alleged ordeal. "We created this story over many bottles of wine that George Lutz was drinking," Weber said. "We were creating something the public wanted to hear about."

And we still do, of course. We love fright flicks. And there's nothing wrong with wanting to make a movie even out of such shabby material as this. Even the halfhearted attempt to present such a story as a "true" depiction of actual events isn't entirely deplorable; it's only silly. We're inclined to go along with it just for the cheap kicks.

What's annoying about this new *Amityville Horror*—more annoying than the original, which was merely brainless and badly made—is that its aim is so low. The movie's only aspiration is to be a jacked-up rejiggering of a name-brand horror "classic." It sets out to be not just schlock, but helpfully prechewed schlock—schlock simply regurgitated. The movie's lack of invention is depressing. It seeks to be little else but a profitable summer diversion, and it seeks to be that by any means necessary.

Unsurprisingly, the lead producer on this project was Michael Bay, the well-known wham-bam specialist, whose previous affronts are several. The script, which is constricted by the demands of the well-known *Amityville* material, is by Scott Kosar—the man who wrote Bay's unnecessary 2003 remake of *The Texas Chainsaw Massacre*. The director, Andrew Douglas, is, like Bay himself, a veteran of the TV-commercial and music-video industry; this is his first feature film.

Douglas creates one memorable suspense sequence high up on the sun-spangled roof of the Amityville house. The scene can't actually be happening the way it seems to be, but it does seem to be happening that way nevertheless—there are no observable signs of computer mediation. Apart from that, though, and a broadly amusing interlude featuring a bong-hitting hot-tramp babysitter, Douglas just rings the familiar horror changes—the drifting ghouls, the hideously contorted faces, the swarming maggots, and the bloody corpse writhing on the ceiling—with the requisite suddenness that substitutes sucker-punch scares for a more psychologically involving variety of fright. The actors who play the Lutzes—Ryan Reynolds (*National Lampoon's Van Wilder*) and Melissa George (*Alias*)—do as they're told; the director requires little more from them than shifting degrees of hysteria, and they dutifully deliver.

So *The Amityville Horror* accomplishes its puny aim. Unconcerned with imaginative effects or the fearful beauty the best horror movies can have, it just slaps you around and leans on the volume and contents itself with keeping you in a state of sustained, unpleasant tension. It's like being poked in the neck with a stick every three or four minutes, over and over and over again. You walk out feeling played and irritable—especially if you've stayed all the way through to the final scene, which is possibly the lamest *Carrie* rip-off ever. Fortunately, the film's real denouement is much cheerier. It begins as you rise from your seat and it ends when you're finally back out on the street. (April 2005)

The X-Files: I Want to Believe

That '90s Show

Who didn't love *The X-Files* in the excitement of its early seasons? Each show put together like a little movie, with witchy scripts, brooding photography, Scully and Mulder rootling around in the foggy woods—for a while in the mid-1990s, it was one of the best things on TV.

I was thinking about this while watching the new *X-Files* movie, which I'm afraid offers little else of its own to think about. Loyal fans of the old series may be puzzled to find that the film, subtitled *I Want to Believe,* is very light in the X department. There are no new mutations of the show's esoteric "mythology," and no monster-of-the-week cheap thrills, either. There's a modest dollop of paranormal activity—a psychic, big deal—but even that is presented as rather iffy. The truth may still be out there; the question is whether anyone apart from Fox Mulder still cares.

The movie opens in snowy West Virginia (snowy British Columbia, actually—why didn't they just set the story in Seattle or somewhere?). A woman is attacked in her home by two scary men and dragged off into the night. Come daylight, we see a broad line of FBI agents trudging across a field of ice behind a shambling gray-haired man who appears to be looking for something. When he drops to his knees, the agents gather round and begin digging. They soon unearth a human arm, minus the rest of its human. Aliens? People-eating ice creatures? Don't get your hopes up.

The gray-haired man is Father Joe (Billy Connolly). Joe is a complicated character: a defrocked priest, a convicted pedophile, a freelance psychic, and an Irishman to boot. He's also a prominent cog in the movie's narrative design. This is a story about belief—"Belief," I mean. Joe still believes in a heavenly beneficence, despite his altar-boy-raping proclivities. Soon he's thrown together with ex-FBI agent Dana Scully (Gillian Anderson), who believes in very little, and exiled FBI agent Mulder (David Duchovny), who'll believe pretty much anything. Scully left the bureau in disgust and has gone back to doctoring at a Catholic hospital. When a blustery FBI agent named Drummy (rapper Xzibit, here saddled with a name I find hard to believe myself) approaches her in search of her old partner Mulder, she reluctantly agrees to seek him out in the remote cabin where he now lives, alone with his beard and his flying-saucer poster. Soon the chase is on. Keep those hopes curbed, though.

There follows a series of killer-snowplow encounters and a creepy maniac who loiters underwater in a public swimming pool (very odd). Bereft of any extraterrestrial overtones, the movie is basically a murder mystery of a rather gruesome sort. In fact, with its sadistic foreigners and grisly surgical shenanigans, it resembles nothing so much as one of the *Hostel* pictures. Longtime *X* fans are unlikely to rejoice at this, and *Hostel* kids would surely be bored by the movie's lack of bare-fanged bloodlust. In any case, the actors are too skilled for simple slaughter porn. The leads seem not to have aged much at all—Duchovny retains his tousled charm, Anderson is still a redhead. And the personable Billy Connolly brings notes of weary self-loathing to his performance that probably weren't all present in the script. *X-Files* creator Chris Carter, here directing his first feature, wobbles occasionally (he goes out of his way to score the lamest Bush joke in the short but populous history of that genre), but his excesses are finessed by cinematographer Bill Roe, a veteran of the TV series, who brings a crisp chill to the outdoor sequences and an infernal glow to the hideous lab scenes.

There *are* a few old-school *X-Files* touches. Bureau buddy Walter Skinner (Mitch Pileggi) puts in a late-inning appearance. Scully and Mulder natter a bit about their ill-fated love child ("I think our son left both of us with an emptiness that can't be filled," says Duchovny, possibly against his will). And there's a passing reference to Mulder's long-lost, alien-abducted sister, Samantha, who's still long-lost. These are the slightest of sops to *X-Files* fans, though. The movie has no idea what it wants to be, and its confusion is embodied in one of the most hilarious lines of the year. Attempting to assess what they've learned from their lackadaisical adventure, Mulder says to Scully, "If Father Joe were the Devil, why would he say the opposite of what the Devil would say? Maybe that's the answer."

What was the question again? (July 2008)

Get Smart

Maxed Out

Why do they keep doing this? Why does Hollywood keep brewing up movies from the exhausted dregs of old 1960s TV series? Like other such questionable projects (*The Avengers*, the excruciating *Wild Wild West*), the new *Get Smart* is uncertain exactly what it wants to be. The original show, created by gag maestros Mel Brooks and Buck Henry, began airing in 1965, in the midst of a spy-movie craze that had been launched by the first three Bond films. That very particular cultural context being long gone, this movie is left with a narrative premise—secret spy agency battles international bad guys with a barrage of spritzy one-liners—that has no contemporary cognate. And so the filmmakers have striven mightily to refashion their antique material into something, anything, else. What they've come up with is an uneasy amalgam of slapstick comedy, halfhearted romance, and, most desperately, rampaging action. The picture has funny passages, though, and if your expectations are bare-minimal, it might occasionally pass for hilarious.

Fans of the original TV show may be puzzled by this lackluster update. But of course they aren't the film's target demo, which is a new audience that's too young to remember the old series and must therefore be courted with more up-to-date inducements. Fortunately, the movie has a sharp cast: Steve Carell as the bumbling spy Maxwell Smart, Anne Hathaway as the beautiful Agent 99, Dwayne "The Rock" Johnson as the stalwart Agent 23, and Alan Arkin as their flustered chief, Chief. A few tokens of the old show have been carried over: Maxwell's silly shoe phone, the malfunctioning Cone of Silence, the telephone-booth entrance to the headquarters of the underground agency, which is still called CONTROL (an acronym that still stands for nothing). But there's no attempt to simulate the 1960s: The story has been relocated to the age of the iPod. Unfortunately, this adds a new layer of implausibility to a tale that was only loosely moored in any recognizable reality to begin with.

The gags that work, however, are almost worth sitting through the ones that don't. (Maxwell's acing of an agency test with an essay on existentialism—"I left that section blank"—doesn't scan when you think about it.) There's plenty of vintage ba-da-bing ("Welcome back. How was the assassination?"), and Carell's gift for physical comedy puts across such slapstick set pieces as a one-man mini-crossbow struggle in an airplane lavatory (don't ask) and an elaborate and surprisingly sweet dance-off in which he partners with the very large and lovable actress Lindsay Hollister. Johnson once again demonstrates an appealing light-comic touch; and the veteran Arkin, now seventy-four, has, of all things, a couple of funny fight scenes.

Unfortunately, Hathaway's character—here upgraded from the adoring sidekick of the TV show to a thoroughly modern butt-kicker—is written with blithe disregard for the need to make at least a little bit of sense. She spends most of the movie sneering at Maxwell, her unwanted new partner, and then, for no persuasive reason, suddenly falls in love with him. Since Hathaway and Carell have no romantic chemistry, this attempt at forcing a relationship is a watch-checking waste of time.

As for the plot, well, it's something about a terrorist scheme to nuke the president of the United States (James Caan) during a symphony concert in Los Angeles. The terrorists here are a vaguely constituted crew of goons bearing no resemblance to the terrorists we know so well today. These people, members of the rival spy agency KAOS, are Russians (I think), although they're led by a character named Siegfried (Terence Stamp, underutilized), who appears to be German. By about halfway through the movie, this strained scenario begins to drag woefully. And a sudden avalanche of road-chase action at the end, despite some muscular stunt work, is a big-bucks climax that seems to come squealing in from another movie. And not necessarily a better one.

Get Smart is a piffling summer diversion. Unsurprisingly, Steve Carell is the best reason to see it. But even his distinctive comic persona— the deadpan puzzlement, the unexpected ray of human warmth—may not be reason enough. (June 2008)

The Last Airbender

Worlds in Collision

Early reviews in the theater full of little kids I saw *The Last Airbender* with were enthusiastic: whoops and wows scattered throughout and a chorus of cheers at the end. The movie is filled with heroic feats, high-kicking martial arts, and elaborate digital imagery, and this is the audience at which it's aimed. Be advised.

Those unfamiliar with *Avatar: The Last Airbender*, the animated series that ran on Nickelodeon from 2005 to 2008, may find themselves straining to track the movie version's live action. The fantasy world of the film is divided into four tribal nations, each devoted to one of the four elements: Earth, Air, Fire, and Water. In each of these tribes there are specialized citizens called "benders," who can manipulate the national element at will. And somewhere there's an Avatar—a spiritual figure, reborn throughout time—who can control all four elements and generally keep peace among the nations.

But the last Avatar disappeared a hundred years ago, allowing the

Fire Nation, led by the glowering Lord Ozai (Cliff Curtis), to embark on a campaign of universal conquest. Ozai's black-armored troops have already exterminated the benders of the Air Nation—all but one. Now the Fire Lord has dispatched his son, Prince Zuko (Dev Patel), to find that elusive individual: the last Airbender. This turns out to be a twelve-year-old kid in a purple cloak and a dusting of runic tattoos. His name is Aang (Noah Ringer), and he's discovered on an ice floe one day by a Waterbender named Katara (Nicola Peltz) and her brother Sokka (Jackson Rathbone). We soon learn that Aang is not only the last Airbender, he's also the long-sought Avatar. Where has he been for the last century? "I ran away from home," he says.

Aang and his new protectors spend the rest of the movie dodging Prince Zuko and a scheming Fire Nation commander named Zhao (Aasif Mandvi) amid great fire lashings and water whips and much tae kwon do posing. There are massed digital ships, rampaging battle rhinos, a wise cave dragon, a six-legged sky beastie, and a friendly flying fruit bat who goes by the name Momo. Among many, many other things.

That's a lot of story. And the movie is so packed (cast of six thousand) and rushed and choppily edited that you soon give up trying to figure out what's happening and just let it drag you along. The picture is crammed with big-budget CGI—it seems determined to command our interest through sheer technological will. But while some of the digital constructions are certainly inventive, at the end we're left feeling wrung out and wearily unamazed.

The most surprising thing about this film is that it was written and directed by M. Night Shyamalan, a man once capable of such twisty delights as *The Sixth Sense* and *Unbreakable*. In the six years since the last of his movies with Disney, Shyamalan has become a wandering refugee, touching down at Warner Bros. to make the very silly *Lady in the Water*, and then at Fox for the execrable *The Happening*. Now he has landed at Paramount, where he acknowledges that he's taking a crack at launching a blockbuster franchise. *The Last Airbender* ends with the iron vow of a sequel. Will Shyamalan's technoid determination be sufficient to keep that promise? Or will the search for a welcoming studio home have to continue? (July 2010)

Last House on the Left

Vintage Violence

At an early point in *The Last House on the Left*, as one or another of a pair of young women was being head-slammed, spit on, kicked in the stomach, ripped with a knife, or raped face-down in the dirt while chortling goons hovered around, I found myself thinking, "It's only a remake, only a remake. . . ."

In fact, this new version of Wes Craven's loathsome 1972 terror landmark is considerably less vile than the original, but also considerably weaker in the "why?" department. Sadistic cinema has come a long way since Craven's debut feature took calculating aim at the grindhouse fringe; now, with the *Saw* and *Hostel* pictures having moved into the multiplexes, the torture-porn bar has been raised dauntingly high. By reining in the depredations somewhat, the Greek director Dennis Iliades, making his first English-language film, has reduced *Last House* to a by-the-numbers revenge tale that seems too halting to get the blood-feast audience really salivating, and too tedious for nondevotees to be expected to endure.

The plot is unencumbered by surprises. A sunny little family—Mom (Monica Potter), Dad (Tony Goldwyn), and teenage daughter Mari (Sara Paxton)—is vacationing at a lake house in the woods. Mari borrows the family van to drive into a nearby town to meet up with her friend Paige (Martha MacIsaac). There, the two girls encounter a glum youth named Justin (Spencer Treat Clark). Justin has some pot, and the three of them repair to the motel room he's sharing with his momentarily absent kinfolk to smoke it. When the rest of the clan returns, we get to meet Justin's escaped-convict father, Krug (introspective Garret Dillahunt, solidly miscast); his psychopath uncle, Francis (Aaron Paul); and a malevolent slut named Sadie (icy Riki Lindhome, of *Changeling*).

The earlier-noted bad things soon transpire. Then a storm comes up, and before long Krug and his crew are stumbling through the rain-whipped forest in search of shelter. They arrive at the lake house, where Mari's unwitting parents unwisely invite them in. Iliadis effectively ratchets up the tension here, but soon Mom and Dad discover what these creeps have done to their daughter and the inevitable orgy of vengeance gets under way, with everything from fireplace pokers to limb-mangling garbage disposals brought into play. It all goes on too long and culminates in a transcendently stupid scene that seems to have been plucked at random from a pile of outtakes and tacked on at the end for no other reason than to provide a farewell burst of gore.

The original *Last House on the Left* is sometimes held up as a bold reflection of the real-life horrors of its era—the Vietnam War, the Manson family, and so forth. Whatever its purported merits, it was a defiantly cruddy-looking picture. This remake (which Craven coproduced) has better color and one memorable image: an overhead shot peering down through teeming rain at a body afloat in the lake, with blood blossoming out in the water around it. The rest of the film is an often murky and occasionally out-of-focus visual wallow. Normally this might be an annoyance. Here, though, you just wonder how much you could really be missing. (March 2009)

WILD THINGS

Like the Vivian Girls of Henry Darger and Gaudí's Park Güell, some movies fit into no preexisting niche. They startle and baffle and sometimes annoy us—sometimes a lot. Three cheers.

Jackass 3D

Bring the Pain

Most of us think of a penis as having two purposes. But as we learn in *Jackass 3D*, the latest anarch-a-thon from Johnny Knoxville and his demented companions, this is a narrow view. In one of the movie's many singular stunts—this one called the Helicockter, I'm afraid—we see that a penis properly equipped with a very long cord can pilot a remote-controlled model airplane high in the sky. At another point, in a demonstration of what would have to be called penis baseball, a ball is pitched, the penis takes a swing (size *does* matter here) and connects, and then—the topper—another player, unrelated to the penis, pops up brandishing the ball in his clenched teeth.

By now, after two feature films and of course the spawning series that ran on MTV for three seasons, the *Jackass* sensibility—wildly violent, jaw-droppingly gross, and state-of-the-art stupid—has become familiar. But the particulars—the individual crazed stunts and antics—remain unpredictable, and often unbelievable; and so this iron-man uproar can still feel liberating. You might never have wanted to see some loon ride a Jet Ski down the side of a rocky hill, or offer up his face to a scorpion attack, or try literally pissing into the wind (as messy as you'd imagine), but when you do, you may find yourself chortling uncontrollably before good taste has a chance to intervene.

The *Jackass* crew remains unchanged from the idiot band that emerged out of the skate-punk world back at the turn of the millennium. Given the broken bones and juddering concussions that are an integral part of their painful trade, this dedication is surprising in itself. Knoxville is still in charge, if that's the word, and lead maniacs Bam Margera, Steve-O, and Chris Pontius are still on board, as are the alarmingly obese Preston Lacy (also credited as a writer, whatever that might mean), and Jason "Wee Man" Acuña, the world's most good-natured dwarf. (One wonders which he found more trying: being slapped with dead mackerels or compelled to don a leprechaun costume.)

Not everything here is a hoot: It's been a *long* time since a guy in a gorilla suit was thought to be funny, and some of the gags are strained setups. But the peak lunacies—like the visiting fart master who plays a trumpet with his butt—are priceless. Disgusting, but priceless. And the decision to shoot the picture in 3-D, while obviously a bid to extend the *Jackass* franchise, was a shrewd one: there are things hurtling off the screen in this movie that are beyond the ken of James Cameron.

Given the fact that most of these men are now in their midthirties (and beyond), one wonders how long they can continue down the *Jackass* path. But then what is it that's kept them going this far? The money? Maybe. (Their first film, the 2002 *Jackass: The Movie*, cost $5 million to make and grossed $60 million in this country alone.) But it would be hard to fake their still-giddy spirit or the affectionate camaraderie that's a part of their appeal. They remain united, it seems, by a single belief: anything for a laugh. As Knoxville says, after being rammed in the gut by an angry buffalo: "*Hahahahaha!*" (October 2010)

Black Dynamite

Ghetto Blaster

Can Black Dynamite fend off the Man and the Mob and the phalanx of wah-wah guitars arrayed against him and fight his way to the Honky House to mete out kung fu justice? *Most likely!*

The new movie *Black Dynamite* is more than just a fond tribute to 1970s blaxploitation films (with echoes of *Enter the Dragon*, too). It's a wild action comedy with a magnetic star (Michael Jai White, last seen in a small role as a snarling hoodlum in *The Dark Knight*) and a scholarly attention to genre detail. Not just the usual purple fedoras, processed hair, and tinted aviator shades, but also the lovable technical defects—the rancid color, the lavatorial lighting, the shifting commitment to focus. The movie is a celebration of cinematic insufficiency.

White, who's built like a tank and possessed of mad kung fu skills, is pretty near perfect in the role of Black Dynamite, an ex-CIA commando just back from the 'Nam and pissed about a bad new kind of smack being funneled into the ghetto by evil ofays. Little kids are getting hooked—helpless little orphans, even. ("Orphans got no parents," BD plaintively observes.) Not only that, there's a strange new brand of malt liquor on the street that's turning . . . never mind—can't blow one of the movie's raunchiest jokes.

On top of all that, some soon-to-be-dead crackers have rubbed out Black Dynamite's brother. So before long, he's making the rounds of local pimps, pushers, and hot brothel mamas with a monster Magnum the size of a lug wrench and a really big set of nunchucks (which he carries around in his *back pocket*). Amid all the ensuing havoc, you'd think there wouldn't be room for a Chinese crime lord called Fiendish Dr. Wu, or an uninviting getaway called Kung-Fu Island, or an armed-and-dangerous doughnut. But you'd be wrong.

There's also room for carnal downtime, naturally, and our man has a smooth way with the ladies. (Sidling up to a hospital nurse, he says, "I think you're runnin' a temperature. Lemme see if I can find the thermometer.") One in particular has caught his eye, a pretty community activist named Gloria (Salli Richardson). She's resistant at first, but Black Dynamite soon lures her back to his ultra-1970s stud pad, where . . . well, let's just say there's no explaining some of the stuff in this movie.

Mostly, though, the picture flies by in a blur of martial arts mayhem and low-budget vehicular pandemonium. (At one point, a car goes sailing off a cliff and blows up *before it even hits the ground*.) The mostly brilliant one-liners whiz past like buckshot. (Checking out Black Dynamite's fab digs, a wowed visitor says, "You must have an eight-track in every room.") And the ending—a hostile encounter in Washington, at the aforementioned Honky House—is spectacularly ridiculous.

Director Scott Sanders wrote the script with White and fellow actor Byron Minns; they shot this thing in three weeks and they've really nailed it. There's no winking irony and no heavy-handed film referencing. The movie's like an actual blaxploitation classic you somehow missed back in the day. Worth catching up. (October 2009)

Scott Pilgrim vs. the World

Big Fun

*S*cott Pilgrim vs. the World is the first movie to bring us, among many other things, on-screen battle scoring, a visit from the Vegan Police, and a really cute kickass girl named Knives. For most of its 112 minutes, Edgar Wright's new comedy lays persuasive claim to being the year's most blazingly imaginative film. Well, okay, along with *Inception*. But Wright's movie is also blazingly funny, something no one has yet attempted to assert about the Christopher Nolan blockbuster.

The picture is a great creative leap for Wright, the giddy parodist behind *Shaun of the Dead* and *Hot Fuzz*. Bryan Lee O'Malley's *Scott Pilgrim* comics began appearing in 2004, and the director latched onto them almost immediately. One understands why it has taken him so long to bring O'Malley's fantastical stories to the screen—the cast, which is deep in talented young actors, must have been difficult to align. Michael Cera plays Scott Pilgrim, mild-mannered bass player in a Toronto punk band called the Sex Bob-omb. Ellen Wong is Knives Chau, his underage girlfriend, and Mary Elizabeth Winstead is Ramona, the mysterious Amazon delivery girl for whom he truly yearns. Then there's Anna Kendrick, as Scott's sister, Stacey, who can't believe her twenty-two-year-old brother is dating a high school girl ("*Scandal!*"); and Kieran Culkin as Scott's gay roommate, Wallace, whose specialty is stealing

Stacey's boyfriends; and Alison Pill as Kim, the monumentally hostile drummer in Scott's band.

The plot, unlike the movie itself, is simple: in order to win the elusive Ramona, Scott must first do battle with her seven previous squeezes—the Evil Exes. The picture is constructed like a vintage video-arcade game, and these contests are wildly psychedelic. One of the Exes, Lucas Lee (Chris Evans in a winningly self-deprecating performance), is a movie star of surprising noncinematic skills (he flings Scott through the air with such force that the skinny suitor lands on a faraway tower). Another, Todd Ingram (Brandon Routh in a blindingly blond wig), is the vegan bass player in a rival band, and he engages Scott in an explosive battle-of-the-basses. The blond-mopped lesbian Roxy Richter (Mae Whitman) is a kickboxing tornado; the Katanayagi twins (Keita Saitou and Shota Saito) are star DJs armed with wall-trembling amplification; and Matthew Patel (Satya Bhabha) is a heavily mascara'd fop who comes flying into a concert to perform a quick dance number with a crew of demon backup chicks and then give Scott a very hard martial-artsy time. Scott dispatches these characters with some ace moves of his own ("I kicked him so hard that he saw the curvature of the Earth!"). But waiting at the end of the line is snaky club owner Gideon Gordon Graves (a preening Jason Schwartzman), the most formidable Ex of all.

Much of the movie's whacked-out humor is the work of the director. Wright's facility with eccentric ornamentation—bursts of canned laugh-track laughter, proudly cartoonish graphics, dreamscape enchantments, and sudden split-screenery—is consistently endearing; and his whiz-bang editing is a marvel throughout. (He's always one step ahead of the viewer, suddenly taking us places we didn't realize we were ready to go to yet.) And the script, which he cowrote, is a feast of deadpan throwaways. ("I've dabbled with being a bitch," says Ramona. "My brother is permanently enfeebled," notes Stacey.)

It's a bit of a letdown, then, that the movie loses its focus toward the end and descends into familiar CGI uproar (the concluding faceoff with Gideon goes on too long). But any movie that can sell us Michael Cera as a hard-hitting hero has already accomplished something unexpected (as has Cera himself, of course). And the entrancing world into which Scott's adventures have been set elicits that rarest of responses: it feels like something new. (August 2010)

Jennifer's Body

Girl Trouble

Just as he's about to rip the beautiful Jennifer's tightly bound body to shreds with a knife, hunky young Nikolai tries to tell her why. Nikolai is the lead singer of an indie band called Low Shoulder. They're desperate to make it big—to be the next Maroon 5. But the world is awash in indie bands, so it's hard. "There are so many of us," he says, "and we're all so cute. . . . Satan is our only hope." In the group's quest for diabolical new management, Nikolai has downloaded a satanic ritual off the Internet. All it requires is a virgin sacrifice. Unfortunately, he's picked the wrong girl: Jennifer's days of sexual innocence are far behind her. ("I'm not even a backdoor virgin," she admits.) So the ritual goes seriously wrong. Instead of leaving Jennifer dead, it transforms her into a snaky-eyed, flesh-eating demon. Oops.

The negative early reviews with which *Jennifer's Body* has been greeted are puzzling. Critics seem irked that the picture's not a full-on horror film or a straight teen comedy or a familiar satirical combination of the two. But the movie has other intentions. It's really about the social horrors of high school for adolescent girls (the guys on hand are clueless bystanders). And with a script by Diablo Cody (her first since the Oscar-winning *Juno*), the picture has a tone—smart and slashingly sarcastic—that's all its own.

Picking Megan Fox to play Jennifer was a sharp move—who better to portray this coldhearted tease and all-around bitch on wheels? ("What's wrong with you," Jennifer asks a classmate, "besides the obvious surface flaws?") And Amanda Seyfried—tamping down her sunny cuteness with bookworm glasses and pulled-back hair—is just right as Jennifer's nerdy best friend, Needy. Jennifer was a monster even before her satanic transformation at the hands of Nikolai (Adam Brody), but Needy has remained loyal to her childhood pal. When Jennifer starts munching on their fellow students, though, Needy has to seriously rethink their relationship.

Director Karyn Kusama (*Aeon Flux*) has given the picture a lustrous look, and there are some wonderfully well edited scenes, like the back-and-forth montage in which we see Needy having sweet first-time sex with her boyfriend, Chip (Johnny Simmons), while Jennifer has her bloody way with the school's timid, lip-ringed goth guy (Kyle Gallner)—who soon learns what goth is really all about.

The movie has a generous ration of gore; but Kusama—possibly with input from *Juno* director Jason Reitman, who produced the film with several associates—maintains solid control over the picture's diverse genre elements. So while Fox suggests nudity even when fully clothed, nobody gets naked in any really ogle-worthy way. And there's a scene in which Jennifer lures the school's star linebacker out into the moonlit woods (reaching into his pants for a purpose very different from what the big lug is expecting) that primes us for some vintage flesh ripping; but then an audience of cute little forest critters gathers around to watch, and suddenly we're somewhere else entirely.

The picture gets a nice kick from its well-chosen soundtrack (Silversun Pickups, All Time Low, even Hole—although *not* that band's own "Jennifer's Body"). But it's Cody's pop smarts that keep the movie bubbling. She knows all about bands and boys, and she never hits a bum note. As Nikolai's satanic ritual is about to get under way, he tells the helpless Jennifer to look on the bright side. "Maybe we'll write a song about you," he says. Perfect.

Sky High

Training Days

This could have been a standard Hollywood bolt job: take one of those coming-of-age teen comedies that John Hughes minted money with back in the 1980s, attach it to the sort of suburban superhero storyline that made *The Incredibles* such a profitable hit, then screw on a few Harry Potterisms for good measure, and—clank, bang—there you have it: a complete mess.

But *Sky High* rises above its motley components, thanks to its nimble director, Mike Mitchell (now forgiven for his part in last year's accursed Yuletide turkey, *Surviving Christmas*), and its winning cast. The veteran actors involved fuel the movie with comic flair; the young ones infuse it with fresh appeal; and the result is a picture that seems familiar, but feels new, too. It's a small, sweet pleasure.

Will Stronghold (puppy-eyed Michael Angarano of *Lords of Dogtown*) has a couple of problems. Not only is he about to start his freshman year of high school, but the school at which he'll be starting is Sky High, where the student body consists entirely of superhero offspring. Being the son of two of the school's most celebrated graduates, the mega-muscular Commander (Kurt Russell) and the high-flying Jetstream (Kelly Preston), Will has a lot to live up to—and, worryingly, he shows no signs of having inherited either of his parents' superpowers.

Sky High, to which Will and his fellow freshmen are transported by a magical bus (you almost expect it to drop all of them off at Hogwarts), floats in a field of clouds high above the Earth. As soon as the students arrive, they're ushered into the presence of blustery Coach Boomer (Bruce Campbell), a retired superhero once known as the Sonic Boom. Boomer proceeds to sort the newbies into two categories. Those who have true superpowers will become heroes; those who don't will be sidekicks, and trained to provide "hero support." Will and his friends have "sidekick" written all over them. Scrawny Ethan (Dee-Jay Daniels) has the dubious ability to turn himself into a puddle. Gangly Zach (Nicholas Braun) can glow like a night-light. And shape-shifting Magenta (Kelly Vitz) can turn herself into . . . a guinea pig.

Will's closest pal, Layla (Danielle Panabaker), who secretly adores him, could easily make the hero cut; she has the power to bend nature to her will. But she refuses to demonstrate it to Coach Boomer. "I think the whole thing's stupid," she tells Will. "Heroes and sidekicks—what is this?" ("High school," Will tells her.)

Since Will has no demonstrable powers of his own, he must join the rest of his friends in sidekick peonage. They form a glum substratum of high school life, enduring the taunts of the school's superbullies and the petty humiliations of the cool kids in the hero clique, chief among them the snooty senior Gwen (Mary Elizabeth Winstead), who, for inscrutable reasons of her own, sets about luring Will away from Layla. There's also a misunderstood loner named Warren Peace (Steven Strait), who is the conflicted son of a superhero mother and a supervillain dad (now in jail, thanks to the Commander). And of course the students must also contend with a staff of oddball teachers, like Mr. Medulla (Kevin McDonald), the pod-headed Mad Science instructor, and Mr. Boy (McDonald's fellow *Kids in the Hall* alumnus Dave Foley), a long-forgotten sidekick who was once more proudly known as All American Boy.

Kurt Russell, who broke through as a child actor himself nearly forty years ago, gives one of the movie's sharpest performances. The Commander's real-world persona is that of Steve Stronghold, a bustling, prosperous, khaki-clad real-estate broker. He and wife Josie/Jetstream keep their supergear stowed away in a downstairs Secret Sanctum, but he's still a gung-ho superhero. He greets Will's friends with a drill-sergeant's bark. ("What's your name? What's your power?") And he's kind of judgmental about the Sky High superyouth of today. "Does that one kid really glow?" he asks Will. "Boy, they've really lowered the bar since I went there." He worries that his son isn't turning out the way he'd hoped

("When I was his age, I could put a truck on my shoulders"), but he strives for optimism. ("He can always go into real estate!")

Can Will find a way to live up to his father's expectations? Can he fend off the brazen Gwen and somehow reinstall himself in the good graces of the heartbroken Layla? And when a scary superthreat arises from an unexpected quarter, can he and his minimally gifted friends somehow manage to superstop it? We know the answers to these questions, but the movie arrives at them in clever and charming ways. It's fun. In fact, it's pretty super. (July 2005)

Team America: World Police

Star Bores

The first thing to be said about *Team America: World Police* is what a well-made movie it is. It's cast entirely with marionettes (save for a clutch of black house cats impersonating panthers), but once you get past the strings appended to their extremities, the picture plays out as a classic action-adventure spy movie, complete with underground lairs, squealing car chases, and exotic foreign locales. And although the scale of the characters is one-third life size, the detailed world they inhabit— replete with puppet barrooms, puppet casbahs, puppet limos, even puppet barfing—is delightfully convincing. It's not a whole lot less "real" than the outré environments of the early James Bond films (which the movie affectionately references). This visual sophistication is a tribute to the underestimated ambitions of the filmmakers, *South Park* creators Trey Parker and Matt Stone, and to their good taste in collaborators, most notably cinematographer Bill Pope (who previously shot all three *Matrix* movies).

As the title announces, *Team America* is a satire of the current international political situation, and of the conviction on the part of the Bush administration that the United States, as the world's sole remaining superpower, should act as a global police force, rooting out tyrants and terrorist cabals wherever they may fester. Parker and Stone have satirized George W. Bush before, in their parody sitcom *That's My Bush!* ("He stole the election, now he'll steal your hearts.") And of course Bush not infrequently satirizes himself. But the president has no puppetized presence in *Team America*. Instead, Parker and Stone have shifted their gaze left and discerned on the other side of the current ideological divide a subject even more ripe for ridicule: the culture of celebrity political pontification.

The famous names and the irksome faces are all here, with strings affixed to their little wooden heads: Alec Baldwin, Tim Robbins, Janeane Garofalo, Martin Sheen, Susan Sarandon, and of course the sublimely clueless Sean Penn. And the story in which they play so comical a part has a familiar shape as well. A brotherhood of murderous Arab terrorists is discovered to be in league with a lunatic dictator, who is selling them weapons of mass destruction. Only Team America can stop them. The Team comprises five special operatives trained in martial arts, psychology, foreign languages, and so forth. Along with their controller, a suave, cocktail-wielding character called Spottswoode, they are headquartered in a swank subterranean hideout in the bowels of Mount Rushmore. Charged with their new mission, and a-clank with heavy weaponry, they jet off to Paris, a naturally suspicious place. There they make their way to a crowded plaza and begin scrutinizing its colorful inhabitants. They quickly zero in on a group of bearded, turban-topped men bearing an odd-looking metal case and murmuring among themselves in Arabic. (Well, it's supposed to be Arabic; it's just gibberish, actually.) One of the Team barks out, "You in the robes! Put down the weapon of mass destruction!" Gunfire breaks out, and soon blood-pocked puppet bodies are sailing through the air. Then Team America gets carried away and also blows up both the Eiffel Tower and the Louvre. Looking around at the wreckage afterward, one of them addresses the stunned Parisian onlookers: "*Bonjour!* It's okay—we got the terrorists!"

The Team moves on to Egypt, where they off more terrorists, but also accidentally blow up some pyramids and—oops—the Sphinx, too.

Meanwhile, back in the States, ABC News anchor Peter Jennings is sourly reporting that Team America has once again put the rest of the world into a serious pout. To clarify the situation for viewers, he solicits the moral expertise of Alec Baldwin, who explains that the terrible things that are happening aren't the terrorists' fault, they're Team America's. Cut to Mount Rushmore, where a raucous demonstration is under way outside the Team's headquarters, led by the corpulent Michael Moore, who is managing to be totally outraged while at the same time gobbling down ketchup-slathered hot dogs with both hands. Then cut to Pyongyang, North Korea, where the delusional dictator Kim Jong Il has been observing all this celebrity indignation with great interest.

Kim, it turns out, is the mad despot who has been arming the Arab terrorists. His machinations have become so obvious they've drawn the attention of the United Nations, which has dispatched mild-mannered weapons inspector Hans Blix to accost the diminutive despot in his vast palace. Blix tells Kim he must turn over his weapons of mass destruction "or else we will be very, very angry with you, and we will write a letter telling you how angry we are." Kim throws him into a pool full of pet sharks, then returns to his plotting. Since both he and the nattering Hollywood film stars want pretty much the same thing—to put an end to the antiterrorist forays of Team America—Kim decides to join forces with the Hollywood knuckleheads and invites them to cohost a world peace conference. The activist actors take the bait and are soon gathered in Pyongyang, where they grow misty-eyed imagining a shiny new world in which people of all nations will see things their way. "We will persuade everyone to drive hybrid cars," says Tim Robbins, "and stop smoking." "We will handle dangerous people with talk," says Baldwin. Sean Penn, for the most part, wanders around muttering, "I went to Iraq, you know." (He eventually has his throat ripped out by a panther.) The moral of the story is encapsulated at the end: "I know you don't like Americans right now," one of the Team members shouts. "But Kim Jong Il is a lot worse!"

It may be best that we pass over *Team America*'s big sex scene, which is . . . pretty hot, actually, for puppets. And let us not dwell on the exquisitely insensitive sequence in which Kim Jong Il laments his friendless solitude in a lilting ballad called "I'm So Ronery." And definitely let us not contemplate too closely the fact that *Team America* is opening on the first day of the Muslim holy month of Ramadan. These are deplorable things—*deplorable*. Although not as deplorable as several *other* things I've left unmentioned. Parker and Stone are virtuosos of insult and ethnic abuse; their wild, what-the-hell comic malice can be thrilling. But it's the pure, focused contempt with which they pile onto the showbiz windbags of stage and screen that's most bracing here. In *Team America*, these posturing savants are so wickedly kneecapped that, in sociocultural terms, they may never walk again. One doubts they'll be offered many rides, either. (October 2004)

STRANGE CARGO

S ome movies not only fit into no known pigeonhole, they seem to have beamed in from an unknown universe. None of the films considered here did much business upon release, but they're still available on DVD, and all of them, I think—well, almost all of them—merit at least a look.

Surveillance

Here Be Monsters

Surveillance started out as a script about witches. Director Jennifer Lynch took a pass at it and has now made a movie about devils—the human kind. The picture is twisted and disturbing and funny, too. Lynch has pushed the material to the wall—she has a gift for violence and perversity, and she never pulls back.

A trail of brutal serial murders has wound its way across the country and now arrived in an isolated, unnamed desert community. The movie begins with a recent atrocity, a man and woman slaughtered at their home. Then there's another bloodbath, out on a lonely highway, which leaves several people dead. We actually don't see this massacre. Not yet. The story gets under way in its aftermath.

Three survivors have been brought to the local police headquarters: a wounded cop named Jack (script originator Kent Harper), a hopped-up young blonde named Bobbi (Pell James), and an eight-year-old girl, Stephanie (Ryan Simpkins). Jack and Bobbi are liars, with much to lie about; only Stephanie has reliable information that could be of help, but she's a kid and nobody pays attention. Soon, to the resentment of the police chief (Michael Ironside) and his men, the FBI takes an interest, and two agents, Sam Hallaway (Bill Pullman) and Elizabeth Anderson (Julia Ormond), show up to take over the investigation.

The movie flips back and forth in time. In a scene set earlier, we observe that two of the cops, Jack and his partner, Jim (French Stewart), are corrupt, half-crazy dirtbags. To pass the dead hours, they sit in their patrol car, parked near the desert highway, and shoot out the tires of selected passing vehicles, which they then approach and detain. The vicious good-cop, bad-cop psych-outs they inflict on these unlucky motorists are among the most alarming things in the movie. Which is saying something.

One of the cars we see the rogue lawmen intercept contains little Stephanie and her family. Then a second car is halted at the same spot, this one carrying Bobbi and her big-lunk boyfriend Johnny (Mac Miller), fresh from a drug rip-off. We don't see what happens next, but soon.

Back at headquarters afterward, the three witnesses are being questioned separately. Stephanie keeps trying to tell anyone who'll listen that she saw something out on the highway earlier: a mysterious white van, a black-gloved hand, blood. Her story doesn't register. Then comes word that three more bodies have been discovered. Agent Anderson and two of the local cops set out for the scene. The picture ends in a bonfire of depravity, played for both shocks and laughs.

Lynch's first movie, the 1993 amputation love story *Boxing Helena*, was critically reviled, and for that and other reasons it has taken the director sixteen years to complete a second one. *Surveillance* has some of the drifting unease we associate with the work of her father, David Lynch (who lent his name to this project in order to help get it made, and who also contributed music to the soundtrack). Some of the visual details (a demented face growling up on a monitor, a crushed bird in the road) have Dad's touch, and a long shot of the highway under a vast sky stacked with clouds recalls his 1999 film, *The Straight Story*. But his daughter has her own ticklingly gruesome sensibility and no reservations about deploying it. She and Harper have cooked up some wicked lines, too. When Agent Anderson threatens the uncooperative Bobbi with a full cavity search, the younger woman says, "I haven't done a girl since art school." Says Anderson: "It's like riding a bike." The movie's fake-out conclusion is something else. It's like falling off a cliff. (June 2009)

The Fall

Dreamwork

The Fall is a movie with a Look. It looks like two hours of high-end perfume commercials. And no wonder: The Indian director, Tarsem Singh, although best known for his 1991 music video for R.E.M.'s "Losing My Religion," and for his previous feature, the outré 2000 creepfest *The Cell*, sustains himself professionally by shooting commercials of the high-end sort. So for the past eleven years, while amassing frequent-flier miles in the service of Levi's, Smirnoff, and Coca-Cola, he also scouted locations for this film in places like China, Brazil, Romania, Egypt, South Africa, Fiji, and Nepal (to name about a third of them). He shot various bits along the way and then, four years ago, began working in earnest, on an indie budget, with a cast of capable, low-profile actors. The result is one of the more gorgeous movies of recent years, and if its ending weren't located about thirty minutes past the point where one might wish it to be, that could have been cause for unqualified celebration.

The story is set in Los Angeles in 1915. Hollywood is in its infancy, and a stuntman named Roy (Lee Pace) is languishing in pain in a small hospital, unable to walk after riding his horse off a bridge while shooting a western. Apart from being paralyzed, Roy also broods about the fact that the movie's leading man, a slick-haired weasel named Sinclair (Daniel Caltagirone), has stolen Roy's girlfriend. A pretty nurse named Evelyn (Justine Waddell) tries to spread a little sunshine, but Roy is feeling suicidal. Then he meets another patient, a five-year-old girl named Alexandria (Catinca Untaru, a Romanian cutie making her first, very good attempt at acting). Roy tries to manipulate Alexandria into stealing a bottle of morphine tablets for him. In return, he says, he'll tell her "an epic story." The girl gets the pills, then has to keep Roy sufficiently preoccupied with inventing the epic that he won't have time to think about offing himself with an overdose.

The story Roy tells sprawls extravagantly. It involves a character called the Black Bandit, whom we see to be Roy himself; a beautiful princess who's a ringer for Nurse Evelyn; and a hateful villain named Odious, who much resembles the sweetie-thief Sinclair. In his search for Odious, whom he intends to terminate, the Black Bandit leads a troupe of loyal fighters—among them, for some reason, Charles Darwin (Leo Bill). Darwin's monkey is on hand, too. And Alexander the Great puts in an appearance early on, lost in the desert wearing a fantastical black helmet with billowing scarlet plumage.

The story evolves in a succession of rich, painterly images. (There's a nod to Escher at one point, and at another, an echo of Edward Hopper's lonely slanting sunlight.) As the Bandit and his men pursue Odious around the world, we're engulfed by uncanny sights. There's a vast blue city. There's a solitary palace in the middle of a lake. There's a tribe of mud men, a hill of black-clad corpses, and a room of polished marble filled with madly whirling dervishes. A wagon moves through the desert on huge wheels within which slaves labor like hamsters. A tree splits open in flames and a dreadlocked man walks out.

There's so much to see and marvel at in *The Fall* that it's hard to keep track of the story, which in any event, as I say, goes on too long. The movie recalls Fellini a little and Jodorowsky a lot; but Tarsem has striking visions of his own. The picture is like a great museum you can't find your way out of—it wears you down. Too bad the gifted director couldn't come up with an earlier exit. (May 2008)

The Saddest Music in the World

The Queen of Beers

As another season of multimedia marketing schemes masquerading as movies gets under way, one casts about for other possibilities, other visions. So if you told me there was a picture playing down the street about a legless female brewery tycoon who wobbles about on see-through prosthetic limbs filled with beer, and who is conducting a global search to find the saddest music in the world, I would probably be slapping down money for a ticket before you even got to the part about the world's most bummed-out cello player, who carries the heart of his dead son around in a jar, "preserved," he says, "in my own tears."

The Saddest Music in the World is a film by Guy Maddin, often referred to, somewhat dismissively, as the Canadian David Lynch. Like Lynch, Maddin, who's been turning out strange little art pictures since 1986, has an affinity for deadpan surrealism and scenic decrepitude. But his distinguishing obsession is with antique visual textures—the primitive, flickery look of old silent films and the soft-focus glow of golden age Hollywood melodramas. Maddin's blown-out, high-contrast black-and-white photography, his stuttery editing, and his shabby deco set touches evoke lost worlds of filmmaking, and they infuse *Saddest Music* with an emotional pull unrelated to its casually absurd story. For a weird movie, it's strangely touching.

We're in snowbound Winnipeg, Manitoba, in the winter of 1933. Winnipeg has been declared the world capital of sadness by . . . somebody. Lady Port-Huntley, the legless brewery owner (Isabella Rossellini), has become excited about the imminent end of Prohibition across the border in the United States, and thus the opening up of a new beer market. Now if only she could find a way to draw international attention to the sad city of Winnipeg—and, not incidentally, to her own fine lager. She already has the ad campaign: "If you're sad, and like beer, I'm your lady."

Thus the contest to find the world's saddest music. Lady Port-Huntley invites musical depressives from around the world to come to Winnipeg and vie for a $25,000 prize. Not surprisingly, in the slough of the Great Depression, they flock: a band of woebegone Mexican mariachis, a foot-stamping Spanish fado troupe, a group of Cameroonian tribal drummers (gouging their flesh in ritual grief), an all-girl Scottish bagpipe team, even a Siamese flute player. ("Nobody can beat Siam," a radio commentator chirps, "when it comes to dignity, cats, or twins.") Two groups at a time go head-to-head with their most doleful laments. The winning act gets to slide down a chute from the stage into a big vat of beer: *ploosh!*

Three of the contestants are related, in complicated ways. Brain-fried piano player Fyodor Kent—a former surgeon, now a local lush—is the father of oily Chester (played by Mark McKinney, of *The Kids in the Hall*), a failed Broadway producer who has returned home with his mistress, a dreamy-eyed amnesiac named Narcissa (Maria de Medeiros, of *Pulp Fiction*). Chester is a scoundrel: He plans to scam his way into the contest, representing the United States, and to win it by whatever sleazy means necessary. ("Sadness is just happiness turned on its ass," he says. "It's all showbiz.")

Chester figures his onetime carnal relationship with Lady Port-Huntley should be helpful. She proves to be a tough sell, though. It was Chester who was responsible for pulverizing one of her legs in a car crash years earlier. And it was his father, Fyodor, another of her lovers, who subsequently decided that the leg should be amputated—and then, in a drunken stupor, mistakenly cut off her remaining good leg, too. (In contrition for this surgical screwup, Fyodor resolved to play the piano in the future only on his knees. In further atonement, he fabricated the glass legs that lifted Lady Port-Huntley up off her stumps.

Meanwhile, also back in town is Chester's older brother, Roderick, the aforementioned supersad cellist. Roderick, who wears dark glasses and an imposing gaucho hat with a long black mourning veil stitched around its rim, now lives in Serbia and performs throughout Europe as

Gavrilo the Great. Apart from hoping to win the contest as the Serbian entrant, he is also searching for his vanished wife, who wandered off after the death of their young son and has not been seen since. You can imagine his astonishment when he lays eyes on Chester's amnesiac girlfriend, Narcissa, and. . . .

Okay, that *is* a lot of plot, I know, and not even all of it. (We'll dispense with Narcissa's gastrointestinal tapeworm, which she sometimes consults for life-path guidance.) The story is happily cracked, but there are also glimmers of moral concern. Roderick is additionally saddened by the public's fading memory of the 9 million soldiers killed in the First World War (which of course got started in Serbia in 1914), and by the fact that he himself is now more distraught by the loss of a single life, his son's. He is sad on top of sad, and if his sadness is absurd, Maddin seems to feel that that's sad, too.

The movie is also a musical, of sorts. (Jerome Kern's swooning 1932 ballad, *The Song Is You*, serves as a melancholy motif.) And it's certainly a logistical triumph: all of the film's sets were constructed in an unheated Winnipeg factory building, with mountains of snow trucked in for icy vérité. You can almost hear the actors cursing the cold, or maybe the director.

The Saddest Music in the World goes on a bit longer than it really should, but it's a movie powered by talent and inspiration and obsessive determination; and as an exercise in style, like Maddin himself, it's unique. (May 2004)

My Winnipeg

Home in His Head

Nobody makes films that even remotely resemble those of Guy Maddin. Over the last twenty years, the Canadian director has created a pictorial language of stuttery, halated imagery—the vintage atmosphere of silent movies—that summons waves of memory and obscure long-ing. In the new *My Winnipeg*, his tenth feature, he brings this style to bear on his snowy hometown, a provincial metropolis about which he has very mixed feelings, and from which he can't seem to escape, at least in his head. As always, his head is an interesting place to visit.

In voice-over, Maddin tells us that he has returned to "snowy, sleep-walking Winnipeg" in order to exorcise its hold on him. "We sleep as we walk, walk as we dream," he says, reaching back into his childhood and his imagination to show us a profusion of local wonders: children tobogganing down a snow-blanketed garbage mound ("the only hill in board-flat Winnipeg"); the Ballet Club, site of séances back in the 1920s, where the founder danced out messages from beyond; a bridge origi-nally built for Egypt, but which "wouldn't fit the river there"; a surreal field of dead horses, their heads poking up through the snow as local folk stroll among them.

We learn about his family, especially his mother, a beautician. ("I've often wondered what effect growing up in a hair salon had on me," he says, "in that gynocracy.") As part of this exorcism, Maddin has rented back his childhood home, restored it to its original glory ("the crummy sofa, the comfy chair"), and hired a group of actors to portray his fam-ily. Since his father is long dead, he arranges, in a dream-state sequence, to have the old man's body exhumed and reinterred under the living room rug. But it's his mother with whom he's most obsessed—"a force from which I can't turn away for long." (Mom is played by eighty-seven-year-old Ann Savage, the unforgettable femme fatale of the 1945 noir classic *Detour*.)

Intermittently throughout the film, Maddin cuts away to a train com-partment where a group of woozy men sway to the lurching rhythms of their conveyance. It's a dark, mesmerizing image. But are the men on their way to Winnipeg, or are they making their escape? Is Maddin among them? Will he ever know? (June 2008)

Rubber

On the Road

The movie: a French production, but in English. The plot: a serial killer rolls into town. The star: a tire.

Quentin Dupieux's *Rubber* isn't as much nutty fun as you'd hope; still, it's a likably odd little film, shot on a consumer-grade SLR camera equipped with a video mode, on a budget that might not cover the wardrobe for a big Hollywood movie. It's a cute riff on the killer-machine horror genre, although the director's interests are mainly meta.

The picture opens with an actor asking us, "In the movie *E.T.*, why is the alien brown? No reason." Then: "In the movie *JFK*, why is the president shot by someone he doesn't know? No reason." Then: "The movie you are about to see is an homage to 'no reason.'"

Thus freed from customary narrative constraints, Dupieux—who wrote, directed, shot, and edited the film—next shows us a group of people on a nearby hill preparing to observe the coming cinematic action through binoculars. ("Is it going to be in color or black-and-white?" a girl asks.) Then we see a cast-off tire squirming to life by the side of a dusty road. The tire has a taste for carnage (for which of course no reason is adduced). After practicing its strange explosive powers on some local wildlife, it moves on to higher vertebrates, following a woman in a car to a shabby desert motel, where the tire checks in—rather violently—and kicks back in a comfy chair to watch a NASCAR race on TV. More bloody explosions ensue. Police arrive and bumble about. The people on the hill keep up a running commentary.

All very cute, and sometimes funny. ("Is the tire gonna get laid?" one observer wonders as the star peeps in on a showering woman.) And the tracking shots, as we follow the remote-controlled menace on its alarming rounds, are pretty impressive. But the movie is short on surprise—it's not really wild enough. Its energy ebbs and it begins to drag. Well before its eighty-five minutes have elapsed, it runs out of road. (March 2011)

The Girlfriend Experience

Sex and the City

S asha Grey isn't the first porn star to attempt a mainstream-movie crossover. Skin-flick pros like Marilyn Chambers, Traci Lords, and Ginger Lynn have all given the higher Hollywood a shot, with middling results. But in Steven Soderbergh's *The Girlfriend Experience*, the twenty-one-year-old Grey—a professed art-film buff who drops names like Godard and Varda on her Web site—makes the most credible transition to date. Playing a high-end Manhattan escort named Chelsea is hardly a stretch for the star of *Sex Toy Teens* and *Strap Attack 6*, but her casting is more than a stunt. With her sleek demeanor and smoky gaze, Grey has real presence; and while the extent of her acting ability is anybody's guess, she's strikingly self-possessed, and she definitely pops on-screen.

Soderbergh shot the movie very quickly in New York last October, when the presidential election campaigns were at full heat and the economy was just beginning to fall apart. The picture is set in the world of self-absorbed urban professionals and their money—about which they're all starting to get very worried. Chelsea's clients are investment advisers, screenwriters, entrepreneurs of various sorts—not the sort of men who want to think of themselves as consorting with hookers. Instead, they call Chelsea, who runs her own one-woman escort service. Chelsea is smart and presentable; they can take her to art galleries and upscale restaurants. ("We had dinner at Blue Hill," she confides to her laptop diary.) They can talk to her about their wives and kids and other problems. She offers them not just a hookup but a more dignified "girlfriend experience." True, they have to pay her—a lot. But then girl-friends are always expensive.

Like her clients, Chelsea is uneasy about her financial situation. She wants to upgrade her Web site to get better Google placement. She might open a boutique. Should she get into gold? She's all about class and polish, but she inevitably has to interact with unsavory lowlifes. A pushy magazine writer (played by veteran New York journalist Mark Jacobson) keeps trying to plumb her personal depths for a profile. The proprietor of an Internet sex site called the Erotic Connoisseur (played with ebullient skeeziness by film critic Glenn Kenny) offers a rave review of her services in exchange for a free sample. Meanwhile, fresh new professional babes are popping up on the escort scene every day, and Chelsea begins to contemplate her sell-by date. She has a live-in relationship with a broad-minded hunk (Chris Santos), but he's just a personal trainer, with his own financial insecurities. Then, unexpectedly, she starts clicking with a new client. Could this be real love, a soul mate thing? Or is it just a boyfriend experience?

Along with directing the movie, Soderbergh shot and edited it, too, and he's given the picture a gleaming, near-abstract beauty. The luxe interiors have a rich glow, and the extensive manipulation of focus (lots of blurred foregrounds) enhances the offhand impressionism of the story. The surfaces are more eloquent than the oblique characters—we have to project ourselves into the film to get much out of it. But the movie conveys a strong sense of time (a past so recent it won't let go) and place (the modern metropolitan money pit). And while Grey either can't or hasn't been directed to express Chelsea's inner reality, she's fascinating to watch. It may be only an actress experience she's providing right now. But she'll be back. (May 2009)

Downloading Nancy

Nancy wants to die. Louis, an S & M creep she met on the Internet, wants to be of service. Albert, Nancy's worm husband, can't figure out what to make of this movie. No, wait—that's us.

Downloading Nancy, a film about self-mutilation, sexual sadism, and dismal fluorescent lighting, features a fearless performance by Maria Bello in the title role and a carefully spare one by Jason Patric, who plays Louis. But the story is so irritatingly jumbled that even the squalid enticements of voyeurism—the painful games involving mousetraps, cigarette burns, and broken glass—are insufficient compensation for the movie's narrative confusion.

Nancy has been married to Albert (Rufus Sewell), a heavily repressed neat freak, for fifteen years, and she's miserable. Because of the violent sexual abuse she suffered as a child, the closest she can come to pleasure is slashing her arms and legs with razors. A sympathetic shrink (Amy Brenneman) tries to help, but Nancy has had it. She can only experience love as a variant of pain and she just wants to end it all.

Bello's control in depicting this character—her crippling timidity, fiery mood swings, and hopeless self-loathing—is formidable. And as Louis—who in a more commercially alert picture might have been a standard nightmare—Patric exerts an impressive restraint. We know Louis is a twisted guy—the walls of his apartment are lined with videotapes of his past sadomasochistic exploits. ("You'll be a whole shelf," he promises Nancy.) But there's a bit more to the character—we learn in a fleeting comment that he has two kids he'll never be allowed to see again—and we notice glimpses of his own pain flickering across Patric's stubbly face and seeping into his deep, mournful voice.

But the movie is nonlinear in a pointless way, flashing forward and then back again and again, and it's often hard to be certain where we are in the narrative. Still, the picture has some supremely strange scenes, the eeriest of which takes place after Nancy has left Albert in order to surrender herself to her new e-mail friend Louis in Baltimore. One day, posing as a computer technician, Louis comes to see Albert at the couple's now half-empty home. Albert lets him in, but as it slowly dawns on him that this is actually the man who has taken possession of Nancy for some sick purpose, their desultory banter builds into heated male verbal wrangling and finally erupts into a vicious physical attack. Here, the first-time screenwriters, Pamela Cuming and Lee Ross (working from a "true story"), show an imaginative dramatic knack. Some praise may also be due to the Swedish director, Johan Renck, another first-timer, for rising above his background in TV commercials and music videos (Madonna, Beyoncé): Apart from an occasional stuttery editing tic, he resists shopworn artiness and maintains the film's bleak mood with grim determination.

Unfortunately, the movie is lit like an operating room (you'd never guess the great Christopher Doyle had anything to do with shooting it), which makes the several scenes of sexual assault and degradation seem even more wretched. That the characters of Nancy and Louis have a recognizable humanity is a tribute to the talents of Bello and Patric. But the part of Albert is weirdly misconceived. Sewell's character is a tight knot of emotional atrophy and oblique seething, and we wonder what his problem is. (He seems to be tormented by things outside the story.) Then we wish he'd go deal with it in some other movie. (June 2009)

Birth

Be My Baby

I admit the scene where the ten-year-old boy strips off his clothes and hops into a bathtub with the naked and waiting Nicole Kidman kind of icked me out, especially when he fixed her with a sultry stare and addressed her as his "wife." That and the scene where Kidman asks him if he's ever made love to a girl and he says, "You'll be my first." I didn't know whether to laugh or leave.

I stuck with it, though, and was relieved to find that Kidman and her little man actually don't have sex in the new Jonathan Glazer movie *Birth*, which is one small thing to recommend it. The film is artfully made, but it's baffling. You wonder what on earth it's trying to say. Then you wonder if it even knows. Kidman plays Anna, a well-to-do Manhattan widow who's been mourning the death of her husband, Sean, for the past ten years. Now she has finally decided to stop moping around and remarry. But then, on the night of her engagement party at her mother's huge Upper East Side apartment, the aforementioned ten-year-old boy (moonfaced Cameron Bright) slips in, takes her aside, and tells her that he is Sean—the reincarnation of her dead husband. Anna finds this preposterous, as who wouldn't, and so do her mother (Lauren Bacall), her pompous fiancé (Danny Huston), and the rest of the party guests. But the child won't be put off, and over the ensuing days he demonstrates an unsettling knowledge of things that only the dead Sean could have known. Nobody is buying this—except, bizarrely, Anna herself. Slowly, she comes to believe that the boy is telling the truth, that he really is her Sean.

Since Glazer's first movie was the bracingly acidulous *Sexy Beast*, and since *Birth* is so elegantly photographed and so boldly, unhastily paced, I kept waiting to see where he was going with this story. And when Anna told little Sean that she'd happily wait eleven years until he turned twenty-one and they could get married—well, I realized where he was going. He was going over a cliff. Slowly, beautifully, trailing clouds of befuddlement. I waved good-bye. (October 2004)

Lars and the Real Girl

Absurdia

Apparently there are people who think this is the feel-good movie of the year. I know I felt really good when the bloody thing ended.

Movies with deluded protagonists usually try to persuade us that their delusions are somehow a good thing—an improvement over real life. In the 1947 *Miracle on 34th Street*, Edmund Gwenn may not really be Santa Claus, but his conviction that he is stirs a heartwarming Christmas glow in those around him. And in the 1950 *Harvey*, James Stewart's belief in a magical friend—a man-size rabbit—serves a similarly sweet purpose.

The protagonist of *Lars and the Real Girl*, however, has fallen in love with a mail-order sex doll. I suppose this premise could be made to work as a movie. The painter Oskar Kokoschka once took up with a custom-made mannequin modeled on the measurements of a woman who'd dumped him, and I'd pay to see that movie. But Kokoschka was a kooky artist. The title character in this film, Lars Lindstrom (Ryan Gosling), is a near-lifeless simpleton with a face of moonlike inexpressiveness (apart from an occasional torpid smile that suggests he's just eaten a really excellent oatmeal cookie).

At first I thought Lars was autistic; later, though, we're told he was emotionally stunted by growing up with a very sad dad. In any case, he's twenty-seven years old and lives in a small, snowy midwestern town, in a converted garage behind a house inhabited by his brother Gus (Paul Schneider) and Gus's wife Karin (Emily Mortimer). A stranger to social skills, Lars nevertheless manages to hold down a job in a nondescript office where he shares a cubicle with a porn-hound named Kurt (Maxwell McCabe-Lokos) and fends off the advances of a girl named Margo (Kelli Garner). Right here the movie waves good-bye to the real world, a place in which women who look like Kelli Garner generally set their sights higher than "dimwit" on the scale of male attractiveness.

When Kurt turns Lars on to Realgirl.com—an actual Web site whose sex dolls come with pre-flattened backs—Lars puts in an order. When the doll arrives, he names it (well, her, I guess) Bianca, and starts introducing the thing around as his girlfriend. Gus and Karin, understandably alarmed, take him to a local psychologist (Patricia Clarkson). Her professional opinion? Ply him with meds? Drive him straight to the bin? No. She suggests that Gus and Karin and everyone else adjust their boringly normal reality to accommodate Lars's sweet delusion. And so before you know it, Lars and his rubbery inamorata are being fondly fussed over by local biddies, toasted at parties, embraced by broadminded churchgoers—in short, they're taking the town by storm. Bianca gets a job in a clothing store (very droll). She volunteers at the hospital. She gets elected to the school board. Can you stand it?

Quite possibly not. Clarkson, Schneider, and Mortimer, three fine actors, are to be saluted for their commitment to indie films, but they're wasted in this one. And Gosling, who was nominated for an Oscar for his performance in last year's *Half Nelson*, can do nothing with the po-faced schlub he attempts to play here. Presumably, those who resonate to a film like this feel it points the way to a better world, one in which rolling around in this sort of sentimental goo can wash away our soul-shriveling cynicism. Don't they worry about their brains dribbling down the drain, too? (October 2007)

Fur: An Imaginary Portrait
of Diane Arbus

Impossible Dream

This odd biopic is an attempt by director Steven Shainberg to illumi-
nate the work of the late photographer Diane Arbus by installing
amid the known facts of her life some outlandish inventions. The movie
is distinguished by Nicole Kidman's game performance as Arbus, and
by the rigorous control of color and framing by cinematographer Bill
Pope (who shot the *Matrix* films) and the rich production design by
Amy Danger (who also designed Shainberg's last feature, the delectably
perverse *Secretary*). That *Fur* collapses into absurdity doesn't diminish
the daring of its concept, although it does call into question the movie's
purpose.

As a photojournalist in the 1960s, Diane Arbus devised a stark new
manner of depicting society's fringe dwellers. Strippers, transvestites,
midgets, nudists, giants, and carnival denizens—all offered themselves
up to Arbus's cool gaze with unsettling candor. "Most people go through
life dreading they'll have a traumatic experience," she once said. "Freaks
were born with their trauma. They've already passed their test in life.
They're aristocrats."

The movie begins in 1958. Arbus and her husband, Allan (Ty Burrell),
a fashion photographer, are partners in a successful commercial photo
business: she styles the models, he takes the pictures. But Diane feels
repressed by her subsidiary role in their marriage; she longs to break
free. One day, a strange new neighbor moves in upstairs, a man named
Lionel (Robert Downey Jr.), whose head is hidden within a baglike knit-
ted mask. Intrigued, Diane makes her way up to his eccentrically fur-
nished apartment (there's a severed foot, a white rabbit, a small bathing
pool). Here, she discovers that Lionel suffers from a disorder called

hypertrichosis, and that beneath his mask and his clothing, his body is entirely covered by long, thick hair.

It is at this point, with the introduction of Lionel, that the picture begins tipping over into ridiculousness. The fictitious Lionel may be intended to suggest the elegant brute played by Jean Marais in the 1946 film version of *Beauty and the Beast*. However, what leaps most quickly to mind, as we watch Lionel padding around his apartment, is the possibility of a previously undiscovered Universal horror movie from that same period: *At Home with the Wolfman*, possibly. With his liquid eyes and creamy baritone, Downey projects an air of fur-ball romantic ardor that has to be seen to be hooted at.

From here on, despite Shainberg's most determined effort to keep playing his premise straight, the picture dribbles downhill. Lionel starts taking Diane out—by bus, by subway, wearing his mask and a pair of purple gloves—to meet his fellow social outcasts. There are Siamese twins, pot-smoking midgets, a whip-wielding dominatrix, and an armless woman who plays the cello with her feet (a startling sight). "This is terrific," Diane says. "I thought you'd like it," Lionel purrs. Inevitably, Diane enters Lionel's apartment one night to find him waiting for her with a pair of scissors, a bowl of water, and a razor. The scene that follows—and the scenes that follow that, and then the big sex scene, and, oh Lord, the gaudy windup on a desolate beach—are of a ludicrousness so untethered that the most reasonable response is derision.

Nothing in the movie is as eerily compelling as the photographs of Diane Arbus, who committed suicide in 1971. Her powers of human witness were uncanny. Eighty of her most psychically resonant photos are collected in the classic *Diane Arbus: An Aperture Monograph*, which can be purchased for approximately the cost of four tickets to see *Fur*. It's an appealing alternative to this pointlessly strange film. (November 2006)

Silent Light

In Another Land

Silent Light, the new movie by the Mexican director Carlos Reygadas, has the feeling of an artifact from another time, or maybe another planet. It's set in a remote Mennonite farming community in rural Mexico, and the actors speak in Plautdietsch, an archaic German dialect that might prove impenetrable even for those who understand modern German. (The picture has English subtitles.) The story is about God's mysterious workings in the arena of human uncertainty; and the very long takes with which the director tells his tale (the opening shot of a vast night sky shading slowly into dawn, amid a rising chorus of insect chatter and treetop bird squawks, goes on for six minutes) puts you in a trance. It will certainly put some people to sleep, but anyone inclined to go with the movie's tidal rhythm will be transfixed.

The movie opens on a farm family—husband, wife, and six children—sitting at a kitchen table, heads bowed in silent prayer. A pendulum wall clock clacks loudly on the soundtrack, eventually joined by the clinking of forks and spoons as the family begins to eat. Not much is said; it's clear that the characters are obscurely distressed. After the mother and children leave on an errand, the father gets up, stops the clock with a finger on its pendulum, sits back down at the table, and begins to quietly weep, at considerable length.

As the father, Johan (Cornelio Wall Fehr), goes about his day—stopping in to seek the counsel of a friend at a service station, paying a troubled visit to his father—we learn the source of his torment. Although devoted to his wife, Esther (Miriam Toews), and their children, Johan has fallen in love with another woman, Marianne (Maria Pankratz), who owns a small roadside café. Their relationship has become physical, and Johan has been conscientious about keeping Esther informed about what's going on. (They do love each other, and she bears this disruptive news with stoic understanding.) Johan's friend thinks Marianne could be the "natural woman" he was meant to be with—that his feeling for her "may be founded on something sacred." His father tells him this temptation is the work of "the Enemy" and insists that the passion will pass. Johan, for his part, is torn: is his attraction to Marianne a signal from God or a moral flaw within himself?

Reygadas is in no rush to resolve any of this. As the story slowly plays out, he settles into a procession of long, quiet scenes—the family bathing outdoors in a rocky pool; the harvesting of hay and milking of cows—with only the most minimal expressive flourishes, like the limpid shot of a drop of dew dripping like a tear off the petal of a flower. The landscape is a flat sprawl of crops and bracken under majestic, ever-shifting skies (the cinematography by Alexis Zabé has a sometimes monumental beauty), and the rooms through which the characters pass have the evocative simplicity of a Vermeer domestic interior. The actors—some of whose chiseled faces might have been modeled on ancient coins—are all amateurs, many of them Mennonites, some of them actually related. But they *are* acting, under the director's rigorous control. In their artlessness, they don't appear to be soliciting an emotional response, but they draw one from us nevertheless. (January 2009)

CRITICAL LIST

H ave we not all had the experience of going to see a movie just because one or another top critic raved about it? And then walking out thinking, "What?" And then thinking, "Is it me, or did that movie actually suck?" This could be a long list. (Remember There Will Be Blood? The Diving Bell and the Butterfly?) But let's keep it to three.

Synecdoche, New York

Nowhere Man

Charlie Kaufman, a screenwriter for whom "brilliant" is the default adjective, is reported to have been peeved in the past with what some directors have done with his scripts (notably George Clooney, with *Confessions of a Dangerous Mind*). Now, with *Synecdoche, New York*, Kaufman has directed one of them himself. The result is a picture that is (a) brilliant, in scattered parts, but also (b) a reminder that every writer needs an editor.

The movie is about failure, decay, and death, pretty much in that order. Oh, and confusion, probably your own. The picture is presented as a comedy, of a Kaufmanian sort, but it's not exactly light on its feet. Philip Seymour Hoffman, usually such a fascinating actor to watch, is here sunk deep in shlubbiness as Caden Cotard, a mediocre stage director who is professionally stranded in the theatrical outback of Schenectady, New York. (Cotard's syndrome, you should know going in, is the psychiatric delusion that one is dead or rotting, or that the world no longer exists.) Caden is obsessed with disease and dying; his wife, Adele (Catherine Keener), thinks a lot about her husband dying, too, but in a hopeful way. Adele is an artist—she paints pictures so tiny they require magnification to make out what's going on in them. When she scores an exhibition of her work in Berlin, she leaves Caden behind but takes their four-year-old daughter along. Not a good sign, but what can Caden do? As someone actually says at one point, "He lives in a half-world between stasis and anti-stasis."

At the local community theater over which he glumly presides, Caden is staging a production of (what else?) *Death of a Salesman*. On his own now, he begins flirting with the bosomy box-office ticket girl, Hazel (Samantha Morton). When Hazel sets out in search of a house to buy, we see that the one she selects is on fire. She takes it. (This house-afire gag is funny the first time we see it; whether we need to see it again is a question to which the answer is no.)

Caden begins to have trouble keeping track of time. When he laments to Hazel that Adele has been gone for a year now, she tells him, "It's been a week." He consults a therapist (Hope Davis), who's not a lot of help. (She recommends to him a novel written by a four-year-old boy: "He killed himself when he was five.") To make things more complicated—although not nearly as complicated as they'll later become—Caden is also being followed by a tall, balding man named Sammy (Tom Noonan). Why? You'll have to be patient.

If I may hurry things along a bit, Caden, who is clearly unencumbered by talent, is suddenly awarded a MacArthur "genius" grant, which will allow him to stage the play of his life—literally—in a huge, hangar-like warehouse in New York. He builds enormous sets that look like . . . New York. He hires actors to play himself and the other people who clutter his existence. He is, you see, *observing* his life rather than *living* it. At one point, Sammy makes a bid for the role of Caden. "I've been following you for twenty years," he says. "Hire me, and you'll find out who you truly are." After a while, cast and crew grow restive—rehearsals have been going on for seventeen years. (So has the film, it almost seems.)

I've passed over Caden's plague of boils, his daughter's green poop, and a lot of other plot eccentricities that I think we can continue passing over. The film's message is stated forthrightly, not to say repeatedly: "I'm very lonely." "The end is built into the beginning." "After death, there's nothing." Anyone unfamiliar with this worldview has never seen a Woody Allen movie.

As the cast and the concept of Caden's play metastasize, there are some surreally funny moments. Many more moments, unfortunately, are surreal in the manner of "What?" And while a number of fine actresses pass through Kaufman's conceptual clamor—Michelle Williams, Jennifer Jason Leigh, Emily Watson, Dianne Wiest—the prosthetic aging makeup with which some of them are spackled and the way in which they continually shift characters make it difficult to tell who's who and what's what and why.

There are parts of the movie that confirm Kaufman's twisty talent as a writer (not that it's ever been in doubt). And the picture is certainly ambitious. But *Synecdoche* is less a demonstration of his ability as a director (which is not apparent) than it is an illustration of why he still needs one. (October 2008)

I'm Not There

Too Much of Nothing

There's a striking sequence in *I'm Not There*, Todd Haynes's new Bob Dylan movie, in which Dylan's besieged mid-1960s artistic transformation is set within the surreal glare of the spa scenes in Fellini's 8½, in which a blocked movie director attempted to work out his own artistic confusion. This is an imaginative melding of period pop-music myth and cinematic iconography, and it resonates memorably. It should also be said that the movie has been made with a clear affection for its subject; that it has some sharp edges, too; and that there are a couple of enterprising performances in it that are worth seeing.

For the most part, though, sitting through this unusual-but-not-a-lot-more-than-that picture, in which six different actors impersonate Dylan in various phases of his career, is like contemplating a package that's arrived in the mail containing something you never ordered and never would. The notion that Dylan's many public personas—as opposed to his songs—merit intense contemplation at this late date seems silly. And yet here they are, on pointless parade: the whey-faced young folksinger Bob; the sharecropper-serenading protest Bob; the turned-on, meet-the-Beatles Bob; and of course the Woodstock Bob of *The Basement Tapes*. Actually, I suppose these multi-Dylans *are* thought-provoking, in a way. I kept wondering, "Why?"

The familiar chronology of Dylan's career has been assembled into a story, of sorts, but it's not particularly compelling; and there's no character development apart from the obvious one of a succession of actors playing the same protagonist. There are only those half-dozen Dylans, wandering in a field of familiar visual cues: the fateful motorcycle crash; the Big Pink and—yikes!—*Renaldo and Clara* references; and, for the Dylan fetishists who will most truly groove on this movie, more oblique touches like a Gorgeous George flyer, a nod to the cover of the *Freewheelin'* album, a glimpse of a faux Moondog rising up in his robes on the streets of Manhattan, and Pete Seeger and Albert Grossman look-alikes wrestling for control of the amplification system during the Dylan-goes-electric contretemps at the 1965 Newport Folk Festival.

The best of the Dylans are Cate Blanchett and Marcus Carl Franklin. Franklin plays the larval Dylan, fresh out of Minnesota, fired up by the songs of Woody Guthrie and spouting playful lies about his train-hopping hobo adventures. Having this Dylan played by an eleven-year-old black kid is an audacious idea, and Franklin embraces it with infectious enthusiasm. He's irresistibly winning; and when he strums up a rendition of "When the Ship Comes In," surrounded by a doting white family in a suburban living room, he's a knockout.

Blanchett brings her extraordinary powers of penetration to the sour, mid-1960s hipster Dylan familiar from D. A. Pennebaker's 1967 tour documentary, *Don't Look Back*. With her skinny suits and wild, plugged-in hair, she gets the character's speed-fueled hostility just right. But there's no point at which you're not aware that this is a woman portraying a man, despite the expertise with which Blanchett attempts it; and since she occupies a central place in the film, the imposture goes on too long and eventually takes on the shape of a stunt, which is basically what it is.

The other Dylans in the picture are nowhere near as interesting—although Ben Wisham brings a droll snap to his brief appearances as a sort of Rimbaud-Bob. Both Heath Ledger, as the love-man Bob, fretting his way through a collapsing marriage, and Christian Bale, as Bob the Protester (and later the born-again evangelizer), are too physically substantial and movie-star handsome: their un-Bobness is distracting. Dullest of all is the extended allusion at the end of the picture to Sam Peckinpah's *Pat Garrett & Billy the Kid*, the 1973 movie in which Dylan made his first appearance as an actor (and to the soundtrack of which he contributed the transcendent "Knockin' on Heaven's Door"). Here the Dylan role is taken on by Richard Gere, of all people, and the rambling story line shuffles past the point of tedium into a complete shambles. (It's also unfortunate that Julianne Moore was cast as the Joan Baez figure in the film—is there anyone less like that bracingly tart woman?)

Because Haynes and his famed cinematographer, Edward Lachman, are so committed to the movie's odd concept, the picture has some value as a well-crafted curio. For most of its length, though, it's merely curious—a different and too-often tiresome thing. (November 2007)

Caché

Puzzling Evidence

This is one of those prickly European art movies that makes you wonder what you've done wrong to deserve it. The Austrian director, Michael Haneke, has a towering disdain for bourgeois intellectuals—the upwardly mobile urban liberals he appears to despise for their smugness, their consumerism, and their unacknowledged racism. But bourgeois intellectuals are the only imaginable audience for a movie like this—you can almost hear them savoring its insights over cocktails at some save-the-wombats fund-raiser.

The movie begins as a mystery thriller, but don't get too excited. It opens with a static shot of a Parisian street—a shot that sits on the screen for so long, you begin to wonder if it's some new kind of postcard with built-in bird chirps. Then it starts to rewind, and you realize that it's actually video footage. The video has been sent to a man named Georges (Daniel Auteuil), the host of a TV book-chat show, and the unwavering shot is of the town house he shares with his wife, Anne (Juliette Binoche), who works in publishing, and their son, Pierrot (Lester Makedonsky). The cassette has arrived accompanied by a crude drawing of a bird with its throat cut. What can this mean? Who's behind it? Anyone hoping for straightforward answers to these questions might want to duck out at this point.

As increasingly unsettling videos arrive at Georges's house, he begins to suspect that they're being sent by Majid (Maurice Benichou), an Algerian immigrant whom Georges knew and mistreated years earlier, when they were both children. He tracks Majid down to an apartment building that's practically as slumped and sorrowful as the man himself turns out to be. Majid says he knows nothing about the videos Georges has been receiving. Georges doesn't believe him and storms out. After he's left, the camera holds on Majid sitting wordlessly at a table. It holds and holds for so long, we begin to wonder if this, too, is surreptitious video footage. Or is it real? What is "real," anyway? And so forth.

There are two really shocking sequences in the movie. One will surely upset the PETA contingent within Haneke's audience. The other—a sudden death—is skillfully horrific. The movie is thick with musings about observation and buried information (the final shot, another long, static take, is like a pop quiz on the meaning of the movie). But the hidden subject of *Caché* (the word is French for "hidden") appears to be France's long and brutal occupation of Algeria and the continuing inhumanity with which the French have treated the Algerians they subsequently allowed into their country to serve as cheap labor. You really should bone up on that history before seeing this movie. Alternatively, you could skip that, and skip this, too. (January 2006)

Twenty Great Lines

As Gore Vidal (who worked in movies) has always been at pains to contend, no matter how important directors and actors may be—or think they may be—they would have little to do without a script. Writers almost always feel themselves undervalued in the film business, despite the fact of their indispensability.

"I killed the president of Paraguay with a fork. How have you been?"

Grosse Pointe Blank (1997), script by Tom Jankiewicz and
D. V. DeVincentis, Steve Pink, and John Cusack

"The only true currency in this bankrupt world is what you share with someone else when you're uncool."

Almost Famous (2000), script by Cameron Crowe

"Listen, strange women lyin' in ponds distributin' swords is no basis for a system of government."

Monty Python and the Holy Grail (1975), script by
Graham Chapman, John Cleese, Eric Idle,
Terry Gilliam, Terry Jones, and Michael Palin

"Love don't make things nice. It ruins everything. It breaks your heart. It makes things a mess. We aren't here to make things perfect. The snowflake is perfect. The stars are perfect. Not us. We are here to ruin ourselves and to break our hearts and love the wrong people and die."

Moonstruck (1987), script by John Patrick Shanley

"It's a Zen thing, like how many babies fit in a tire."

Waiting for Guffman (1996), script by
Christopher Guest and Eugene Levy

★★★★★★★★★★★★★★★★★★★★★★★★★★★★★★★

★★★★★★★★★★★★★★★★★★★★★★★★★★★

"We'll begin with a reign of terror, a few murders here and there. Murders of great men, murders of little men. Just to show we make no distinction."

The Invisible Man (1933), script by
R. C. Sherriff, from the H. G. Wells novel

"Aristotle was not Belgian. The central message of Buddhism is not 'every man for himself.' And the London Underground is not a political movement. Those are all mistakes, Otto. I looked 'em up."

A Fish Called Wanda (1988), script by John Cleese

"You know, I don't think I've got it in me to shoot my flatmate, my mum, and my girlfriend all in the same night."

Shaun of the Dead (2004), script by
Simon Pegg and Edgar Wright

Summer: "We've been like Sid and Nancy for months now."
Tom: "Summer, Sid stabbed Nancy seven times with a kitchen knife. I mean, we have some disagreements, but I hardly think I'm Sid Vicious."
Summer: "No, I'm Sid."

(500) Days of Summer (2009), script by
Scott Neustadter and Michael H. Weber

"I'm not questioning your powers of observation. I'm merely remarking upon the paradox of asking a masked man who he is."

V for Vendetta (2006), script by the Wachowski Brothers,
from the graphic novel by Alan Moore

★★★★★★★★★★★★★★★★★★★★★★★★★★★

★★★★★★★★★★★★★★★★★★★★★★★★★★★★★★★★

"Clark Kent is how Superman views us. And what are the characteristics of Clark Kent? He's weak. He's unsure of himself. He's a coward. Clark Kent is Superman's critique on the whole human race."

Kill Bill: Vol. 2 (2004), script by Quentin Tarantino

"Do you think you might agree not to marry me? And do you think not being married to me might be something you could consider doing for the rest of your life?"

Four Weddings and a Funeral (1994), script by Richard Curtis

"I have come here to chew bubblegum and kick ass. And I'm all out of bubblegum."

They Live (1988), script by
Frank Armitage, from a short story by Ray Nelson

"If you want me to keep my mouth shut, it's gonna cost you some dough. I figure a thousand bucks is reasonable, so I want two."

Miller's Crossing (1990), script by Joel Coen and Ethan Coen

"This is the captain. We have a little problem with our entry sequence, so we may experience some slight turbulence . . . and then explode."

Serenity (2005), script by Joss Whedon

"I'll meet you at the place near the thing where we went that time."

Broadcast News (1987), script by James L. Brooks

"You are far weirder than someone merely into S & M. At least they have a tradition. We have some idea what

★★★★★★★★★★★★★★★★★★★★★★★★★★★★★★★★

★★★★★★★★★★★★★★★★★★★★★★★★★★★★★★★★★

S & M is about. There's movies and books about it. But so far as I know, there is nothing to explain the way you are."

Barcelona (1994), script by Whit Stillman

"Did you have a brain tumor for breakfast?"

Heathers (1988), script by Michael Lehmann

"You're not the Antichrist. You're only a malcontent who knows how to spell."

Quills (2000), script by Doug Wright

"All you of Earth are idiots."

Plan 9 from Outer Space (1958), script by Edward D. Wood Jr.

★★★★★★★★★★★★★★★★★★★★★★★★★★★★★★★★★

DECLARATIONS OF INDEPENDENCE

J ust because it's an indie is no guarantee of a film's quality, of course. Very often you may find yourself spending two hours with a clan of twentysomethings moping around bemoaning the burdens of being twentysomething. But independent film is still the place where you're likely to find the freshest approaches to filmmaking. The occasional encounter with chronicles of whiney youth is a bearable price to pay.

(500) Days of Summer

Crazy Love

(500) Days of Summer is a breezy first feature by former music-video director Marc Webb, and it's nothing like what you'd dread: it's light and airy and filled with surprises. The picture was written by two hot up-and-comers, Scott Neustadter and Michael H. Weber, who clearly know more about life than what's taught in screenwriting courses. And while what they've created is a love story, it's a love story of an unusual sort. As a voice-over tells us at the beginning of the film, "This is not a love story."

The picture could be pigeonholed as a romantic comedy, but it's not about finding the right person—it's about finding the wrong one. It's also about the pitfalls of infatuation: how it misguides us, while at the same time driving away the object of our desire, who, inexplicably, doesn't share our heart-bursting love jones.

The two leads, Zooey Deschanel and Joseph Gordon-Levitt, long-time friends in real life, are an ideal match—they have the perfect chemistry for a tale in which the chemistry between their characters has to be a little off. He plays Tom, an architecture student who, following school, drifted into a job as a crafter of platitudes at a Los Angeles greeting-card company and has never moved on. She's Summer, the new girl in the office. The other guys in the shop all take their shot at her (and reassure themselves when she doesn't respond that she must be a lesbian or something). Then one day when Tom's in an elevator, listening to some music on his iPod, Summer steps in. She hears the tuneful buzz leaking out from his headphones, taps him on the arm, and says, "I love the Smiths." Then she gets off. Ka-boom—Tom has suddenly found his dream girl. Or, as he soon puts it, "I know she's the only person in the entire universe who can make me happy." Uh-oh.

The writers keep the story hopping by telling Tom and Summer's story out of sequence, as a sort of Cubist narrative. The movie begins at Day 290, and then skips around to Day 4, Day 321, and so forth. At the outset, Summer acknowledges Tom's interest but is up-front about where she's coming from. She thinks love is a fantasy, a delusion. "I'm not really looking for anything serious," she says. "Is that okay?" Their relationship doesn't blossom, exactly, but it evolves. There's a kiss in the copy room, a tipsy karaoke night, a hand-holding romp through an Ikea showroom (very funny), and—finally—sex. In fact, *shower* sex. As far as Tom's concerned, this is the real deal—he and Summer are a couple. She declines to put a name to whatever it is they're doing, though. "Who cares?" she says. "I'm happy. Aren't you happy?"

Of course not. He's miserable. The girl of his dreams remains, maddeningly, just out of reach. He can't *possess* her. A buddy tries to help, talking about his own longtime girlfriend: She's "better than the girl of my dreams," he says. "She's real." Tom's not listening.

Zooey Deschanel's searchlight eyes have never been bigger and bluer than they are here, and we understand why Tom would be instantly smitten. But she's a subtle comic actress, and her performance as Summer—maneuvering around Tom's romantic effusions without coming right out and hurting his feelings—is a careful balancing act. And Gordon-Levitt—a born leading man—deploys his trademark tousled charm very shrewdly: His Tom isn't stupid, he's just blind. Who hasn't been here?

We keep hoping things will go right for these two—aren't they perfect for each other? But slowly we begin to suspect that they might not. Any shameless rom-com director would slap a happy ending on this picture and ship it off to chickville. Webb and his writers have more interesting things in mind. We keep hoping, though—couldn't there be *some* sort of romantic salvation at the end? Well, maybe. Sort of. (July 2009)

D.E.B.S.

Where the Boys Aren't

D.E.B.S. is surely the best—okay, the only—teenage lesbian superspy movie to date. It's sweet and surprising, and funny in a cheerfully offhand way. You root for it to work, and it does, pretty much. In a year that's been littered with expensively undistinguished big-time product, this film is a happy reminder of what can be done by clever people with a small budget and a lot of enthusiasm.

The premise is cute, but don't be afraid. Hidden inside the annual SAT test, it seems, is a secret, government-funded subtest that identifies girls who have special talents for lying, cheating, fighting, and killing. High scorers are taken to the secret paramilitary D.E.B.S. academy, where they're trained in the arts of espionage and the wearing of short plaid skirts. (D.E.B.S. stands for "Discipline, Energy, Beauty, Strength"—anything for a zippy acronym.)

At the end of four years of training, blond, brainy Amy Bradshaw (Sara Foster) is questioning her commitment to the program, and to her lunkhead fellow-spy boyfriend, Bobby, with whom she has recently broken up. ("He was just so boring.") Amy tries to keep her D.E.B.S. doubts from the other members of her squad: tough-girl Max (Meagan Good), ditzy little Janet (Jill Ritchie), and chain-smoking French sexpot Dominique (Devon Aoki). But Amy's personal issues are sidelined when it's learned that the world's most dangerous supervillain, Lucy Diamond (Jordana Brewster), who went underground after masterminding a failed plot to sink Australia a few years earlier, is back on the scene. The D.E.B.S. are dispatched to bring her in.

Lucy, a sleek brunette with a seductive smile (under a lot of lip gloss), is having problems of her own. It's been two years since she was dumped by her last girlfriend, and she's lonely. Her concerned henchman, Scud (Jimmi Simpson), is trying to fix her up with a beautiful Russian assassin, but Lucy's nervous. "Why is it I can hold the whole world hostage," she asks him, "and I'm scared of going on one stupid blind date?" "Because," Scud replies, with a wonderfully straight face, "love is harder than crime."

Unbeknown to Lucy, her dinner date with the brassy blond assassin takes place under the eyes of the D.E.B.S., who are stationed—preposterously, of course—on swings hanging high above Lucy's table. (Squinting down at the decked-out villainess, Janet says, "I have that sweater she's wearing, in taupe.")

The date goes badly. In fact, it ends in gunfire. But in the course of the ensuing confusion, Lucy comes face to face with Amy—and it's love at first sight. For Lucy, at least. Amy has never considered the possibilities of gay romance. She is, however, writing a thesis on the notorious Lucy for a course called Capes and Capers: Gender Reconstruction and the Criminal Mastermind, so she's not entirely uninformed on the subject. Lucy spirits Amy and Janet (who has drawn the interest of the lovable Scud) to a faraway bad-guys bar, where they bond over beers and Lucy and Amy nearly kiss—to Janet's horror. ("You're so busted!" she squeaks.)

Amy eventually realizes she really is drawn to Lucy, to the amazement of her fellow D.E.B.S. ("You're not as boreeng as I thought," says the deadpan Dominique, in her dense French accent.) Will the star crime fighter and the internationally infamous evildoer ever get together? What about Janet and Scud? And what will Amy do about the doltish Bobby, who's still sniffing around? ("Listen," he says, "I been thinkin'. That lezzie thing? Kinda hot.")

Is this a dumb movie? Hey—was *Charlie's Angels* a dumb movie? *D.E.B.S.* is of course a takeoff on that film (there's even a Charlie figure, played by Michael Clarke Duncan), but it has none of the preening air of big stars slumming with junky material. It has appealing actors, some good lines, and a nice little soundtrack, too (Goldfrapp, the Cure, the Only Ones). It's good-natured and romantic, and, best of all, maybe, there's nothing winkingly "hip" about it. Which is pretty hip. (March 2005)

Savage Grace

Family Romance

The real-life Baekeland family had it all: money, murder, incest—a nightmare domestic trifecta. Barbara Baekeland was a beautiful one-time model and sort-of actress. She had married up from her modest Boston origins, securing a union with the brilliant and handsome Brooks Baekeland, heir to an enormous plastics fortune. Their son, Tony, was similarly brilliant, but troubled (in fact, schizophrenic, as it turned out). Rejected by his emotionally remote father, Tony bonded inseparably with his boozy, social-climbing mother, who took pictures of him naked in the bathtub and encouraged him to read passages from the Marquis de Sade to startled party guests.

Unburdened by any need to work, the Baekelands were dedicated expatriates, traipsing endlessly from London to Paris to various luxury accommodations in Italy, Spain, and Switzerland, dragging their son along. Eventually, it became clear that Tony was gay, a fact that disgusted his father. Barbara attempted to reorient her son, bringing in young women to go to bed with him. When these efforts failed, she had sex with Tony herself. One afternoon in November of 1972, at their home of the moment in London, Tony stabbed Barbara through the heart with a kitchen knife. When police arrived, he was on the phone ordering Chinese takeout.

This horrific narrative was recounted in great detail in 1985, in a nearly five hundred-page oral history called *Savage Grace: The True Story of a Doomed Family*, by Natalie Robins and Steven M. L. Aronson. In adapting that book into a ninety-seven-minute movie, director Tom Kalin has discarded all but the most telling moments. We see Barbara (Julianne Moore) and Brooks (Stephen Dillane) in New York in 1946, dressing for dinner at the Stork Club. Barbara is drinking and chattering and clearly getting on her icy husband's nerves, as is their squalling infant son. We see them in the Spanish resort of Cadaques in 1967, where the now-teenaged Tony (Eddie Redmayne) is having a tentative heterosexual encounter with a girl named Blanca (Elena Anaya). When he brings Blanca home to meet his parents ("like a kitten that has killed his first mouse and laid it at your feet," Barbara says), his father immediately takes an interest in the girl and soon runs off with her. Later, when Tony finds his mother in bed with a bisexual companion named Sam (Hugh Dancy), he climbs under the covers with them. In Paris the following year, Barbara—her loveless marriage now over—slashes her wrists in despair, and a short while afterward, in one of the film's eeriest images, we see Tony tenderly smoothing ointment over her stitches.

The movie ends in London, of course, where Barbara seduces her son for the first time, on a living room sofa. The scene is shot with an unblinking objectivity that's chilling. Before long, during a pointless argument over a long-dead pet dog, we see the murder, which is depicted in a virtuoso sequence of smothered emotional release.

Julianne Moore dives into her role with fearless abandon, unleashing gales of foul-mouthed rage and erotic calculation in her portrayal of a woman who's both smart and pathetic. And Eddie Redmayne, with his fleshy lips and carefully flat delivery, is a perfect foil—Barbara's helpless partner in a fatal family dance. Director Kalin, best known for his only previous feature, the 1992 film *Swoon*, bathes much of the picture in gorgeous Mediterranean light (it was partly shot on the Costa Brava), a ravishing visual strategy for a story of such dark struggle.

In the aftermath of Barbara's 1972 murder, the real Tony Baekeland was sent to Broadmoor, an English hospital prison for the criminally insane. He was released in 1980 and returned to New York to live with his maternal grandmother, whom he soon also attacked and stabbed. (She survived.) He was then imprisoned on Rikers Island, where in March of 1981 he committed suicide by suffocating himself with a plastic bag. In reviewing *Savage Grace*, the book, the late William F. Buckley Jr., who moved in some of the same social circles as the Baekelands, called it, unsurprisingly, "a story of spectacular decadence." He also observed, more incisively, that "seldom has there been so devastating an exposure of the consequences, for the most sophisticated people, of failure in the simplest duties of love." (May 2008)

Before Sunset

Walkie Talkie

*B*efore Sunset, the new Richard Linklater movie, was shot in fifteen days and completed for a fraction of what Columbia is spending just to advertise *Spider-Man 2*. But while the picture consists almost entirely of two people walking around Paris and talking, it's an exhilarating film.

The sole characters, Jesse and Celine, appeared earlier in Linklater's 1995 film, *Before Sunrise*. Played then as now by Ethan Hawke and Julie Delpy, they were strangers on a Eurail train—a wandering young American and a French graduate student—who got off in Vienna and walked around and talked and talked and slowly, over the course of fourteen hours, sort of fell in love. They had to part before sunrise, but each promised to return to Vienna in six months to see where this nascent relationship might take them.

In *Before Sunset*, nine years have passed. Jesse is now a writer living in New York with his wife and four-year-old son. He has written a successful book about that long-ago one-night romance in Vienna, and on a European tour to promote it, he visits a Paris bookstore to autograph copies and be interviewed by a clutch of journalists. Glancing up at one point, he's startled to see Celine standing off to the side. Quickly winding up an interview, he goes over to greet her. He's scheduled to get on a plane back to the States in just a few hours, but there's time to do something, he says. Maybe just go for a walk.

Strolling through the cobbled streets and leaf-strewn byways of the city, they fall back into an easy intimacy. Celine claims not to be really clear about the details of their long-ago night of love; Jesse remembers the brand of condoms they used. "Do I look different?" she asks. "Well," he says, laughing and having fun with her, "I'd have to see you naked."

Celine works for the environmental organization Green Cross. She has relationships with men—she's in one now—but they always seem to fizzle out. She's restless. She's read Jesse's book and found it strange "being part of someone else's memory." She says, "When you're young, you believe there'll be many people you can connect with. You get older, you know it'll only happen a few times."

Jesse tells Celine he loves his son, but that he and his wife aren't happy together and haven't been for a long time. It's a melancholy observation, not a come-on. He simply wishes he and his wife could have the better lives they both deserve, with other people. He says, "Do you think if we never wanted anything, we'd never be unhappy?"

Celine wonders about the six-month reunion that never happened nine years ago. Did Jesse actually return to Vienna for it? No, he says. She's visibly relieved—she wanted to make it, but her grandmother died and it became impossible to keep the date. As it turns out, though, Jesse knows she didn't make it—because he *was* there. He really cared. He still does. But does she? And is there enough time to find out before his flight leaves?

This eighty-minute movie is a marvel of artful compression. The dialogue, which was written by Delpy, Hawke, and Linklater, seems once again so spontaneous that it comes as a surprise to learn that the film was in fact tightly scripted and rigorously rehearsed. (A necessity: Linklater was determined to shoot the picture in very long, uncut takes.) In standard movie terms, nothing really happens—no one gets shot, nothing blows up. But there's a rich sense of life actually unfolding, unmediated, right before our eyes. It's a hypnotic experience.

For a film like *Before Sunset* to open up against *Spider-Man 2* seems like a death-wish move. Without substantial promotion, how large an audience can it possibly draw? And as Linklater himself said during a visit to New York last week, "If you don't have a great opening weekend, you go down in history as a bad movie."

But this is a very good movie, and good movies can always live on:

in repertory theaters, at midnight screenings, on DVD. It's always possible you might see it at some future point, I suppose. But it's for sure you can see it right now. (July 2004)

In Search of a Midnight Kiss

L.A. Story

In Search of a Midnight Kiss is a romantic comedy with a seductive glow, and it's considerably more ambitious than the usual indie festival fodder. The story concerns a gigless screenwriter named Wilson (Scoot McNairy), a transplanted Texan adrift in Los Angeles, who hasn't had a date in six years. Now, with the holidays at hand, he faces the annual prospect of being alone on New Year's Eve. Egged on by his DJ roommate Jacob (Brian McGuire), whose relationship with his own live-in girlfriend Min (Kathleen Luong) is annoyingly blissful, Wilson taps out a call for help on Craigslist: "Misanthrope seeks misanthrope." It draws one weird phone response:

"Are you the misanthrope?" asks the girl on the other end of the line.

"Yes. Are you the misanthropee?"

"I dunno. I had to look it up."

Such is the movie's verbal tilt, a procession of testy jousts that's consistently funny even if it tells us a little less about the characters than it does about the word-crafting facility of director Alex Holdridge, who wrote the script.

The girl on the phone turns out to be Vivian (Sara Simmonds), a moonfaced blonde in cool boots and big black shades who's oddly over-revved and seriously lacking in interpersonal skills. She's auditioning potential male companions to fend off a lonely New Year's Eve herself, and she allots Wilson the number four slot on her list of possibilities. They meet at a café and find themselves instantly incompatible. Nevertheless, Vivian gives Wilson until 6:00 p.m. that evening to win her over. They spend most of the rest of the movie walking around Los Angeles while the desperate slacker presses his case.

The movie unavoidably recalls Richard Linklater's walk-and-talk classics, *Before Sunrise* and *Before Sunset*. Holdridge doesn't bother attempting to replicate Linklater's long, intricately constructed takes; but in the same way that Linklater guided us through the less-traveled paths around Vienna and Paris, his fellow Austin filmmaker guides us through parts of Los Angeles that are rarely seen on movie screens: out-of-the-way parks, abandoned theaters, glaring subway stations, and grotty downtown lofts. Wilson begins the journey as a reflexive pessimist ("I think L.A. is where love comes to die"); but Vivian, despite her borderline hostility, begins to lighten him up. She's an actress, she says (unemployed, of course), and since he claims to be a screenwriter, why doesn't he write her a juicy part—"Something sexy and edgy. Something where I get to use a knife."

The picture is also indebted to Woody Allen's 1979 *Manhattan*, in which cinematographer Gordon Willis set a standard for black-and-white photography that's rarely been matched since. Here, Holdridge's cinematographer, Robert Murphy, ranges through a carefully graduated grayscale from eye-popping whites to deep rich blacks; and his inventive framing enlarges the story in interesting ways—tilting up the sides of sun-drenched buildings, he shows us the city the way Wilson and Vivian are beginning to see it, as if discovering it for the first time.

Holdridge is less addicted to trite sex gags than many other indie directors, but he has his moments, and while they're sometimes funny, they disrupt the tone of the movie. And his take on love—which basically boils down to "What the hell is it, anyway?"—leads to a conclusion so airily ambiguous it almost floats away into film-school pretension. Still, *Midnight Kiss* is a tidy accomplishment, not just for Holdridge and Murphy, but for the adroit McNairy, whose shambling charm carries the movie at just the right level of warm confusion, and for the subtly skilful Simmonds, who's a complete sweetheart. (Her moving explication of something called the Lost Shoe Project, accompanied by a haunting visual montage, is one of the movie's loveliest sequences.) On top of all this, Holdridge, in a transport of inspiration, wraps up the picture with a *Scorpions* song—and it *works.* How indie is that? (August 2008)

2 Days in Paris

French Disconnection

Among the many amusing things about *2 Days in Paris* is that Julie Delpy—the enormously simpatico French actress who wrote, directed, edited, and scored it and who stars in it with Adam Goldberg—raised the money to make it by telling prospective backers that what she had in mind was a film along the lines of *Before Sunset*, the 2004 Richard Linklater picture in which she starred with Ethan Hawke. This was a shrewd pitch. *Before Sunset* (the sequel to Linklater's 1995 *Before Sunrise*, in which Delpy and Hawke also starred) was a *succès d'estime* with a unique romantic bloom. It was also cheap to make—the movie consisted of two people walking and talking their way around Paris. And the talk was marvelously alive; it felt as if the actors were making it up as they went along. By suggesting that the *Before Sunset* magic could be conjured again, even without the participation of Linklater and Hawke (with whom she had cowritten the Oscar-nominated script), Delpy got her funding (less than $200,000). Then she went out and made this exceptionally funny relationship movie.

The plot is simple. Marion (Delpy), a French photographer, and her boyfriend, Jack (Goldberg), an American interior designer, have just finished a two-week vacation in Venice and are en route back to their home in New York. Before flying out, though, they'll be spending two days in her hometown of Paris. They've been together for two years, and they feel committed to one another, but they're still very different people. Jack is a wisecracking urban neurotic, a hypochondriac who fears food poisoning in foreign parts and always feels a migraine coming on. He's also grindingly self-centered: Waiting in line for a taxi, he tells a group of lost American tourists in line ahead of him that the Louvre is actually too nearby to justify cab fare and directs them down the street and around a corner. Actually he has no idea where the Louvre is, but he gets the next taxi, which is all that matters.

Marion, on the other hand, is sweet and generally serene, an angel of accommodation. Or so she seems to Jack, and to us at first. But now that they're together on her native turf, he begins to see her in a new and disturbing light. Everywhere they go, whether to a party with her old friends or just walking down the street, they seem to encounter one or another of Marion's ex-lovers. There appear to have been many. One of these former swains, in the worldly European manner, shares a sexual anecdote about her with Jack; another one appears in a photo he finds in one of her old books—a party picture of a naked guy with a balloon attached to what is usually a balloon-free appendage. Jack grows paranoid. Since he only speaks about ten words of French, all of them badly, he's frozen out of the verbal interaction on which he thrives and begins to think that everyone is laughing at him. He's not entirely wrong.

Jack makes a halfhearted attempt to enjoy Paris, though, dragging Marion off to the Père Lachaise cemetery to see the grave of Jim Morrison. (He has no interest in the Doors, he admits—he's just "a huge Val Kilmer fan.") But then, when they're in a restaurant, Marion spots another of her exes, a cad who once coldly dumped her. As Jack watches in complete bafflement, she begins to berate the man, and soon her goading escalates into a near-fistfight, which gets them bounced from the premises. Jack is appalled—who *is* this woman he thought he knew so well?

The movie is an eloquent demonstration of the chaos of relationships both romantic and familial, and of the troublesome interpenetration of our past and present lives. It is also hilarious virtually from start to finish. Unlike *Before Sunset*, in which the liberated flow of the language couldn't really conceal the elegance of its artifice, the dialogue here has the messy splutters and miscues of real interaction, real life. Delpy, who plays her age (thirty-five at the time of filming) with rumpled élan, is a master of impromptu lines and stuttery emotion; and Goldberg (her actual ex-boyfriend) has possibly never been as caustically funny as he is here—with his snarly smile and air of permanent exasperation, he's an uproarious study in transatlantic cultural panic.

Can Jack and Marion's relationship be saved? Can anybody's? Are romantic liaisons not all basically the same, "with ups and downs," as Marion says, "and in-betweens, mostly"? (August 2007)

(Untitled)

Sound and Vision

Adrian Jacobs (Adam Goldberg) is a prickly young composer on the New York experimental-music scene. His compositions, which he performs with a trio in sparsely populated theaters, are a clamor of kicked buckets, crackling bubble wrap, and sudden ensemble shrieks. "I just hate all his work," a critic says, behind his back. But Adrian is intransigent. "Harmony," he says, "was a capitalist plot to sell pianos."

Unlike Adrian, who's forced to take demeaning supper club gigs to pay the rent, his brother Josh (Eion Bailey), a painter, is flush with success—his canvases fetch $10,000 each. True, they're insipidly sunny abstracts that are bought by the yard for indifferent display in hospital lobbies and corporate boardrooms. Still, their endless salability has made Josh one happy artist—or has it?

Josh's paintings are the gold mine that keeps Madeleine Gray (Marley Shelton) and her Chelsea art gallery going. Her commissions on his work allow her to promote the edgier artists she really loves—like the coarse Ray Barko (Vinnie Jones), who expresses himself with stapled cats and whole stuffed cows. But Ray is getting restless. He's being courted by a rival gallery with promises of higher sale prices. Worse yet, Josh, too, is growing restive. He wants his canvases to be acknowledged as real art, not just commercial decor, and he's pressuring Madeleine to mount an exhibit devoted solely to his work—or else he'll move on as well.

The artsy avant-garde is always ripe for satirical targeting, and director Jonathan Parker's new movie, *(Untitled)*, has a lot of fun with it. What makes the picture more interesting than it might have been if it were just a ritual trashing of familiar stereotypes is its commitment to the idea that the significance of a work of art can only really be judged by posterity. In the here and now, most artists of a radical creative bent—whatever their merits may ultimately prove to be—must often weather public incomprehension and financial injustice. Adrian's music may sound like nothing more than noise, but he feels its structure in his head, and he's baffled that no one responds to it.

The movie derives a lot of energy from its skillful cast. Goldberg, with his serious beard and helmet of dark hair (he peers up from under it like some querulous sea creature), perfectly embodies downtown disgruntlement. And the photogenic Shelton gets completely inside the ambitious ice queen Madeleine—this woman may not have a real-world heart, but her love of new art is genuine. Lucy Punch has a sweet, fuddled charm as the reed player in Adrian's concert group. Zak Orth is amusing throughout as a wealthy, taste-free collector who's never heard of Matisse but knows that trendy new work can be a solid investment. ("Art does not look as good when it goes down in value," he says.) And Ptolemy Slocum brings a wonderful stuttery presence to the role of Monroe, a new conceptual artist who's even more out-there than Ray, and may soon displace him. ("I think I want what I want to say to go without saying," he says.)

(Untitled) is a very funny film, especially in episodes like the make-out scene in which Adrian attempts to extricate Madeleine from her au courant clothing and is nearly defeated by its welter of fashionable clamps and buckles. But the movie also has moments of delicate feeling. There's a vibrant scene in which Adrian, after an illuminating talk with an acclaimed older composer, goes home to try something new: putting aside his usual commitment to listener confrontation (but retaining his avoidance of anything so corny as a tone center), he sits at a piano constructing a new piece that's seductively harmonic without compromis-

ing his bristling artistic integrity. The music carries him away, and us along with it. (October 2009)

Hard Candy

Wrong Girl

Jeff Kohlver (Patrick Wilson) is a thirty-two-year-old California fashion photographer whose carnal interest in the teenage girls he shoots begins to fade around the time they turn fifteen. As *Hard Candy* opens, we find him cruising an online chat room in his nightly search for younger stuff. In fact, he's in the process of reeling one in. She's fourteen years old—just right—and we see their conversation scrolling up on his computer screen. "Whatcha doing now?" he asks. Her response couldn't be more perfect: "Besides fantasizing over you?" After a bit more flirting, the girl agrees to meet him at a local diner; her big sister can drop her off.

The girl's name is Hayley (Ellen Page), and at the diner Jeff spots her immediately. She's a pretty, brown-eyed, freckly kid, her dark hair cut tomboy-short. She's sitting at the counter eating a piece of chocolate cake and reading a book about the sad, screwed-up life of the late actress Jean Seberg. As an intriguing conversational gambit, Hayley tells Jeff that Seberg "slept with all the wrong people. I'm only gonna sleep with the right people." Jeff insinuatingly dabs a smear of chocolate off her lip with his finger, then tells her he has a recent concert by Goldfrapp—a group he just loves—recorded on MP3. It's back at his house. Hayley, apparently a Goldfrapp enthusiast also, agrees to go home with him to hear it.

Jeff's place is sleekly modern. Hayley marvels at the blown-up photos of young women on his walls. Jeff pulls a vodka bottle out of the fridge and makes them each a screwdriver. He shows Hayley his little photo studio. Knocking back her drink, she tells him, "Why don't you get out one of your cameras and see what you can get out of me." Then she goes to the kitchen to pour a pair of refills. Circling around her, sipping his drink, Jeff suddenly feels woozy, then worse; then he collapses to the floor. When he wakes up, he's tightly bound to a chair. Disoriented, he figures this must be some kind of kid joke. He asks Hayley, standing nearby and seeming somehow different now, "Why did I get tied up first, if this is the game we're gonna play?" She's not smiling anymore. "Jeff," she says, "playtime is over. It's time to wake up."

Hard Candy has a luscious conceit: in the same way that Jeff is a pedophile who preys on little girls, Hayley is a little girl who preys on pedophiles. She's fixated on the recent disappearance of one little girl in particular, and she seems certain that Jeff knows something about it— maybe all about it. She's already told him that her father is a doctor, and when she pulls out a scalpel and some green surgical scrubs from her bag, we can see that she's serious about extracting the truth from him.

The movie has a peculiar intensity—it's boldly unpleasant, but it's also fascinating, and funny, too. Mocking Jeff's faux musical hipness and his cheesy MP3 ploy to get her back to his house, Hayley tells him, "You used the same phrases about Goldfrapp as they do on Amazon .com. Plus," she says, "I fucking hate Goldfrapp." Jeff and Hayley are both a little out of focus. Jeff may be a predator, but the chummy come-on he uses to seduce his young marks really is appealing. (And Patrick Wilson, who plays him, bears a strikingly out-of-place resemblance to the amiable Kevin Costner.) Hayley, for her part, shows no evidence of being a victim herself, a girl bent on personal revenge. Her cool calculation in stalking and bagging Jeff suggests something more cold-blooded behind her sweet angel face. She's a little frightening herself.

First-time feature director David Slade (best known for the videos he's made with such bands as System of a Down and Stone Temple Pilots) captures the actors' emotional nuances in probing close-ups, and he maintains firm control of the film's formal elements, especially its color design. (The chilled-out decor in Jeff's house has sparse dabs of richly saturated color—arterial red and a bright, peachy orange—and as the camera glides around the premises, these hues loom forth to fill the screen.) Slade also manages the considerable task of generating enough suspense to hold our interest in a movie that essentially consists of two people talking (although often in the midst of the most alarming actions). In this the director is valuably assisted by playwright and first-time screenwriter Brian Nelson, whose dialogue has a bright, acrid tang. (Gloating about the ruinous embarrassment that would be attendant upon any public disclosure of Jeff's vile erotic activities, Hayley tells him, "You're a headline waiting to happen.")

The movie's flaws are mainly a matter of plausibility. A long middle sequence in which Hayley threatens and then begins to carry out a terrible punishment is too luridly contrived to be believable. And even though Hayley has told Jeff that she's had him under surveillance and knows that his neighbors are all away, it turns out that one of them is very visibly in residence right next door. (She's played by Sandra Oh, of *Sideways*, and she comes knocking at a really inconvenient moment to deliver some Girl Scout cookies Jeff has ordered.)

It's a powerful film, though—it wrings you out. And it's a fine showcase for the Canadian actress Ellen Page. She was a very young-looking seventeen when the movie was shot, but her emotional command—morphing in an instant from fresh, coltish charm to icy-eyed menace—is extraordinary. We have no idea where Hayley is going at the end of the movie, but we suspect that Page is on her way to some large sort of stardom. (April 2006)

Interview

Shock Therapy

*I*nterview is a movie in which nobody gets shot, chased, or bashed in the face and nothing blows up; and yet it's exciting to watch. The story is a shadow play of predatory deception. The characters aren't very nice, and they evolve in unexpected ways. The dialogue cuts like a razor, and the two lead performances, by Steve Buscemi and Sienna Miller, have an intense emotional focus.

This is the fourth feature directed by Buscemi (who also cowrote the script), and it's composed of elements so intricately interlinked that to give away too many of them would be a disservice to prospective viewers. Basically, it's a New York media story about celebrity, disenchantment, and simple human cruelty. Buscemi plays a sour, middle-aged magazine writer named Pierre, a onetime war correspondent now reduced to conducting fluff interviews with famous faces. His latest assignment is a blond starlet named Katya (Miller), a young woman known less for her work (a teary TV series and the occasional slasher movie) than for her sex life and variable breast size.

She's an hour late for their interview in a trendy restaurant, and their encounter goes downhill from the moment she arrives. Pierre is openly contemptuous of Katya and all that he thinks she represents. He has never watched her TV show or seen any of her movies (even though he's been given a DVD of one of them and has it in his bag). She has a thick skin about this sort of media hostility; she's gotten used to it. But Pierre is insufferable, and before the interview even gets started, Katya decides it's over. She calls for the check. When it comes he reaches for it. "I have an expense account," he says. She snatches it away. "I have a bank account," she says.

Something unexpected happens and they wind up back at her huge loft. They start drinking and they don't stop. Pierre is openly scornful. "You're a rich, spoiled brat who can turn on the charm," he tells Katya, "but that's not the same as having talent." Then, when she drifts away to take a phone call, he opens the laptop on her kitchen table and clicks into a diary she keeps on it. He's shaken by what he reads. When she returns, he tries to apologize for his animosity. She seems to melt a bit, but soon they're going at each other again. The ebb and surge of their verbal parrying has an impacted rhythm: she wants him gone but doesn't actually throw him out; he wants to leave but never quite makes it to the door.

Their probing into one another's lives becomes obsessive. Katya suggests they tell each other their darkest, most shameful secrets. She tells hers, and it's shattering. He tells one of his, and it's a shock; then he tells another, the big one, and it's ghastly. At this point, we realize that our initial assessment of these two people was completely off-track. But then, before long, we realize that our second assessment was equally wrong. The end of the film is a body slam that comes out of nowhere.

Interview is an English-language adaptation of a 2003 movie by the late Dutch filmmaker and controversialist Theo van Gogh. In 2004, van Gogh collaborated with the Somalian writer Ayaan Hirsi Ali on a provocative film about the subjugation of women in fundamentalist Islamic societies. In November of that year, the director was shot dead and mutilated on an Amsterdam street by an Islamist assassin. At the time, van Gogh had been planning to remake three of his earlier movies in English, relocating their locales to New York, a city he loved. After his death, his producer, Gijs van de Westelaken, joined with American producer Bruce Weiss to complete this project posthumously, under the rubric *Triple Theo*. Of the New York actor-directors to whom they offered the films, Buscemi was the first to sign on. (The other two movies will be made by Stanley Tucci and John Turturro.)

I think we can assume that the pugnacious tone of *Interview* derives from van Gogh's original picture; and that at least a skeletal amount survives of the original Dutch script, by Theodor Holman. But Buscemi and his cowriter, David Schechter, have refurbished the story with sizzling idiomatic English. And because the picture essentially consists of two people in a room talking and was shot in van Gogh's gritty low-budget style (with three digital cameras, over the course of nine nights), it draws you in like a well-mounted stage play.

Steve Buscemi is one of the most amiable of actors. Who hasn't relished his underplayed performances in films like *Ghost World* and *The Island* and the recent *Paris, Je T'Aime*? Here, though, he creates a character from which all warmth has been purged, and his self-loathing malice and inexhaustible dishonesty are hypnotic.

The movie's most gripping revelation, however, for anyone who hasn't been following her career, might be Sienna Miller. Here's an actress who's been delivering uniquely shaped performances over the last three years in pictures that not a lot of people have gone to see: the bubbly *Casanova*, the unloved *Alfie* remake, and most recently the underrated 1960s biopic *Factory Girl*. In none of these films has she coasted on the beautiful reality of being Sienna Miller. She always seeks out new character shadings and camera strategies, and she always delivers. Her performance in *Interview*—a combustible mixture of dubious vulnerability and icy calculation—seems unlikely to be bettered by any actress who ends up competing for an Academy Award this year. Couldn't she be one of them? (July 2007)

World's Greatest Dad

Choked Up

World's Greatest Dad is that uncommon thing, an original vision. The movie is quite dark, but it's also funny and emotionally probing—an ambitious mix of narrative elements. As in his last film, *Sleeping Dogs Lie*, writer-director Bobcat Goldthwait centers his plot on a shocking incident—a teenager's death by autoerotic asphyxiation. But like *Dogs*, which used a brief bout of trans-species sex to trigger its story, this movie is about subsequent repercussions, not the linchpin act itself.

Among other impressive things, Goldthwait has found a use for the often irritating Robin Williams. Here, Williams plays Lance Clayton, a lifelong aspiring writer who has never managed to get published. He's a timid high school poetry teacher whose classes are most notable for their many empty seats. He's also carrying on a love affair—or at least a sex affair—with a pretty young art instructor named Claire (Alexie Gilmore), although the middle-aged Lance has no more idea what she sees in him than we do.

Lance is a single dad who lives with his teenage son Kyle (Daryl Sabara)—one of the foulest kid characters in movie history. Kyle is mean, hostile, and abusive to everyone around him, not least his father. He hates music (thinks it's "gay"), hates movies—hates everything, in fact, but the nastiest sorts of Internet porn, which he watches incessantly, hunched forward with a strap tied tautly around his neck. Catching him at this one night, Lance meekly attempts to have a fatherly discussion about it, but Kyle just snarls at him.

When Kyle finally takes his porn obsession too far and chokes to death, Lance is left with an embarrassing scene on his hands. So he tidies things up to make it look as if Kyle hanged himself. He even writes a suicide note for his son—a long, melancholy message to all those the apparently misunderstood Kyle has left behind. Soon the suicide note shows up on the Internet, where it's seen by Kyle's schoolmates—all of whom loathed him in life but now realize he had a beautiful, sensitive side, too. Soon they're wearing Kyle buttons; Kyle posters appear. Lance, now inspired, begins churning out further "Kyle" writings. Before long book deals come pouring in, and offers for TV appearances. Lance is at long last launched as a writer.

One scene in particular highlights Williams's technical expertise as an actor. After Lance's book—a supposed collection of Kyle's prose—has been published, he appears on an Oprah-like TV show to promote it. Coached by one of the show's producers to "just go with it" if he feels himself starting to cry on-camera, Lance does indeed begin tearing up under the host's shameless prodding. What's remarkable about the scene is that Lance isn't actually crying—he's having a hysterical giggling fit. The host and the studio audience see only the grief they want to see; but *we* see what's actually happening and how beautifully Williams blurs these two emotional states.

Lance finally secures the literary acclaim he has always wanted, but of course it's secondhand. He also has the renewed affections of Claire, who'd been drifting off toward another, more popular teacher. But Claire's a weird lady, and Lance's only real connection—a new one—is with an old neighbor woman who shares his enthusiasm for marijuana and zombie movies. Where can all of this be going?

Goldthwait keeps the movie's unexpected twists coming all the way to the end—a splendid achievement. It's fitting that *World's Greatest*

Dad was coproduced by another gifted writer-director, *Donnie Darko* auteur Richard Kelly. The movie is a true indie, made, no doubt, for practically nothing (in Seattle). But in a time of endless big-budget studio recycling, it stakes out a fine small place all its own. (August 2009)

Solitary Man

Star Time

Ben Kalmen is a man who had it all: pots of money from his high-end auto franchise, a beautiful wife and daughter, a lavish Manhattan apartment, the works. Then, because he's a complete fool, he started throwing it all away. As *Solitary Man* begins, he seems intent on completing that mission.

Kalmen is an off-putting character, an ethically oblivious sixty-year-old man who slavers after every woman who wanders within range of his come-ons, the younger the better. The triumph of Michael Douglas's performance in this role is that he plays Kalmen as exactly what he is—a creep—and yet keeps us with him, wondering if this downward-bound hustler can possibly come to his senses before he hits bottom—and whether we should care. As was the case with Jeff Bridges in last year's *Crazy Heart*, Douglas reveals himself here as a veteran actor, familiar from dozens of other movies over the last forty years, who's still capable of doing his best work—who can still surprise us.

The picture opens with a flashback: we see Kalmen being told by a doctor that he has a heart problem and should return for further tests. That was six years ago, and Ben never went back—physical infirmity doesn't fit in with his self-image as a big-city business stud. He subsequently pulled a financial scam in which a lot of people got hurt, and his reputation never recovered—one day he was on the cover of *Forbes* magazine, dripping success, the next he was pictured in *The New York*

Times in handcuffs. He spent all of his money on the lawyers who barely kept him out of prison.

Now we find Kalmen living in an apartment he can't afford, hitting up his daughter (Jenna Fischer) for loans, and trying to maintain a breezy façade for the sake of his adoring grandson (Jake Siciliano), whom he begs not to call him Grandpa. He's also dating a well-to-do divorcée named Jordan (Mary-Louise Parker) and struggling to win the approval of her teenage daughter, Allyson (Imogen Poots), which has so far not been forthcoming. Things aren't going well for Ben, but they could be worse. Soon they will be.

Douglas acutely conveys the personality flaws of which Kalmen is so blindly unaware. Ben is the kind of aging hotshot who still wears black ties with black shirts and who butts into other people's conversations in order to talk about himself, and the actor gets this overbearing boor-ishness just right. The supporting cast is pretty much perfect, too. Fischer is especially moving as a woman torn between love for her father and a growing need to banish him from her life; Poots is memorably astringent as a girl who's wised up way beyond her years; and Susan Sarandon makes nicely underplayed appearances as Ben's ex-wife, who's observing his southward spiral from afar. Most surprising, perhaps, is Danny DeVito, who gives a charming performance as Kalmen's only true friend, the owner of a diner near the college Ben attended in his long-gone youth.

Hovering above the picture is our awareness of a certain resemblance between Ben Kalmen and the man who plays him. Like Ben, Michael Douglas is a highly successful businessman (among the many movies he's produced is the 1975 Oscar-winner *One Flew over the Cuckoo's Nest*) with a onetime reputation for hard partying. It seems likely that his well-known past has informed his portrayal of Kalmen, and there's an element of bravery in his taking on of such an unsympathetic character. Unlike Jeff Bridges (until recently), Douglas already has one Academy Award as an actor (for the 1987 *Wall Street*). It's too early to bother speculating about whether he could win another one for his performance here (not that it matters). But he's in the running. (May 2010)

FOREIGN PARTS

Foreign films don't draw an adventurous moviegoing crowd the way they once did, back in the New Wave days of the 1960s. Maybe there just aren't as many adventurous moviegoers anymore. And of course a reflexive resistance to subtitles always plays a part. So most of the pictures here, I think, deserve a larger audience than they were able to draw during their theatrical runs. One of them, The Reader, isn't actually "foreign" in the usual sense: The director and two of the movie's stars are English. But the film is drawn from a German novel, it's largely cast with German (or Swiss, in the case of Bruno Ganz) actors, it was shot in Germany (and Poland), and its theme is uniquely German. It also has a thematic connection with the other three German films considered toward the end of this section. Not all of the movies included here deal with such somber material, and one of them is an unabashed genre romp. Which is to say that wherever you look in the wide world of filmmaking, it often feels a lot like home.

Elegy

Dark Passage

Ben Kingsley is gazing with admiration at the unhaltered breasts of Penélope Cruz. As are we. "I adore them," he says. We understand.

In *Elegy*, a new movie by the Spanish director Isabel Coixet (*My Life Without Me*), Kingsley plays David Kepesh, a middle-aged New York lit professor and man-about-media who has an unquenchable thirst for the smartest and prettiest of his female students. Cruz is one of these, a beautiful young Cuban American named Consuela Castillo, who has a highly informed taste in art and culture. Having gotten carnal formalities out of the way, Kepesh is falling in love with her, which is not the way these things usually go with him.

Kingsley's boney, goatlike presence contrasts alarmingly with Cruz's luxuriant beauty, but this is as it should be. It's not physical attraction that draws her to him; it's his mind and, despite his cold, priggish self-regard, his emotional possibilities. The two actors are opposites in every way, and they're perfect together.

Kepesh is a transplanted Brit, an Oxford product who came to the States in the 1960s to sample the sexual revolution and stayed to continue sampling it. Apart from his classes, he has a radio book-chat show, makes occasional TV appearances as a celebrity literatus, and sometimes reviews plays for *The New Yorker*. His accomplishments are wearyingly extensive. He plays the piano well and is also a talented photographer, developing his own prints (black-and-white only, of course) in a very professional darkroom in his elegant apartment. He is a rock of self-sufficiency, his only intimate acquaintances a Pulitzer Prize–winning poet named George O'Hearn (Dennis Hopper, in one of his warmest performances) and a successful businesswoman named

Carolyn (Patricia Clarkson), with whom Kepesh has been sleeping on a no-strings basis for twenty years.

Kepesh has a failed marriage buried deep in his past and a now-grown son, Ken (Peter Sarsgaard), who's still bitter about his parents' divorce and his father's abandonment. ("Only one of us could make it over the wall," Dad says, with icy nonchalance.) Kepesh has never had time for Ken or anyone else, and he's alarmed that Consuela is breaching the walls of his carefully organized isolation. When she tells him, at his urging, about a three-way sexual tryst she had at age seventeen, he becomes retrospectively jealous. He's convinced some younger man will steal her away from him: "I know," he says, "because I once *was* that younger man."

Kepesh is wrong about this. Consuela really does love him; she wants a future with him. But for all his womanizing, he has little real interest in the opposite sex ("When you make love to a woman, you get revenge for all the things that defeated you in life"), and his consuming jealousy finally drives her away.

The movie, which is based on a 2001 novella by Philip Roth, is a model of formal control. The images—Kepesh sitting in stony silence in his richly shadowed apartment; Consuela presenting herself to him in the nude, as if to Manet at his easel—are elegantly composed. The carefully scaled color palette by cinematographer Jean-Claude Larrieu infuses the story with atmosphere, while the soundtrack sighs with Bach, Satie, and Chet Baker. At the end, after a long absence, Consuela steals back into her ex-lover's life, this time bearing a terrible secret. The news she brings, on a rainy New Year's Eve, is devastating, and the picture takes a sudden, unforeseen turn. Can anything ever again be the same? For Consuela, definitely not. And possibly not for Kepesh, either. But that, in the movie's moving denouement, is the good news. (August 2008)

Terribly Happy

Town Without Pity

Talk about tough towns. The remote Danish village that Copenhagen cop Robert Hansen finds himself transferred to in *Terribly Happy* is more than just unwelcoming: it's deeply creepy. The marshal who preceded Hansen in this job has mysteriously disappeared, and the rustics who congregate at the local tavern whisper and leer whenever the new arrival walks in—they seem to know more about him than they should. There's also a little girl who walks the empty streets in the dead of night pushing a babyless stroller, and a desolate bog on the outskirts of town where somebody's car is slowly sinking into the muck.

The movie is wonderfully warped. There are overtones of horror and noirish depravity that recall both the 1973 *Wicker Man* and Shirley Jackson's 1948 short story, *The Lottery*. But *Terribly Happy*, which was Denmark's submission in the foreign-language category for this year's Oscars (and is scheduled to be remade in English), has a mind-tickling fascination of its own. Working from an adaptation of an Erling Jepsen novel by screenwriter Dunja Gry Jensen, director Henrik Ruben Genz builds tension in oblique increments. We see that the downcast Hansen (Jakob Cedergren) isn't quite right in the head himself—he screwed up in Copenhagen (exactly how, we don't learn till late in the film), and this reassignment to the faraway village of Skarrild is his only chance to salvage his career. The troubled cop is already taking antianxiety medication—with which the local doctor (Lars Brygmann) is oddly eager to keep him well supplied—and the director presents the flat, featureless landscape as an emblem of his isolation.

The villagers have their own sinister way of doing things. Delinquent children are smacked around rather than turned in for civilized judicial discipline, and their elders encourage Hansen to follow suit.

Troublesome wives are similarly dealt with. When an attractive woman named Ingerlise (Lene Maria Christensen) turns up in Hansen's office to show him the bruises inflicted by her husband, the town bully (Kim Bodnia), the marshal urges her to file a complaint—something she's unwilling to do. Instead, she starts coming on to him, in classic femme-fatale fashion, luring Hansen to what seems very likely to be his doom.

The picture is suffused with a sense of menace, and it's so artfully constructed that it gives you the sweats right up to the end. What's going on in this strange place? What are these people hiding? And who can Hansen trust? He'll be damned if he knows. (February 2010)

Broken Embraces

Love in Vain

Lena, Mateo, and Ernesto are caught up in a vintage film noir triangle. Lena (Penélope Cruz) is a willful beauty with a lurid secret. She lives in luxury with the much older Ernesto (José Luis Gómez), a wealthy Madrid businessman, but is falling under the spell of Mateo (Lluís Homar), a celebrated movie director, who has cast her in his latest picture. Ernesto, ruthlessly possessive, has arranged to become the film's producer and has assigned his unstable son (Rubén Ochandiano) to shoot a video documentary about the making of it—footage that allows Ernesto, back in his mansion during Lena's increasingly frequent absences, to track her deepening relationship with Mateo.

Pedro Almodóvar's *Broken Embraces* is a rapt essay in film noir atmosphere—the classic black-and-white fog of desperation, treachery, and impending disaster—which the director has transmuted into carefully calibrated color. Each scene is a rich mélange of muted hues; but virtually every scene is also daubed—in a shirt, a car, a pair of gleaming high-heeled shoes—with a splash of red: the color of lust and danger, and of course blood.

The movie begins in the present day, but its story is rooted, in the noir tradition, deep in the past. When we meet him at the outset, Mateo is a blind man living alone. No longer able to direct films, he has adopted the pseudonym Harry Caine, under which he continues to fashion successful scripts. For him, the famous Mateo of years before is dead, killed in the car crash that left him sightless more than a decade ago. Lena, we notice, is no longer around; and Mateo has just learned that his old rival Ernesto has died.

Mateo is tended by his longtime production manager, Judit (Blanca Portillo), and by her son, Diego (Tamar Novas), who acts as his typist and, when Mateo ventures outside, his eyes. One day, Diego prods the older man for a story he has always avoided telling—the story of what happened to Mateo and Lena, and what part Ernesto played in it. As Mateo reels back the years, we learn of Ernesto's mounting jealousy and the terrible revenge that he pursued; and we watch as Mateo and Lena flee to the long black beaches of the Canary Islands in a doomed attempt to evade it.

Almodóvar's script is ingenious, guiding us in measured steps through the story's unfolding secrets. There's a brilliant scene involving Ernesto and a lip reader whom he's hired to put words to the silent footage of Mateo and Lena that he's watching—a narrative interrupted when Lena slips into the room behind him and begins speaking the missing words herself. And there's a wonderful moment when Mateo and Diego are batting around script ideas and Diego comes up with one for a new kind of vampire movie—an idea that's actually so good you can imagine screenwriters on both sides of the Atlantic scurrying to their computers to turn it into an actual movie.

Almodóvar is such a master of framing, pace, and visual texture that even if this film had no plot, it would still be a pleasure simply to register his images as they pass before our eyes. (A shot of two lovers in a carnal rumpus under a shroud of bedsheets might have been lifted out of a lost Magritte painting, and a kitchen scene in which we see a fallen tear run down the side of a plump red tomato is so original a flourish we can't help but smile.) The actors restrain themselves entirely to servicing the story; and Cruz, in her latest collaboration with the director, remains such a gorgeous camera subject that her emotional eloquence as an actress still comes as a happy surprise.

Broken Embraces is as much about movies (it's seeded with references to Fritz Lang, Jules Dassin, and Roberto Rossellini) as it is about the elegantly tied knots of its plot. At the age of sixty, Almodóvar, still a fertile and seductive artist, remains intoxicated by the medium his work has so long adorned. (November 2009)

Dogtooth

Strange Daze

*D*ogtooth is an art movie from Greece that's so open-ended that you wonder while you're watching if all of its meaning has dribbled out the backdoor. For the first twenty minutes or so, anyway. Then a story begins to cohere, and the picture, already strange, becomes very creepy.

Three nameless siblings, two girls and a boy, apparently in their late teens, live in a remotely located house with their father (Christos Stergioglou) and mother (Michele Valley). In the sizable grounds outside there are palm trees and a swimming pool and a high wooden fence that rings the entire property. The kids, we eventually realize, have never been allowed to venture beyond this barrier.

Inside, there's a television set, but it's used only to show boring family videotapes shot by the father. There's one telephone, but it's hidden at the back of a shelf—the kids have never seen it. Their days pass blandly. They are homeschooled by their mother in a most unusual way. Her vocabulary instruction imparts the information that a carbine is a bird and a zombie is a little yellow flower. Occasionally the father has his son (Hristos Passalis) and two daughters (Aggeliki Pappoulia and Mary Tsoni) get down on all fours and bark like dogs.

The father is a boss at a nondescript factory. We see him one day arriving home in his Mercedes with an employee, a young woman named Christina (Anna Kalaitzidou), who has been blindfolded for the drive. The father takes her into his son's bedroom and leaves. Christina and the son shed their clothes and have perfunctory sex. (The sex and the full-frontal nudity in the movie have the arousing quality of a calculus lecture.) When they're done, the father takes Christina back to the factory.

The movie offers small islands of incident. When a stray cat finds its way onto the property one day, the son responds violently. (PETA people will want to avert their eyes at this juncture.) The siblings explore each other's bodies in a bathtub, wordlessly, as if tracing the shapes on statues. When Christina, on another of her regular visits, sneaks into the bedroom of one of the girls, offering a small gift, the girl says, "What do I have to lick?"

Can there be any escape from this bizarre existence? Theoretically, yes. The children have been told they can leave home as soon as their canine teeth—their dogteeth—fall out. The kids don't realize that this means never. Not in any natural way.

The story is hypnotically inscrutable. Is it an indictment of home-schooling? Of middle-class paranoia? Of what? The distinctively talented director, Giorgos Lanthimos, offers no answers, or even suggestions. He observes the family with placid objectivity. When someone in a facial close-up is doing something with his hands, we don't see them. When a character stands up out of frame, the camera stays put. (The shots are beautifully composed.) Even at the end, when we're hoping for a jailbreak moment, the director leaves us hanging, in squirming uncertainty. The movie is irritating and disturbing, and when it's over we want to put it behind us. It just won't stay there. (June 2010)

Let the Right One In

Blood in the Snow

Let the Right One In, a luminous new vampire movie from Sweden, creates a fresh sensibility for a timeworn genre. Here the old darkness has been banished, and in its place all is light: shining snowscapes, clean, bright interiors. Daubs of red and flashes of artful violence are very carefully placed. The tone is muted and beautiful.

Twelve-year-old Oskar (Kåre Hedebrant), with his blond mop of hair and his sad pale eyes, is an emotional invert, bullied at school, falling through the cracks of his parents' divorce at home in a Stockholm suburb. Late one night a strange girl (Lina Leandersson) moves into the apartment next door, accompanied by a tormented-looking man who could be her father. The girl is a disheveled madonna, peering out from under a curtain of dark hair through eyes with huge irises. In a yard the following night, she appears out of nowhere. "I can't be your friend," she tells Oskar. "I want to be left alone." Says Oskar: "So do I."

Of course neither of them really does. They're each melancholy loners who've finally found a friend. The girl, Eli, is twelve years old, too ("more or less," she says). She's a little scruffy, and she smells weird, and she goes coatless and sometimes shoeless in the bitter cold. But Oskar is awkwardly drawn to her, and she—suppressing a powerful urge for the first time—to him. One day he wanders through the open door of her apartment; no one is there, only a note. "I'm in the bathroom," it says. "Please don't go in. Want to hang out tonight?"

The picture is built on a procession of extreme, radiant close-ups, and it has scenes of startling originality: a character suddenly bursting into flames, an attack of terrified house cats, a very long shot (so long you might miss her in the distance) of Eli scrambling up the side of a building. There's blood seeping into the snow, too, of course, and one hideous mutilation; but there are no shock cuts, no cheap thrills, and there's very little sucker-punch music, either—only an occasional wash of somber strings or a lone piano.

Everything is background to Oskar and Eli's strange story. He falls more and more in love with her even as it dawns on him what she really is; and she toughens him against his classmate antagonists and teaches him how to grow up—something she can never do. At the quiet, glorious conclusion, the movie's cryptic title finally settles onto it like a cool breath of poetry. (October 2008)

Dead Snow

From Norway, with Nazis

The combination of Nazis and zombies isn't new. The 1977 *Shock Waves* is a hardy genre cult item; and while I haven't seen the German *Golden Nazi Vampire of Absam: Part II*, which was released into instant obscurity last year, Jean Rollin addressed the Nazi gut-muncher theme in his 1981 *Zombie Lake*, as did fellow horror vet Jesús Franco that same year with *Oasis of the Zombies*. Both of these directors, as you may know, screwed it up. So while the Norwegian *Dead Snow* may not be the first exemplar of its tiny genre, I think we can safely say that it is, by default, one of the best.

Young director Tommy Wirkola has a knowing fondness for gore history, but not in the preening fanboy manner so common in English-language horror films. Wirkola is a bit more subtle—a stray *Evil Dead* mention here, a *Braindead* T-shirt there. And he and Australian cinematographer Matthew Bradley Weston have put a lot of effort into giving the movie a stylish look.

But enough of that. Two vans full of vacationing med-school students are driving up into the snowy mountains of somewhere-in-Norway to spend their Easter break at a remote log cabin. In another departure from common practice, these youths are not all hunks and babes. One of the four guys is standard-issue handsome, but the other three are geeks and wiseacres. (One's a horror nerd: "How many movies start with a group of friends on the way to a cabin?") The three women (a fourth is en route, skiing cross-country—uphill, presumably) are entirely presentable, but you don't feel it's imperative that they get naked. (Well, maybe.)

So they arrive at the cabin. They party and flirt. Night falls and there's a knock at the door—a snow-dusted old geezer wanting a cup of coffee. He comes in and tells the kids a story about World War II Nazi invaders and their brutal depredations among the local populace. As the war wound down, these goons were driven off into the woods, never to be seen again. But their malign spirit still haunts the mountains: "There is an evil presence," the man says. Then he leaves. As we soon learn, he really should have stayed. The rest of the film is an exercise in cautionary instruction. Never hike off to an outhouse to have sex when big groaning creatures are lurching around outside. Never pitch a tent in a zombie neighborhood. And don't stand too close to windows unless you want your face ripped right off your skull. The zombies are what you'd expect—gray-skinned and droolly, their once-spiffy uniforms sorely in need of laundering. They're very fast-moving, though. The students do their best to fight the creatures off with hammers, scythes, and Turbo Saws, but some of them still end up with their intestines swinging from trees.

The movie definitely delivers in the gore department—it's hard to imagine who could want more in the way of ripped throats, knife-poked eyeballs, and amputated extremities. There's also a subterranean ice cave filled with Nazi memorabilia and, nestled among the helmets, a startling severed head. (Cross-country girl won't be coming after all.) The movie's problem—you knew there had to be one—is its uncertain tone. It's smart and funny in parts (there's a hilarious bird-throttling moment), but genre demands keep leading it off in predictable directions. And although it only runs ninety minutes, the picture goes on too long—especially at the end, when the zombies keep coming and coming and never seem to quit. Another downside, for some, will be the English subtitles. But even if it's not a great movie, it's trying for something a little different, so let's be appreciative. And hey: Nazi zombies! (June 2009)

The Girl with the Dragon Tattoo

Swede Sensation

Lisbeth Salander may be the first punked-out nutjob heroine in the mystery-thriller genre. She's a computer wizard with a talent for hacking, and in the sensational Swedish film *The Girl with the Dragon Tattoo*, she's a mesmerizing presence.

Lisbeth (Noomi Rapace) works for a Stockholm security firm. In the course of researching a client's case, she becomes involved in the complex affairs of Mikael Blomkvist (Michael Nyqvist), a crusading journalist who specializes in ripping the lid off crooked financial shenanigans. Mikael has just lost a big libel suit and has decided it would be best to resign from *Millennium,* the investigative magazine of which he is also publisher, and get out of town for a while. He accepts an offer from a reclusive industrialist named Vanger (Sven-Bertil Taube) to write a history of the man's famous family empire. But when he arrives at Vanger's mansion on a remote, snowy island, he learns that the man despises most of his family's members and is convinced that one of them was responsible for the mysterious disappearance of his beloved niece, Harriet, some forty years earlier. Mikael's real job is to find out who that was.

Lisbeth, who followed Mikael's legal tribulations in the press, is convinced he was set up (he was). Hacking into the laptop he has taken with him on the Vanger assignment, she learns what he's actually up to and decides she can help.

The story is fat with characters, most of them various Vangers, some of them back-in-the-day Nazis, one of them possibly a murderer.

There are *Silence of the Lambs* overtones as Mikael and Lisbeth attempt to connect Harriet's disappearance to a series of long-unsolved murders elsewhere in the area; and Mikael's discovery of crucial clues in a group of photographs taken the day Harriet vanished—clues that he slowly, methodically links together—is memorably suspenseful.

It's a movie in which there's a lot going on, almost all of it interesting. But Lisbeth, with her hostile glare, her dead-black hair, her many piercings, and a full-back tattoo that gives the picture its name—is the film's most compelling presence. We learn that she did something terrible when she was a child (exactly what it was only slowly becomes clear), and that she spent time in a mental institution. Since her release, she's been under the control of state-appointed guardians, the latest a man named Bjurman (Peter Andersson). Bjurman is a repulsive sleaze who annoyingly monitors Lisbeth's activities, controls her finances, and subjects her to hideous sexual assaults. Realizing there would be no point to turning him in—who would believe a crazy girl's story?—she instead devises a more direct response; and her return to Bjurman's apartment with a Taser and a tattoo needle has to be one of the most electrifying revenge scenes ever put on film. We're appalled, but exhilarated—this guy, after all, really deserves it.

The movie is based on a novel with the more pungent Swedish title *Men Who Hate Women*, by the late Swedish journalist Stieg Larsson. The book is the first of a bestselling Millennium trilogy that Larsson wrote but didn't live to see published. (He died in 2004.) With its intricate plot and vivid characters, this film version must surely be headed for an English-language remake. The two succeeding books in the Millennium series have already been filmed in Swedish, and will soon make their way to this country. The return of Lisbeth Salander—damaged, angry, and brilliant—is now keenly awaited. (March 2010)

The Girl Who Played with Fire

Middling

The good news about *The Girl Who Played with Fire* is that hacker-punk avenger Lisbeth Salander is right at the center of it. In *The Girl with the Dragon Tattoo*, the first movie drawn from Swedish author Stieg Larsson's Millennium trilogy, Salander (Noomi Rapace) was slightly peripheral, a sort of cyber sidekick to investigative journalist Mikael Blomkvist (Michael Nyqvist). Here, she's the focus of the story, which is more of a straight-ahead thriller, and, unsurprisingly, she's a treat to watch.

At the end of the first film, Salander had taken off to the Caribbean with millions of dollars of bad-guy cash. Now she's back in Stockholm, paying a visit to her sleazy social worker custodian, Bjurman (Peter Andersson), whose last encounter with his angry ward left him with a new appreciation for Tasers and some unexpected tattoos.

Meanwhile, Blomkvist has commissioned a sensational story for his magazine by two young reporters—a blockbuster exposé about sex trafficking that incriminates a score of government big shots. Then the reporters are murdered, and Salander's fingerprints are found on the gun that killed them. The gun belonged to Bjurman, and it turns out he's dead as well.

Salander is suddenly on the run, and she's determined to find the truth about the murders. Blomkvist is, too—he's convinced his odd little friend is innocent. The story expands into areas of espionage, corruption, and sexual abuse, with a towering white-haired killer lumbering into the action in the service of a vile Russian thug. We also learn about the devastating childhood incident that landed the young Salander in a mental institution (and gives the movie its name).

Although there's an abundance of things happening, the best parts of the film are pure Lisbeth. She takes her Taser along to pay a visit to another sex pig (they're her mission in life) and leaves him tied up like a very sad clown. She takes on a trio of greasy bikers and leaves them deeply wishing she hadn't. We also get a glimpse of her sensitive side (who knew she had one?) in an artfully shot lesbian sex scene. Noomi Rapace owns this iconic character, and even though we're getting more of her here, we can't get enough.

The bad news about the movie is that it's not well made. It's a chopped-down Swedish TV movie, and it looks it. Niels Arden Oplev, who directed the first film, is here replaced by its second-unit director, Daniel Alfredson, who brought along a new writer and cinematographer, too. The picture is flat and disjointed, and some of its gaudier elements (the white-haired killer might have drifted in from an old Bond movie) aren't as much fun as you keep wishing they were. There's also the usual ungainliness of any middle installment of a movie trilogy— we have to wait for the story's ambiguities and unanswered questions to be clarified in the final film, *The Girl Who Kicked the Hornet's Nest*, which is due out here in the fall. The bad news about that picture may be that it was also made by Arden, back-to-back with this one. Lisbeth Salander's most formidable opponent may turn out to be her director. (July 2010)

The Girl Who Kicked the Hornet's Nest

Killer Queen

It's no mystery why Stieg Larsson's three Millennium novels have sold some 40 million copies worldwide. The late author's anticorporate politics and stern feminism must resonate with many readers, especially in Europe, and his juicy genre plot trappings—murder, sex, conspiracy, revenge, and, what the hey, vintage Nazis, too—are probably an even bigger draw. But what's really catapulted this sprawling trilogy onto the heights of international bestsellerdom is its unforgettable central character: the bisexual psycho-punk cyber sleuth Lisbeth Salander, girl of our twistiest dreams.

Noomi Rapace, the actress who plays Salander in the three Swedish films made from Larsson's books—*The Girl with the Dragon Tattoo*, *The Girl Who Played with Fire*, and now *The Girl Who Kicked the Hornet's Nest*—is uniquely effective in the role. She's wiry, guarded, and entirely iconic, and it's hard to imagine anyone else playing the part. (We wish Rooney Mara well in David Fincher's English-language remake of the first film, currently under way.) Rapace, with her deadpan stare and flat-black thatch of goth-girl hair, easily carries all three movies; but like the books on which they're based, the films are of variable quality. *Dragon Tattoo*, released here earlier this year, offered the unrepeatable thrill of introducing Salander in full kickass form, although the story was so crowded with contending characters that you missed the scorecard to which your tickets should surely have been affixed. It was a terrific beginning, though.

The next two pictures, however, put into production before receipts from the surprise-hit opener came pouring in, were shot for Swedish television, with a new director, Daniel Alfredson, taking over the mini franchise from Niels Arden Oplev. Salander was more central to *The Girl Who Played with Fire*, which opened here last summer: We were drawn deeper into the brutal childhood trauma that consigned her to a mental institution, and Rapace remained a gripping presence. But the movie felt like a TV rush job, trashy-looking and awkwardly made, and it didn't seem to bode well for the concluding installment.

So it's an unexpected surprise that *The Girl Who Kicked the Hornet's Nest* is such a rousing wrap-up. The movie is a straight-ahead thriller, filled with corruption, perversity, and smash-bang action scenes, and it almost—although not quite—justifies its two-and-a-half-hour runtime. It opens (need I say "spoiler alert" here?) where the last film left off, with the bullet-riddled Salander being airlifted away to a hospital after having taken an axe to the vicious Russian Cold War spook Zalachenko (Georgi Staykov), who, adepts will recall, is actually her detestable father. The diminutive avenger is now in a classically tight spot, unjustly accused of murder, menaced by a sicko shrink who wants to put her back in the bin, and targeted for termination by Zalachenko's shadowy controllers in the Swedish intelligence service. And still lurching about around the edges of the action is the murderous goon Niedermann (Mikael Spreitz), who's most unfavorably disposed toward Salander himself.

Fortunately, her quasi partner and protector, the crusading journalist Mikael Blomkvist (Michael Nykvist), is determined to clear Salander by publishing her life story—filled with appalling sexual abuse and dark political chicanery—in a special issue of his investigative magazine, *Millennium*. This further inflames the intelligence heavies, and soon the story grows thick with deadly assassins, bent medicos, excitable bikers, a considerable amount of courtroom cat-and-mousery (and rather talky hospital interludes), and a heavy-duty nail gun that's put to alarmingly inventive use.

It's fitting that this final Salander movie doesn't end in a burst of sunny transformation and high fives all around. The conclusion does, however, leave open the possibility of a sequel, and one can imagine the temptation of cutting Salander loose from Larsson's books and launching her into a series of unrelated films in Bondian perpetuity. This seems unlikely to happen, though. Rapace has already been cast in Guy Ritchie's *Sherlock Holmes* sequel, and there are mumblings of her possible involvement in Ridley Scott's *Alien* prequel. The actress is moving on. But the character, now headed for Hollywood, may be here to stay. (October 2010)

The Reader

Small Fry

The Nuremberg war crimes trials of top Nazi leaders, which got under way in the fall of 1945, brought forth a procession of incomprehensible monsters. But another series of trials, conducted two decades later in Frankfurt, West Germany, focused on a more lumpen collection of Holocaust enablers—the orderlies, adjutants, and lower-level SS thugs who helped run the Auschwitz death camp in Poland, where more than a million people were exterminated. There were no women among this group of defendants, but Hanna Schmitz, the fictional character played with spellbinding precision by Kate Winslet in *The Reader*, is clearly of their ilk.

Unlike other Holocaust-related films being put before us this year—*The Boy in the Striped Pajamas* and the forthcoming *Good*, for example—*The Reader* makes no case for the common humanity we purportedly share with Nazi functionaries. (In *Good*, especially, the decision to become a Nazi is presented as an ill-considered career move.) Instead, the picture gives us a protagonist who elicits little sympathy. Hanna is dumb, sullen, and obscurely troubled—although not, as it turns out, by anything she did in the war. She's a pathetic human being, and Winslet plays her that way unflinchingly.

Roughly like the German novel on which it's based, *The Reader* tells the story of a fifteen-year-old boy named Michael Berg (David Kross), who falls into a casual affair with a thirty-six-year-old streetcar ticket taker in 1958. This is Hanna. She finds Michael collapsed outside her apartment building one day with the beginnings of scarlet fever and guides him back to his home. After recovering, he returns to her cheerless apartment to thank her. It's cold, and she tells him to bring a scuttle of coal up from the basement. He comes back covered with coal dust. "Take off your clothes," she says. "I'll run you a bath." He strips and steps into the water. When Hanna returns with a towel for him, she's naked, too.

In return for sex, Hanna asks only that Michael, who's studying Latin and Greek in school, read to her. So he brings over books and begins reading aloud from the work of Horace and Sappho, as well as Chekhov and D. H. Lawrence. Hanna is transfixed; Michael is in love. One day, though, Michael comes to Hanna's apartment and finds her gone, with no word left behind.

He doesn't see her again until the early 1960s, by which time he's a law student at a Berlin university. Michael is part of Germany's first postwar generation, a vast cohort of young people who are trying to come to grips with the inconceivable crimes against humanity that their elders either committed or countenanced during the Hitler years. Opinions differ strongly. A law professor (Bruno Ganz) contends that no matter how abominable the Nazis' undertakings were, a decent society must still be ruled by law: "The question is never, 'Was it wrong?' It's, 'Was it legal?'" Some of Michael's fellow students are infuriated by such nitpicking and disinclined to let their parents' generation off the hook for any reason. "What is there to understand?" one of them angrily asks. "Everybody knew." The professor takes them to observe a trial of minor SS members—a group of women who had worked as guards at Auschwitz. Here, Michael finally lays eyes on Hanna again. She's in the dock.

Listening from the courtroom's back benches, Michael learns that Hanna was one of those responsible for singling out prisoners for extermination at Auschwitz, and that she took part in a death march in which dozens of inmates were burned alive in a locked church. In these riveting scenes, Winslet plays Hanna as a trapped and baffled animal. She testifies that she was unemployed in 1943, when she heard the SS was seeking people to work as guards at Auschwitz. It was just a job. Sending selected prisoners to the ovens? "The old ones had to make way for the new ones." Refusing to unlock the doors of the burning church so the terrified inmates could escape? "Our job was to protect the prisoners. There would have been chaos." Looking at the judge, she asks, "What would you have done?"

Hanna is set up as the sole perpetrator of these crimes by her devious fellow defendants, who, twenty years after the events in question, now look like happy, harmless hausfraus. Hanna has a secret that might at least contextualize her actions, but she's too ashamed to admit it, and the court sentences her to life in prison. Michael knows her secret, too, but realizing that the woman he once loved is someone he never actually knew, he says nothing.

The movie suffers from its disjointed structure, which flashes back and forth between the young Michael's experiences with Hanna and his ongoing connection with her as an adult (when he's played with recessive concern by Ralph Fiennes). And some viewers will understandably reject any attempt to understand, even if in no way to exonerate, a Nazi executioner. But Winslet, I think, surmounts such objections with the exacting focus of her performance. Her Hanna, dim and uneducated, is a moral illiterate—a witting but uncomprehending participant in the abominations of the Final Solution. That she could have been anybody is one of the Holocaust's many indelible horrors. (December 2008)

A Woman in Berlin

War Diary

Rape is one of the oldest horrors of war, but movies rarely deal with it in any depth. Now comes *A Woman in Berlin*, a German film that takes wartime rape—and associated gray areas of resistance and collaboration—as its subject. The film asks an agonizing question: in a situation in which women become spoils of war, to be raped and beaten at the enemy's whim, what are their options?

The movie begins on April 26, 1945. The end of the war in Europe is less than two weeks away. Soviet forces are on the outskirts of Berlin, the bomb-blasted German capital, where Adolf Hitler, locked away in his bunker, is in raving denial. (Four days later he'll commit suicide.) When the Soviets break through and take part of the city, its civilian residents are at their mercy. They have good reason to be terrified. Over the past four years, Nazi invaders, storming the Soviet Union, killed millions of Russian soldiers and civilians, often monstrously. (Later in the film, a young Russian tells how Nazis captured his village and killed all the children—stabbing them, throwing them against walls, beating in their skulls. "I saw it," he says numbly.) Now the victorious Soviet troops, pouring through the streets of Berlin, are in a vengeful frame of mind.

The movie's protagonist, played by Nina Hoss, is a woman called

Anonyma. (The picture is based on a 1954 memoir of the fall of Berlin by Marta Hillers, a woman who lived through it and chose at the time to remain anonymous.) She is a journalist, well educated, who over the course of her career has been stationed in London, Paris, and Moscow (where she added Russian to her list of languages). Her husband, Gerd (August Diehl), is a German soldier currently stationed elsewhere. As the story gets under way, we find her huddled in the basement of an apartment house with a number of other frightened people, mostly women.

The random raping begins almost immediately, with Russian soldiers, fueled by the alcohol they've been denied in combat, dragging off young women, very old ones, and girls not even in their teens. After being raped three times herself, Anonyma makes a desperate decision: in order to maintain some vestige of personal autonomy, she tells us, "I swore that nobody would touch me unless I let them." And so in order to approximate a human connection, she greets the next soldier who approaches her with a smile and has sex with him voluntarily. "We'll survive," she tells another woman. "At all costs."

Anonyma soon finds a powerful protector, a Russian major named Andreij (Yevgeni Sidikhin). Like her he is intelligent and cultivated (he's a classical pianist). She begins sleeping with him, and they fall into something that might have been love in another context. Soon Andreij is bringing supplies—scarce food, wine, sugar—to the decrepit apartment in which Anonyma and some other Germans have found shelter. Andreij deplores the rapes being perpetrated by Russian soldiers outside, and he assigns some of his men to guard these people. Soon the soldiers are reviling him as a traitor, and before long he's transferred out of Berlin. Around this time Anonyma's husband returns home from the lost war. In a gesture of candor, she allows him to read her journals (from which Hiller's book was later assembled). He's appalled. "It's disgusting just to look at you," he says and storms off.

Is Anonyma a detestable collaborator, willing to do anything to find favor with her country's occupiers? Or is she just a woman forced to defend herself in the absence of civilized alternatives? The question is further clouded by certain facts about Marta Hillers that are only alluded to in the movie but are well known in Europe (where her book was a bestseller upon its reissue in 2003). As a German who was free to travel during the Hitler period, Hillers obviously had privileged connections with the Nazi government and even wrote propaganda for it. Should we withhold our sympathy? Or should we be gratified that she had the professional skill to record an appalling experience that was shared by many other women with less compromised backgrounds? Who can judge? And how? (August 2009)

Sophie Scholl

Lost Voices

Sophie Scholl: The Final Days, Germany's nominee for this year's Academy Award for Best Foreign Language Film, is a true story that doesn't ask any questions—the movie is spare and straightforward. But it provokes a question unavoidably. While most of us are quick to assert our beliefs and opinions, how quick would we be if doing so were dangerous—if standing up were certain to mean we would be brutally cut down?

The movie begins on the night of February 17, 1943, with Sophie Scholl (Julia Jentsch), a twenty-one-year-old student at the University of Munich, making her way through streets hung with Nazi banners to a secret workshop where her brother, Hans (Fabian Hinrichs), and two friends are producing anti-Nazi leaflets. They are all members of the White Rose, a student resistance movement dedicated to rousing other young Germans to rise up and overthrow the Nazi regime. This is the last meeting the group will have. Sophie has six days left to live.

The Hitler dictatorship is now in its ninth year, and its barbarism is in full, appalling flower. Germany's Jews have been officially stripped of their rights and ordered to wear yellow stars in the streets. A government euthanasia policy, initially intended to eradicate mentally and physically handicapped children, has been expanded to include adults, and at a half dozen killing clinics around the country, "elite" Nazi SS soldiers have tested a new, experimental method for their termination: poison gas. This having proved efficient, the mass gassing of Jews has begun at a death camp in Poland called Auschwitz. Like Poland, such other countries as Czechoslovakia, France, Denmark, Norway, and the Netherlands have fallen before Nazi invasions, and Germany is now at war with Great Britain, the United States, and other Allied nations.

Hans Scholl and three other members of the White Rose have recently returned from tours of duty as conscript medics on the Eastern Front, where they witnessed SS troops murdering Jews indiscriminately in Poland and the Soviet Union. Their second White Rose leaflet, which was mailed out to academics and pubs in late 1942, noted that "since the conquest of Poland, three hundred thousand Jews have been murdered . . . in the most bestial way. Here we see the most frightful crime against human dignity, a crime that is unparalleled in the whole of history." White Rose leaflet number five, distributed in early February of 1943, decried the Nazis as "a criminal regime" and implored Germans to stand up and cast them off. "In the aftermath," the leaflet warned, "a terrible but just judgment will be meted out to those who stayed in hiding, who were cowardly or hesitant."

Now, on this last night of the White Rose, it is decided that a freshly printed leaflet number six will be distributed within the University of Munich itself. It will be an insanely dangerous mission—Nazi informers are everywhere. But Hans Scholl volunteers for the job, and Sophie insists on going with him.

Early the next morning, February 18, Hans and Sophie enter the university carrying a small suitcase stuffed with leaflets. Scurrying through the empty hallways, they place stacks of them at random along the floors. Thinking they've finished, they prepare to leave, but then realize there are still some leaflets left. They turn back and mount a staircase, and Sophie tosses a sheaf of leaflets off a balcony onto the main concourse below, just as students and staff are beginning to pour into the building. She is spotted by a janitor, a Nazi stooge, who calls the Gestapo. Sophie and Hans are arrested and taken to secret-police headquarters.

What follows is based on the official record of the hours of interrogation of Sophie Scholl conducted by Robert Mohr, a Gestapo inquisitor who is seen by the filmmakers as more of a by-the-book policeman than a Nazi ideologue—a contemptible but unimpassioned collaborator. He and Sophie face each other across an imposing desk in his bleak office. Mohr (Alexander Held), in a gray suit and a bow tie, is for the most part quietly bemused. He has a son just one year younger than Sophie, and he doesn't think Sophie is guilty—complicit, yes, but probably just led astray by her brother. Sophie admits nothing. As Mohr peppers her with questions—about why she was at the university so early that day, why she was carrying the suitcase, who else was involved—she stares him straight in the eye and deftly improvises an alibi he can't crack.

Sophie claims to be apolitical herself but allows that there are things happening in Germany about which a more political person might feel disgust. Mohr tells her she is "confused." The Jews aren't being wiped out, he says, they're simply "emigrating." "You have to realize," he says, "a new age is dawning." Sophie disagrees. Erupting in frustration, Mohr shouts, "Without law, there is no order. What can we rely on if not the law?" Sophie mildly replies, "Your conscience. Laws change. Conscience doesn't."

Meanwhile, the Gestapo has been gathering evidence at Sophie's apartment that implicates not only her and her brother but also another member of the White Rose, Christoph Probst (Florian Stetter), a young married father of three. He, too, has been arrested. Finally, in their last confrontation, Mohr presents Sophie with a document signed by Hans—a confession, in which he claims sole responsibility for the leafleting operation. Mohr tells Sophie that if she will just admit she was misguided and renounce any anti-Nazi beliefs, she will avoid punishment. She refuses. Is she confessing her guilt? "Yes," she says, "and I'm proud of it."

On February 22, Sophie and Hans and Christoph Probst are brought to trial—a travesty conducted before an audience of Gestapo thugs and presided over by the infamous Nazi judge Dr. Roland Freisler (André Hennicke), a screaming lunatic in crimson robes who also acts as prosecutor and jury. (This scene is taken from the official trial transcript.) By prearrangement with Hans and Sophie, Probst claims that he became involved with the White Rose while in a state of severe depression and pleads to be spared for his children's sake. Freisler tells him he's not worthy to be a father. The judge makes it frothingly clear that he views the defendants as mere insects buzzing ineffectively about the great body of National Socialism; but when Hans steps forward to testify, he tells Freisler, "If you and Hitler weren't afraid of our opinion, we wouldn't be here."

Finally, Sophie is brought to stand before the court. After Freisler has delivered himself of another barrage of hysterical invective, he asks her, "Aren't you ashamed?" Sophie says, "No." And to the courtroom at large, she adds, "You will soon be standing where I stand now."

The verdict for all three defendants is guilty, of course, and the sentence, death. Shockingly, they are told that they will be executed forthwith. A prison matron nervously allows them to share a last cigarette together, and then we follow Sophie into the last room she will ever see. I will not describe the scene.

The director of *Sophie Scholl*, Marc Rothemund, has kept the horror of the Nazi period carefully muted in this film. There are no vicious beatings or bloody tortures. The prospect of inescapable doom that hangs over the heads of the three main characters is chilling enough. We marvel at these young students, who had a whole life left to live but who gave it up for a belief—when all around them, others had given up the belief itself instead. Will there always be people capable of such courage? And in similar circumstances, how likely is it that we would be among them? (February 2006)

The Baader Meinhof Complex

Apt Pupils

The Baader Meinhof Complex is an explosive movie about a German student terrorist gang of the 1970s and the wave of arson, robbery, kidnappings, and murder with which they shook their country's government, in the process triggering exactly the sort of right-wing oppression against which they claimed to be crusading. The picture was a deserving Oscar nominee earlier this year for Best Foreign Language Film, and in its weaving together of the intricacies of righteous social ferment and the bloody reality of what the gang wrought, it's a fascinating achievement.

The Baader Meinhof Group, as the gang was called in the press (they styled themselves the Red Army Faction, or RAF), was led by Gudren Ensslin (played here by Johanna Wokalek), a blond parson's daughter turned steely-willed Marxist revolutionary, and her charismatic boyfriend, Andreas Baader (Moritz Bleibtreu), a petty thief and intellectual primitive with a taste for fast cars (usually stolen) and guns and a grand vision of himself as a Brandoesque action-movie hero. Ulrike Meinhof (Martina Gedeck, of the Oscar-winning *The Lives of Others*) was popularly portrayed as the group's other leader, but was essentially a subsidiary propaganda minister—a famous left-wing journalist who found herself drawn into the gang's violent orbit after being confronted with the hypocrisy of her revolutionary rhetoric in print when measured against her failure to join in armed action herself.

The picture takes us from Baader and Ensslin's first operation—an arson attack on two Frankfurt department stores—through all the subsequent bank robberies, kidnappings, shootings, bombings, and gun battles, as well as the group's training in the Middle East with Palestinian terrorists (who didn't appreciate their casual attitude toward nudity and sex). In one gripping section of the film, we see the capture of the RAF's top leaders in 1972 and their imprisonment in Stuttgart's specially fortified Stammheim prison, where, during a chaotic trial (the dialogue in these scenes is taken from the trial transcripts), they were all found guilty of various murders and other crimes and given life sentences.

Ulrike Meinhof committed suicide in prison, and in 1977, the other RAF leaders followed suit. (The guns that were found in their cells had almost certainly been smuggled in to them by their lawyers, who were fellow radicals.) By this point, the group had developed a large national youth following, which formed a "second-generation" RAF and carried on the group's murderous legacy for years. These homicidal successors didn't announce their disbanding until 1998.

Like similar political ideologues of the period—the Weather Underground in this country, the Japanese Red Army, and the Italian Red Brigades—the Baader Meinhof Group forged early links with Arab terrorist organizations and helped fashion a Western template for urban-guerrilla action. Arising out of the worldwide antiwar protest movement of the late 1960s, the group had justifiable grievances: they were the children of the Nazi generation, appalled by what their parents had done during the Hitler period and outraged by the number of former Nazis who had insinuated themselves back into positions of social power after the Second World War. But the RAF, like the other national terror groups, operated under a fundamental delusion—that the proletariat they sought to lead into armed revolt actually had any interest in following them.

Baader Meinhof is the most expensive German-language movie ever made in that country (it cost $20 million), and the outlay is apparent in the film's production values (parts of it were shot in Rome and Morocco) and in the top-flight direction by Uli Edel, who masterfully orchestrated a cast that included more than 120 speaking parts and more than 6,000 extras. The three lead actors are superb, especially Wokalek, who's both sultry and scary, and Bleibtreu, who speaks the universal language of movie star magnetism. (August 2009)

THE COMIC-BOOK CONQUEST

Filmmakers have always been drawn to comic books as a source of colorful characters and clear, lively stories. The Blondie and Dick Tracy features and Batman serials of the 1940s were popular undertakings, as were the Jungle Jim pictures (starring Johnny Weissmuller, fresh from bestriding another vine-draped precinct as Tarzan) in the 1950s. The modern mania for comic-book movies could be said to have gotten under way with Richard Donner's 1978 Superman and to have swelled further with the release of Tim Burton's innovatively dark Batman in 1989. Today, all manner of comic-book characters throng movie screens, dwindling in impact, if not in box-office appeal, as filmmakers plumb the lower depths of the comic-book barrel in search of new profit centers. More up-to-date comics have gotten the Hollywood treatment, too, although with variable results. I should note that one of the movies reviewed here, Coraline, is based, not on a comic, but on a novella by comic-book auteur Neil Gaiman, which was later turned into a graphic novel. The rest of these films were lifted straight (more or less) from the multi-paneled pages.

Spider-Man 3

Tangled Web

Superheroes aren't supposed to burst into tears, are they? Or go all huggy at the drop of a mask? And their girlfriends—I don't recall any of them ever breaking into song, do you?

Well, director Sam Raimi's third installment of the *Spider-Man* saga gives us all of this, as if someone had asked for it. The series has always had a prominent emotional component—the teenage isolation felt by nerdy protagonist Peter Parker (Tobey Maguire); his love for his dear old Aunt May (Rosemary Harris); his longing for the seemingly unattainable girl next door, Mary Jane Watson (Kirsten Dunst). Here, though, these sweet narrative ingredients ooze over the line into pure syrup. At the screening I attended—which was filled with real people, not just movie reviewers—I thought I detected an actual slump of puzzlement at the end, as the movie's final scene sank into a bog of unexpected mush.

There's too much story, is the problem. (The movie is a good fifteen minutes longer than the preceding films, and it feels longer still.) And as cool as they may be individually, there are also too many villains. Flint Marko (Thomas Haden Church), who mutates into the shapeshifting Sandman after stumbling into the middle of a molecular-physics experiment, is an interestingly conflicted bad guy—a guilt-ridden ex-con who was only trying to save his dying daughter when he robbed and accidentally killed Peter's beloved Uncle Ben years earlier. And the black-suited Venom (Topher Grace) is a fine razor-toothed horror—an evil anti-Spider-Man. But then Peter's erstwhile friend Harry (James Franco) is still on the scene, too—he's taken over his late father's Green Goblin franchise and, wrongly convinced that Peter killed the old man, is sailing around Manhattan on his New Goblin surfboard in search of payback. (In a flourish typical of a script that's willing to wheel in dying daughters, Harry's menace is conveniently neutralized, for a bit, by a sudden bout of short-term amnesia.) And as if all of this weren't jeopardy enough, Harry's dad (Willem Dafoe) is still around as well, stirring up trouble from beyond the grave. ("Make him suffer!")

Exacerbating this overload of villainy is a small black ball of outer-space gloop called a symbiote, which falls to Earth in a mini-meteor one night, not far from a tree where the now-an-item Peter and Mary Jane are snuggled in a big Spidey web, mooning up at the stars. Soon this insidious goo has taken over Peter's body, compelling him to sexy-up his hairstyle and turning him into an obnoxious disco stud who vamps around town with a demented leer for every passing babe. (Watching the straight-arrow Peter go to the dark side is funny at first; but the caricature gets pretty broad, and the routine goes on too long.) The symbiote naturally has a malign affect on Peter's Spider-Man persona, too. He finally manages to shed the thing, but inadvertently drops it onto a smarmy rival, Eddie Brock (Topher Grace with blond highlights), turning him into the aforementioned Venom (minus the highlights, but with the razory teeth).

In a way, it may be good that there are so many bad guys. Otherwise, we'd have to endure even more of the gas-passing colloquies that litter the script (written by director Raimi and his brother Ivan, along with *Spider-Man 2* screenwriter Alvin Sargent). The scenes with Aunt May are particularly bromidic this time around ("Learn to forgive yourself," she sagely advises); and even Peter ("People really *like* me now") has become problematic, his bashful sweetness shading over into arrested development. Most tiresome, though, is Mary Jane, who is given little more to do than whine and shriek throughout the movie. M. J. is now an actress, and as the film opens, she's won the lead role in a Broadway musical—a part from which she's fired after opening night. (We're supposed to sympathize with her, and we do; but we also sympathize with the show's director, who, like us, has heard her sing—Dunst isn't a bad vocalist, exactly, but she's not Broadway.) From this point on, Mary Jane becomes very *needy*, and there's little relief from her po-faced pouting until Venom gets his hands on her, at which point the shrieking kicks in.

Spider-Man 3 reportedly cost more than $250 million to make—possibly twice as much as the first film—and a lot of the money obviously went to the battalion of effects technicians who brought their computers to bear on the labor-intensive Sandman (who can morph from a raging tornado into a Kong-size golem) and on the movie's many action sequences. There's a spectacular, sky-high battle between Spider-Man and New Goblin early in the picture that's seamlessly kinetic—vintage Raimi—and a clever bit in a subway where Spider-Man shoves Sandman's granular head up against a train that's barreling by and shears off half his face. But a lot of the digital tumult becomes numbing after a while, and the inevitable shots of Spidey leaping around the concrete canyons of New York remain as cartoony as ever.

The actors elevate the material to some extent. Thomas Haden Church, in particular, brings real feeling to his portrayal of a man with no place left to run. Bryce Dallas Howard makes a dewy-fresh series debut as Spidey admirer Gwen Stacy, and James Franco and Topher Grace are too skillful ever to be mistaken for mere hunks. It's also fun to see *Evil Dead* star Bruce Campbell popping up in another Raimi film—even if his cameo here, as a sniffy maître d' in a French restaurant, is shoehorned into a scene that goes on much too long.

But it's hard to imagine where else Maguire and Dunst can go with their characters—there's not much more we need to know about them. And Raimi may have reached the end of his creative investment in the series in any case. All three are being very vague at the moment about returning for *Spider-Man 4*—something I think we can take to be semaphored salary negotiations. Since the conclusion of this picture would seem to make another sequel a certainty, will Sony not marshal boatloads of cash and contract perks in order to secure the services of this core trio one more time? How the filmmakers will deal with the conceptual bloat that's now set in, however, may be a more pressing question, and no matter how much money this picture mints, it'll have to be answered. As Mary Jane observes at one point, "Everybody needs help sometimes. Even Spider-Man." (May 2007)

Kick-Ass

Moppet Mayhem

Sitting through *Kick-Ass* is like seeing a Tarantino movie for the first time: Terrible things are happening on-screen—a musical ear removal, a nasty basement-geek episode—and yet, somehow, they're breathtakingly funny. Tarantino's discursive tone and giggly humor allow us some distance from the horrors he works up. *Kick-Ass* director Matthew Vaughn isn't as jokey as Tarantino—he plunges us straight into the bloody mayhem. But his movie's juicy comic-book colors and exuberant fight choreography still distance the action from any possible real world and anchor it firmly in comic-book fantasyland, converting the mayhem into high-spirited fun.

The picture is wonderful in a number of ways. It marks a welcome return to form for Nicolas Cage, who portrays the vigilante crime fighter Big Daddy in the halting, campy cadences of Adam West in the old *Batman* TV series. (Who else would have thought of such a thing?) And it features a door-busting breakthrough performance by Chloë Grace Moretz, eleven years old at the time the movie was made, who plays Daddy's little Hit-Girl as a knife-happy mini martial arts avenger capable of reducing a room full of mobsters to wet, dripping sashimi. The movie isn't really about Hit-Girl, but it's Hit-Girl who runs away with the movie.

The story is nominally focused on Dave Lizewski (Aaron Johnson), a teenage dweeb who longs to make a difference in the world. Dave's high school pals laugh when he floats the idea of becoming a superhero, but he goes ahead and buys a cheap green wet suit for a costume and sets out to fight crime anyway. This doesn't go so well at first—an initial street-thug encounter puts him in the hospital—but he soon gets the hang of it, sort of, and after administering rough justice to another group of bad guys in front of a crowd of cheering teens, he finds himself transformed into a YouTube celebrity, reborn as Kick-Ass. This notoriety brings him to the attention of Big Daddy and Hit-Girl—who have their own crime-busting agenda—and then to the notice of drug lord Frank D'Amico (Mark Strong) and his son Chris (Christopher Mintz-Plasse), another dweeby kid with his own superhero sideline, as Red Mist (he drives a slick red sports car called the Mist Mobile).

The movie isn't just faithful to the gore-soaked *Kick-Ass* comic-book series by Mark Millar and John S. Romita Jr.; in some ways it's an improvement. The film went into production just as the comics began publication, and it's more of a collaboration with Millar and Romita than it is a standard adaptation of their work. This allowed Vaughn to tweak the material in beneficial ways, adjusting Big Daddy's backstory to more gratifying effect, which among other things sweetens up a subplot involving a high school babe named Katie (Lyndsy Fonseca), after whom Dave pathetically lusts. And presumably Millar was responsible for some of the picture's comic-geek flourishes: Spider-Man creator Steve Ditko gets name-checked at one point, and at another we're offered a passing glimpse of a theater marquee advertising *The Spirit 3*—a movie one hopes will never be made.

The picture advances in a series of rousingly staged set pieces, the most memorable of which is a furious Hit-Girl attack on D'Amico's gangster-packed penthouse headquarters—a bloody whirl of bullets and butcher knives and even an unexpected bazooka. The violence is rippingly horrific (Vaughn had to finance the film himself after every studio he approached passed on it), but it's also, for the most part, explosively funny. (Although a gruesome moppet beatdown toward the end was an ill-advised step too far.)

There have been some outraged complaints among critics in Britain, where the film opened a few weeks ago, that Moretz is exploited in this picture in ways that only a pedophile could find appealing. I don't think so. She's not sexualized in any way, and the gross epithets she's called upon to deliver are, after all, only words (and coming from such a pint-size character, they're shockingly funny). Most pertinently, Hit-Girl is not a victim. When Kick-Ass, in the aftermath of a battle that almost went wrong, tenderly inquires about her future prospects, she tells him, "I can take care of myself." After all, she says, "I saved your sorry ass." (April 2010)

Fantastic Four

Colorless Quartet

First the bad news: there could be a sequel to this movie. The good news: with any luck, there won't be.

Fantastic Four has been cooked down from the unending Marvel Comics series, which began in 1961. A movie version has been making the development rounds for more than a decade, so this picture has been a long time coming. Not nearly long enough, though.

Ioan Gruffudd (*King Arthur*) plays scientist, inventor, and clueless dork Dr. Reed Richards. In search of funding for a rocket trip to study a space storm of some sort firsthand, he approaches a snotty rival from his MIT days, Victor Von Doom (Julian McMahon), who is now a snotty industrial billionaire. Victor agrees to finance Reed's expedition in return for 75 percent of the scientific spoils. He'll also be coming along for the ride and bringing with him his "director of genetic research," Sue Storm (Jessica Alba). Sue happens to be Reed's ex-girlfriend. (She's still miffed, and we are dumbstruck, that he failed to realize that her one-time offer to play house meant that she really liked him.) Sue will be bringing along her brother, hotshot pilot Johnny Storm (Chris Evans), while Reed will be making do with the company of his gruff pal, Ben Grimm (Michael Chiklis).

Despite all the genius on board, the group's spaceship gets creamed by the cosmic storm. Plummeting back to Earth, the brave little band discovers that this extraterrestrial calamity has, as Sue pertly puts it, "fundamentally altered our DNA"—to the point where they must quickly come up with some superhero names. Sue, who is suddenly able to render herself invisible, will become . . . let's see . . . Invisible Girl! No, wait—that was her original name in the long-ago Marvel comics. Now she must be—Invisible Woman! And Reed Richards, who has acquired the ability to distend his body into all kinds of stretchy shapes, shall become . . . Plastic Man? No, wait—Plastic Man is a DC Comics character who's been around since the 1940s. Something else. Okay, Reed will henceforth be known as—Mr. Fantastic! Johnny Storm, now able to burst into flame at will, is easy: the Human Torch. And Ben Grimm, who has been turned into a hulking—indeed, Hulk-*like*—man-mountain, will have to settle for just being called the Thing.

While not technically a member of the cliquish Fantastic Four, Victor Von Doom needs a supername, too—he is, after all, turning into metal and shooting death rays out of his fists. Only a minor moniker-adjustment is needed here: Victor becomes Dr. Doom.

And so the stage is set for superdoings both heroic and villainous, although rarely interesting. The Thing head-butts a speeding truck. Johnny learns to fly and becomes such a hothead that Sue tells him, "You were at 4000 Kelvin—any hotter and you'd be at supernova!" Reed discovers that shaving's a lot easier when you can pull your cheek out like a handful of taffy. ("Hey," says Victor, when Reed begins melting during a heated confrontation, "why the long face?")

Comic-book movies should be fun, of course, but they also need a little soul: Spider-Man is sad but stoic; Batman is troubled and broody. The X-Men are . . . well, the X-Men are a lot more dynamic and vividly individuated than this pallid crew of superfolk. The Fantastic Four talk too much, and apart from some slick effects—mainly involving Mr. Fantastic and his ability to slide his flattened hand under a locked door or lasso his arm out to scrawl formulae down at the end of a long laboratory chalkboard—the wow factor in this movie is minute. Ioan Gruffudd is too bland to bring much vitality to the transformed Reed Richards; and Jessica Alba, as the ads for the movie make curvaceously clear, is used mainly for decorative effect. (Why is her supersuit the only one that shrank at the superlaundry?) As the Human Torch, Chris Evans has comic charm to spare, but there's something uncompelling about a character who's composed mainly of flames. And while Michael

Chiklis, as the Thing, manages to project emotional shifts using nothing but his eyes, the bunch-of-boulders body suit in which he's encased remains a distraction—he's a guy wearing a bunch-of-boulders body suit.

Only Julian McMahon's nefarious psycho, Dr. Doom, shows iconic promise here, especially after he dons his hooded cloak. If for some reason there had to be a sequel to this movie, it'd be best if he were the only one of this crew in it. (July 2005)

Fantastic Four: Rise of the Silver Surfer

Wipeout

I saw *Fantastic Four: Rise of the Silver Surfer* with members of its target demographic, which is to say, kids within hailing distance of their teens. They loved it. They laughed and applauded, and at the end they cheered. They really had a good time.

For those who've moved on into other demographics, however—and seen a lot more movies—it should be noted that this is an action flick with not a lot of action. There's virtually none in the first third, which is largely devoted to wedding planning. (Really.) The picture is also overloaded with CGI of a very familiar sort. The Silver Surfer himself—one of the more beloved figures of the Marvel Comics universe—is nothing but; and while he looks great, and the producers went to the expense of bringing in Peter Jackson's WETA Digital effects shop to help whip him up, anyone who's seen Willem Dafoe and James Franco hanging ten around Manhattan in the *Spider-Man* films won't be inordinately impressed. This is a superhero movie with a crippling lack of superness.

The Fantastic Four have become a cuddlier bunch since we last saw them. Having dispatched brainiac bad guy Victor Von Doom (Julian McMahon) in the first film, they're now looking to kick back. Stretchy-man scientist Reed Richards (the still-tepid Ioan Gruffudd) is about to marry the occasionally invisible Sue Storm (very blond Jessica Alba); and walking-rockslide Ben Grimm (the affable Michael Chiklis) is in full nuzzle mode with his actually-not-just-metaphorically blind girlfriend, Alicia Masters (talented Kerry Washington, well-paid, we hope). Only Sue's fireball brother, Johnny (Chris Evans), remains eager for action. Which is eventually forthcoming.

The big wedding is derailed when Reed gets a PDA "cosmic radiation" alert in the middle of the ceremony. A pinballing meteor has been wreaking weirdness around the world—triggering snow in Egypt, snuffing the lights in L.A., really bad stuff. Turns out this is the Silver Surfer (mo-capped CGI star Doug Jones, of *Hellboy* and *Pan's Labyrinth*), an advance man for "Galactus, Destroyer of Worlds." (In the Marvel comic in which he debuted back in 1966, Galactus was an imposing badass with a complicated metal helmet; here he—or it—is just a computer-spawned intergalactic blizzard of the so-what variety.) After an airborne chase through New York's Holland Tunnel (a pale descendant of a much cooler sequence in *Men in Black*), Johnny Storm's fiery superpower starts going haywire. It doesn't take a genius to figure out what's happened, but resident genius Reed explains anyway: "Your encounter with the Surfer has affected your molecules." Why? Because the silver guy has "the ability to convert matter and energy." This sort of comic-book science would be fun if the lines were delivered with satirical snap, but the colorless Gruffudd isn't the man to do that.

Then Victor Von Doom reappears, and our hopes for the movie momentarily rise. That hopeful moment soon passes, though—Dr. Doom is given insufficient room to deploy his evil flamboyance. Instead he is imposed upon the Fantastic Four as a new teammate by a special-ops military commander (Andre Braugher), who's obviously unaware that movie generals have been wasting their firepower on invincible alien invaders since the 1950s. The movie limps along for a bit (it only runs ninety-two minutes) and finally comes to an unspectacular conclusion.

Fantasy pictures needn't be bound by the constraints of real-world logic, but they can't survive the blandness by which this one is smothered. The sunny visual design lacks atmosphere, and the score (by John

Ottman) is as perfunctory as the team's trademark superpowers (the hulking Ben still has the ability to hold up really heavy things, and Sue Storm still excels at fancy *take-that!* hand gestures). The jokes are pretty thin, too. Mild chuckles arise when the Four, boarding a flight to New York for the wedding, are downgraded from first class to economy (Ben naturally gets a middle seat). But we immediately wonder why they didn't just make the trip in their flying Fantasticar. About halfway through the movie, I wished I had one myself. (June 2007)

Catwoman

Tail End

Because *Catwoman* isn't as bad as you might expect, it's not as much fun as it might have been. Executed with the right sort of cinematic ineptitude, this story about a woman who turns feline after being breathed upon by a weird cat and then sets out to foil a nefarious plot involving nefarious beauty cream—well, in the right hands, this could have been a mirth bomb for the ages. But no. *Catwoman* is a little too clever and a little too well executed—or at least expensively executed—to qualify as classic dreck. Plus it stars Halle Berry in the title role, strapped into a black leather catsuit straight out of an old 42nd Street bondage reel, and this tends to short-circuit critical contemplation of the film's inadequacies. At first, anyway.

Berry plays Patience Philips, a shy, aspiring New York artist who pays the rent by working in the ad department of a big cosmetics company called Hedare. The story begins, as she says in an opening voice-over, "on the day that I died." First she encounters a strange cat (an Egyptian mau, it turns out—a breed that was *once revered by pharaohs*). In the course of attempting to rescue this brooding quadruped from a precarious perch outside her living room window, Patience attracts the attention of a passing police detective, Tom Lone (Benjamin Bratt). In the process of assisting Patience, Tom winds up in her apartment, and we know they're going to hit it off when he looks at one of her paintings and says, "Kind of reminds me of early Chagall—elegant, but whimsical." We want to smack him, but Patience is smitten.

Cut to the headquarters of the Hedare company, where Patience is working on the ad campaign for a revolutionary antiaging beauty cream called Beau-Line—or Bee-o-leen, as the employees say it. I wondered at first why the filmmakers hadn't consulted a French person to correct this mangled pronunciation; then I realized that the director—a man who goes by the single name Pitof—*is* a French person, and that the head of the beauty company is played by the French actor Lambert Wilson, his trademark sneer still in place after heavy use in the last two *Matrix* movies (in which he portrayed that tiresome character called the Merovingian).

When Patience learns that Beau-Line is addictive and will turn a consumer's skin into "living marble," she is marked for death. But she doesn't die. Well, she *sort of* dies, but she's reborn—as a cat. Or a catlike person, anyway. She starts hissing at dogs and gorging on sushi and saying things like "*Purrr*-fect." She also starts doing things I don't think cats are actually capable of, like crawling across ceilings and knocking down doors. But I guess that's okay in a movie in which we're initially expected to accept that somebody who looks like Halle Berry can't get a date.

Implausibilities aren't the problem in a comic-book picture like this. The problem is that the movie feels so spiritless and secondhand: The fight scenes, however elaborate, are standard-issue wham-pow; and the swooping shots of Catwoman leaping across rooftops are pure *Spider-Man*. And although director Pitof is best known (in France, anyway) as a digital-effects supervisor (this is only the second movie he has directed), the CGI is limp: Much of what passes for Manhattan here is achingly fake, and at least one close-up of a cat's head looks like it was scanned off a greeting card.

Halle Berry must savor this sort of action role; and while she can't manage much romantic chemistry with Benjamin Bratt, she does shoot off some sparks—and some lively jump-kicks—with Sharon Stone, playing a discarded trophy wife who is, shall we say, not a cat person. This isn't a really bad movie, but it leaves you wishing it had the vulgar pizzazz of a much worse one. (July 2004)

Elektra

Starpower Outage

Jennifer Garner's Elektra character was the second-best thing in *Daredevil*, the 2003 movie in which the modelesque assassin made her debut. (The best thing, of course, was the part where the picture ended.) Now she's the second-best thing once again, in her own movie, the only really good thing about which is the fact that Ben Affleck's pallid Daredevil character makes no appearance in it. (The ending of this film is such a dribbly disappointment, it doesn't even qualify as a pleasure-by-default.)

Elektra must be the pokiest superhero movie of the current comic-book-flick revival. There's an awful lot of walking about and brooding and staring out to sea. Occasionally a character will sigh, or maybe raise an eyebrow. At one point, the three leads sit down to have dinner, and we get to watch. (Oh boy.) There are bad guys, of course, but more often than not, we have to wait for them to show up. And wait. And wait. Sitting through some of the more torpid parts of this picture is like cooling your heels at the DMV.

Unsurprisingly, there's a skeleton of a cool fantasy story here (the Elektra character was created for Marvel by Frank Miller in the early 1980s), but the clatter of its fleshless bones is dispiriting. Suffice it to say that the sword-wielding Elektra, who was clearly deceased at the end of *Daredevil*, is back, don't ask how. ("I died once," she mutters, without further elaboration.) She's been hired by the Hand, a group of semi-supernatural rub-out specialists, to terminate a man named Mark Miller (Goran Visnjic) and his cute teenage daughter, Abby (Kirsten Prout), who are holed up in a big house on an island somewhere. Elektra dutifully lines these two up in the sights of her sniper-scope (which is affixed to a risibly ornate bow-and-arrow rig—can't she afford a rifle?), but then decides not to go through with the hit. The Hand, hearing about this, dispatches a team of assassins to do the job, among them a guy named Tattoo (his torso full of tats teems with evil life), another called Stone (a big bulletproof fellow), and a menacing babe named Typhoid, who wears a push-up bra and, in addition, turns people to stone. (You'd think that would be Stone's job, actually, but . . . whatever.)

Meanwhile, Elektra is consulting with her martial arts sensei, Stick (the sonorous Terence Stamp), who's headquartered, rather oddly, in a pool hall. Stick says things like, "Don't look for your opponent—know where he is." He's not much help. So Elektra rejoins Mark and Abby, and they wait for the dispatched assassins to attack. And, as I say, wait and wait.

The attack finally comes, of course. But the action scenes are so brazenly secondhand they might provoke a class-action lawsuit. A sword fight conducted in a roomful of floaty white sheets is clearly a rip from *Hero*. Elektra's slow-mo dart-dodging (the villains have no gun budget either) is yet another feeble reprise of the once-nifty *Matrix* bullet-time effect. And the inevitable panoply of wire-borne leaps and drifting kung fu kicks has never seemed less fresh.

With one exception, the actors are fine. Goran Visnjic has an appealing thoughtful-hunk presence, and Kirsten Prout is plucky in an agreeably unirritating way. (She suggests a pint-size Renée Zellweger.) And it's too bad that the uncredited Jason Isaacs, that virtuoso hambone, best known for his portrayal of the hissable Lucius Malfoy in the *Harry Potter* pictures, is dispatched so early on.

But these performers labor in vain. Because *Elektra* is becalmed by the po-faced Jennifer Garner, whose inexpressive performance sucks the air out of just about every scene in the movie. After two hours, as the picture peters out, little Abby asks Elektra, "Will I see you again?" Elektra's response suggests the depressing possibility of a sequel—something for which we'd be *happy* to wait. (January 2005)

Sin City

Town Without Pity

Of all the hard-boiled crime writers who followed in the wake of Dashiell Hammett and Carroll John Daly, the hardest-boiled was surely Mickey Spillane. Mike Hammer, the private eye Spillane introduced in his first book, *I, the Jury*, in 1947, wasn't just another bruised urban romantic, a knight in corroded armor like Raymond Chandler's Philip Marlowe. Hammer was a brute. Mayhem was his business, and justice, sneeringly meted out to the human scum among whom he moved, was whatever he decided it to be.

Spillane is the presiding spirit of the *Sin City* comic books that Frank Miller began writing and drawing in the early 1990s—stories in which scantily clad women get smacked around and sometimes like it and a prolonged bloody beating is likely to be the least of a protagonist's torments. Spillane's pungent idiom (presenting a buxom barroom babe, for example, as "a tomato in a dress that was too tight a year ago") echoes throughout the *Sin City* stories. One of their battered antiheroes, the blockheaded Marv, even looks like Mickey Spillane (who actually played Mike Hammer in a 1963 film version of one of his novels).

What made the *Sin City* comics an instant sensation in the fanboy subculture was not just Miller's mastery of the literary elements of the hard-boiled world—its relentless violence, barbed-wire dialogue, and bleak emotional landscape—but his innovative artwork. His *Sin City* panels—bursting with muscular black-and-white imagery and raked with striations that suggested antique Japanese woodcuts—were a bold achievement in comic-book art. Three of these stories—*The Hard Goodbye*, *The Big Fat Kill*, and *That Yellow Bastard*—are now the basis of a technically arresting movie by Robert Rodriquez (with Miller himself brought on board and credited as codirector). But the film's central effect is to force us to confront the fundamental nature of what Miller's comics pass off, in a more distanced way, as kinky, retro-hip kicks. It's not a pretty picture.

After a brief introductory sequence that's essentially an homage to the famous final scene in Spillane's *I, the Jury*, Rodriguez starts parading Miller's three stories past us. These brutal tales all take place in grubby, corrupt Sin City, and they're united by sadism. Bruce Willis plays an honest cop at the end of his career who's determined to rescue a little girl from a vicious sex maniac (the reliably repellent Nick Stahl). Mickey Rourke, walled off behind a mask of prosthetic rubber, is the brutish, Quasimodo-like Marv, who's determined to avenge the only woman who's ever shown him any kindness. (A whore, of course, who's been murdered, of course.) And Clive Owen, in an odd haircut whose damp bangs flap limply on his forehead, is a journalist of some sort in pursuit of a rotten cop called Jackie Boy (Benicio Del Toro, with a screwy prosthetic leer), who's on his way with a pack of drunken bootboys to the "Old Town" district of Sin City, there to wreak havoc on its female inhabitants. (All whores, of course.)

The movie's violence—the endless beatings of bound and helpless men, the smashing of women's faces, the whipping of a young girl in a flimsy slip, the repeated plunging of a man's head into a colorfully unflushed toilet, the hacking of heads and limbs, and the unprecedented sight of a man's genitals being grabbed and ripped right off his body—is so unrelentingly demented that when somebody pauses to punch out a hapless dog, it's almost a Disney moment.

Rodriguez makes much of the fact that, through digital simulation and the draining of color from the images (leaving only the occasional flash of an emerald eye or a crimson puddle of blood), he has precisely replicated Miller's canonical, hypernoir environments from the comics. (The actors performed on empty soundstages; the nonexistent surroundings were later injected by computers.) Rodriguez says this as if he thinks no one saw last year's *Sky Captain and the World of Tomorrow*, which presented a richer and more resonant synthetic world. *Sin City* is all style, but, by design, it's all Frank Miller's style. Miller already directed the film in his original drawings, and so apart from blocking the shots and angling the camera and signing the checks for the CGI guys, it's hard to discern the substance of Rodriguez's contribution. He's certainly cemented his status as fanboy number one, though.

I like movie violence as much as the next person. But I like it to have more snap and tingle than this sense-deadening slop. Rodriguez has transferred Miller's comics to the screen with an iron literality. The images now move, but they don't go anywhere. The picture is stuck in Sin City. And for two hours and ten bucks and no good reason, so are we. (April 2005)

The Spirit

Darkman

With his new movie, *Sin City 2*, Frank Miller does a strange disservice to the work of the late Will Eisner. Miller reveres Eisner (he published a book of conversations with the older man in 2005, shortly after Eisner's death), but then most comic-book artists do. Eisner brought a new mood to the comic-book panel; he was the creator of the eye-grabbing "splash page" and the godfather of the graphic novel. And the Spirit—that noirish urban crime fighter with the bitty mask and the big fedora—was his most famous creation. But in bringing this character to the screen, Miller, as both writer and director, has imposed his own muscle-bound graphic style on Eisner's more pliant comic-book world and practically obliterated it. The movie is actually called *The Spirit*, of course, but Eisner fans are likely to be puzzled.

This wouldn't matter much if the picture had a spirit of its own. But it lurches about in search of a narrative structure—it's a procession of splash-page set pieces. They look great; but as was the case with *Sin City*, Miller's first film foray (on which he was credited as codirector with Robert Rodriguez), the dark, airless digital environments in this movie, with their drained colors and black-slab nightscapes, soon grow monotonous. And the story's not strong enough to stand up under the oppressive stylization.

In Eisner's comics of the 1940s and early 1950s, the Spirit battled many villains. Here, blandly portrayed by Gabriel Macht, he's up against just one of them: the Octopus. In the comics, this character was little more than a set of evil eyes and gloved hands—he was never fully revealed. In the movie he's revealed to be Samuel L. Jackson, which turns out to be another problem. Jackson brings what have become his usual psycho-badass mannerisms to the part, and Miller is disinclined to rein them in. The result is Jackson's most embarrassingly self-indulgent performance, an extended eruption of hambone megalomania. (When the Spirit tells the Octopus, "I'm gonna kill you all kinds of dead," you *so* wish you could help out.)

The Octopus is determined to lay his hands on a vase containing the blood of the mythological (and therefore presumably bloodless) Heracles. Assisting him in this quest are his hot science-girl sidekick, Silken Floss (Scarlett Johansson) and a bevy of chuckling cloned thugs (all played by Louis Lombardi). The Spirit gets backup from Central City's top cop, Commissioner Dolan (Dan Lauria), who knows his real identity, and from Dolan's smart, perky daughter, Ellen (Sarah Paulson). Complicating matters are the mysterious Sand Saref (Eva Mendes)—the Spirit's childhood sweetheart, long since gone bad—and such ambient babes as Plaster of Paris (Paz Vega) and Lorelei Rox (Jaime King). All of the women in the picture melt into puddles of adulation at the Spirit's approach, which is odd: Macht has been directed to give such a limp, jokey performance that the rest of the movie practically runs him over.

Some of the scenes, like an extended Spirit-Octopus beatdown, sprawl and sputter. Others, like the one in which we see Jackson and Johansson suddenly marching around in Nazi regalia, come out of nowhere and quickly return there. Johansson gives her lines a nice sarcastic spin, and Mendes is suitably steamy, but all of the actors are underserved by the director, who seems to have been preoccupied with the film's visual design. Miller is certainly a filmmaker who knows what he wants to do. Why he had to do it to the Spirit is a question he really ought to be asked. (December 2008)

The Losers

Trouble Boys

The Losers is the kind of action movie in which two bikini babes can inexplicably pop up in the middle of a firefight and everybody on-screen is too busy dying to even notice. It's also the kind of action movie in which the sight of a helicopter being shot down while carrying small children to safety is followed by a close-up of a teddy bear smoldering in the wreckage. I'm not sure exactly what kind of action movie that is, but this is it.

It's a comic-book picture (Andy Diggle's Vertigo series ran from 2003 to 2006), but one that's a little too short on wild satire (as opposed to peppery one-liners) to be outrageous fun and a little too under-funded to offer any really rousing fireballs or other techno-tumult. The premise—good-bad guys versus bad-bad guys—is hardly new, and here it's muddled with outré James Bond elements. If it weren't for some of the actors, the film would collapse into its unbridled commotion.

Jeffrey Dean Morgan (of *Watchmen*) plays Colonel Clay, the leader of a CIA team of black-ops specialists on a drug-lord hit mission in the Bolivian jungle who are betrayed by a scheming government sleaze called Max (Jason Patric). Clay's men are the usual assortment of dark-arts wizards, adept at demolition, assassination, and computer hijinks. There's the wisecracking Jensen (Chris Evans), the paranoid Roque (Idris Elba), the sweet-natured Pooch (Columbus Short), and the squinty-eyed Cougar (Óscar Jaenada). The boys have gone to ground in a jungle village, soaking up the local cockfights and bar floozies, when they're approached by the mysterious Aisha (Zoe Saldana, of *Avatar*), a pistol-packing beauty so kick-ass that "the CIA has a standing kill order on her." Aisha offers to smuggle the vengeful team back to the States (in dummy coffins, no problem) and lead them to the conniving Max, whose luxurious lair is located in Los Angeles. Clay, who has a taste for dangerous women, agrees to this, and off they all go.

The movie is dimmed by a certain geographical homogeneity. Apart from the Miami sequences—including an implausible South Beach assault in which a giant chopper-borne magnet lifts a truck right up off the street (pure Bond)—the bulk of the movie was shot in Puerto Rico, which has to do double duty as Mumbai, Dubai, Houston, and New Mexico, as well as Bolivia and L.A. (The various faux locations are distinguished by highway-style signs awkwardly embedded in the imagery.) Some scenes look as if they were shot on random construction sites.

There's also the plot, which is unclear even by action-movie standards. There's some business about a "sonic dematerializer" (capable of sinking whole islands into the sea), and some "next-generation" weapons called "snukes," and millions of dollars that have gone missing (many of them into Aisha's personal bank account). If the action were more engaging, this narrative jumble might not matter. But it matters.

Fortunately, Morgan grounds the movie (as best he can) with his grizzled charm, and Evans contributes some lively comic riffs. Best of all, maybe, is Patric, whose supercilious Max is a camp megalomaniac in the classic Bondian mode, dementedly bent on world domination (or at least on "engineering a global terrorist conflict") and determined to do it with maximum flamboyance. (At one point we see him swanning around on a beach with a pretty subordinate scurrying alongside holding a parasol over his head. When she falters in the sand, he shoots her in the face.) Patric is a hoot in this role (he seems to be channeling the sniffy Dirk Bogarde villain in the 1960s spy spoof *Modesty Blaise*), but his character would be more at home in a different movie. Here, Max throws the rest of the film's familiar action-flick derring-do into unflattering relief. In an attempted sequel setup at the end, Clay says, "I'll be seein' you, Max." Given the low wattage of most of what's come before, though, we doubt that he, or we, ever will. (April 2010)

The Incredible Hulk

Anger Management

Nobody much cared for Ang Lee's take on the Hulk five years ago—too thoughtful. So Marvel Comics—now rolling out movies on its own without the annoyance of studio partners siphoning off profits—is taking another shot. This time, the accent is on damage, as it should be. Psychological complexities and other distractions are presumably being held for *Ghost Rider 2*, which I'm afraid actually is in the pipeline. But let's not torment ourselves.

Anyone even glancingly familiar with the last forty-six years of Hulk lore will need no prep to grasp *The Incredible Hulk*. Research scientist Dr. Bruce Banner (Edward Norton this time out) is still plagued by the effects of a gamma-ray overdose that turns him into a rampaging mass of angry green muscles whenever he gets upset—or even when he thinks a little too heatedly about his girlfriend, Betty Ross (Liv Tyler). As the movie opens, Banner is hiding out in Brazil, studying martial arts in an effort to keep his pesky temper under control and trading encrypted e-mails in his off hours with a scientist back in the States named Sterns (Tim Blake Nelson), who's working on a Hulk antidote. Banner is on the down-low because a megalomaniacal U.S. Army general called "Thunderbolt" Ross (William Hurt) is hot on his trail. Ross—who is also Betty's father, talk about a bummer—wants to use whatever it is that ails Banner to create a legion of "supersoldiers" for purposes that may not be altogether well intentioned. Spearheading Ross's search for the young physicist is a psycho subordinate named Emil Blonsky (Tim Roth).

I know it's pointless to nitpick superhero movies, in which plausibility is a suspect notion, but I had a problem with Blonsky. First of all, he was born in Russia and raised in England—and yet he's now a captain in the U.S. Army (not just attached to it, in the manner of Peter

Sellers's Captain Mandrake in *Dr. Strangelove*). He also has longish hair and Hollywood-issue face stubble, and he slouches around as if there were twenty pounds of rocks sewn into the seams of his disheveled uniform. If the writers (Zak Penn and Norton himself) were determined to make this character such a schlub, they might have used his slovenliness to explain why Blonsky is still only a captain at the advanced age of thirty-eight. But no: Blonsky claims that the reason he hasn't been promoted is that he doesn't *want* to be—he's a fighter, not a desk jockey. Please. If Blonsky were so intent on being a warrior, why didn't he just become an enlisted man? It's the grunts who do most of the fighting.

While we're on the subject of implausibility, I must also say that I found the computer-generated Hulk to be insufficiently cool. Obviously it's difficult to weave a humongous green guy into live action in any completely convincing way; but this big-screen iteration of the Hulk is pure video game. Speaking of which, so is a lot of the mayhem—especially an endless street smackdown between the Hulk and Blonsky's own savage alter ego, the Abomination. Cars go hurtling through the air, rockets are fired, snarling behemoths swat them away. Didn't *Cloverfield* already do this with about one-fifth of the budget?

Even Norton is problematic here. Being such a fine actor, he's overqualified for a simple monster romp. He brings fresh gestures and shades of feeling to his character; but especially in the first third of the movie (which is a little slow), this emotional filagree takes up room that might be filled more enjoyably with damage.

In any case, the actor who ends up owning the movie is Robert Downey Jr. He's only in it for a minute, at the end, and he's not even credited; but when he strolls up to General Ross in a barroom, deploying his Tony Stark persona from *Iron Man*, and announces that he's "putting a team together"—well, you realize that this okay-but-not-great movie is only a way station en route to that most tantalizing of Marvel Comics destinations, *The Avengers*. Four years and counting. (June 2008)

300

Exiled in Guyville

Robert Rodriguez's *Sin City* was an eye-frying accomplishment—the movie lifted Frank Miller's stark noir fantasy world up off the comic-book page and deposited it straight into your face. Zack Snyder's film version of *300*—Miller's 1998 graphic-novel re-creation of the bloody battle of Thermopylae in 480 B.C.—surpasses that feat considerably. Snyder's movie actually improves upon Miller's celebrated graphics. Here, the shadows are denser, the colors more intensely concentrated. Every image throbs with drama—even the steely, shifting skies are troubled and turbulent. You feel you're truly in another world. The film's concerns, like those of Miller's book, are narrow: it seeks only to submerge you in a sea of heroic brutality. It does just that one thing, but it does it with feverish expertise.

The story recounts the invasion of ancient Greece by an enormous army, a quarter-million-men strong, under the command of the Persian god-king Xerxes (Rodrigo Santoro). Several thousand Greeks, few of them seasoned soldiers, hasten to the narrow mountain pass at Thermopylae, hoping to obtain from this cramped corridor a tactical advantage over the enemy's sheer numbers. For two days they manage to repel the invaders. On the third day, a treacherous shepherd betrays the Greeks' position, and as the Persians climb up behind and begin to surround them, the leader of the defenders' most battle-hardened contingent, the Spartan king Leonidas (Gerard Butler), sends the bulk of the Greek forces home to mount rearguard defenses while he and his three hundred men remain at Thermopylae to fight on against impossible odds, to a guaranteed death.

Snyder has watered the testosterone in which Miller's comic series was marinated with some less ferocious diversions. He cuts away from the battle occasionally to return to Sparta, where Leonidas' wife, Queen Gorgo (Lena Headey), struggles to foil the treachery of a duplicitous councilman named Theron (Dominic West). There's also some lurid debauchery in a harem and a visit to a mountaintop where a group of hideous degenerate priests contemplate the erotic writhings of a beautiful young Oracle. (One of them stoops to lick her head with his diseased tongue—nice.) Apart from those moments, though, the movie is all blood and guts and raging spectacle. Spears rip through chests, heads fly off necks, and gouts of blood spurt through the air. There's a tree filled with arrow-pierced corpses and a wall of bodies stacked fifteen feet high, waiting to be pushed over onto unsuspecting Persians. The mayhem is hyperstylish and unburdened by deep thought or serious issues.

Chief among the movie's indelible images is the nine-foot-tall Xerxes himself, who is carried into battle on a platform, complete with throne, by a detachment of Immortals—a particularly vicious breed of soldiers in eerie silver masks and black turbans. With his shaved chest and plucked brows, and his baubles, bangles, and nose rings, Xerxes exudes a sexual presence that's too deliriously campy to qualify as ambiguous, and he brings a giddy frisson to every scene he's in. Equally memorable is his monstrous executioner, a flesh-mountain of a man whose forearms have been honed into blades. And there's an extraordinary sequence in which Xerxes' invading fleet of ships is swallowed up by the sea, a high-tech advance in big-screen naval imagery.

It's great that there's so much to watch in *300,* because there's not a lot to contemplate. The story seeks to elucidate a single idea: that some things are worth not only fighting for but dying for; that selfless heroism is a core value of human civilization. It's hard to argue with this, although occasionally you might long for a little elaboration, if not nuance. But then another severed head goes flying by, and the thought passes. (March 2007)

Surrogates

Double Trouble

In *Surrogates*, nobody goes to work anymore, or even leaves the house much. Instead, lifelike robo-mannequins are dispatched to undertake the day's business while their operators sit at home with headsets and watch. These surrogates tend toward white-bread perfection—blonder of hair, bluer of eye, and hotter of bod than their owners—and they can also be purchased in any race (or gender) desired. Imagine the benefits, let alone the possibilities. Cops and combat soldiers would no longer need to risk their real lives. Communicable diseases would fade away, along with various sorts of prejudice. (That hot guy your surrogate just picked up in a club might actually be some leering lardo sprawled at home on his living room sofa.) Life—or at least "life"—would be good.

The movie makes significant alterations (mainly of gender and motivation) in the Robert Venditti comic books on which it's based; but these changes, for a change, actually enhance the story. Bruce Willis plays Greer, a veteran FBI agent, and Radha Mitchell is Peters, his partner. Like everyone else, they send their pretty, glazed surrogates to the office every day, while their authentic selves—older and more life-worn—monitor the action remotely. Their latest case involves the murder—well, the destruction—of a pair of sexy young surrogates by a killer using a mysterious weapon that also snuffed out the surrys' operators at home. (According to the manufacturer, a sinister enterprise called VSI, this was supposed to be impossible.)

The two agents soon become involved with Canter (James Cromwell), the shadowy creator of surrogate technology, and with a dreadlocked anti-surry firebrand called the Prophet (Ving Rhames), who's determined to eradicate it. There's also a hotshot programmer named Bobby (Devin Ratray), whose cutting-edge software could save the ever-darkening day, and an FBI honcho named Stone (Boris Kodjoe), who's even more unlike what he seems than is usual in this shifting world. The investigation takes an unexpected twist after a hell-bent chase in which Greer's surrogate is destroyed, forcing Greer himself to take over the case in the flesh.

Director Jonathan Mostow (*Terminator 3: Rise of the Machines*) knows how to stage maximum-wreckage action sequences (with pronounced *Terminator* overtones), and he's added some cute passing details not present in the comics, like the surrogate recharge booths we glimpse on a street corner. But he never roils the story's despairing mood with standard FX uproar. Greer's melancholy home life is movingly depicted (his aging wife, played by Rosamund Pike, stays locked in her bedroom while her forever-young surrogate keeps the disconsolate Greer company); and there's a wonderful moment when Greer's own surrogate returns home after a taxing day, pours a drink for the real Greer, still zoned out next to his operating gear, and then retires to his surry storage cabinet like a self-hanging suit.

Willis is allowed to act in this movie (he's not just another action android), and, as usual when given the opportunity, he's expertly effective. His Greer is a man slowly waking from a terrible dream. He's beginning to register the horror of the surrogate phenomenon—the way in which people have happily outsourced their humanity to high-tech automatons (there's also a new line of surrys in the works for children), and the impossibility of ever knowing who you're really dealing with in the world of surrogate interaction. The movie is a mystery thriller filled with sleek computerized doppelgängers, but it's really about the pleasures of the flesh. (September 2009)

Wanted

Bullet Time

Here we have a movie that is not a remake. Remember those? And while *Wanted is* a comic-book movie, the director, Kazakh filmmaker Timur Bekmambetov, has wisely dumped a lot of the schoolboy nihilism that made Mark Millar's six-issue miniseries a disagreeable read. The picture has other problems, but at least they're fairly original ones.

The plot: James McAvoy plays Wes, a Chicago office drone who hates his loser life: the dead-end job, the hump-busting boss, the whiny girlfriend who's boffing his best pal. Stopping by a drugstore one night, Wes is accosted by an exotic stranger called Fox (Angelina Jolie), who informs him that his father, whom he'd thought long dead, was in fact alive until yesterday. "The man who killed him is behind you," she says, shifting her eyes toward a sinister figure back among the shampoos and ointments.

There follows a wild shootout-and-car-chase sequence featuring some of the most enormous guns in the history of big-screen pandemonium. The killer, a guy named Cross (Thomas Kretschmann), escapes, and eventually Fox hauls the now-battered Wes off to a dilapidated textile mill, which turns out to be the headquarters of an ancient fraternity of assassins. These hit folk—bear with me—trace their origin back a thousand years to a group of medieval weavers, who discovered within the warp and weft of the cloth produced by their magical loom a binomial code revealing the names of dangerous people who needed to be preemptively rubbed out before they could fulfill their evil destiny. Transported to Chicago, the loom is still weaving today, and the rubouts continue. Okay. Wes's late dad was a member of this homicidal elite—in fact, he was the best of them—and the time has come for Wes

to embrace his lethal heritage, join the team, and track down and terminate the elusive Cross. All of this in the service of maintaining a "balance of justice" in the world. Something like that.

Bekmambetov, best known for the Russian neo-vampire movies
Night Watch and *Day Watch*, here helms his first big-budget English-
language film. He is a director for whom the term "over the top" is a goal,
not a shortcoming. Some of his action effects would surely make a bang-
boom specialist like Michael Bay quiver with admiration. I don't think
I've seen anything quite like the moment when Angelina Jolie, at the
wheel of a hot red kill-mobile, comes screeching sideways toward James
McAvoy and scoops him up through the open passenger-side door like a
jai alai ball. Or the wonderfully preposterous sequence in which McAvoy
is blocked from blowing away a bad guy by the bulletproof windows of
the man's limo, and Jolie, once again at the wheel, stomps the gas and
rolls their car up and *over* the limo so that McAvoy can shoot the creep
upside-down through an open sunroof.

Great stuff. Too bad the director seems interested in little else beyond virtuoso mayhem—after an hour or so, *we* start feeling blown
away. And I kind of wish Bekmambetov hadn't dropped one of the
more enjoyable elements of the comics—in which the assassins are actually a league of supervillains, complete with costumes—and had instead toned down Wes's assassin-training regimen, which entails an
endless series of brutal, bloody beatings. Bekmambetov isn't much of a
stylist, either. So, while the movie owes a large debt to *The Matrix* (lots
of slo-mo "bullet time," among other things), he's unable to approximate that film's sleek visual design. I also found it a little difficult to
accept McAvoy as a seething action man (I can't dispell the memory of
his simpering faun in the first *Chronicles of Narnia* movie), and even
harder to buy Morgan Freeman, of all people, as the head assassin. And
it's not much fun to see the vibrant Angelina Jolie trapped within a character as inexpressive as the stone-faced Fox.

Bekmambetov has a flamboyant talent for this sort of picture, no arguing that; and *Wanted* is certainly more rousing than many another action movie unspooling at the omniplex right now. But the film's agitated

camerawork and one-note cacophony grow monotonous; and while its conclusion leaves open the possibility of a sequel, I suspect that open is what it'll remain. (June 2008)

Stardust

Slack Magic

Stardust is an attempted magical fantasy with so much going for it— splashy cast, budget-gobbling digital designs—that you wonder while you watch it why it isn't going anywhere more, well, magical. Based on Neil Gaiman's 1997 comics series, the movie is stuffed with wonders— all manner of witches and spells and general faerie whatnot, plus a sky-borne pirate ship that sails the bounding clouds. But the story sprawls, and it's sometimes confusing (seven scheming princes, with names ranging from Primus to Septimus, are especially hard to keep track of). There are some funny moments, and director Matthew Vaughn, who cowrote the script, also works up some expensively impressive images. (Although even the best of these, the aerial inventions, were just as imaginatively conveyed in the low-budget *Sky Captain and the World of Tomorrow*.) The movie's intended sense of enchantment never achieves real wonder, which leaves it stranded in the lowlands of whimsy.

The story is set in Olden Times (the late 1830s, in Gaiman's original tale), in the English country village of Wall, so named for the stone barricade that separates it from the magical kingdom of Stormhold next door. A young man named Tristan (Charlie Cox) longs to win the heart of a local beauty named Victoria (Sienna Miller), and as a token of his devotion vows to catch a falling star for her. He boldly crosses the wall into Stormhold to do this. Meanwhile, the king of Stormhold (Peter O'Toole) is dying, and his sons are contending with one another to inherit his crown. (Some of the brothers have already been dispatched by their more ruthless siblings, but the deceased hang around as a sort of ghostly black-and-white chorus.) The princes' expiring father decrees that whichever one of them can locate a lost ruby necklace shall be the next monarch, and off they ride in search of it.

Tristan finds the star he needs, but it turns out really to be a beautiful girl named Yvaine (Claire Danes), who's fallen to Earth with the ruby necklace in her possession. Three witches hear about this star-girl's arrival, and they determine to capture her and cut out her heart in order to restore their own vanished beauty. One of these cackling hags, Lamia (Michelle Pfeiffer), is selected to undertake the mission and is made temporarily presentable with the remaining shreds of the last heart she and her sisters secured for this purpose long ago. Much chasing, curse casting, and flame hurling ensue, and then ensue some more. Director Vaughn knows how to keep this cinematic contraption rattling along; getting it to stop, though, was clearly a problem. (The movie is just over two hours long.)

The actors are generally engaging and seem to be having fun. Michelle Pfeiffer brings diva authority to her witchy machinations. (Every time she works some magic, she loses a bit of her borrowed beauty. At one point, she casts a spell and her boobs sag.) And Claire Danes, who bears a distracting resemblance to Gwyneth Paltrow here, has a fine celestial deportment (stressed a little too nudgingly, perhaps, with an overlay of digital glow). Mark Strong brings a dashing caddishness to the role of Prince Septimus, the most dogged of Yvaine's royal pursuers; and Ricky Gervais, as Ferdy the Fence, dealer in stolen lightning bolts, gathers up his two brief scenes in a big silly beaver hat and walks off with them.

Unfortunately, there are some crucially weak links in the cast, too. Charlie Cox is a suitably handsome lead, but his appeal seems a little too unformed at this point to anchor such a star-filled picture. Much worse yet, Robert De Niro has taken Gaiman's kindly Captain Alberic, leader of the sky pirates, and turned him, for no reason at all, into Captain Shakespeare, a mincing transvestite, complete with red boa, petticoats, and fluttery fan. This could be the most grotesque performance of De Niro's career; it's flabbergastingly unfunny.

In the *Stardust* production notes, the filmmakers unwisely cite *The*

Princess Bride as a model for their own picture—a ruinous comparison. Not only was that 1987 film incomparable in its limber wit and larky charm, it was also half an hour shorter than this one. In fact, you might want to rent *The Princess Bride* and watch it again. It'll give you something to do instead of watching this. (August 2007)

Coraline

Mommy Dearest

Henry Selick's *Coraline* puts 3-D technology to glorious new use. Turning away from the cliché poke-in-the-eye thrills of many previous 3-D films, this sumptuous stop-motion picture—truly years in the making—uses the form to draw us deep into the complex layers of its animated world, where we marvel at the gemlike colors and swirling perspectives. That the picture was created one painstaking film frame at a time adds another dimension of wonder.

The movie is based on the 2002 fantasy novel by Neil Gaiman. Gaiman is an admirer of Selick's *The Nightmare Before Christmas* and *James and the Giant Peach,* the two stop-motion movies the director made under the aegis of his friend Tim Burton. So as soon as the author had finished the manuscript for *Coraline*, he sent it to Selick—a fine idea, as we now see.

The story has a rich emotional core. Coraline Jones (voiced in the film by Dakota Fanning) is an eleven-year-old girl who has just moved with her parents from Michigan to a remote and rambling old house in Oregon. Her mom (Teri Hatcher) and dad (John Hodgman) are writers, preoccupied with deadlines and bookish contemplation. Coraline, friendless in her new surroundings, feels neglected. A bumbling local boy named Wybie (Robert Bailey Jr.) makes himself available for acquaintance as Coraline scouts the nearby hills and fields, but she rejects him as an annoyance. There are also two apartments in the new house, and their occupants are exceedingly strange: a pair of ancient vaudeville ladies called Miss Spink (Jennifer Saunders) and Miss Forcible (Dawn French), and, on the top floor, a bulbous Russian, Mr. Bobinsky (Ian McShane), who maintains an elaborate mouse circus and feasts on beets.

Wandering through the rooms of her new home one day, Coraline discovers a small door that opens onto a brick wall. Later, in a dream, she makes her way through the door and crawls down a long passageway into what turns out to be an alternate world, complete with much-improved versions of her parents. The Other Mother here has all the time in the world to cook wonderful things for Coraline, and Other Father is endlessly attentive to her wants and desires. They're perfect. ("Everything is right in this world," her second dad says.) Oddly, though, both of these ideal elders have black buttons installed where their eyes should be.

Coraline shuttles back and forth between the two worlds—sometimes in the company of a droll cat (Keith David), who sometimes speaks. When Other Mother suddenly demands that Coraline remain in this new world—and be equipped with button eyes of her own—the picture takes on a tone of lyrical dread.

The movie's wonders begin with Coraline herself. She's not the saucer-eyed cutie of so many animated fantasies, but a budding punkette of very contemporary spirit (and blue hair). And the new world she moves through is a riot of visual delights: ridable grasshoppers, incandescent night gardens, and a fantastical piano that plays its player. There's also an extended mouse-circus scene with Bobinsky and his lively rodents that required more than two months to animate and must surely establish a new benchmark in stop-motion filmmaking; and a spectacular theatrical performance by the two ancient neighbor ladies— before a large audience of carefully individualized Scottish terriers— that can only be seen, not adequately described.

Early stop-motion films—most famously those animated by Willis O'Brien (the 1933 *King Kong*) and later by Ray Harryhausen (the 1958 *Seventh Voyage of Sinbad*)—had a herky-jerky dynamic that's now a part of their charm. Selick's film—each minute of which required nearly a week to create—has a seamless flow, down to its last drift of fluttering fabric and pane of delicately dusty glass. It's a movie of consummate technique that vividly evokes the terrors of childhood. Is it too dark and scary for children? (When Other Mother suddenly rears up in hideous fury, you know you've left the nursery.) Maybe, a little bit. But as any kid will tell you, that's a recommendation. (February 2009)

Jonah Hex

Dead Man Walking

Jonah Hex is about as anti- as a hero can get. It's not just his chewed-up cowboy hat, his bullet-riddled duster, and his perma-surly disposition. It's the melted skin running down one side of his face and the ugly flesh hole next to his mouth (which makes whiskey drinking a messy enterprise, but not—as we see just before he shoots up a barroom full of bad guys—an impossible one).

In distilling thirty-eight years' worth of DC comics for *Jonah Hex*, the new movie, director Jimmy Hayward and his writers have produced a lumpy soup of western action and supernatural shenanigans, heavily spiked with narrative confusion. The story leaps back and forth in time, and while the picture is sometimes funny, possibly intentionally, at some points it's anybody's guess what's going on.

In playing Jonah, Josh Brolin is stuck with a character whose facial constriction reduces him to little more than a walking bad attitude—he's like Clint Eastwood's Man with No Name in the old Sergio Leone westerns, but without the warmth.

The time is just after the Civil War (at least when it's not *during* the Civil War). We learn that Jonah was framed for the betrayal of his Confederate battle unit, which resulted in the death of his friend, Jeb Turnbull (Jeffrey Dean Morgan). Jeb's demented father, Quentin (John

Malkovich in full cuckoo mode), retaliated by killing Jonah's wife and son and disfiguring Jonah's face with a red-hot branding iron. Now (or sometimes now) Jonah roams the West as a badass bounty hunter, his only love connection a beautiful whore named Lilah (Megan Fox). When Ulysses S. Grant (Aidan Quinn), president of the newly reunited States, learns that Turnbull is creating a "superweapon" that will be a "nation killer," he recruits Jonah to stop him.

Our battered hero is well equipped to do so. After a close call with death some years back, Jonah was left with one foot in the spirit world; and so while he spends much of the movie being shot and beaten, he appears to be unkillable. He's also attended by a pack of hellhounds ("I wouldn't try to pet 'em if I was you") and has the useful gift of bringing dead men back to life with a touch of his hand. ("I'm sorry I killed you," he tells one corpse, after raising him from the grave. Says the dead guy: "I'd better be getting back underground.") Jonah also has a taste for esoteric weaponry—saddle-mounted Gatling guns, dynamite-firing crossbow pistols—and a talent for dodging bullets by simply leaning back a bit to let them fly by (past our madly rolling eyes). The lovely Lilah is no slouch in the slick department, either: when she and Jonah are handcuffed to an overhead pole, the cuffs suddenly snap free and she brandishes a lock pick. "My mama didn't raise no fool," she says. (To which we reply, "What the hell?")

Despite the picture's wall-to-wall uproar—train-jackings, bullet storms, incessant detonations—there's little excitement to it. The action is furious from the outset and remains at that level throughout, diluting its intended effect. And the dialogue, which I take to be satirical, doesn't mesh with the film's heavy violence. Like its half-dead protagonist, the movie never comes completely alive. (June 2010)

30 Days of Night

Tired Blood

Steve Niles's *30 Days of Night* comic-book series, which got under way in 2002, worked a new twist on the vampire genre. In the opening issues, a group of hungry bloodsuckers discovered the existence of Barrow, Alaska, the northernmost town in the United States. Since the sun deserted this remote habitation for one whole month every year (in the comic, anyway), the light-loathing vampires decided to travel to Barrow and spend those thirty sunless days feasting on the locals.

It's a fun premise, but of course limited: vampires attack; townsfolk die; survivors hide, flee, hide somewhere else; and so on. To keep the series stalking along, Niles added interwoven subplots, the first of which involved a survivor of the Barrow slaughter who escaped to Los Angeles and tried to raise anti-vampire consciousness. This and subsequent narrative elaborations effectively fended off monotony.

Unfortunately, in the new movie adaptation of *30 Days of Night* (which Niles had a hand in scripting), the filmmakers have been forced by the time constraint to focus exclusively on the Barrow invasion. Since the picture runs nearly two hours, the continual gut ripping and face chewing and scampering and holing up soon become very monotonous, and we start to notice things like the actors' breath, which sometimes is seen to be condensing in the cold air and sometimes isn't. There's also the vampire language, an approximately Balkan tongue (they sound like they're gagging on a cheek steak), which was a source of audible amusement among the audience with which I saw the movie.

Being limited to killing, dying, or fleeing, there's not much the actors can do with their characters. Josh Hartnett brings his usual bland amiability to the role of Eben Oleson, the Barrow sheriff, and Melissa George is very blond (and feisty, too) as his wife, Stella. But even fitted out with barracuda fangs and splatters of blood, Danny Huston seems too nice a fellow to be the vicious head vampire, Marlow (a name that makes you wonder why he doesn't speak English). Mark Boone Junior brings snorts of life to the picture as an angrily resistant Barrow resident, but he's lost in all the hide-and-seek commotion. And while Ben Foster, as a sort of vampire advance man, briefly enlivens the film with his mad-eyed malevolence, he's not around long enough to salvage this oddly lifeless enterprise.

Director David Slade—whose last movie, the bracingly nasty *Hard Candy*, couldn't have been more different from this one if it were a musical set in Bermuda—maintains an atmosphere of shivery tension in the beginning. But he's too faithful to the sometimes incoherent visual style of the comics (which were drawn by Ben Templesmith), and so a lot of the vampire-attack action amounts to little more than repetitions of bloody, snarling violence. In addition, a big-deal confrontation between two powerful vampires turns out to be nothing more than a routine action-flick smackdown. The final scene, a lyrical blend of love and sunburn, is nicely done. But by then our interest has drained away. (October 2007)

The Green Hornet

Buzzkill

A superhero movie can be smart, funny, and action-packed, too—*Kick-Ass* demonstrated that. Smart-ass, jokey, and loud, however, isn't the same thing. Which is what *The Green Hornet* demonstrates.

Although Sony denies it, one can imagine the studio's dismay upon first seeing this mess. The picture was originally scheduled for release last summer; then, in order to (what else?) convert it into 3-D, it was rescheduled for December 23, in the midst of the profitable holiday season. Now, here it finally is, in the depths of January. Where it belongs.

The movie's setup—wealthy newspaper publisher turns masked crime fighter in league with his Asian chauffeur sidekick—remains unchanged from the story's origin in 1930s radio and its subsequent iterations in comic books, movie serials, and a one-season 1960s TV show (which introduced Bruce Lee as the sidekick). A feature-film version has been in the works for years, with George Clooney, Nicolas Cage, Kevin Smith, and Hong Kong action-comedy director Stephen Chow attached at various points. What we have here, at long last, is a movie directed by the whimsical Michel Gondry (fondly known for *Eternal Sunshine of the Spotless Mind*, not so fondly for the wifty *Science of Sleep*); scripted by Seth Rogen and his writing partner, Evan Goldberg (they also wrote the superior Rogen vehicles *Superbad* and *Pineapple Express*); and starring Rogen as the crime-fighting publisher, Britt Reid, and Taiwanese pop star–actor Jay Chou as Kato, the sidekick. Chou, despite sometimes indistinct line readings, brings charm and energy to the proceedings; Rogen brings Rogen, and not a lot else, which is one of the picture's several problems.

The movie opens with some quick backstory. Browbeaten as a kid by his rich father (Tom Wilkinson), Britt grows up into a bratty wastrel, devoting his life to drunken carousing. When his dad suddenly dies of a mysterious bee sting, Britt decides to shape up. He begins to take an interest in the family newspaper, the *Daily Sentinel*, as a vehicle for exposing crime and corruption. Then, after an encounter with some street thugs, he decides on a more direct approach. Teaming with Kato, the family retainer, auto mechanic, and gadget-meister, he dons a disguise—a small black mask and vintage fedora, which disguise nothing—and becomes the Green Hornet, bringing vigilante justice to bear on the local crime lord, Chudnofsky (Christoph Waltz, setting aside the Oscar he won for *Inglourious Basterds* and giving the movie's wittiest performance).

Back at the *Daily Sentinel* offices, Britt soon acquires a new secretary, Lenore Case, played by Cameron Diaz. Lenore is a onetime journalism student who now improbably works as a temp. Okay. But she is also not the hot young babe Britt was hoping to hire. When she reveals her age, her new employer is crudely derisive: "Thirty-six?" Britt says.

"We'll have to build a ramp." This ungracious emphasis on the ten-year age difference between Rogen and Diaz (who's unflatteringly photographed to look weathered throughout), short-circuits whatever romantic interest might have leavened the boycentric plot, and leaves the story to sink beneath Gondry's rampant visual chaos—endless lashings of slo-mo kung fu and Britt-Kato bickering, and more gunfights, explosions, and woefully generic car chases than even a much better movie might bear. The tedium swells as the narrative dwindles.

Britt's throwback hat and mask suggest a more useful direction the movie might have taken. Would it not have been better as a cool retro yarn set in the period of the Hornet's origin, with snappier dialogue and a more noirish atmosphere? A comic-book movie is nothing without a style, and setting this one in the familiar environs of present-day L.A. buries it in blandness. Similarly, the Hornet character, lacking any tragic flaw of the Bruce Wayne variety, or superpowers along the lines of Peter Parker's, needs some sort of compensating brio. Rogen is never less than likable, but his trademark brand of funny, with its casual, throwaway delivery, is insufficient to create a vivid character. He ends up with no alternative but to play himself.

Special note must be made of the picture's pitiful 3-D conversion, which rivals that of *Clash of the Titans* for pure ineffectuality. You don the requisite 3-D glasses and then spend the rest of the movie wondering why you bothered. When the end credits—which were actually created in 3-D—finally roll, they really pop out at you, and you wonder why the whole movie didn't look like this. Then you wonder why the jokers responsible for such techno-flummery would think you should pay an extra five dollars for such a lackluster visual experience. Talk about crime lords. (January 2011)

LOOKING FOR LOVE

How frustrating is it to fall completely in love with a movie, and then to realize that no one else is going to see it, that it's slipped through the cracks of public awareness? And by the time you've managed to talk up one of these films to people you know, it's disappeared. You can blame this sort of thing on limp promotion, bad release-scheduling, or the fact that for most of every year there are just too many movies competing for people's attention (and that going to see them is just too expensive to allow for experimentation). But I've been heartened to discover that at least three of the films here—Sunshine, Zodiac, and The Fountain—have spawned enthusiastic cults. The rest await enthusiasts of their own.

The Fountain

Space Odyssey

In his dazzling new movie, *The Fountain*, director Darren Aronofsky reaches deep into the historical past and far out into the future to tell a story of endless love and its struggle against the constraints of human mortality. The picture is intoxicating—the images have a luminous psychedelic beauty—and the film's themes emerge elegantly out of the story's intricately looped trilevel structure. (Aronofsky wrote the screenplay from a story he created with Ari Handel.) It's a new kind of science-fiction movie and, unusually for that boys' club genre, possibly a great date movie, too. Mainly, though, as used to be said back in the Roger Corman days, it's a trip.

Unlike Stanley Kubrick, whose *2001: A Space Odyssey* this film might be said to resemble, Aronofsky has cast his picture with compelling actors. (For his *2001* leads, Kubrick settled for Keir Dullea and Gary Lockwood—two icons of inexpressiveness.) Hugh Jackman plays three incarnations of a character called Tom Creo; he's teamed at each stage of the story with Rachel Weisz, as Izzi, the woman he loves. We first see them in sixteenth-century Spain, where Izzi is the fictitious Queen Isabel and Tom is Tomas, her loyal conquistador. Isabel, who has been seeking the secret of eternal life, the fabled "fountain of youth," is menaced by the growing power of the Inquisition—the Grand Inquisitor has condemned her for heresy and vowed that she will die. But another loyal subject, a Franciscan monk named Father Avila (Mark Margolis), has just returned from the New World to report the existence of a tree of life, a Mayan *axis mundi* that unites Xibalba, the mythical Mayan underworld, with the earth and the heavens above. Isabel dispatches Tomas to return with Avila and a band of fellow conquistadors to find this tree, which, like the Tree of Life described in the biblical book of

Genesis, is thought to be a source of immortality. "When you return," Isabel tells Tomas, "I shall be your Eve, and together we shall live forever."

Five hundred years later—which is to say, now—research scientist Tommy Creo is desperately seeking a cure for the cancer that is killing his young wife, Izzi. He has learned of an ancient tree in Central America whose bark has properties that might be useful in combating the disease. But Izzi has already come to accept her death as a part of life, and she wishes that instead of frantically seeking a cure to save her, Tom would spend more time with her while she lives. She herself has been passing her remaining time writing a book about the Maya, called *The Fountain*. One night, while they're sitting on a rooftop with a telescope, she points out to Tom a nebula wrapped around a dying star. The Maya called it Xibalba, she says—the place where dead souls go to be reborn.

Shuttling ahead to the year 2600, we find Tom, a spiritual astronaut now, ascending through far galaxies in a globe-shaped spaceship that also contains a large tree—ascending toward Xibalba and the answer to the mortal question that has haunted him throughout his previous incarnations.

The Fountain is a movie of stunning imagery that reverberates ingeniously across the picture's millennial span: falling snow mirrors the stars falling away outside Tom's spaceship; rings of betrothal echo the rings of the Tree of Life. There's also a Mayan priest wielding a flaming sword (like the fiery sword the God of Genesis planted in the Garden of Eden after banishing Adam and Eve) that's a powerful symbolization of stark, primitive mysticism. The outer space effects are particularly inspired, creating a drifting, gelatinous aura through which Tom's ship rises like an intergalactic elevator. (They're the work of the Oscar-winning English micro-photographer and optical-systems developer Peter Parks, whose footage of petri-dish-size chemical reactions have been blown up to cosmic proportions—an eloquent effect.)

The Fountain isn't the sort of movie one might have expected from the man who made the harrowing 2000 drug-addiction elegy *Requiem for a Dream*. But then *Requiem* wasn't the sort of movie anyone would have expected from the maker of Aronofsky's first feature, the sci-fi noir *Pi*, either. The director's attempt to say something meaningful in such an emotionally and visually arresting way appears to have prompted some critical snickering already. Whatever. *The Fountain* will almost certainly endure. (November 2006)

Zodiac

Out of the Past

This haunting film by David Fincher is both eerie and, at several points, really frightening, too—just what you want from a serial-killer movie. Most impressively, though, over the course of its two hours and thirty-five minutes, the picture lays out an enormous amount of information about the Zodiac murders in the San Francisco Bay area in the late 1960s, a ten-month spree by a still-unknown assassin that became the inspiration for the 1971 Clint Eastwood movie, *Dirty Harry*. *Zodiac* is thick with procedural detail, but it goes down smoothly—we never feel like we're being force-fed. And what the movie demonstrates most memorably is how an overabundance of raw data—police reports, expert speculation, conflicting witness statements—can spread not illumination but increasing uncertainty.

Like Jack the Ripper, who despite his enduring renown actually murdered only five people during his brief rampage in 1888, the Zodiac, as he called himself, was a small-scale eliminator. He, too, is credited with just five killings (although there may have been more). But the reason his crimes continue to resonate is that, like the Ripper, he made the media an accessory to his depredations. The letters and mysterious ciphers he mailed to the *San Francisco Chronicle* and other local newspapers—usually beginning with the salutation, "This is the Zodiac speaking"—creeped people out in a new way.

The movie begins on the night of July 4, 1969, in Vallejo, California, with holiday parties in progress and fireworks lighting up the suburban sky. At a deserted teen parking spot far from the festive hubbub, a young man and woman (Lee Norris and Ciara Hughes) are sitting in their car talking. Donovan's "Hurdy Gurdy Man" is playing on the radio. Then, quietly, a second car glides up behind them. It just sits there. After a while, it drives off. An uneasy moment passes. But then, along with the two kids, we see headlights in the distance. The second car is coming back.

Fincher stages this first Zodiac attack with a careful minimum of pulp frenzy. We can't quite make the killer out; and he's no clearer in a pay-phone booth a bit later when he calls in his crime to the police. ("I also killed those kids last year," he tells the cops offhandedly.) The murderer subsequently mails letters to three newspapers, each missive containing part of a complex cipher which the Zodiac claims contains his identity, and which he demands that the papers print. At the *Chronicle*, this draws the interest of hard-drinking hotshot reporter Paul Avery (Robert Downey Jr., never more flamboyantly entertaining than he is here) and a geeky editorial cartoonist named Robert Graysmith (Jake Gyllenhaal). (The movie is based on two books about the Zodiac case written by the real Graysmith.)

The Zodiac's cipher turns out to be a stumper—the FBI, the CIA, and the NSA all take a shot at cracking it, and all fail. Then an amateur code breaker deciphers it. The murderer says he enjoys killing, and he believes that his victims will all become his slaves in the hereafter.

Fincher gets the picture's period details precisely right—the jaunty little hipster neckerchiefs and thick leather watchbands; the big clackety electric typewriters in the *Chronicle* newsroom—without spotlighting them. And the pop music that floats through the film avoids the usual groaning clichés. (Three Dog Night's "Easy to Be Hard" is oddly perfect for the opening scenes; also apt, later on, are the Oliver version of Rod McKuen's sappy "Jean" and the jailbait anthem "Young Girl," by Gary Puckett and the Union Gap.)

The story advances in a series of intense set pieces. There are the actual killings, of course—one of them, on the sunny bank of a lake near Napa, is unforgettable, conveying an inhuman brutality without descending into all-out gore. And there's a sinister late-night encounter in a basement between Graysmith and a strange little man named Bob Vaughn (Charles Fleischer), who may—or may not—actually be the Zodiac.

The last likely Zodiac killing, of a San Francisco cab driver, takes place in October of 1969. But that isn't the end of the case. Two San Francisco police detectives, Dave Toschi (Mark Ruffalo) and Bill Armstrong (Anthony Edwards), keep pursuing leads as the years mount up—and so does the freelance enthusiast Graysmith, who becomes increasingly obsessed. There's no shortage of suspects, many self-admitted, most of them bogus. But as the passing hunches and puzzling indications proliferate, one man stands out—a bald, doughy child molester named Arthur Leigh Allen (John Carroll Lynch). Is he the Zodiac? Toschi and Armstrong definitely like him as a suspect—especially after a bizarre confrontation at the oil refinery where Allen works (an ingeniously constructed scene). Despite their most determined efforts, though, they can't make all the evidence fit. The movie's point of view—which is the point of view of Robert Graysmith—is that Allen is the man. And even though the Zodiac case was never solved, Fincher manages the considerable feat of bringing the picture to a satisfying narrative conclusion.

Zodiac bears little resemblance to Fincher's hyperviolent 1995 serial-killer hit *Se7en*. This film is more ambitious and much more subtle—it's an essay in ambiguity. And while it's a long picture, it doesn't feel that way. I wanted it to keep going, like the Zodiac case itself, which continues to fester to this day. (March 2007)

In Bruges

Hit Parade

Ken and Ray are two Irish hit men who've just botched a job in London, a rub-out gone wrong in which Ray did something horrible. Their English employer, a psycho crime boss named Harry, orders them to blow town till things cool down. For reasons known only to him, he dispatches them to the twinkly medieval city of Bruges, in Belgium. There, Harry orders Ken to do something horrible. Harry being quite horrible himself, Ken feels he should probably comply.

In Bruges is the first movie by the celebrated Irish playwright Martin McDonagh, who also wrote the script. It's an electrifyingly funny take on the Euro-gangster flick. Cut loose from his urban mooring, the volatile Ray (Colin Farrell) is miserable in his touristy new surroundings. As he tells Ken (Brendan Gleeson), "If I'd grown up on a farm, and was retarded, Bruges might impress me. But I didn't." Ray is sour and hostile. He hates the Gothic architecture, hates the perfumed lager on tap in the pubs ("One gay beer!" he barks at a bartender); he even hates all the famous Belgian chocolate on offer.

Ken, on the other hand, older and mellower, quickly turns tourist himself. With map in hand, he drags Ray through the cobbled streets and across the swan-dotted canals to climb the thirteenth-century bell tower and visit the even older basilica, said to be a repository of some of the actual blood of Jesus. Ray doesn't get it. Still haunted by his bloody bungle in London, he just wants to hit the bars and get hammered. Soon, however, he finds himself caught up with a Dutch film crew, a surly midget, a couple of hookers, and a spritely drug dealer named Chloë (an effervescent performance by Clémence Poésy, who played Fleur Delacour in *Harry Potter and the Goblet of Fire*).

Meanwhile, the excitable Harry (Ralph Fiennes) keeps calling from

London with, as we soon learn, a disturbing message. When he encounters difficulty conveying its seriousness, he decides to put in a personal appearance; and when he finally arrives in Bruges, about two-thirds of the way through the movie, the story ratchets up from a merely startling series of shootings and smackdowns to a new level of cutthroat comic delirium.

McDonagh is a master of bristling dialogue and sudden bloody violence, and he doesn't cheat the story by softening it. He shows us what it was that Ray did in London, and it *is* horrific—beyond the pale even for a hired gunman. We share Ray's self-loathing. But we also can't help laughing at the ways in which Ray externalizes his disgust, turning it like a fire hose on everyone around him and blowing them away with streams of rancid verbal aggression.

The three lead actors are exemplary. Gleeson centers the wild proceedings with melancholy warmth. And Fiennes, here in full Cockney honk, is a caustic blend of suburban family-man crime executive and full-on sociopath. (Dickering with a local gat merchant, he says, "I want a normal gun for a normal person.") Even in this robust company, though, Colin Farrell stands out. Gnawing at a thumbnail, swatting a midget, squinting about in paranoid confusion, he's magnetically funny. It's nice to be reminded, after some recent professional miscalculations, what an appealing and resourceful actor he is. Even *Alexander* can now be forgiven. (February 2008)

The Brothers Bloom

Liars in Love

The Brothers Bloom is set on a planet somewhat like our own, but way wackier. The Bloom brothers of the title—Stephen (Mark Ruffalo) and, well, Bloom (Adrien Brody)—have been ardent swindlers since they were kids. (They appear to have been born wearing shifty little black suits and ties.) Stephen is the brains of the team—he composes elaborate schemes as if they were short stories, each one a chapter in an ongoing compendium of cons. His younger brother, Bloom, is always the protagonist. As we join them in the middle of their latest scam, in Berlin, Bloom is chafing under the dictates of his brother's never-ending narrative. "I've only lived life through these roles that aren't me," he complains. He wants to break free, to live "an unwritten life." Not yet, Stephen says.

The boys relocate to New Jersey to case a new job. They're accompanied by their assistant, a mysterious young Japanese woman called Bang Bang (Rinko Kikuchi, the troubled teen in *Babel*). Bang Bang's face is a mask of deadpan disgruntlement—she seems to have been waiting all her life for a punch line that's never arrived. She only speaks three words of English; one of them is "Campari." Still, she's "an artist with nitroglycerin," as Stephen notes, and thus handy to have around.

The Blooms' new mark is Penelope (Rachel Weisz), a rich, lonely nut-job who lives alone in a vast mansion. Penelope has a variety of unusual talents. She can play every musical instrument. She can build model boats inside of bottles. She can juggle chain saws on stilts. She has also created a pinhole camera out of a watermelon, and she calls herself an "epileptic photographer." She really shouldn't drive, but that doesn't stop her. She's the Blooms' kind of gal.

The movie is wonderfully weird. It has one foot planted in the real world (well, *a* real world—the Balkan locations in which the picture was shot give it a tangy unfamiliarity) and the other foot waggling out over the edge of a cliff. Cons sprout up within cons. Bloom is supposed to pretend to fall in love with Penelope so she can be fleeced of her money. But Penelope has so much money, she can afford to be fleeced—she doesn't care. In fact, she finds the con the Blooms are trying to run on her so exciting she wants to join them and become a con artist herself. At this point, Bloom actually does fall in love with her, which screws everything up. Or does it?

On a boat to Greece, they encounter an outsized Frenchman named Melville (Robbie Coltrane). Under a boldly artificial starry-night sky, he whispers to Penelope of Bloomian deceit. But then he turns out to be part of a con, too—one involving smuggled antiques and a shadowy character called the Argentine. Soon they all end up in Prague, where they have an unwanted encounter with an old Bloom colleague, the one-eyed Diamond Dog (Maximilian Schell). The attempted con blows up in their faces. The lovesick Bloom retreats to an island aerie in Montenegro. Penelope returns to New Jersey. But not for long.

Rachel Weisz gives what may be her freest and funniest performance in this movie. Her Penelope is a ditz with a plan—a giddy combination. Kikuchi is also a surprise—she wields disdain like a just-declassified comic weapon. Ruffalo's generous restraint allows these two to shine, but he also puts an expert spin on every off-kilter line that comes Stephen's way. (Recalling a woman he once loved: "pale skin, long feet . . ."). And while Brody's slumpy borzoi charm isn't to everyone's taste, he's right for Bloom, a guy so frazzled by unending deceit that he can never be sure he's not conning himself.

The picture is a small triumph for Rian Johnson, who wrote and directed it. Johnson's first film, the hard-boiled high school noir *Brick*, delivered more promise than payoff. Here, working in a form of low-budget, high-style surrealism that may be all his own, he pulls off a neat trick. Along with all the dizzying non sequiturs and near-subliminal sight gags, he's given the movie a real heart; and at the story's peak, we see the four main characters for what they really are—a family. A non-con at last. (May 2009)

Lemony Snicket's A Series of Unfortunate Events

The Kids Are All Right

Anyone familiar with Daniel Handler's mock-gothic *Series of Unfortunate Events* novelettes, which he writes under the pixilated pseudonym Lemony Snicket, will be aware that the three Baudelaire orphans, teenagers Violet and Klaus and toddler Sunny, have been left a lot of money but have also, alas, been left in the care—well, the clutches—of a distant relative called Count Olaf, who wants to kill them and snatch their inheritance. This movie is based on the first three books in the Snicket series—*The Bad Beginning*, *The Reptile Room*, and *The Wide Window*—and given the picture's open-ended conclusion, it seems clear that the filmmakers are hoping for a franchise. (Eleven installments of the *Unfortunate Events* book series have been published so far, and two more are projected.) I wish them success.

In some ways, this feels like a Tim Burton movie. Burton himself wasn't involved (Brad Silberling directed), but the film's cinematographer, art director, and production, costume, and makeup designers have all worked with Burton, some of them extensively; and so the picture's bleak vistas, dilapidated mansions, and decrepit characters create an agreeably scruffy Burtonian ambiance.

Jim Carrey gives one of his less exhausting performances as Count Olaf, a spindly, moth-eaten stick figure who might have been raised in a wind tunnel—his goateed chin juts out ahead of the rest of his face, while the blown-back crown of his head pulls in the opposite direction. Olaf is an actor by trade, a very bad one, and a windfall is just what he needs to finance his raggedy theatrical troupe. He's unctuous at best, and transparently insincere, and when the Baudelaire siblings are delivered to the door of his ramshackle dwelling by the executor of their estate, Mr. Poe (Timothy Spall), Olaf touchingly vows, "I will raise these orphans as if they were actually wanted."

The grown-ups in the story—among them such other relations as the viper-collecting adventurer Uncle Monty (Billy Connolly) and the frazzled Aunt Josephine (Meryl Streep)—are oblivious to Olaf's malign intentions. But the Baudelaire kids have his number from the get-go, and they improvise nifty escapes from his murderous scenarios. They're well-equipped to do so. The oldest of the siblings, Violet (played by the beautiful sixteen-year-old Australian actress Emily Browning), is an inventor—the creator, according to Snicket, of such things as "a bed that makes itself, an automatic harmonica player, and a device that can retrieve a rock after it has been skipped into the ocean." Her younger brother, Klaus (fourteen-year-old Liam Aiken, precociously charismatic), is a bookworm brimming with arcane knowledge. And the youngest (and maybe funniest) of the trio, the hilariously subtitled baby Sunny (played by alternating twins Kara and Shelby Hoffman), mainly likes to bite things—a handier specialty than you might anticipate.

Count Olaf locks the children in a car parked in the path of an oncoming train, but they outwit him and escape. They similarly avoid being eaten by giant leeches and blown off a cliff into the chilly waters of Lake Lachrymose. These adventures are all part of a larger story—something about mysterious fires and curious brass spyglasses—but we get only hints of it here. At the end of the picture, you're surprised not to see the words "To Be Continued" pop up. A sequel is definitely called for. This first movie is gorgeous to look at. Jim Carrey really is very funny, and Browning and Aiken are almost certainly stars-to-be. May they shine again in a second installment. (December 2004)

Sunshine

Born in Flames

Danny Boyle's *Sunshine* brings a new look to the sci-fi genre. The spaceship on which we travel here is headed not into some vast black void, but out toward the sun. Its mission: to deliver a nuclear jolt to that dying star in order to save the Earth from descending into terminal winter. The presence of the sun—which sometimes floods the screen with its fierce, fiery plasma—triggers an awe in our minds that's different from the dark horrors of other space epics. It bathes the story in a beautiful, frightening light.

The year is 2057, and the ship, the *Icarus II*, is 55 million miles from Earth as the picture begins. Its mission has already been attempted once before, seven years earlier, by another ship, the *Icarus I*. That expedition was never heard from again. The *Icarus II* has a crew of eight, six men and two women, each of them a specialist: a physicist (Cillian

Murphy, who narrates the story), a biologist (Michelle Yeoh), and a medical officer (Cliff Curtis), as well as a captain (Hiroyuki Sanada), a pilot (Rose Byrne), a navigator (Benedict Wong), a communications chief (Troy Garity), and an engineer (Chris Evans). Theoretically, these people can all survive this desperate mission and make it back to Earth. Realistically, though, they know there'll be no return trip.

Predictably, they're a mixed bunch. The biologist, Corazon, has a soothing tranquility—she tends the ship's "oxygen garden," a sizable enclosure filled with greenery, which also provides food for the crew. But the introspective physicist, Capa, and the abrasive engineer, Mace, rub each other the wrong way and sometimes come to blows. The medical officer, Searle, closely monitors their flare-ups. But Searle himself is experiencing turbulent epiphanies about the sun to which their ship is drawing ever nearer. Then the *Icarus II* detects a signal, a distress call, originating from a place far off their course. It's coming from the *Icarus I*.

Sunshine naturally builds upon breakthrough films of the sci-past: the *Alien* movies and of course *2001: A Space Odyssey*. As in those pictures, you know that the crew members here are fated to be picked off one at a time, and you know why: they're not alone. But the malign presence in their midst isn't a slavering monster or a mad computer; it's something more imaginative. The picture stays with you. Some of its imagery—like a crew member sinking down in surrender to join others who have already given up their struggle—may become a permanent part of your pictorial memory. This is a movie that really enriches the genre of which it is now a radiant part. (July 2007)

Duplicity

The Lying Game

f Clive Owen had taken over the role of James Bond, rather than Daniel Craig, the result might have been a movie like *Duplicity*. This second feature by writer-director Tony Gilroy (*Michael Clayton*) is devilishly complex and consistently funny. Owen and his costar, Julia Roberts, playing a pair of scheming freelance spies, don't overdrive their star power, but their wisecracking chemistry lights up the picture. And the story is so tricky that at the end even some of the characters aren't quite sure what's happened. Neither are we (until we've squinted back over it a bit), but we're too tickled to care.

CIA agent Claire Stenwick (Roberts) and Ray Koval (Owen), of Britain's MI6 (Bond's old outfit), have hooked up romantically and professionally and decided to "go private"—into the lucrative realm of corporate espionage—in order to score enough money to retire in the high-flying style to which they've become accustomed. (Claire figures $40 million should do it.) They don't really trust each other, and as the movie's pranks and double-crosses pile up, we begin to feel the same way about both of them.

Ray and Claire have hired themselves out to a big soap-and-lotions corporation run by a ruthless mogul named Garsik (Paul Giamatti), who's at war with a rival outfit helmed by the slick, silken Tully (Tom Wilkinson). Claire has infiltrated Tully's operation and discovered that he's on the verge of a major commercial breakthrough—a game-changing product that'll reap tons of money. Garsik is determined to steal Tully's secret formula for whatever this concoction is and do the reaping himself. Ray and Claire are on hand to help him—or are they? Also in the mix is Garsik's crack backup team, led by a wily operative named Duke (Denis O'Hare), as well as a slob-genius chemist named

Ronny (Christopher Denham) and a winsome travel agent named Barbara (Carrie Preston, walking away with one of the movie's funniest scenes). You can't imagine how complicated all of this gets.

Like the Bond films, and the *Bourne* movies, too (Gilroy was a key writer on all three of those), *Duplicity* logs extensive flight time, touching down everywhere from Dubai and the Bahamas to London, Rome, and Zurich, with brief layovers in Miami (where we learn a bit about the unexpected espionage opportunities in the frozen-pizza industry) and, uh, Cleveland. The dialogue is zesty throughout: when Claire accuses Ray of having seduced a female target, his wounded reply is, "That's my cover."

The picture has a unity of wit and structure that could only have been achieved by a sharp writer who's also a fine filmmaker. (One with excellent taste in collaborators, too—you could put your brain on snooze and have a perfectly fine time savoring the rich color and elegant camera moves of cinematographer Robert Elswit, one of several *Michael Clayton* alumni who worked on the picture.) Apart from the clever plot choreography, one of Gilroy's smartest strategies was to allow Roberts to dial down her all-devouring smile in favor of a more deadpan, reactive performance, which allows Owen's comedic agility to take wing. Are Ray and Claire really in love, or just in league? We're never entirely sure. "I think about you all the time," he declares, in a moment of possible passion. "I think about you even when you're with me." (March 2009)

Gone Baby Gone

Darktown

To all the usual gratifications of a neo-noir private-eye thriller—betrayals, evasions, corruption, and gunfire—*Gone Baby Gone* adds a new wrinkle in the realm of moral ambiguity. The picture is an impressive achievement by its first-time director, Ben Affleck, who also cowrote the script (based on Dennis Lehane's 1998 novel), and for his brother, Casey Affleck, whose compact star performance follows on the heels of his virtuoso turn in *The Assassination of Jesse James by the Coward Robert Ford*. This actor is clearly on a career roll.

Casey Affleck plays Patrick Kenzie; Michelle Monaghan is his partner and longtime girlfriend, Angie Gennaro. They're private investigators who work the blue-collar streets of Boston's Dorchester district. When a four-year-old girl named Amanda McCready is abducted, they're drawn into the investigation by her agonized uncle, Lionel (Titus Welliver). Patrick and Angie's involvement in the case doesn't sit well with Captain Jack Doyle (Morgan Freeman), the cop in charge, who doesn't feel he needs any help; and it's equally irritating to an abrasive detective named Remy Bressant (Ed Harris, never better).

As a neighborhood boy, however, Patrick is uniquely situated to provide assistance. For one thing, he already knows that Amanda's mother, Helene (Amy Ryan), is a junkie and a lush and a sometime drug mule for a sinister dealer called Cheese (Edi Gathegi); and he learns that she was doing lines in a dive-bar bathroom the day her daughter disappeared. Patrick also has useful connections in the local dope trade, among them a blustery kingpin named Bubba Rogowski (Boston rapper Slain, born to the role). Soon the soft-spoken PI is putting two and two together—a big drug rip-off, a grisly torture-murder—but nothing adds up. And the clock is running out: as Doyle notes, kidnapped children who aren't found within a day or two generally aren't found at all, alive anyway. This is day three.

Patrick is a straight arrow in a bent world, but in a horrific sequence in the house of a middle-aged cokehead couple (Mark Margolis and the formidable Trudi Goodman), he discovers that he's capable of terrible actions he never thought possible. Angie tries to reassure him afterward, but Patrick is tormented by what he has done—and more determined than ever to get at the truth behind the abduction of Amanda McCready, now probably dead. Working his connections, he learns unsettling things about Doyle, Bressant, and Lionel; and when he finally cracks the case, he feels compelled to do something that even Angie can't sanction.

Ben Affleck, a Boston native himself, has infused the movie with a strong sense of place, from the faces of the people on the streets to the Beantown cadences in which they speak. He's uncommonly good at handling action, and he's also fluent in the rhythms of intimacy. (Working with a master of low-key emotion like his brother helps a lot.) The two most impressive set-piece scenes in the film are both extended monologues: one by Lionel, falling off the wagon in a neighborhood bar, and the other an electrifying disquisition by Bressant, laying out for Patrick the moral necessity of sometimes doing things that seem completely wrong. ("You gotta take a side," he says. "If you take little kids, if you beat little kids, you are not on my side.")

The end of the picture is both disturbing and, in terms of traditional narrative conventions, deflating. The movie's true conclusion, however, takes place in our heads after the movie's over. The uncomforting message is that sometimes doing the right thing can be the worst thing to do. Are there no alternatives? That's the disturbing part: sometimes, no. (October 2007)

PLEASE SHOOT ME

Movie reviewers see a lot of movies, of course. Some of them are great, others not bad at best. But the odds dictate that many will be altogether otherwise. And in some particularly wretched cases, the odds against them even being made would have seemed insurmountable. If only . . .

Death Race

Bad Max

The most astonishing thing about *Death Race*, an over-amped action movie otherwise wholly free of astonishment, or even much passing interest, is the presence in its cast of Joan Allen. And apart from the fact that she's actually *in* this damn thing—togged out in exactly the sort of dark, tailored suits she wears in the *Bourne* movies—she is also called upon to utter the most baffling line in any recent film. To wit: "Okay, cocksuckers, fuck with me, and we'll see who shits on the sidewalk." This from an actress who's been nominated for three Academy Awards.

If I tell you that *Death Race* was directed by genial schlock purveyor Paul W. S. Anderson, the man who cluttered the world with *AVP: Alien vs. Predator* and *Resident Evil*, that may be all you need to know about this dismal flick. But let's press on regardless.

The movie is set in a hellhole prison—it looks like a vast abandoned foundry—that houses (what else?) "the worst of the worst": murderers, rapists, personal-injury lawyers, what have you. Allen's character, Hennessey, is the warden of this place—or as one lowlife puts it, watching her walking to her office right through all the scumbags, "the baddest ass in the yard." She also presides over an event called Death Race, a sort of armored NASCAR tourney in which the fearsome autos are equipped with all manner of cannons, flamethrowers, even napalm, and driven by guys with handles like Machine Gun Joe (Tyrese Gibson, looking very 50 Cent) and the Grimm Reaper (Robert LaSardo).

Death Race is beamed out worldwide on the Internet; it's wildly popular, and Hennessey gets hot watching the site hits click up into the multimillions. There's a problem, though: her reigning champion, a mysterious subhuman called Frankenstein, grievously banged up in the last Death Race, has quietly died of his injuries. Fortunately, since Frankenstein always wore a scary metal mask and never spoke, he can easily be replaced—and Hennessey has just the man for that purpose: a real-world racing star named Jensen Ames (Jason Statham), who was framed for the murder of his wife and now resides in Hennessey's nightmarish lockup. Ames is persuaded to get behind the mask and is paired with a hot female "navigator" (don't ask) named Case (Natalie Martinez). Before you can say "cue mayhem," the Death Race is back under way.

Statham, the English Vin Diesel, does most of his acting with his brow muscles, which may overqualify him for this picture. He glowers and broods, beats and gets beaten, while all around him tanklike hot rods are screaming through the bullet-filled air and buying the farm in billowing fireballs. Once upon a time, car chases were a highlight of any serious action movie (come back, George Miller!); here they are its entire substance, which will make *Death Race* a source of interest only for those who've never seen one.

The movie is notionally based on the 1970s grindhouse classic, *Death Race 2000*, which starred David Carradine and the pre-*Rocky* Sylvester Stallone. But that film had elements of satire and sparks of humor amid the carnage. *Death Race*, with its monotonous leeched color, is grim and laughless, and Anderson pushes his stuttery cameras so close-in to the action that it's often a strain to discern exactly what is going on. Or, if it need be said, to care. (August 2008)

Hannibal Rising

The Doctor's Not In

If this picture were a little more ludicrous, just a shade more inane, it might be fun to watch. Unhappily, that is not the case. *Hannibal Rising*, the latest greedy squeeze of the once-beguiling Dr. Lecter story, looks pretty great, thanks to cinematographer Ben Davis and Oscar-winning production designer Allan Starski (*Schindler's List*). And director Peter Webber (*Girl with a Pearl Earring*) provides some jazzy angles on the action, and he keeps things moving. But the screenplay, by Lecter auteur Thomas Harris (who cooked up this script and his new novel of the same title at about the same time), is very silly from the start; and it's so dull you wish the old Anthony Hopkins Hannibal, who does not appear in this film, would drop by and liven things up in some suitably gruesome manner.

The movie is a prequel: It proposes to show us the awful events that turned Hannibal Lecter into the silky serial killer we came to adore sixteen years ago in the movie version of Harris's *The Silence of the Lambs*. But this is a fundamental violation of the character—as the good doctor himself once said, "Nothing happened to me. *I* happened." Even though we really don't need to know, though, the movie fills us in.

It begins in 1944, in war-torn Lithuania, where Nazi bombers are swooping down on Castle Lecter, the family manse. Little Hannibal's aristocratic parents are killed, and he and his even littler sister, Mischa, are captured by a gang of local looters, led by a wildly depraved psychopath named Grutas (Rhys Ifans). The weather is cold, and the looters are hungry—*very* hungry. In a fit of drooling desperation, they grab an axe, lead the adorable Mischa out the door, and before you know it—soup is served! This incident was already alluded to in the last installment of the Lecter saga, the dreadful *Hannibal*. Knowing more about it is not especially illuminating, and focusing on it turns the rest of the movie into a revenge thriller of a gory but entirely unthrilling sort.

Hannibal escapes the looters, and we find him eight years later in a Russian orphanage, where he's grown up into a French actor named Gaspard Ulliel (unpersuasive as the Hopkins Hannibal in embryo, despite an occasional appropriation of the older actor's behavioral tics in the role). Before long, he makes his way to France, to the country estate of an uncle, south of Paris. There he learns that the uncle has died, but that his Japanese widow is very pizzazzily alive. Her name is Lady Murasaki (Gong Li), and she graciously takes Hannibal in. (World-lit majors will recall that a Lady Murasaki was also the author of the ancient Japanese text called *The Tale of Genji*, which among many other things concerns a young prince who falls for his stepmother. This bookworm showboating is more than usually strained and pointless.)

In the basement of her chateau, Lady Murasaki amusingly maintains a full-dress shrine to her ancestors, complete with flickering lanterns, an ornate samurai sword, and a towering suit of ancient armor—the helmet of which, inexplicably, features a mouth opening (not a desirable thing in battle, one would think) with three little bars vertically inset. This prefiguring of the iconic muzzle worn by the captive Lecter in *The Silence of the Lambs* is entirely nonsensical. But then what are we to make of all the wild boars waddling through this film? Are they meant to prefigure the voracious swine that were the silliest plot element in *Hannibal*? They remain ridiculous.

Lady Murasaki trains Hannibal in martial arts, for no pertinent reason, and soon starts coming on to him. (Hannibal backs away: "I promised my sister," he says, bafflingly.) After utilizing the samurai sword to carve up an obnoxious butcher (slicing off his cheeks to make tasty campfire kabobs), Hannibal moves with his patroness to Paris, where he enters medical school and starts boning up on anatomy. He also learns that he's being trailed by a suspicious cop, Inspector Popil (Dominic West), a character whose po-faced melancholy introduces a new level of monotony into every scene he enters. Before long, despite Lady Murasaki's flowery entreaties ("Hannibal, memory is a knife—it can hurt you"), he sets out in search of his sister's killers. Much bloodshed ensues, none of it as stylishly transgressive as the guard-clubbing scene in *The Silence of the Lambs*. There is some frightening dialogue, though. (Bad guy to Hannibal: "What did I do to you?" Hannibal: "Apart from eating my sister?")

Most of the murderers turn out to be—I think I've got this right— headquartered on a river barge in Fontainebleau, along with a collection of battered girls they've kidnapped and now hold captive for sport and torment. There's a wonderfully daffy scene here, in which we come upon the vile Grutas lolling in a soapy bath, with a bruised beauty crouching by the tub, carefully shaving his chest. (Rhys Ifans, an actor of beaming sweetness in other roles, is so deliciously rotten in this movie that you desperately wish he were in a different one.) Soon, the defiant Grutas and the vengeful young Lecter are facing off, and scriptwriter Harris—a fine crime novelist whose prose started hurtling off the rails with *Hannibal*—really outdoes himself:

Grutas: "Answer me this. Would you have fed me to your little sister because you loved her so much?"

Hannibal: "Yes."

Grutas: "There you have it. Love. I love myself as much."

Some of the dialogue in this movie is so barmy, I half suspect that Ifans, at least, was playing it for laughs. If only the rest of the cast had been encouraged to follow his lead. It's hard to imagine how the Hannibal Lecter character could survive this dismal film, certainly not without the reinstatement of Anthony Hopkins. (And if Hopkins was up for the film version of *Hannibal* six years ago, he might still be game for anything to which a paycheck is attached.) But what could possibly follow *Hannibal Rising*? *Hannibal Stretching*? *Hannibal Yawning*? *Hannibal Meets the Wolfman*? Stay tuned, I'm afraid. (February 2007)

The Lake House

You've Got Mail

Dr. Kate Forster (Sandra Bullock) is moving out of the house she's been renting, a gleaming, glass-walled affair overlooking a lake in the Illinois countryside, to start a new job in a Chicago hospital. She leaves a letter for the next tenant in the old-fashioned metal mailbox affixed to a post in front of the place. Please forward her mail to her new address, it says. Oh, and about those odd paw prints painted on the wooden walkway—they were there when she moved in.

Next we see a young architect named Alex Wyler (Keanu Reeves) moving into the lake house. He reaches into the mailbox and retrieves Kate's letter. He looks around. He doesn't see any paw prints. Later, on a trip to Chicago, when he tries to drop off some mail at the apartment house address Kate left, he finds only a construction site, where an apartment house is being built. How can this be?

It's simple, actually, in a madly convoluted way. Kate is living in 2006. But Alex is living, on exactly the same day at all times, in 2004. Does this relationship have a future, so to speak?

The Lake House, which is based on a South Korean film that's living in the year 2000, rings every possible brain-wrenching change on this premise. When Alex starts sprucing up the house, for example, his dog trots through a roller-pan of paint he's using and scampers up the walkway, leaving behind odd little paw prints—the very ones that Kate is, or was, or will be talking about two years later.

Kate and Alex continue corresponding via the magical mailbox. Neither rain nor sleet nor time itself can stop the celestial post office from delivering their missives—and with a promptness beyond the ken of earthly mailmen. (No sooner does Kate slip a letter into the box than the little red metal flag attached to it pops up, and there inside is Alex's reply.) They long to meet, and finally they do, at a party two years ago. There, they even kiss. But she of course has no idea who he is; her then-boyfriend intervenes, and the moment passes. Finally, Alex adventurously suggests that they have dinner together. She picks a swank Chicago restaurant that's so popular, reservations have to be made weeks, even months—no, *years*—in advance. (This is pretty funny, actually.) Alex tells Kate he'll see her tomorrow night. (Her tomorrow night—he'll presumably spend the next two years getting dressed for the big date.)

Does he show up? Can you bear the suspense? We can see how a charming romantic movie might have been erected around this woozy premise, but *The Lake House* isn't quite it. It's not just the dialogue that does it in. ("You never told me how beautiful you are," Alex moistly intones, in one of the many epistolary voice-overs that nudge the story forward.) And it's not the clutter of extraneous characters, either. (Alex has a crusty father from whom he's estranged; and a brother who's, well, his brother; and a sort-of girlfriend who hangs around for a while.) It's not even the bits of undigested plot logic. (Wouldn't Kate figure out that since Alex was alive in 2004, he's probably still around, and simply look him up in the phone book? Or what about installing a much larger mailbox and crawling into it herself?)

What finally sinks the film is the puzzling lack of heat between the two principals. Reeves and Bullock were of course first teamed in the 1994 hit *Speed*—the picture that made her a star and gave him the action-movie cred he subsequently brought to *The Matrix*, five years later. They've apparently remained friends. But their few scenes together here are limp and dawdling, and when they're apart they spend way too much time moping about and gazing soulfully out of windows. Despite her unexpectedly tart performance in *Crash* last year, Bullock remains an unexpressive dramatic performer; she seems lost without a wise-crack to work with. (It is also, as always, difficult to accept that a character played by a cute movie star would be lonely and dateless in a big city.) Reeves maintains a bluff, amiable appeal throughout, but when he breaks down in tears at one emotionally manipulative point, you wonder if maybe he's just reached the end of his tether in trying to keep track of the plot.

"What's it like in the future?" Alex asks, early on. "Oh, we all wear shiny metal jumpsuits," Kate quips. Now *that's* an interesting idea for a movie, one that might be fun to watch. As opposed to this one. (June 2006)

The Tourist

Road to Nowhere

*T*he Tourist is a movie that achieves a dreadful perfection. Everyone involved in it—not just the stars, Johnny Depp and Angelina Jolie, but also the director, the cinematographer, the score composer, the various writers and makeup artists, and possibly even the gaffer and the craft-service cooks—all of these people have conspired, all at once, to do their very worst work. The French and Italian accountants who conjured up the foreign tax breaks that enabled the making of this $100 million picture have much to answer for as well.

Jolie plays a woman of mystery named Elise. We meet her in Paris, where she is under observation by a van full of French security operatives. In a sequence of attempted brevity that is nevertheless much too long we see her receiving a note at a sidewalk café sent by an equally mysterious man named Pearce (her onetime lover, it later turns out). The note tells her to board a train to Venice and while en route to pick out a passenger who "looks like me" and to sit with him on the trip. Those who unwisely choose to see the movie will learn that this plot point utterly scuttles the film's preposterous conclusion.

The man Elise selects is a vacationing schoolteacher named Frank Tupelo (Depp). Frank can't believe his luck. Nor can we. While Elise, with her beige-on-beige designer ensembles and her heavy impasto of powder and paint, suggests an alien eminence from Planet Fashion, possibly on her way to a 1980s photo shoot, Frank is a lumpy schlub with a droopy tangle of hair that suggests Jack White at the end of a long day. Will these two fall in love? Next question.

In Venice, Elise takes Frank to her glittering six-star hotel, where they spend a chaste night together. In the morning, Elise is gone, and in her place is a gang of Russian thugs in search of the elusive Pearce. Oddly, the Russkis' boss (Steven Berkoff) is actually British. Why should this be? Well, as someone limply explains, he "surrounds himself with Russians." Ah.

There follows an awkwardly conceived chase sequence, with Elise piloting a boat through the canals of Venice. Since she is also laboriously towing behind her a second boat with Frank on board, this episode lacks the sort of splashy zing we have every right to expect. The Russians, in hot pursuit, are convinced that Frank is actually Pearce—the man who ripped off a huge sum of money from their angry chief. A team of English security ops who are monitoring the action know better, but by this time we've lost our will to care. The story continues on to a fancy-dress ball, where one of the most ridiculous dance interludes in recent memory takes place. I'll not go into it, or on any further.

More interesting than the movie itself, by far, is its backstory. Tom

Cruise, Charlize Theron, and Sam Worthington were all at one time attached to this project, but all of them, presumably after getting a look at the script, bailed. Similar second thoughts were had by a number of directors, including the estimable Lasse Hallström. This left the field to the German director Florian Henckel von Donnersmarck, best known for his first feature, the grimly engrossing Cold War drama, *The Lives of Others*, which won a Best Foreign Film Oscar five years ago. Here, helming material that cries out for the continental esprit of a Hitchcock or a Stanley Donen, he comes up with results that are once again, but in a different way, grim.

Jolie and Depp have no chemistry whatsoever: They look as if they've *just* read the script, and they go about their business with the twinkling elan of two actors waiting for their checks to clear. Not that the script, in which Henckel von Donnersmarck also had a hand, offers them any alternative. The picture has exactly two funny lines in it; the rest of the dialogue is crushingly flat. At one point Depp asks, "What made Pearce think he could take on a guy like that?" And Jolie replies, "It's just the way he is." Elsewhere, Jolie actually utters the line, "I wish we'd met in another life, Frank." Or maybe another movie. (December 2010)

Lady in the Water

Glug

M. Night Shyamalan says the story line of *Lady in the Water* originated in a bedtime fairy tale he improvised for his children. Possibly it would work better as a movie if we were all in bed with the kids and could fall asleep in comfort about a third of the way through. With any luck, the picture's reception will serve as a wake-up call for its gifted but drifting director.

Shyamalan exploded into the big time in 1999 with his wickedly intricate third film, *The Sixth Sense*. He followed that with a moody comic-book fantasy, the sadly underrated *Unbreakable* (a classic origin story that still cries out for a sequel). Problems started cropping up in his 2002 feature, *Signs*, a space-invasion yarn in which the director made the mistake of bringing his shadowy aliens too far into the light. (They turned out to be little green men, only bigger.) Then, in 2004, came *The Village*, which many viewers found to be an infuriating audience cheat.

Shyamalan has now parted ways with Disney, which released his last four films, because the studio exhibited insufficient enthusiasm for making this one. One understands the company's reservations. The thirty-five-year-old director here appears to be staking a very large claim, possibly stoked by too-frequent contemplation of his earlier press notices, as an artist who can take even the wispiest narrative material and, through sheer technical and imaginative facility, make it vibrate with meaning. If this was in fact his intention, he has failed utterly. The picture not only dispenses with the clever plotting that distinguished his most popular films; it also turns its back on some of the basic elements that make movies fun to watch.

The story overflows with absurdities. The protagonist, played by Paul Giamatti, is ridiculously named Cleveland Heep. He's the superintendent of an apartment-building complex in the Pennsylvania hinterlands— a place that's pointedly called the Cove. Its tenants are a lifeboat-style assortment of colorfully quirky individuals: an unassimilated Korean woman and her hyper-Americanized daughter; an Indian-American writer (Shyamalan's largest role yet in one of his movies); a black crossword-puzzle fanatic; a nice lady who loves animals; a grumpy recluse who loves nobody; a Puerto Rican bodybuilder who exercises only the right side of his physique, for some reason; and a sour-faced newcomer who turns out to be a film critic. (Anyone who remembers the vitriolic reviews rained down upon *The Village* will know this character must come to an unpleasant end.)

Cleveland finds an ethereal-looking girl gurgling around in the courtyard pool one night. She says that her name (I couldn't make this up, and I'm amazed that Shyamalan did) is Story (Bryce Dallas Howard). She's a "narf," a creature from "the Blue World," who's taken up residence in a cubbyhole beneath the pool. She has journeyed here to locate a person who's fated to do something of major consequence for the world. (Guess which character this turns out to be.) Now she has to make her way home again on the back of the "Great Eatlon" (a big eagle), whose arrival she anxiously awaits. Meanwhile, she's being menaced by a "scrunt," a nasty, grass-backed, hyena-like creature that looks very much like the lawn when it lies flat amid the shrubbery outside. The scrunt is in turn menaced by the "Tartutics," a trio of fierce, monkey-esque beings who hide in the trees. Got that? I didn't think so.

What does all this mean? Not much—not anything, actually, although Cleveland becomes convinced, for the most unconvincing of reasons, that the key to the whole boring mess is contained in an ancient Korean folktale, and that the Korean mother upstairs, who unfortunately speaks no English, knows all about it.

I won't go on, although Lord knows, Shyamalan does. The story is exceedingly dull; to become involved in it would require not just a suspension of disbelief, but a suspension of most mental faculties altogether. The characters are little more than broad-stroke doodles (an apartment full of heavy smokers is especially uninteresting), and despite the efforts of such able actors as Giamatti, Jeffrey Wright, Sarita Choudhury, Bill Irwin, and Mary Beth Hurt, they serve little purpose other than to illustrate the movie's leaden family-of-man theme. Such action as there is comes in the form of simple boo-level startlements; and apart from one brief, peppery monologue by the ill-fated film critic (played by Bob Balaban), the dialogue is a desultory verbal blur. After a while, you marvel that the actors can be bothered to continue giving voice to it.

Lady in the Water is a bewildering misstep for a director of Shyamalan's talent. Its flaccid pretension suggests a radical misunderstanding of his strengths as a filmmaker; and the key role he's written into the picture for himself suggests an unattractive arrogance. Since the man seems determined to make his movies as nearby as possible to his farm and family in rural Pennsylvania, it must also be said that the Keystone State greenery is starting to look familiar—haven't we seen that dumb bush, that same damn tree, before? Maybe it's time for Shyamalan to venture farther out into the world, and to show us a little more of it. Nobody's going to want to see more of this. (July 2006)

The Happening

Night Falls

I don't want to say *The Happening* is a bad movie. Well, yes, I do; in fact, consider it said. But it's bad in more than just an everyday, sure-does-suck kind of way. Director M. Night Shyamalan's last picture, *Lady in the Water*, based on a bedtime story that put everybody to sleep, was a bad movie plain and simple. *The Happening*, on the other hand—with its what-the-hell plot, lobotomized dialogue, and consequent B movie performances—is worse, in a way, because littered among its many baffling passages are brief, vivid demonstrations of what a skillful filmmaker Shyamalan can be. And has been. I'd say "will be again," too, but by now we're starting to wonder.

The movie gets off to a good creepy start on a sunny morning in New York's Central Park: people strolling the lanes, wind rustling the trees. Suddenly, the strollers all come to a halt, rooted in place. A lone scream is heard in the distance, then, nearer by, a fearful voice: "Is that blood?" Then a woman sitting on a bench pulls out a stick that's knotted in her hair and jams it into her neck. What's going on? Well, as one character says shortly thereafter, prefiguring the verbal fizz to come, "There seems to be some sort of event happening."

Very soon it's happening to the movie's four main characters: a Philadelphia science teacher named Elliot (Mark Wahlberg), his wife Alma (Zooey Deschanel), their math-teacher friend Julian (John Leguizamo) and Julian's eight-year-old daughter Jess (Ashlyn Sanchez). Wahlberg, Deschanel, and Leguizamo are all miscast, although in fairness, it's hard to imagine any actors who wouldn't feel stranded in the motivational morass of Shyamalan's script. We're given vague indications that Elliot and Alma have been squabbling, but this turns out to have no import for the story. Alma and Julian keep exchanging devious looks, as if they might be having an affair, but this eventually amounts to nothing either. And in what may be the movie's most risible plot thread—although that's a large statement—Alma keeps getting unwanted calls on her cell phone from someone named Joey. "You have to stop calling me," she hisses during one such intrusion, clearly ashamed and panicked. What's going on? We find out when she finally decides to come clean with her husband. Joey, it seems, is one of Alma's work colleagues. One night, she and Joey went out and had dessert together, and Alma never told Elliot. Again: she snuck off with this guy and they had dessert together. Did I mention that Elliot wears a mood ring?

As the mysterious suicide epidemic rages up and down the East Coast (but nowhere else, go figure), Elliot, Alma, and little Jess flee for the Pennsylvania countryside, the destination of choice in most Shyamalan movies. There they spend much too much time trudging through otherwise empty fields, as if they'd just wandered into an especially uneventful soccer game. The picture's tedium builds up like silt. But then, usually when you least expect it, the director will suddenly unleash a jolt of startling imagery: bodies raining down out of buildings; corpses hanging like Spanish moss from the tree canopy over a lonely road. There's also a scary encounter with a crazy old lady (Betty Buckley) in a remote farmhouse that suggests hair-raising possibilities for a better movie than this one.

And what's been causing all the suicides? Global warming, of course. Yes, really! Well, sort of. There's a lot of stuff about disappearing bees and angry plants and other such silliness, but in the end, Shyamalan reaches back into the mustiest recesses of the 1950s sci-fi tradition to bring forth an explainer: a doctor who earnestly informs us, "This was an act of nature we'll never fully understand." If I were the guy who made this movie, I would have thought that was hitting a little too close to home. (June 2008)

RocknRolla

Mobbed Up

How bad can the world economy be if people are still giving Guy Ritchie money to make movies? On the tenth anniversary of his breakthrough with *Lock, Stock and Two Smoking Barrels*—a film about the near-incomprehensible doings of a group of London toughies with names like Dog, Plank, and Barry the Baptist—Ritchie is back with *RocknRolla*, a film about the almost entirely incomprehensible doings of a group of London toughies with names like Waster, Tank, and Fred the Head. Given the crash-and-burn of his last mob job, the utterly incomprehensible *Revolver* (with French Paul, Fat Dan, and Lord John), the time would seem to have come for Ritchie to stop making this movie.

The plot of *RocknRolla* can be suggested in only the most impressionistic terms. There's an old-school bad guy named Lenny (Tom Wilkinson, channeling Bob Hoskins in *The Long Good Friday*) and a new-school Russian bad guy named Uri (Karel Roden, revisiting the shady Russki he played in *The Bourne Supremacy*). There are also a pair of low-level gangsters named One Two and Handsome Bob (Gerard Butler and Tom Hardy), and an unlikely pair of club owners named Mickey and Roman (Jeremy Piven and Chris "Ludacris" Bridges), and a nest of gamblers called the Wild Bunch, and a crafty accountant named Stella (Thandie Newton), and a drugged-out rock star called Johnny Quid (Toby Kebbell), who happens to be Lenny's stepson (not that it matters). Suave Mark Strong plays Lenny's enforcer, Archie, and gives the only interesting performance in the movie.

What are all these people up to? Hard to say. There's a whole bunch of money involved, of course and, rather oddly, a "lucky" oil painting that Uri has loaned to Lenny, for reasons that only a screenwriter (that would be Ritchie) could care about. Naturally it goes missing. In addition, there is a pit full of imported American crayfish (!) into which misbehaving miscreants are lowered for disposal. This is the silliest plot kink since the evil Mason Verger schemed to feed Hannibal Lecter to a pen full of giant killer hogs in *Hannibal*.

Ritchie has once again made a movie with far too many characters in it and way too little of much interest for them to do (or, Lord knows, say). The picture aspires to the usual stylish savagery, but it mopes and drags. Why Ritchie didn't just go ahead and remake *The Long Good Friday* this time around is a puzzlement. (And it's too late now: *Death Race* director Paul W. S. Anderson is at this very moment in the process of trashing that little Cockney-gangster classic—he's already relocated the action to Miami.)

A career rethink is definitely in order for Ritchie. His take on the mean streets of London was never especially convincing. *RocknRolla* demonstrates that he's been married to the mob for way too long. (October 2008)

Flawless

Bland Theft

Even though it wasn't intended to be a comedy, the new jewel-heist movie *Flawless* is nevertheless entirely hilarious. Consider this: Michael Caine, playing an ambitious janitor (!) named Hobbs, has obtained the code to open a huge vault at the London Diamond Corporation, inside of which lies "one of the largest single deposits of riches in the world." Hobbs intends to break in there and fill up his workingman's thermos bottle (!) with jewels. But the vault is situated at the end of a very long basement corridor, which is monitored by a security camera up near the ceiling. How can Hobbs make it all the way down that corridor, pause to dial in the code, pull open the vault's enormous door, and slip inside without being seen?

Simple, really. As Hobbs makes his way toward the vault, in full view of the camera, the guard whose job it is to watch the monitor on which Caine's appearance is now evident suddenly becomes distracted—by a biscuit! Which he proceeds to eat, very, very slowly. By the time the guard looks up again, Caine has disappeared inside the vault. What luck!

But wait. Having slipped inside the vault, Hobbs must of course somehow slip back out again. Impossible? Not at all. As he makes his way back down the corridor—once again, in full view of the security camera—the guard watching the monitor suddenly becomes engrossed in . . . a cupcake! Which he nibbles, once again, very slowly.

It gets better. Hobbs has obtained the vault code from a disaffected company executive, a prim Englishwoman named Laura, who's played by Demi Moore (!). (Okay, toward the end of the movie we're informed that she's actually an American who went to Oxford and stayed on. Unfortunately, this introduces a new level of improbability.) Laura obtained the code from the home of the company's chairman. How? Well, while she was rooting around in his den during a cocktail party at which she was a guest, she heard footsteps approaching and quickly scurried up some stairs to a dark balcony. The chairman entered and crouched down in front of his safe. If only Laura could see what numbers he was going to enter to open it. Looking around, she noticed a pair of opera glasses *lying on the railing right in front of her*—what luck! She used these to eyeball the safe's combination as the chairman dialed it and then, after he'd left, pilfered the vault code from inside.

It gets better. How did Hobbs peg the high-toned Laura, of all people, as a perfect potential partner in this heist? Well, she'd just been passed over for promotion for the umpteenth time, and she was bitter about it. How did Hobbs know this? Because Laura, an ice queen with no friends, vented her feelings by writing them down in letters and addressing them—to herself! Hobbs simply intercepted these missives, somehow, and made his approach. Naturally, a preliminary meeting was then in order, and what better place to hold it than in a movie theater, where the unlikely duo's incriminating conversation, conducted at normal walking-down-the-street volume, drew not the slightest no-

tice from their fellow patrons, who were as absorbed in the movie being screened as if it were a cupcake.

It's not finished getting better. Hobbs doesn't just steal a thermosful
of diamonds from the vault; he steals its entire contents—enough jewels to fill a good-size truck. I won't reveal the method by which he does
this; let's just say it's entirely hilarious. Then Hobbs—who, again, is a
lowly janitor—anonymously hires a top-tier corporate lawyer to negotiate a ransom demand for the diamonds with the company chairman.
I guess this could happen.

The movie is sluggish and juiceless, which is surely why it's only
now creeping into theaters, two years after it was shot. Michael Caine
is always good, but here he has to deal with Demi Moore, which must
have been a challenge. And any attempted thriller that makes the miscalculation of failing to show us how the heist is being brought off will
have a lot to answer for on the great day of cinematic reckoning. (Hobbs
enters the vault, then leaves it, and we see nothing of what he did inside
until the end of the film, when there's a quick flashback recap.) At least
the picture's title is apt—as a work of seamless implausibility it is, indeed, without any redeeming flaw. (March 2008)

Filth and Wisdom

Absolute Beginner

Madonna makes her directorial debut with a three-hour movie
that . . . no, wait—it says eighty-four minutes here; surely a mis-
print. Anyway, Madonna makes her directorial debut with what seems
like a very long movie about, well, filth and wisdom, I suppose. Or as
narrator-star Eugene Hutz puts it, "Without filth, there can be no wisdom." As deep thoughts go, this seems too feeble to provoke much in the
way of actual thought, let alone to hang a movie on, but let us, unlike the
film, move right along.

The setting is London; the focus, three friends. Juliette (Vicky Mc-Clure) is determined to save disease-ravaged African children by stealing bottles of pills from the pharmacy in which she works and . . . what? Mailing them off to general delivery, Zimbabwe? Not clear. Holly (Holly Weston) is an underemployed ballerina who's persuaded to try stripping to pay the rent. (The pole-dancing scenes in which she features seem like an attempted comment on the objectification of women's bodies; but then the scenes themselves objectify women's bodies— although not nearly as much as pole-dancing aficionados might hope.)

And then there's A. K. (Hutz), a lushly mustachioed layabout who pays *his* rent by conducting S & M sessions (heavy on the caning) in his ratty apartment and sitting in an empty bathtub dispensing gaseous aphorisms straight to the camera. ("He who licks a knife will soon cut his tongue." "If you want to reach the sky, fuck a duck and learn to fly.") Hutz, of course, is the leader of the gypsy-rock band Gogol Bordello, a group on which Madonna dotes and which gets lots of exposure here. As a frontman, he's an energetic performer. As a constant presence in the movie, however, he is deeply, maddeningly tiresome. After his seventh or eighth wearying epigram ("There is more to love than words— for instance, the back of a woman's neck"), you want to leap onto the screen and start caning *him*.

Why Madonna should want to pursue her love of movies beyond simply appearing in them and into the realm of directing (and producing) is a mystery. She's brought some helpful pros on board to help out: cinematographer Tim Maurice-Jones is a longtime associate of her soon-to-be-ex-husband, Guy Ritchie; and Dan Cadan, who appears to be taking the fall for the script, is a onetime Ritchie assistant who has also worked on electronic press kits for two of his movies. But who should be credited for the awful lighting (the movie is lit like a lavatory), and the clichéd overhead shots of people morosely curled up on beds, and the puzzling decision, midway through the movie, to suddenly start styling Vicky McClure to look like Jean Seberg in Godard's *Breathless*? I'm afraid we know. (October 2008)

The Hottie and the Nottie

Trial by Dire

There's no point in being too hard on *The Hottie and the Nottie*. It isn't the kind of movie you go into expecting much, and you won't be going into it anyway, I'm guessing, and you won't be alone in not doing so. Still, the picture manages to deliver so much less than even the tiny bit you might anticipate (a weak chuckle, even a wan smile) that it's almost notable.

The film is said to star Paris Hilton. This is not entirely accurate. Paris Hilton is *present* in it. She's not entirely terrible. She actually has an almost fresh, wholesome glow in her early scenes; it isn't until later that she starts reverting to the glazed red-carpet smirk with which we're all familiar. Still, Hilton has no more business being in a movie than she does in, say, a recording studio. Her brittle media persona is all she has to work with; characterization is simply not something for which she's equipped.

First-time feature director Tom Putnam seems to have anticipated this very large problem. The picture is designed to revolve *around* Hilton, in the manner of a maypole dance. The other actors frolic about with the flat dialogue and desultory action, leaving the nominal star to simper and coo at the center of it all in a consistently uninteresting way.

The story is silly, which needn't have been a drawback—it might have served as the basis for a frothy romantic fantasy. Unfortunately, the script (by first-timer Heidi Ferrer) is limp and witless and somewhat repellent. A loser named Nate (Joel David Moore) has nursed a yen for a pretty grade-school classmate named Cristabel (Hilton) for twenty years. Back in the day, all of the little boys' interest in Cristabel was deflected by her best friend, a snaggle-toothed, mole-flecked, snot-dripping horror named June (Christine Lakin). And when Nate tracks the grown-up Cristabel to

Los Angeles, he discovers that not only is she hotter than ever but that June—now losing her hair, on top of everything else—is still her gate-keeping best friend.

Apart from the fact that women who look like Paris Hilton do not have best friends who look like road-show Quasimodos (a truth regularly demonstrated by Hilton herself in her well-chronicled adventures with fellow celebutantes) and do not fall for gawky oddballs like Joel David Moore (an engaging comic actor who's shipwrecked in this mirthless picture), there's something unsavory about turning a character afflicted with disfiguring medical problems into the butt of numbskull ugly-girl jokes. Offputting on another level is the notion that the hideous June could attract the amorous attention of a godlike stud (Johann Urb) and then, of course, be transformed by him and his money into a hottie herself. No amount of modernist irony can revivify this ancient plot contrivance.

A couple of laughs might have helped. But while it abounds with listless gab and meandering scenes, *The Hottie and the Nottie* is almost entirely fun-free. Watching it is like watching a wall. The picture runs about ninety minutes, and could easily lose twenty. Make that thirty. It'd still be sixty minutes too long, though. (February 2008)

Charlie St. Cloud

Dead Zone

Charlie St. Cloud sees dead people. Which would be the ideal audience for this movie. Although the story line of *Charlie St. Cloud* has some nice love-after-death twists, and the imagery—gleaming harbor-town nightscapes and sleek sailboats scudding across the water—has been sleekly rendered, the picture is becalmed by its star.

Charlie (Zac Efron) lives for sailing, and as the movie opens, in his briny hometown on the Washington coast, he's preparing to leave for

Stanford University in the fall on a sailing scholarship. Despite his re-semblance to Zac Efron, Charlie doesn't have a girlfriend. He's entirely devoted to his mother (a minimal appearance by Kim Basinger) and especially his little brother, Sam (Charlie Tahan, talented beyond the call of cuteness). Sam lives for baseball, and Charlie coaches him with daily pitching practice in a clearing in some nearby woods. Charlie tells Sam he'll always be there for him. But then there's a car crash; Sam is killed, but Charlie, although briefly flatlined, survives.

Five years later, we find Charlie working as a caretaker at the local cemetery. He canceled his Stanford plans because . . . well, because he told Sam he'd always be there for him. And Sam *is still there,* turning up in the woods every evening for their regular pitching sessions. Presum-ably Charlie has decided to spend the rest of his life as an undead-baseball coach. But then he meets the beautiful Tess (Amanda Crew), an avid sailor herself, who's gearing up for an around-the-world race in her ele-gant yacht. As Charlie and Tess fall in love, Sam, with no other earthly pursuits to occupy his time, watches them with growing unease (possibly even observing the movie's lone sex scene, a coupling so discreet it barely rises to the level of PG-13). "I could feel you forgetting me," he tells Char-lie. "Without you, I feel myself start to disappear."

This basic plot conflict grows even slushier following a second trag-edy, which introduces another level of trite ambiguity. Unfortunately, despite the best efforts of Tahan and Crew (who injects some fizz into the otherwise turgid proceedings), the real love story at the heart of the picture is between Zac Efron and director Burr Steers's camera. Efron, such a charmer in last year's *17 Again*, is a woebegone mope here, acting mainly with his burnished tan and his bioluminescent blue eyes, which all too often well with tears. Charlie stares out to sea. He stares into his soul. He suffers and suffers, and his muffled torment, even when back-grounded by glorious coastal sunsets, grows oppressive. We want Efron to jack this character up to another emotional level, to manifest some personality, but he just keeps wallowing in heartbreak. The movie is a peculiar throwback to Hollywood melodramas of the 1940s. Charlie keeps seeing dead people (there's also a deceased buddy on hand), and we're left watching a lifeless movie. (July 2010)

Atlas Shrugged

Where Is John Galt?

It's a blessing, I suppose, that Ayn Rand, who loved the movies and actually worked extensively in the industry, isn't alive to see what's been made of her most influential novel. The new, long-awaited film version of *Atlas Shrugged* is a mess, full of embalmed talk, enervated performances, impoverished effects, and cinematography that would barely pass muster in a TV show. Sitting through this picture is like watching early rehearsals of a stage play that's clearly doomed.

The movie is especially disappointing because Rand's 1957 book, while centrally concerned with ethical philosophy (and inevitably quite talky), has a juicy plot that, in more capable hands, might have made a sensational film. (That possibility, alas, may now be closed off.) The story concerns strong-willed Dagny Taggart, who's fighting to save her family railroad, Taggart Transcontinental, from the inept leadership of her brother, James, a moral weakling, and from the metastasizing reach of government regulation. Dagny finds a kindred spirit in Henry Reardon, a principled industrialist who has formulated a new kind of steel that Dagny intends to use in upgrading Transcontinental's decaying tracks. She and Reardon are opposed at every turn by collectivist politicians and corporate titans corrupted by their addiction to the government teat. Meanwhile, the nation's most productive businessmen, demoralized by rampant political interference, are vanishing one by one from the public scene. And a mysterious figure named John Galt appears to have something to do with this.

The film was obviously a labor of love for producer John Aglialoro, a multimillionaire Randian who held movie rights to the book for eighteen years and made every effort to set it up as a professional production. (Angelina Jolie was famously attached at one point.) Then, last year, with his option running out, Aglialoro decided he had no choice but to make the movie himself. He quickly hired Brian Patrick O'Toole, a writer of low-budget horror films, to work with him on the script, and an actor, Paul Johannson (of TV's *One Tree Hill*) to direct. He also managed to sign some seasoned professionals for the cast: Graham Beckel (*Brokeback Mountain*) in the role of oil magnate Ellis Wyatt; Edi Gathegi (from the *Twilight* movies) in the part of Dagny's loyal lieutenant Eddie Willers; and two veterans of Coen brothers films, Michael Lerner and Jon Polito, to play political fixer Wesley Mouch and the collusive corporate sleaze Orren Boyle.

Unfortunately, Aglialoro then cast a pair of TV actors in the key roles of Dagny and Reardon. Taylor Schilling (*Mercy*) is an appealing performer, but she's not really equipped to project Dagny's passionate determination; and Grant Bowler (*True Blood*), an actor of low-key warmth, is too unassertive to hold the screen as the uncompromising Reardon. It may be unfair to judge these two on their work here—they don't seem to have been given much in the way of useful direction, and they've been set adrift in a succession of poorly blocked and shot scenes. Because of budget constraints, presumably, the whole movie seems underpopulated; and the one big party sequence is so low on energy that it resembles a casting call for which the auditioning actors have turned up already in costume. There's quite a bit of narrative padding and a woeful lack of action. We see rather too much footage of sleek trains speeding through the countryside (assisted at times by surprisingly crude computer generation), and there are lingering shots of hilly, verdant landscapes shoehorned into the proceedings to no purpose. (At one point there's even a close-up of a flower.)

Anyone not familiar with Rand's novel will likely be baffled by the goings-on here. Characters spend much time hunkered around tables and desks nattering about rail transport, copper mining, and the oil business. A few of these people are stiffly virtuous ("I'm simply cultivating a society that values individual achievement"), but most are contemptible ("We must act to benefit society" . . . "a committee has decided" . . . "We rely on public funding"). These latter creeps should set our blood boiling, but they're so cartoonishly one-dimensional that any prospective interest soon slumps. We *are* initially intrigued by the recurring question, "Who is John Galt?" But since the movie covers only the first third of the novel (a crippling miscalculation), we never really find out, apart from noting an anonymous figure lurking around the edges of the action, togged out in a trench coat and a rain-soaked fedora like a film noir flatfoot who's wandered in from a very different movie.

Rand's book is set in an unspecified future that bears a startling resemblance to our own here and now. There's a stock market collapse, much populist demagoguery and union thuggery, and chaos in the Middle East that has driven gas prices to $37 a gallon (which purportedly explains the resuscitation of railroads as the only affordable transport for passengers and freight). The book is set in an unspecified future; the movie relocates the story to the year 2016, but it might as easily have been next week. These sociopolitical similarities might have been more rousing if they had been punched home more dramatically. The occasional bursts of TV news footage employed here don't really do the job.

Although Rand's novel is well over a thousand pages long, one can't help wondering if, with a radically compressed script, it couldn't have been turned into a tightly edited two-and-a-half-hour film—into a real movie, in other words, not just a limply illustrated literary classic. Now we may never know. Which is too bad. But the picture is too lusterless to stir much indignation. Instead, it leaves us feeling, in Rand's words, "the merciless zero of indifference." (April 2011)

Repo! The Genetic Opera

Schlocky Horror Show

Anyone intent on reviving the rock opera, that most misbegotten of pop-music genres, should consider two things. The first would be, don't do it. The second, if one were determined to do it anyway, would be the need for songs—brief musical compositions of sufficient sturdiness to ensure that they won't be forgotten while they're still being sung. With *Repo! The Genetic Opera*, director Darren Lynn Bousman has obviously ignored the first of these precepts, and his songwriting collaborators, Terrance Zdunich and Darren Smith, haven't been successful in observing the second. The result is a work that stirs retrospective appreciation of the mock-bombastic Meat Loaf. Meat Loaf, you'll recall, had songs.

The movie has metastasized from a 2002 stage play written by Zdunich and Smith and directed by Bousman. It's set in a postapocalyptic world in which millions have died in an epidemic of organ failures, and a biotech company called Geneco has arisen to sell transplantable organs to needy survivors—and to repossess those pricey innards whenever the owners fall behind in their payments. The scalpel-wielding characters who carry out these grisly interventions are called repo men. One of them is secretly a doctor named Nathan Wallace (Anthony Head, of the *Buffy the Vampire Slayer* TV series), who's been forced into this vile sideline by Geneco founder Rotti Largo (Paul Sorvino). Largo is terminally ill himself and determined not to let his lucrative organ business pass into the hands of his good-for-nothing children (one of them played by Skinny Puppy frontman Ogre; another, with unwarranted enthusiasm, by Paris Hilton). Instead, he wants to bequeath his empire to Wallace's daughter, Shiloh (Alexa Vega, of the *Spy Kids* films), because her late mother was, as he sings in one of many tuneless interludes, "once very dear to me." The plot thickens like a blood pudding. The movie's art direction (by Anthony A. Ianni) and production design (by David Hackl—like Ianni and Bousman, a veteran of the *Saw* movies) are deliriously flamboyant. The city in which the story is set is dank and tainted, shrouded in endless night. The lighting leans heavily toward a supersaturated blue, the characters skulk about in a fog of halation, and the visual quality is otherwise pure point-and-shoot. Wardrobe designs are goth, of course—lots of black leather S & M gear, with much mascara and lipstick all around—and the city itself is a lurid digital chowder of grim streets and dark graveyards spread out in the shadow of the towering Geneco headquarters. All of this might have been fun, sort of, were it not for the grinding metal guitar riffery upon which—this being a rock opera—the characters' every word must be conveyed.

Thirty years after *The Rocky Horror Picture Show*, there's nothing shocking about the thirdhand decadence on display here. What really startles are some of the unexpected performers lunging around in the murk. What could Paul Sorvino have been thinking as he blustered through the din, trailed by a long gray ponytail, belting out lyrics like "Maggots, vermin—you want the world for nothing!" And how did actual singer Sarah Brightman—Andrew Lloyd Webber's onetime wife and muse—feel about being tricked out as some sort of pop-eyed Elvira puppet? The songs aren't all dreadful—one of them, "Seventeen," is a lively arena-punk anthem that Vega delivers with near Avril Lavigne–like energy. But the tunes are for the most part formless, and many of the lyrics have the flat slap of words that should simply have been spoken, not sung. ("Didn't I tell you not to go out?" Wallace bellows at his sheltered daughter, in response to which she warbles, "You did! You did!") The picture runs ninety-eight minutes, and it starts feeling too long about three-quarters of the way in. It feels unnecessary from the beginning. (November 2008)

Repo Men

Internal Affairs

Any picture that recalls one of the worst movies of 2008 is off to a bad start. *Repo Men* isn't as teeth-grindingly terrible as *Repo! The Genetic Opera*—there are no songs, for one blessed thing—but the plot holds no surprises (apart from a semiclever twist at the end that will appeal to fans of the downbeat); and despite all the gore splattered about, the film is surprisingly bloodless.

It's set in the familiar Future World that's come down to us from *Blade Runner*: Chinese signage fills the streets and blimp-borne billboard ads cruise around up above. Jude Law (squandering his charisma) and Forest Whitaker (likewise his charm) are Remy and Jake, lifelong friends now working for the Union, a company that manufactures high-end artificial organs—kidneys, lungs, eyes, ears, pick a body part—and sells them to desperately ill consumers on installment plans. As a smarmy sales honcho named Frank (Liev Schreiber) explains to prospective clients, the arrangement is simple: the company installs the new innards, the consumer makes monthly payments. The downside of the deal—the consumer falls behind, the company uninstalls—is something that Frank says "almost never happens."

That's a lie, of course—the recycling of repossessed organs is how the company makes most of its profit. This is where Remy and Jake come in, cruising around town with special gadgets that allow them to spot deadbeats on the streets and then, armed with Tasers and a fearsome array of surgical cutlery, chase them down and repossess the pricey organs right on the spot. It's a bloody business, but Remy and Jake love their work: "Some whimper, some cry, some even laugh," Remy observes with a giggle. But then one repo job goes wrong, Remy is gravely injured—and he wakes up in the hospital with a new heart and an installment plan of his own.

This all might have been a lot more fun if first-time director Miguel Sapochnik had resisted the urge to turn the picture into an action-chase movie of a very standard sort. There's lots of flailing violence—hacksaw battles, hammer attacks—but it's stylelessly blunt. And there are few time-outs to consider the story's social implications: When we meet a woman named Beth (Alice Braga), whose entire body—apart from her kissable lips, in which Remy has taken an interest—is apparently overdue for repossession, we wonder what it must now mean to be human (another echo of *Blade Runner*).

The movie has no interest in such questions, which is okay—or would be if it weren't otherwise so predictable (will Jake be assigned to track down and terminate his old pal, do you think?) or if it had a more distinctive sci-fi look. The urban chaos in which Remy and Jake go about their grisly work is a grim environment, with none of the dystopian enchantment of . . . oh, say, *Blade Runner*. There's a lovely sequence in a recording studio in which Remy arrives to repossess the heart of a famous singer (RZA) and winds up telling the man how much he's always loved his music (as he unpacks his sinister tool kit). And there are a few funny bits, like the repo man who's bummed about being stuck on perpetual "ear duty." But the movie's cheap jokiness muddles whatever tone the director might have intended. When Remy and Beth, in frantic search of a high-security portal known as the "pink door," finally come upon a wall sign bearing a directional arrow and, I'm afraid, the words "Pink Door," you wish there were someone around to slap. Or at least come up with some bloody songs. (March 2010)

The Number 23

Mathematical Uncertainty

Dogcatcher Walter Sparrow (Jim Carrey) is being driven mad by the number 23. He has been launched into this obsession by a strange little book called *The Number 23*, which his wife, Agatha (Virginia Madsen), gave him for his birthday. It's a novel or a memoir or something, written by a man named Topsy Kretts (get it?). He was apparently driven mad by the number 23, too.

And no wonder. When you think about it, the number 23 is *everywhere*. Like, did you know that William Shakespeare was born (maybe) and died on April 23? And that Kurt Cobain was born in 1967 and died in 1994, and that the numerals in each of those years add up to 23? And that the Latin alphabet has 23 characters? And that the Tool album *10,000 Days* has a track called *Viginti Tres*, which is Latin for—that's right—23. And hey, this *is* interesting: add up the number of letters in the names Jim Carrey and Virginia Madsen and what do you get? Right again! Best of all, if you divide 2 by 3 you get .666!

The "23 Enigma," has been doodled forth in the goof-cult religion called Discordianism, and elaborated in the 1975 *Illuminatus!* trilogy by novelists Robert Anton Wilson and Robert Shea. The number's usefulness in linking all sorts of things in vaguely conspiratorial webs of coincidence derives from the fact that 23 is a prime number, and that it's composed of two digits that are themselves the two lowest prime numbers. I'd go on, but you can Google this stuff as well as I can.

What does it all mean? Not much; nothing useful anyway. But it's fun, in a too-much-time-on-your-hands way. Unfortunately, the same can't be said of this movie.

As Walter starts burrowing into the mysterious book, he learns that the author, as a boy, created a crime-busting alter ego called Detective Fingerling. Soon, in his dream life, Walter starts turning into this character. His shoulders blossom with thick black tattoos. He takes up late-night saxophone. He finds himself in a hot relationship with an S & M enthusiast named Fabrizia (also played by Madsen), and he encounters another woman called the Suicide Blonde (Lynn Collins), who's obsessed with the number 23 herself. The Sparrows' amiable friend Isaac (Danny Huston) starts appearing, too, in the guise of a sinister Dr. Phoenix. It's all very noir, or at least very dark. (The cool, inky cinematography is by Matthew Libatique, best known for his work with Darren Aronofsky.)

There's also a murdered woman named Laura Tollins (Rhona Mitra), whose body has never been found; and an ominous facility called the Nathaniel Institute; and a vicious dog called Ned (n being the fourteenth letter of the alphabet, e being the fifth letter, and so on). There's also a twist to the book: the story only goes up to Chapter 22—after that, where Chapter 23 should be, there are just blank pages, waiting to be filled in.

Jim Carrey plays all of this straight, if that's the right word—his tired, twenty-million-dollar-man buffoonery is nowhere in evidence. This strategy of setting aside his rubbery comic persona worked for Carrey in *Eternal Sunshine of the Spotless Mind*; but that film had an intriguing comic structure provided by screenwriter Charlie Kaufman. *The Number 23* relies on a script by first-time screenwriter Fernley Phillips, and while it's frenetically enterprising in trying to keep all sorts of narrative balls in the air, its complexity bogs down into murky complication. You also start to wonder just how crazy someone could be driven by this number-23 business. A certain sort of person might be transformed into an unusually tedious geek, maybe, but a murderer?

The director, Joel Schumacher, works up a juicy, lurid atmosphere, but the picture is cramped and airless. You wait for it to really take off, but it never seems able to find its way out of all the claustrophobic rooms and corridors. The plot points sort of connect, eventually (well, some of them do); but after the movie ends, you don't feel like it's added up to much. And you're pooped from doing all the math. (February 2007)

Burlesque

Strip-Clubbed

Midway through the glitter storm of *Burlesque*, there's a moment of calm in which Cher, playing the owner of an L.A. show palace, consoles an unhappy dancer with a line that will surely prove deathless. Addressing the younger woman with mom-like concern and an impressively straight face, Cher utters these words: "How many times have I held your hair over the toilet while you threw up everything but your memories?" And you wonder, where are those hair-holding hands when *we* need them?

The movie is a classic train wreck. The dialogue falls upon the ear like baseball bats. The story—girl flees hick town to chase stardom in the big city—is an exhausted cliché. And the imagery pillages any number of old musicals, from *Gentlemen Prefer Blondes* to *Cabaret* (which it rips off with unblushing gusto). But then, midway through the picture, it suddenly becomes clear—well, I *think*—that *Burlesque* is something more than just a mind-fogging travesty. It's a "fond tribute" to the Hollywood song-and-dance form, with all of its snappy chatter and blinding pizzazz. Great.

The plot: having escaped the Iowa sticks, aspiring singer Ali (Christina Aguilera) does the usual jobless pavement pounding until she comes upon a Sunset Strip nightclub called the Burlesque Lounge—from the outside a shabby dive, on the inside a Vegas-y glitz pit complete with lightly clad chorines and laughably elaborate sets. The owner, a deadpan lady named Tess (Cher), turns Ali away at first; but, inevitably, the spunky lass brazens her way up onstage and knocks everybody out with her gotta-dance-gotta-sing gifts. "How do you do that?" asks the blown-away stage manager (Stanley Tucci, in an extension of the fluttery grande dame accessory he played in *The Devil Wears Prada*). "I dunno," Ali says. "I just do it." Says Tess: "I'm gonna go up to my office and plan a whole new show."

Ali's ascent at the lounge displaces its former star, Nikki (Kristen Bell), who of course plots revenge. Also wading into the mix are a rich clubgoer named Marcus (Eric Dane), who has immediate eyes for the hot new talent; a hunky bartender named Jack (Cam Gigandet), who'd like to make some moves, too, if only his long-distance fiancée weren't in the way; and the club's heavily mascara'd emcee (Alan Cumming), who fulfills the filmmakers' *Cabaret* fetish in a leering musical interlude with two pliant tarts. (Cumming won a Tony Award in the near-identical role in the 1998 stage revival of *Cabaret* on Broadway.)

The eye-rolling silliness of the musical genre is also much in evidence. At one point, Ali is compelled by dubious circumstance to move into Jack's apartment, where they wander around in various states of undress. (There's no nudity in this PG-13 film, unless you count some briefly bared male buttocks.) Despite the close quarters, though—and Ali's obvious erotic interest—Jack keeps finding entirely unconvincing reasons to fend her off. And then there's the abundant vocalizing: whenever Ali opens her mouth to sing, her voice is suddenly engulfed in big-time reverb—even when she's nowhere near a microphone. If you can't just go with this sort of thing, you're at the wrong movie.

Director Steve Antin (who also scripted) is fortunate to have Cher to anchor these gaudy proceedings with her serene diva presence, which keeps the movie from helicoptering off into the camp ozone. (And I'm guessing it was Cher who wheeled in Diane Warren—composer of her

1989 hit, "If I Could Turn Back Time"—to whip up the old-school power ballad, "You Haven't Seen the Last of Me.") But the real star, of course, is Aguilera, here making her feature-film debut. Her huge, booming voice has been an alarming marvel ever since her Mouseketeer days back in the early 1990s. Now she's a belter in a tradition going back to Ethel Merman, but with distinctly modern flourishes (she wields melisma like a weapon). She's prone to overkill, beating "Something's Got a Hold on Me," the old Etta James hit, into gasping submission; but dialing down a bit, she delivers an acceptably sultry rendition of Mae West's "A Guy What Takes His Time." Admirers of this diminutive powerhouse, and of musicals generally, may eat this movie up. Unbelievers, on the other hand, will probably go on unbelieving. (November 2010)

The Boondock Saints II: All Saints Day

Sloppy Second

Having been unable to sit through the 1999 *Boondock Saints* in its wretched entirety, I've been surprised to see it become a "cult hit" on DVD. A wave of Blockbuster-enabled fan enthusiasm has propelled the film into the top twenty of all catalog titles currently on sale, and to number twelve in Blu-ray unit sales. So shut my mouth.

Now comes director Troy Duffy's flatulent sequel, *The Boondock Saints II: All Saints Day*. Ten years in the contemplation! It doesn't feel quite that long to sit through in its wretched entirety (which I did this time), but I still can't imagine any but the most easily entertained being willing to do so.

The new movie opens where the last one left off, more or less. Twin brothers Connor and Murphy MacManus (Sean Patrick Flanery and Norman Reedus), having fled their native Boston after wreaking vigilante havoc among the local mobsters, are now hiding out in Ireland—in very silly fake beards—with their father (Billy Connolly). We know we're in Ireland because Dad wears a big cable-knit sweater and slices potatoes into a little pot over a cozy hearth fire. (He also murmurs things like, "Peace, they say, is the enemy of memory.") When word arrives from Boston that a priest has been murdered and coins placed over his dead eyes (the boys' old calling card), they decide to head back to Beantown to clear their names and wreak more havoc. Along the way they pick up a disciple, a scrappy Mexican American named Romeo (Clifton Collins Jr. in an alarming mullet), whose specialties are bare-knuckle brawling and pop-eyed buffoonery.

Awaiting these three when they arrive in Boston are a trio of local detectives (their specialty is remarkably bad acting); the new Mafia don, risibly called Concezio Yakavetta (Judd Nelson!); and a spike-heeled FBI agent named Eunice Bloom (the usually charming Julie Benz, of *Dexter*—here, for some reason, doing a drawling, dead-on impression of Kyra Sedgwick's character in *The Closer*).

What follows is woefully garbled, thanks to the script (by Duffy and his brother Taylor—so memorably abused in the priceless Duffy documentary *Overnight)* and the ham-handed direction. There's endless gunfire, of course; and the word "fuck" is flung around with a frequency that rivals that of simple prepositions. There are a number of baffling conceptions (Eunice turns up in cowboy garb at one point, twirling a six-shooter) and snoozy interludes (like a Russian roulette encounter between Connolly and a mob hit man). And there are whole scenes that don't play at all—preeminently the one set amid apocalyptic flames and gun roar in which we meet an aged Mafia overlord who says things like "Eet is in za blood" and who turns out, upon close inspection, to be . . . Peter Fonda!

Duffy's way with dialogue remains tone-deaf. ("I am so smart," Eunice says at one point, "that I make smart people feel retarded.") And while he continues to preen himself on his political incorrectness ("I hail from colorful people," Romeo notes), it may be time to rein in his homo-anxiety ("Does that amuse you, queerbait?"), or people might start to wonder.

Duffy also pads the action shamelessly. A fantasy scene in which we see our heroes invading a drug factory and blowing away its occupants is immediately followed by the actual invasion, pretty much the same, but with slapstick comic touches appended. Similarly, a chaotic bar-room shoot-out is followed by a pointless slow-motion reprise.

The first *Boondock Saints* movie was dismissed by its detractors as secondhand Tarantino, but that now seems imprecise. This picture is more like thirdhand Tarantino—which is to say, secondhand Guy Ritchie. Since Ritchie himself appears to have moved on, there may be a minor market vacancy that Duffy can aspire to fill. Harboring any dream larger than that, though, would be inadvisable. (October 2009)

NICOLAS CAGE

Yes, the man is a category unto himself. *Wayward scion of the Coppola clan, amasser of yachts, castles, whole Caribbean islands, and many other things it turned out he couldn't really afford, Cage is one of the great without-a-net highfliers of our time. He's such a fine actor (see* Moonstruck, Matchstick Men, *and of course* Leaving Las Vegas, *for which he won an Oscar) that his willingness to appear in pictures that can only be called crap is baffling. (Con Air? The Wicker Man? It's a long, saddening list.) Presumably his multimillion-dollar squabble with the IRS in 2009 exacerbated this tendency. In any case, a lot of onetime fans have given up on him. Personally, I've decided to just sit back and enjoy his flick-picking excesses, the more appalling the better. Even in the worst sort of dreck, Cage's simple love of acting always shines through (he never gives a lazy, tossed-off performance). This sort of ironic appreciation will have to do, I'm afraid, until the man comes to his senses. If he ever does.*

Ghost Rider

Flameout

The best that can be said about this movie, which is quite bad, is that it's not a complete surprise. Having already underwhelmed us with another B-team Marvel superhero in the Ben Affleck oddity *Daredevil*, director Mark Steven Johnson now attempts to resuscitate an even more obscure figure: the chopper-borne "Devil's bounty hunter," Ghost Rider. The problem with both of these characters is that their superpowers lack epic zing. Daredevil is blind. Ghost Rider bursts into flame. Where can you go with these attributes? Tumbling down a flight of stairs? Into the home heating business?

Apparently (I had to look this up), Ghost Rider started out as a cowboy character named Carter Slade back in 1967. He was retooled as a motorcycle menace called Johnny Blaze in 1972 and went on to have a ten-year run in his own comic-book series. If it weren't so low on the list of things wrong with this movie as to barely justify utterance, I'd suggest that trying to squeeze both of these characters into one film was unwise. Only the most unbalanced fanboy could possibly care. Everyone else will just be confused. I think I get it now, kind of, but it's still confusing.

Briefly: 150 years ago, the first Ghost Rider was dispatched by the Devil to retrieve a contract signed by a village full of people who'd agreed to sell him their souls. The fiery cowpoke found those villagers, but then took off with the contract, and the Devil's been looking for it ever since. I should mention here that the Devil—"Mephisto," he's called—is played by Peter Fonda in full, fruity Prince of Darkness drag (floor-length evil-master greatcoat, skull-knobbed cane), under a carapace of hair spray so thick it would require hammers of the gods to crack it. Now—which is to say 150 years later—Mephisto is back, and for reasons I won't go into, because they're too boring, he has a claim on the soul of Johnny Blaze (Nicolas Cage), a motorcycle stunt rider with a traveling carnival. (The carnival is a musty device, but the movie plays the midway scenes as if they were thunderous NASCAR rallies.) Mephisto now wants Johnny to find the long-missing contract. But so does Mephisto's evil son, Blackheart (Wes Bentley), freshly cast out of Heaven with three of his demon cronies and itching for action.

Johnny is a whimsical character. In fact, whimsy is about all there is to him. He loves to watch TV, especially if there's a show about monkeys on. He loves the Carpenters. ("Shh," he tells a gabby friend as the soft-rock duo coos in the background, "you're steppin' on Karen.") And while he doesn't drink, he does like to suck up jellybeans out of a martini glass. These arbitrary quirks don't rise to the level of funny even if you stack them on top of one another, which the movie does. And Johnny's offbeat superpower—he turns into a skeleton and erupts in flames whenever there's evil around—is so haplessly computer-generated, it's little more than a cartoon.

Why does a skillful actor like Cage lower himself to appear in pop junk like *Ghost Rider*? The director appears to have no facility for guiding actors, and so Cage is reduced to screamy-face bellowing in some scenes and in others to croaking out lines like "I am speaking to the fire element within me." He's also been burdened with a ratty black hairpiece that sits on his head like a crow on a phone pole. He deserves better but seems to have forgotten that.

But where were we? Ah, yes. So it's Johnny versus Mephisto, and Mephisto's son, Blackheart, and Blackheart's nasty friends. Rallying to Johnny's side are his childhood sweetheart, Roxanne (Eva Mendes), who's now a TV news babe; his amiable pal Mack (Donal Logue); and a mysterious cowboy named . . . Carter Slade (Sam Elliott). Much devilment ensues—lots of Johnny tearing around on his flaming bike, lots of sultry mugging from the heavily powdered Blackheart, occasional cameo campiness from Mephisto. But the action is flat and awkwardly staged—it's tumult striving for excitement and failing to attain it.

Apart from the silly story, the movie is oppressive on a couple of other levels. Many of the scenes are lit like a TV sitcom, and there's a romantic restaurant interlude that seems to be taking place in an airport departure lounge. (There's also a sequence in which Johnny is biking his way through a fake foggy bayou that just has to be some sort of Ed Wood tribute.) And the music deserves special mention—it's a tasteless gumbo of pummeling synth-rock, sub-Journey arena dreck, and a witlessly employed ZZ Top tune. Just when you think you can't watch this movie anymore, you realize you also can't stand to listen to it anymore. Fortunately, this being the land of the free, you don't have to do either. (February 2007)

Next

Writer Blocked

The novels and stories of the late Philip K. Dick have already provided the basis for eight movies, some of them very good (*Blade Runner*, *Minority Report*), some so-so at best (*Imposter*, *Paycheck*), and at least one of them godawful (*Screamers*). *Next*, the latest such undertaking, is definitely so-so at best; but it also falls into a new category of PKD adaptations—if "adaptation" is the word. For this curious project, writer and producer Gary Goldman (who'd previously worked on *Minority Report* and *Total Recall*, another PKD-based movie) acquired the rights to a 1954 Dick short story called "The Golden Man." Then he threw away the story, replaced it with an unrelated narrative of his own devising, changed the title, and shopped the resulting property to Saturn Films, a production company run by Nicolas Cage. Cage's reaction to Goldman's PKD-free script is quoted in the movie's press notes: "I admire Philip K. Dick; he's edgy and uncompromising, and his unique voice in writing translates successfully to films."

This is a bizarre thing to say about a story that has nothing to do with Dick's "unique voice," or with his writing, really. "The Golden Man" is set in a near-future world in which the government is trying to stamp out pockets of mutant beings who've been born to human mothers. One of these creatures, eighteen-year-old Cris Johnson, raised in secret on a secluded family farm, has the mutant ability to see thirty minutes into the future and to pre-adjust his actions in relation to events that are about to happen. He falls into the hands of a government "deviant" squad, but with his ability to foresee their every attempt to hold him, he soon escapes and disappears into the night. He leaves behind a woman whom he's managed to impregnate.

"The Golden Man" has the hallmarks of scores of other sci-fi yarns Dick churned out for pulp magazines in the early 1950s, its rough style reflecting the author's trying financial circumstances. But it also has the distinctive PKD imaginative hooks that make his work so compelling. The story raises questions without stating them. What is Cris Johnson's purpose? Where is he really from? Where has he gone? What will become of the pregnant woman he's left behind, and to what will she give birth? It's a neat little tale. It might make a good movie. *Next* is not that picture, though.

There's nothing blasphemous about making major alterations in a Philip K. Dick story, of course—Shakespeare gets defiled all the time, why not PKD? Dick's fiction, all brain waves and hallucination, already has the feel of raw material. But what's the point of going to the trouble of acquiring a PKD property and then discarding it in order to make yet another generic Hollywood action movie? Why bother slapping Dick's name onto the credits? It's not entirely accurate to say that nothing of the original story survives in this film—the protagonist, played by Cage, is still named Cris Johnson, and he still has the gift of precognition (although now he can see only two minutes into the future, not half an hour). But everything else here is new, and for no interesting reason.

One can almost hear the ghost of Philip K. Dick crying out at the news that Cris has been transformed here into a small-time Las Vegas magician, working a seedy downtown casino under the stage moniker Frank Cadillac. (The name, he says, is a tribute to two of his favorite things, one of which is Frankenstein.) We first meet Cris sitting at the counter of a diner, sipping a martini. Then we see him at the casino foiling an attempted heist that he sees coming from two minutes away. Gun-wielding security goons at first think *he's* the bad guy, so Cris, as though determined to prove them correct, takes off. There follows a funny scene in which he gingerly snakes his way through the casino, dodging his pursuers by various precognitive means. Then comes a slam-bang car chase that wouldn't have been out of place in a 1970s TV cop show. This ends with Cris pulling into a hideout-garage of some sort where, to our complete startlement, Peter Falk is waiting. "You can't keep stealin' cars," he says, with grizzled wisdom. "That's not a life." Then Falk disappears from the story, never to return.

Meanwhile, the FBI is on Cris's trail, too, led by tough top agent Callie Ferris (Julianne Moore in a nonregulation, near-waist-length ponytail). She and her team have been spending a lot of time watching Cris's magic act (who says the feds have their priorities all wrong?), and they can't figure out how he does his mind-reading tricks. Therefore, they've decided they desperately need his help on their latest case. It seems that terrorists have stolen a nuclear bomb from the "Russian Federation," and have brought it to Los Angeles, where it is even now being prepped to inflict mass destruction. Since Cris can see two minutes into the future, they want him to . . . well, I'm not sure what they expect him to do, actually.

Back at the diner again, a hot number named Liz (Jessica Biel) enters, and Cris starts making passes at her. Each one fails, but with this two-minutes-into-the-future thing, he's able to start over again each time, until he finds an approach that works. Soon the two of them are cruising through the desert in her van, on their way to a bucolic Indian settlement where Liz sometimes teaches. As they exchange meaningful looks beside a towering waterfall, with cute little kids scampering amid the sunbeams, we can feel the movie begin to sag irreversibly.

It droops further when Liz and Cris, having known each other for all of about twenty-four hours, fall head over heels in love, or at least into bed, at a mountaintop motel. (Cris thinks Liz is "the one," since she somehow enables him to see more than two minutes into any future in which she figures.) I realize the sight of Jessica Biel returning from a shower wearing only a towel might short-circuit anyone's eloquence, but you kind of wish Cris could come up with something snappier than a poleaxed "You're beautiful." Or that Liz might muster a comeback more responsive than, "Wow." But hey, they're in love. You can tell: when he says, "I like rain," she says, "I like rain, too."

Despite the fact that one of the movie's big destructo sequences soon erupts—with Cris being pursued down the side of the mountain by an avalanche of logs, boulders, vans, trains, possibly whole buildings and mountain trolls, too—the movie edges ever closer to tedium. The digital action is loud and no doubt expensive, but a lot of it is familiar from the sort of TV commercials in which people walk around in real time as slo-mo mayhem erupts all around them. The director, Lee Tamahori (*xXx 2: The Next Level*), hasn't managed to impose a visual style on the chaos—the endless running and shouting, the machine-gun hotfooting played out on dull rooftops and in even duller loading bays—so the action has no lift to it. And whenever the generic tumult comes to a brief, blessed halt, bad dialogue rushes in to fill the void. At one point, Moore—impossibly miscast in a Bruce Willis–type role—tries to talk down a terrorist: "Release the hostages," she shouts. "You can get out of this." Says the terrorist: "Don't patronize me!"

Next isn't as flamboyantly bad as Cage's last movie, *Ghost Rider* (which made a ton of money, something this sucker is unlikely to do). But you know you're in for not much when Cage starts out the picture wearing that doleful, please-pat-my-head expression he adopts whenever there's nothing going on that places any demand on his fondly remembered acting talent. Here, it's an expression he never has cause to shed. It's possible that less interesting things could be done with this ungainly material, I suppose. But only if there's a sequel. (April 2007)

Bangkok Dangerous

Thai Die

Top-flight international assassins are all pretty much the same: dead of eye, grim of lip, armed to the teeth. They move through a world of steely blue light and more than average rainfall, and they have souls of deepest noir, trusting no one, needing no one. The hit master played by Nicolas Cage in *Bangkok Dangerous* doesn't even need a last name. Just call him Joe. Or maybe—since he pointedly observes that "No one knows who I am"—don't.

Like all such lethally omnicompetent characters, Joe services a worldwide clientele. ("The Russians swear by him," says a subthug admiringly.) But he wants to quit the game before he becomes a target himself. So he accepts one last, lucrative commission: eliminating some bothersome rivals for a Bangkok crime boss. I don't think it diminishes Joe's talent for termination to suggest that luck—or maybe just the script's oblivious disdain for logic—plays a large part in his deadly undertakings. For example, one of his designated victims is taking a nighttime swim in a small garden pool, closely watched over by a bodyguard. How likely is it that Joe would be able to slip into the pool himself, accost his target, pull him down underwater, and hold him there until he drowns—without Joe drowning himself? And then, of course, he has to make an unavoidably sloshy getaway unspotted by the hovering bodyguard. Which he does. That's how good Joe is.

Cage demonstrates that Joe is a cold, unfeeling killing machine by dispensing with pretty much all but one of the facial expressions that actors traditionally find useful in creating characters. For such a total pro, though, this master assassin is surprisingly undiscriminating about the help he hires. When he sees a street hustler named Kong (Shahkrit Yamnarm) relieving a tourist of his wallet, he immediately brings this complete stranger on board as his trusty assistant. Why? Says Joe, "Maybe it's because—and this is strange—when I looked in his eyes, I saw myself."

We can see that Joe is a man with a Claymore mine where his heart should be; and yet a chance encounter with a beautiful deaf-mute pharmacy clerk named Fon (the exquisite Charlie Young) turns him instantly into a puddle of lovelorn goo. We know that she's won his Claymore because it is here that Cage brings a second facial expression into play. (He also brings it along with him on a tea-sipping visit to the house of Fon's mom—one of the movie's sillier scenes, which is saying something.)

I won't even go into the elephants. Well, yes, I will. Joe is something of an elephant magnet—they sidle up to him in a colorful marketplace; they sway bashfully on the other side of a pond he's peering into. The movie informs us that elephants are symbols of luck in Thai culture— good luck when their trunks are raised high, bad luck when they're pointing down. Joe has an elephant print hanging on a wall in his sleek hideaway apartment, and Kong notes that its trunk is dangling downward. A little later, when bad luck starts piling up, Joe returns to the print and realizes what has to be done. After a moment of contemplation, he reaches out, very carefully, and *turns it upside down*. There.

Bangkok Dangerous is an English-language remake of a 1999 movie of the same name by the same directors, Hong Kong siblings Danny and Oxide Pang (*The Eye*). This picture has all the raucous death and destruction an action fan might want, but it's a glum, grainy film, and so generic that you wonder what several of the characters are doing walking around when you could swear that they—or genre stereotypes very much like them—were already blown away in some previous action exercise. What Cage—such a fine actor when the mood's upon him—is doing wasting his time in listless junk like this is anyone's guess. Has somebody installed a Claymore where his brain used to be? (September 2008)

Bad Lieutenant: Port of Call New Orleans

Drug Bust

Do fish have dreams? Do they dream of ominous iguanas, perhaps? Or maybe the break-dancing souls of freshly capped gangsters? More to the point, will Nicolas Cage ever make another movie that makes sense? Judging by his new one, *Bad Lieutenant: Port of Call New Orleans*, and considering his current financial straits, the prospects seem dim.

The director—the esteemed Werner Herzog, stupefyingly enough—claims never to have seen Abel Ferrara's original 1992 *Bad Lieutenant*, and I think we can take him at his word. The Ferrara movie, which I'd recommend seeing before—or better yet instead of—this one, concerns a viciously bent New York City cop; and Harvey Keitel, in the title role, is the embodiment of rank, skeezy corruption. In Herzog's take on the story, the action has been relocated, for no reason at all, to New Orleans, "in the aftermath of Hurricane Katrina." Cage, in full rant-and-glower mode, plays Lieutenant Terence McDonagh, whose self-assigned duties include stealing drugs from the police evidence room, tooting up with his hooker girlfriend (Eva Mendes), and barging around town with a huge handgun stuffed right in the front of his pants, like a walking Smith & Wesson commercial. I doubt that rude laughter is what the director was going for, but it's continually elicited.

The plot, which staggers around like a drunken tourist without a map, has McDonagh tracking a local drug lord called Big Fate (rap graduate Xzibit, very persuasive), whom he suspects of blowing away a group of freelance smack merchants. There was one witness to the wipe-out, a little kid named Daryl (Denzel Whitaker). McDonagh can't find him, so he confronts the boy's godmother (Irma P. Hall). She won't give him up. But then, in a moment of blinding convenience, Daryl just steps into the scene, reporting for plot duty.

Soon McDonagh and Daryl and a dog who has also drifted into the story are off to Biloxi to find the hooker girlfriend, Frankie. They locate her at a hotel, where one of her clients (Shea Whigham) has not only beat her up but is continuing to lash her with bad acting. Then young Daryl disappears. Then a mob enforcer named Marco (Eugene Gratz) shows up. McDonagh has accumulated serious gambling debts, and Marco wants him to hand over $50,000. Wriggling out of that tight spot, McDonagh decides to stash Frankie at the country home of his alcoholic father (Tom Bower) for safekeeping. There McDonagh shows her "my special place"—a room where he once played pirates as a kid and also, very sadly, lost a sterling silver spoon he's never been able to find again.

McDonagh's life is further complicated when suspicious Internal Affairs officers come down on him and confiscate his gun. Our man is pissed: "A man without a gun is not a man," he says. (He also says things like "I'll kill all of you till the break of dawn, baby," and "No, thank you, we're going to stick with our sparkling water.") By this point, we've already made the acquaintance of the aforementioned iguanas, lazing on a coffee table in a crowded room, where only McDonagh can see them. And soon we witness the break-dancing soul rising from the body of a slain bad guy. These are supposed to be hallucinations, I guess. But when McDonagh leaves the coffee-table room, the lizards remain behind, in continuing full view. And when he shoots the dancing soul, it falls to the floor, adding existential ambiguity to the picture's already abundant confusions.

Cage can't take the whole rap for this muddled picture. He puts a lot of energy into his performance, and he does get an occasional good line. ("Everything I take is prescription . . . except for the heroin.") But unlike Keitel in the original movie, he's too personable to pass for a complete scumbag. And the script, by William Finkelstein, gives him little but nonsense to work with. Then there's Herzog's direction, which is anything but rigorous. (One of his shots, framed between the gaping jaws of an alligator, is something you might expect from a first-year film student, not an internationally renowned director.) The movie wraps us in a fog of torpid indifference. By the time McDonagh finally recovers his silver spoon, you may realize you've lost something of your own. Two hours' worth of it. (November 2009)

Season of the Witch

Cursed Again

The movies of Nicolas Cage are a crapshoot by now. Fans of this fine but wayward actor never know what to expect when they enter the theater. A winner like *Matchstick Men*, *The Weather Man*, or *Leaving Las Vegas*? Or dire junk like *Con Air*, *Bangkok Dangerous*, or the extra-silly *Ghost Rider*? Cage's determination to work a lot, plus his shaky taste in scripts and his heavy debt to the IRS, practically guarantee there'll be more of the latter sort of picture than of the former.

His latest, a medieval sorcery exercise called *Season of the Witch*, falls somewhere between these two poles, although it inclines more toward the flaming-motorcyclist school of cinema than that of the heartbroken alcoholic. It's a good-looking film (much of it was shot in the Austrian Alps), but heavily derivative. The pestilential villages and grimy peasants on view have an unmistakably Pythonian cast, and there are resounding echoes of Ingmar Bergman, Mario Bava, *The Name of the Rose*, various Hammer horrors, and even, in one big CGI monster bash, if you can imagine, *Gremlins*.

The time is the mid-fourteenth century. A weary knight named Behman (Cage), having bailed out of the latest Crusade in disillusion-ment, is returning home from the Holy Land in the company of a fellow warrior named Felson. Arriving back in Europe, they are greeted by the scourge of the Black Death at its ghastly peak. Soon they're seized as de-serters and tossed in a dungeon. Then a plague-ridden cardinal (Christopher Lee, unrecognizable behind a face full of bulging pustules) offers them freedom in exchange for undertaking a mission—transporting a young woman (Claire Foy) thought to be a witch to a faraway mountain-top abbey where the resident witch experts will render judgment as a pro forma prelude to dispatching her in some appropriately hideous way.

Behman and Felson accept this deal and set off with the alleged witch confined in a sort of cage-coach. They are accompanied on their journey by another sad knight (Ulrich Thomsen), a nervous priest (Stephen Campbell Moore), a peasant guide (Stephen Graham), and an all-purpose valiant youth (Robert Sheehan). The caged girl is by turns sweetly appealing and weirdly malevolent. Could she really be a witch? The peasant guide thinks so. ("Kill the bitch!" he suggests.) Behman is having none of that, though, and the group proceeds on its way through snowy mountains and fog-choked forests. En route, they are attacked by wolves, possibly of the demonic variety. Finally they arrive at the remote abbey, only to find that nobody's home. Nobody inclined to offer a warm welcome, anyway.

The movie is plagued by an unrelenting mildness. The is-she-or-isn't-she witch question generates minimal suspense, and the attempted supernatural thrills are subverted at every turn by witless anachronisms. Apart from the name of Perlman's character (is "Felson" not a moniker more appropriate to a sitcom second banana than a hardy warrior?), there are lines of dialogue that land with a thud far short of amusement. "I've saved your ass a hundred times," for example. Or, "We're gonna need more holy water!" My favorite crops up in the middle of an early battle scene, when Felson turns to Behman amid the fray and says, "I'm building up a powerful thirst," and Behman replies, "You're buying, my friend!"

The movie consists of little more than its elaborate production design. (The director, Dominic Sena, is a music-video veteran and previously directed Cage in the lamentable *Gone in Sixty Seconds*.) Cage is a pro, and he gives an actual performance, unfortunately to no avail. His character may be on a mission, but the picture—being released into the traditional January graveyard for doomed movies—is on its way to a funeral. (January 2011)